Beginnings of
Interior Environments

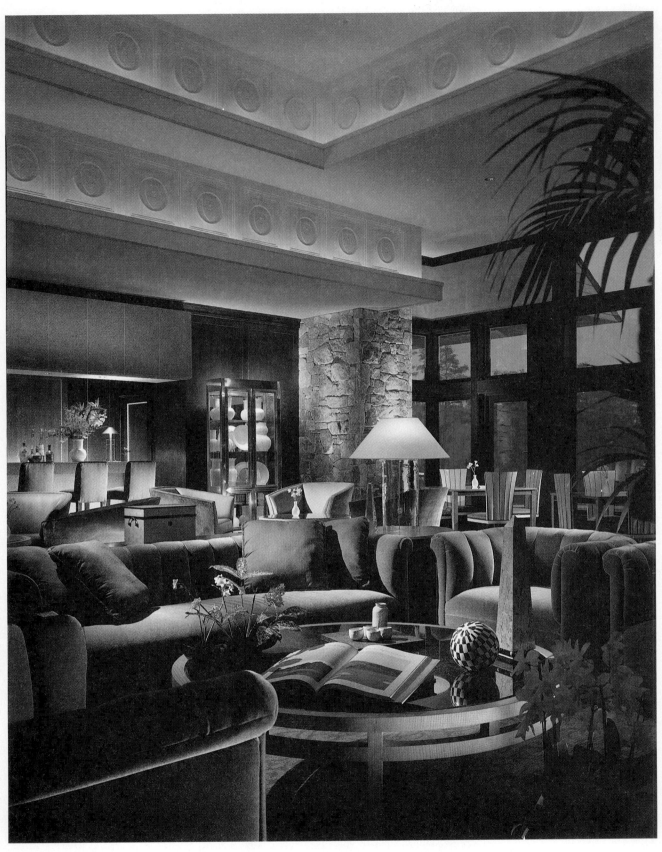

Designers from the United States frequently work with international clients. This members' lounge at the Northampton Golf Club in Akita-Akita, Japan, is highlighted by ceiling soffits that incorporate the club's logo. Warm and comfortable furnishings add to the relaxed ambience. (Interior design: Design Continuum, Inc. Photograph by Robert Miller Photography.)

Beginnings of Interior Environments

Eighth Edition

Phyllis Sloan Allen

Miriam F. Stimpson   Brigham Young University

Lynn M. Jones, ASID, IIDA, IDEC   Brenau University

Prentice Hall
Upper Saddle River, New Jersey

Library of Congress Cataloging-in-Publication Data

Allen, Phyllis Sloan.
  Beginnings of interior environments / Phyllis Sloan Allen, Miriam
F. Stimpson, Lynn M. Jones. —8th ed.
    p.   cm.
  Previous eds. published under title: Beginnings of interior
environment.
  ISBN 0-13-082390-1
  1. Interior decoration Handbooks, manuals, etc.   I. Stimpson,
Miriam F.   II. Jones, Lynn M.   III. Allen, Phyllis Sloan.
Beginnings of interior environment.   IV. Title.   V. Title: Interior
environments.
  NK2115.A59 2000   99-36535
  728—dc21   CIP

Editor: Elizabeth Sugg
Developmental Editor: Gianna M. Marsella
Editorial Assistant: Delia Uherec
Production Editor: Mary Harlan
Copy Editor: Sheryl Rose
Design Coordinator: Diane C. Lorenzo, Karrie Converse-Jones
Photo Coordinator: Sherry Mitchell
Text Designer: Dianne Schaefer/Books by Design
Cover Designer: Dan Eckle
Cover photo: ©Robert Miller Photography
Production Manager: Pamela D. Bennett
New Illustrations: Carlisle Graphics and Carol Platt
Director of Marketing: Debbie Yarnell
Marketing Manager: Shannon Simonsen
Marketing Coordinator: Adam Kloza

This book was set in Garamond by Carlisle Communications
and was printed and bound by R. R. Donnelley & Sons
Company. The cover was printed by Phoenix Color Corp.

Printed in the United States of America

10 9 8 7 6 5 4 3 2

ISBN: 0-13-083290-1

Prentice-Hall International (UK) Limited, *London*
Prentice-Hall of Australia Pty. Limited, *Sydney*
Prentice-Hall of Canada, Inc., *Toronto*
Prentice-Hall Hispanoamericana, S.A., *Mexico*
Prentice-Hall of India Private Limited, *New Delhi*
Prentice-Hall of Japan, Inc., *Tokyo*
Prentice-Hall (Singapore) Pte. Ltd., *Singapore*
Editora Prentice-Hall do Brasil, Ltda., *Rio de Janeiro*

Dedication

To all beginning interior designers who desire to enrich the quality of life through the respectful use of our earth's resources; may each of you come to appreciate the earth's gifts and use them wisely in your future interiors.

Preface

The field of interior design encompasses a unique blend of art and science. I have always told my students that successful designers construct a balance between their left and right brains. The designer's goal in any interior should be to *analyze* the needs and desires of the client, and then through the *synthesis* of this information create a healthful and safe environment that enhances the client's quality of life. It is the mission of this text to assist beginning designers in achieving this goal.

Significant Changes in the Eighth Edition

The eighth edition of *Beginnings of Interior Environments* discusses foundation information that assists the reader in understanding the nature of interior design and the practice of the interior design profession. The text continues in the tradition of earlier editions as a brief and practical approach to understanding interior design. Although previous editions focused primarily on residential design, this edition expands readers' awareness of commercial design as well. The eighth edition also includes new information on green design, universal design, and aspects of multicultural awareness.

The most significant changes to the text include an introductory chapter focusing on the design process and scope of services, as well as career options in the design field. The historical section has been condensed into a pictorial essay, and follows the first chapter. A new chapter has been added on construction, systems, and codes, as well as an updated discussion on lighting. The space planning section of the text has been expanded to include two chapters focusing on designing from the *inside out,* based on the user's spatial needs. The final chapter briefly discusses the business aspects, ethics, and outlook of the interior design profession.

Special features are dedicated to green design solutions, and design scenarios are located throughout the text. Nearly 500 new images or illustrations have been incorporated.

Text Overview

The following synopsis of each part of the text is repeated in the Introduction to ensure that students understand the broad knowledge base required of interior designers.

Part I, "Introduction to Interior Environments," discusses the history of the design profession and reviews in detail the process by which interior designers complete an interior space. Drawings and drafted plans demonstrate the use of visual communications. A pictorial essay on the history of style will familiarize students with significant eras of design that influence today's interiors.

Part II, "Design Fundamentals," establishes the basics for the study of design in all creative fields. Color is given special attention because of its complexity. Part II emphasizes the principles and elements of design that guide designers in technical and decorative design decisions.

Part III, "Building Systems," emphasizes the architectural, electrical, and mechanical aspects of design. This section assists future designers in understanding the visual communications needed to collaborate with electrical, mechanical, and structural engineers, the client, and the rest of the design team.

Part IV, "Space," addresses both the technical requirements and the creative dimensions of planning the layout of furniture and rooms. Designers learn to read floor plans by thinking and visualizing in three dimensions (3-D). These chapters encourage designers to recognize space as *volume* and to design from the *inside out.*

Part V, "Furnishings, Fabrics, and Background Elements," provides a foundation for understanding the multitude of selections available to designers.

Finally, **Part VI,** "The Profession of Interior Design," discusses the steps required to become a professional member of the interior design industry. It reviews basic business practices and the ethics and outlook of the profession.

Ancillaries and Supplements

As an additional education tool, the *Instructor's Manual* accompanying the text develops standard test questions and practical studio design problems. Also available is a Student Packet, which contains assignments and plates for students to execute in color paints.

Acknowledgments

Special appreciation is extended to the photographers, designers, architects, and manufacturers who contributed images and information for this text. Truly one of the most rewarding experiences of working on this text was opening the packages containing these wonderful images sent by so many talented professionals. The design community has been so very helpful sharing pertinent information and materials. I am particularly grateful to Karen Downs at *Southern Accents,* Bob Shimer at Hedrich-Blessing, and Robert Thien of Atlanta for their extensive film contributions.

Many individuals have assisted in the effort of verifying information. Several practicing designers and educators (listed below, but who were anonymous to the author) reviewed chapters for accuracy and readability. I appreciate their candid and constructive comments and have altered much of the text based on these reviews. I am particularly grateful to whoever paid special attention to the material on design history. Reviewers included

- Patricia G. Allen, Portland Community College
- Reed Benhamou, Indiana University
- Stephanie Clemons, Colorado State University
- Marcia Gonzales, Scottsdale Community College
- Janet Lacek, Brenau University
- Nancy Lickson, Kingwood College
- Jerry L. Nielson, University of Florida
- Joy K. Potthoff, Bowling Green State University
- Susan Reedy, Michigan State University
- Jane D. Reagor, Tennessee Tech University
- David L. Rodgers, Indiana University of Pennsylvania
- Suzanne Watkins, Chaminade University of Honolulu

LuAnn Nissen was particularly insightful and I appreciated her words of wisdom as I started this project. The following individuals deserve special recognition for their assistance with their respective areas of expertise: Jason Haner (carpet), Shelly Hughes (design scenario 1), Janet Morley (textiles), Michael Hinton (CRI), and Carol Platt (modern design history). Also, the accomplished freehand renderings of the space planning process and three-dimensional volume development are from the creative hand of Carol Platt. Paul Petrie, Marcia Davis, Charles Gandy, and Roger Godwin served as a constant source of encouragement, vision, and stability throughout my design career. I value their insights.

Elizabeth Sugg, Brad Potthoff, Gianna Marsella, Mary Harlan, Sheryl Rose, Carol Sykes, Mary Evangelista, and all the folks at Prentice Hall have shown a unique dedication to the publishing of this text. Mary Harlan, Carol Sykes, and Sherry Mitchell have been particularly resourceful and attentive to the visual aspects so critical to the success of the eighth edition. Mary Evangelista went beyond the call of duty to secure permissions to reuse photos, and Gianna Marsella served as a guiding source throughout the writing process. For all their efforts, I am truly grateful.

To my colleagues in ASID, IIDA, IDEC, and at Brenau University, as well as to my students, I express my wholehearted appreciation for your support, motivation, and understanding—particularly just before a deadline. To my dearest friends and family in Georgia, Indiana, and on the North Fork, I appreciate the space (both physical and psychological) all of you allowed for my husband and me to complete the text. (Special thanks is extended to the Secrest clan for the solar power that allowed us to continue working over the summer.) To my parents, Verle and Nona Fiegle, I express an additional deepfelt gratitude for the tenacity and dedication that you instilled in me. These characteristics have helped immensely.

Finally, to my husband, Philip, I cannot adequately express my sincere appreciation for the hundreds of hours (taken from our personal time) that you spent wordsmithing, typing, calling, and generally assisting with the organization of this text. For your spirit and sustained encouragement, I am forever indebted.

Lynn M. Jones

Lynn M. Jones, ASID/IIDA/IDEC, knew she wanted to pursue interior architecture at an early age. In grade school she developed house plans on graph paper and raked leaves or shoveled snow into floor plan patterns; furniture in her room was always on the move. Lynn graduated from Purdue University magna cum laude with a Bachelor of Science in Environmental Design, and at age 23 became NCIDQ certified. She earned her Master in Historic Preservation from University of Georgia with a summa cum laude designation. Her thesis, The Design of National Park Visitor Centers: The Relationships between Buildings and Their Sites, *took Lynn and her husband to more than 100 National Park locations.*

Lynn worked full-time as a designer in Atlanta for several years, focusing on hospitality and commercial office design. She has served as an educator since 1984 and opened her own business, Jones Interiors, in 1989 to coincide with her educational endeavors. Her work has received awards from ASID, AIA, and IDEC. She was named outstanding faculty member at Brenau University in 1993, where she has served as Interior Design Program Director since 1988 and is presently Chair of Art and Design. Lynn spends her summers at a remote homestead in northwest Montana, where she finds inspiration and respite in the beauty and simplicity of nature.

Brief Contents

Contents

PART III BUILDING SYSTEMS 100

The Construction Process 101
Site Selection and Development • Footings and Foundations • Framing • Sheathing, Roofing, and Interior Building Systems • Finish Materials

PART IV SPACE 144

Form and Space 145
Space Planning 145

Beginnings of
Interior Environments

Introduction to Interior Environments

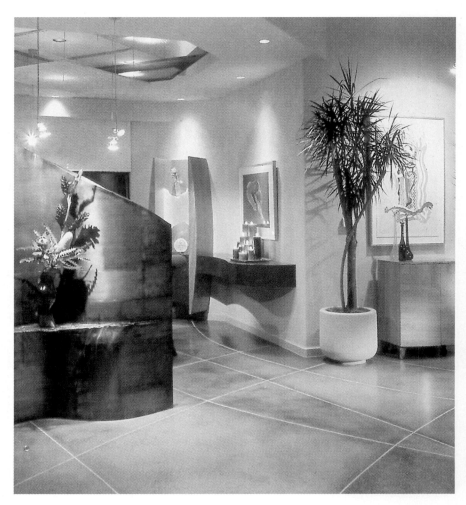

Figure I.1 *The creative use of concrete has greatly evolved since its beginnings in Roman history. Concrete floors can be custom colored and patterned, as seen here, or they may also be textured. Patterned floors help to delineate space. Designs can be applied to existing or new floors, both inside and outside. (Courtesy of Bomanite Corp.)*

Throughout history humans have organized and enhanced their surroundings to meet their physical and psychological needs. Tools and products were developed and refined to perform specific tasks. Furniture, fabrics, and finishes changed to meet people's needs. The physical arrangements of rooms, furnishings, and mechanical and electrical systems have relocated based on aesthetics and function. Today, the interior design profession incorporates a broad scope of services offered to a wide variety of clients (Figure I.1).

Definition and Responsibilities of an Interior Designer

The following definition, developed by the National Council for Interior Design Qualification, demonstrates the scope of the interior design profession:

For the purpose of improving the quality of life, increasing productivity, and protecting the health, safety, and welfare of the public, the Professional Interior Designer

- analyzes the client's needs, goals, and life and safety requirements
- integrates findings with knowledge of interior design
- formulates preliminary design concepts that are appropriate, functional, and aesthetic
- develops and presents final design recommendations through appropriate presentation media
- prepares working drawings and specifications for non-load-bearing interior construction, materials, finishes, space planning, furnishings, fixtures, and equipment
- collaborates with licensed practitioners who offer professional services in the technical areas of mechanical, electrical, and load-bearing design as required for regulatory approval
- prepares and administers bids and contract documents as the client's agent
- reviews and evaluates design solutions during implementation and upon completion.

Interior designers are responsible for developing interior environments for people of all ages and abilities, including the elderly, children, and those who are temporarily or permanently disabled. Designers must understand the complexities related to the diverse needs of these clients. The concept of **universal design** focuses on creating spaces and furnishings to meet the needs of individuals regardless of age and ability. Interior designers must be able to integrate the needs of a wide variety of individuals into a particular space.

Designers may also be required to coordinate interiors that are welcoming to a multicultural community. Different cultures view color and space in a variety of ways. Sensitivity to individuals' tastes and cultural preferences permits designers to suggest the appropriate design solutions for these clients (Figure I.2).

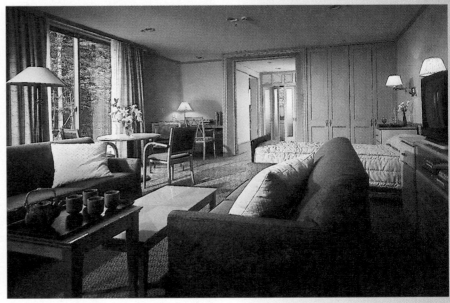

Figure I.2 *Designing for the elderly requires sensitivity to special needs. This continuing care retirement facility, located in Sun City Kanagawa, Japan, also required special research into multicultural awareness. (Architect/Designer: Hellmuth, Obata & Kassabaum, Tokyo and San Francisco. Photograph by Jaime Ardiles-Arce.)*

Interior designers also are responsible for protecting the environment by using sustainable resources whenever possible. Designers should develop design solutions that promote environmental considerations, and should use and specify products that are recycled and can be recyclable. The use of sustainable products and the development of environmentally sensitive interiors is called **green design** (Figure I.3).

The terms *interior decorator* and *interior designer* have had various

A.

Figure I.3 *This house, called the Sun-catcher, is constructed from used tires packed with dirt and stacked to form the walls. The walls are covered with stucco to create a Southwest adobe interior. Windows face south to aid in the solar design. A, exterior; B, entry hall-way, looking back toward the front door; C, living area. (Architect/Designer: Michael Reynolds. Photograph by Philip A. Jones.)*

B.

C.

meanings. *Interior design* is the profession that embodies the above definition and responsibilities. (Some prefer to call it *interior architecture.*) *Interior decorating,* or the embellishment of interior finishes and the selection and arrangement of fabrics and furnishings, is an important component of interior design. As defined by NCIDQ, however, "the interior designer is qualified by education,

experience, and examination to enhance the function and quality of interior spaces, and to insure the health, safety, and welfare of the public."

It is important to emphasize that although the designer may be responsible for the decorative design solutions for load-bearing walls, the practice of interior design does not include the structural design of buildings. Design-

ers collaborate with a team of allied professionals, especially when working with mechanical and electrical systems and construction components.

Relationship with Allied Professions

While developing a new or renovated interior for a client, a designer works as

Figure I.4 *For this laboratory, a computer-aided design software program created interior views for preliminary presentation to the client. Visual interpretation is a critical skill required of designers. The computer allows the space to be viewed from various angles and helps clients (and designers) visualize the solution prior to construction. (Architect/Designer: Talka & Connor.)*

a member of the design team. Interior designers may work with architects, builders, decorators, landscape architects, mechanical, electrical, and structural engineers, and product and graphic designers. Designers are also likely to work with other professionals including lighting and sound specialists, historic preservationists, and a wide variety of other specialized contractors in interior finishes, fabrics, furniture, and products. The success of a job depends on communication and collaboration among these design professionals.

Knowledge Required by Interior Designers

In order to perform competently and communicate effectively with the allied professions, designers must acquire a broad foundation of technical and decorative knowledge.

Part I, "Introduction to Interior Environments," discusses the history of the design profession and reviews in detail the process by which interior designers complete an interior space. Drawings and drafted plans demon-

strate the use of **visual communications** required of all design professions. Students using this text as a part of an introductory design course may be required to start drafting or to work with **computer-aided design** (CAD) software (Figure I.4). Also in Part I, a pictorial essay traces the history of style, showing how past eras influence interiors.

Part II, "Design Fundamentals," establishes the basics for the study of design in all creative fields. Color is given special attention because of its complexity. Part II emphasizes the principles and elements of design that guide designers in technical and decorative design decisions.

Part III, "Building Systems," emphasizes the architectural, electrical, and mechanical aspects of design. Lighting solutions are particularly important in interior spaces. This section assists future designers in understanding the visual communications needed to collaborate with electrical, mechanical, and structural engineers, the client, and the rest of the design team.

Part IV, "Space," addresses both the technical requirements and the creative dimensions of planning the layout of furniture and rooms. Designers learn to read floor plans by thinking and visualizing in three dimensions (3-D). These chapters encourage designers to recognize space as *volume* and to design space from the *inside out.*

Part V, "Furnishings, Fabrics, and Background Elements," provides a foundation for understanding the multitude of selections available to designers. For example, designers need to know the advantages and disadvantages of selecting cut-pile carpet over level-loop carpet or flat latex paint over semigloss alkyd.

Finally, Part VI, "The Profession of Interior Design," discusses the steps required to become a professional member of the interior design industry and reviews basic business principles and ethics. The text concludes with an outlook for the profession.

Understanding Interior Design

Figure 1.1 *This warm and inviting space welcomes guests into the Carolina Inn lobby and makes them feel pampered. Hospitality design requires designers to create interiors, not only for their clients—the hotel owners— but also for the clients' client—the hotel guests. (Architect/Designer: The Glave Firm. Photograph by Robert Miller.)*

The profession of interior design is relatively new. It evolved during the latter half of the 19th century and the early 20th century, and then fully emerged following World War II. Interiors designed prior to the establishment of the profession as it is known today were executed primarily by furniture designers, painters, cabinetmakers, sculptors, architects, and others active in the decorative arts.

Development of the Interior Design Profession

In the 1850s, authors became deeply interested in how human comfort was affected by sound principles of design. At the time, the Industrial Revolution (particularly in Europe) was producing a variety of poor-quality household goods. Many individuals condemned the use of the machine to create inferior products and designs.

William Morris and the Arts and Crafts movement in 1860s England advocated "good design for everyone." English author and moralist Charles Eastlake wrote *Hints on Household Taste* in 1868, one of the first books on interior decoration. In the United States, American Arts and Crafts movement leader Gustav Stickley published *The Craftsman* at the turn of the century, featuring numerous articles on home design. In the late 19th century, various publications such as *Godey's Lady's Book*, *Harper's New Monthly*, *Harper's Bazaar*, and *Ladies Home Journal* advocated more tasteful interiors. As early as 1890, Candace Wheeler published an article entitled "Interior Decoration as a Profession for Women." Later that decade, Edith Wharton and Ogden Codman wrote *The Decoration of Houses*, which was intended to show that the purpose of interior decoration was to bring out the proportions of a well-designed room. W. C. Gannet wrote a privately printed series of essays called "The House Beautiful," from which in 1896 a magazine of the same title derived its impetus and was first published. Soon, other home decorating periodicals appeared on the market.

Elsie de Wolfe

Although there were many relatively unknown decorating shops and private decorators in America and Europe at the turn of the century, one of the most famous individuals to offer interior decorating services to the public was New York actress Elsie de Wolfe, who had expert knowledge of French furniture and antiques. Her decorating expertise could transform a room with a somber, cluttered, Victorian feeling into one with a light, airy, eclectic French design (Figure 1.2).

In 1901 Elsie de Wolfe began her business as "America's first professional interior decorator." Through her efforts, along with the work of others during this period, including Nancy McClelland, English decorator Syrie Maugham (known for her "white" interiors), Dorothy Draper (who wrote a decorating advice column), Rose Cummings, and later Billy Baldwin (who was known as the "Dean of Decorators"), the profession of interior decorating was established.

A.

B.

Figure 1.2 *A dining room designed by Elsie de Wolfe early in her career is shown in A. The lighter, refreshing redesign (B) of the same room exemplifies de Wolfe's later design character. (Photographs from the Byron Collection, The Museum of the City of New York.)*

Frank Lloyd Wright

Whereas Elsie de Wolfe focused on the embellishment of surface decoration and the placement of furniture and accessories, Frank Lloyd Wright, an architect working in the early 1900s, brought to the profession an integration of structure and design. Wright was concerned with the planning of space, its function, and its relationship to the structure. He defined spaces based on furniture arrangements rather than enclosures. His integration of furnishings, light, construction materials, ornamental detail, and structural materials formed what he called **organic design.**

In the Robie House (Figure 1.3), as in all his prairie-styled homes, Wright emphasized the fireplace. Materials used on the exterior of the home were brought inside to become part of the hearth. The hearth became the heart or core of his homes, symbolizng the strength of the American household.

Other progressive designers and architects, in both America and Europe, saw the need to integrate the exterior of a structure with the interior spaces and furnishings. Designers also began to integrate acoustical and lighting solutions into their designs during this era.

Following World War II, the explosive growth of commercial and residential development created a greater demand for interior design services. Americans wanted more efficient and aesthetically pleasing private and public environments—and were willing to support a new profession that would implement that desire.

Professional Design Organizations

The establishment of professional interior design societies began in the 1930s with the development of the American Institute of Interior Decorators (AIID), which gave credibility to the new profession. In order to be a member of the

A.

Figure 1.3 *In the plan of the 1909 Robie House (A), Frank Lloyd Wright's emphasis on the fireplace as the heart of the home is evinced by its central location. B shows an interior view of the home from the dining room looking into the living room. The bank of windows to the left pulls the outdoors into the home. (Frank Lloyd Wright drawings copyright © 1998 The Frank Lloyd Wright Foundation, Scottsdale, AZ. Photo courtesy of The Frank Lloyd Wright Archives, Scottsdale, AZ.)*

B.

organization, individuals were required to have a combination of education and experience. The society emphasized continuing education programs, a code of ethics, outreach to the community and students, and collaboration with related professions.

After World War II, the nonresidential or contract market developed. Decorators were designing hotels, offices, and retail establishments. Space planning became a focus of the decorating community. For many the term "decorator" no longer fit, and in 1957 the National Society of Interior Designers (NSID) was formed, the second professional design organization in the United States. In 1975 the two organizations merged to form the American Society of Interior Designers (ASID). Presently ASID has 20,000 professional members and 13,000 industry affiliates.

Various other professional organizations developed throughout the 1970s and '80s. In the 1980s and '90s, a movement called the "Unified Voice" was created to bring all competing professional interior design organizations under one umbrella. In 1994, three organizations (the Institute of Business Designers, the Council of Federal Interior Designers, and the International Society of Interior Designers) merged to form IIDA, the International Interior Design Association, with approximately 9000 members. Both ASID and IIDA require the passage of the National Council of Interior Design Qualification (NCIDQ) exam as one requirement for professional membership. More information about these organizations is discussed in Part VI, "The Profession of Interior Design."

The Design Process/ Scope of Services

Knowing where to begin with a client, what information to obtain, and then how to proceed through the installation and evaluation of the completed space is a comprehensive task. Designers follow the **design process** to ensure creative and comprehensive design solutions that satisfy clients' needs and desires (Table 1.1).

Designers may use a variety of terminologies to describe the design process or the methods of completing a project. All terminologies or methods center on the analysis and synthesis of the design solution.

Analysis focuses on discovery. Analyzing a design project requires gathering information, understanding goals and objectives, researching related codes and other technical data, comprehending the design problem, and defining the design criteria. Once this information has been assimilated, designers begin to synthesize the solution.

Like the analysis phase, the *synthesis* phase also requires an immense amount of contemplative thought. Designers stretch their imaginations and develop alternative solutions to the design problem. Only then does the designer return to the analysis phase to select the best solution and refine it to meet the client's needs. The designer creates, selects, and produces design presentations by way of visual communications for the client's review. Based on the client's feedback, the designer will return to the analysis phase to rethink or retool the solution.

The design process is dynamic and cyclical, allowing the designer to create interiors that are responsive to particular situations. The analysis and synthesis of the design problem form the basis for all creative design solutions.

In some projects, phases of design may be combined or condensed, and in other projects (particularly residential) the phases may occur simultaneously. The following discussion utilizes the terms frequently employed by the practicing professional.

Initial Client Contact

The initial client contact is an integral part of the design process. It is through the initial meeting(s) that designers and clients evaluate their compatibility. Designers evaluate whether the project fits their firm, time frame, and staff load. Clients evaluate previous projects related to their needs completed by the firm. Both the client and the designer should interview each other to look for a cooperative blend. Proposals are reviewed and contracts are secured.

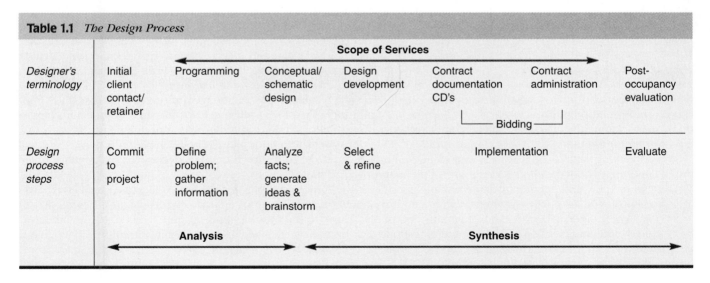

Table 1.1 *The Design Process*

		Scope of Services					
Designer's terminology	Initial client contact/ retainer	Programming	Conceptual/ schematic design	Design development	Contract documentation CD's	Contract administration	Post-occupancy evaluation
					└─── Bidding ───┘		
Design process steps	Commit to project	Define problem; gather information	Analyze facts; generate ideas & brainstorm	Select & refine	Implementation		Evaluate
	←─── **Analysis** ───→		←──────────── **Synthesis** ──────────────→				

Programming

The **programming** phase is the information-gathering phase. Designers identify and analyze the needs and desires of the client, usually through personal interviews. In a residential project, the designer should meet with everyone in the household. In a commercial project, the president or facilities planner may serve as the client contact, or this person may appoint a committee or team to work with the designer. Typical questions relate to design preferences, space needs, and the interrelationships of spaces and departments. A typical residential programming questionnaire or client profile can be found in Appendix A.

Designers also review existing conditions or items (furniture, artwork, etc.) that are to remain. Furniture and other artwork may be inventoried and photographed to help the designer assimilate all the information. An example of a furniture inventory sheet can be found in Appendix B. If the interior space already exists, the designer also develops a floor plan of the space. Sometimes clients have floor plans (a measured drawing produced by the architect or builder of the home or office), but frequently the designer will measure and draw a plan of the interior space. The floor plan is the first step in developing visual communications for the client.

During this programming phase the designer researches life safety codes (fire codes) and universal design requirements, and begins coordinating with other specialists if necessary. As in all the phases of the design process, the designer will be reviewing the budget and schedule and making recommendations for changes.

By the end of the programming phase, the designer should fully understand the scope of the project and be able to produce a *design concept statement* outlining the broad-based requirements of the project. Depending on the scope of the design project, the programming phase may take one afternoon (if the client only needs a small bathroom remodeled, for example), or it could take months (for a commercial client with several hundred employees). In general, 5 to 15% of the time in a design project is spent in programming. As with all other design phases, the designer reviews the final programming information with the client and incorporates their feedback before proceeding to the next phase of design.

Conceptual Design

During the **conceptual** or **schematic design** phase, designers formulate preliminary broad-based concepts. Design decisions regarding the character, function, and aesthetics of a project are presented to the client for approval.

When working with a client who is remodeling a home, the designer may show the client a preliminary floor plan indicating where new and existing furniture would be located. The designer would also present the client with a few fabric and paint samples indicating the conceptual direction of the color palette and design scheme. The client can respond to the plan and selections before the designer spends hours selecting the specific new sofa and exact fabric.

In a commercial project, or a residential project requiring an entire custom home design, the designer may begin by developing a **matrix** (sometimes called a *compatibility matrix*) indicating the relationship of particular individuals, departments, or spaces (Figure 1.4A). Another tool is the **bubble diagram** to help the designer and the client visualize the requirements of the space (Figure 1.4B). The bubble diagrams can lead to the **blocking diagram** that helps to establish the flow and arrangement of rooms and the outline for the perimeter of the building (Figures 1.4C and D). A designer who is working with a multistory house or high-use office complex may develop a **stacking diagram** (see Design Scenario) to help evaluate what departments or rooms are located on each level. As with the smaller residential project, the designer ultimately puts all this information on a floor plan to illustrate the layout of the space. This process is called **space planning.**

Also during conceptual design, the designer selects sample color chips for reference to the color palette, fabrics, and/or furniture for the design scheme. The designer may also prepare a preliminary three-dimensional drawing or a perspective to help the client visualize the proposed new space. As with the floor plan and preliminary furniture plan, all of these diagrams, drawings, and sketches add to the process of visual communication.

The designer prepares all of this conceptual design documentation while considering the life safety and building codes, universal accessibility codes, green design options, and budget (all of which are discussed in later chapters). Only after presenting these designs to the client *and* receiving client approval will the designer move on to the next phase of the design process. The conceptual design phase consumes from 15 to 20% of the time in the total design process.

Design Development

The **design development** phase is also a creative phase. During this phase all the furniture, fabrics, finishes, hardware, and lighting fixtures are selected for the client's review. Space planning of rooms and furniture arrangements is refined based on feedback from the client's review of the conceptual design. Designers may develop art, accessory, graphic, or signage programs. Walls, windows, doors, fireplaces, stairs, and ceiling designs are defined and detailed where necessary. This entire array of information is shown to the client via a presentation.

A small residential project presentation may include photographs of selected pieces of furniture and actual samples of fabrics, floor coverings, and wall treatments along with a presentation floor plan. More likely, however, the client will be taken to a showroom or a decorative arts center to view specific selections.

A more complex residential project or a commercial project usually requires a series of presentation boards that illustrate the interior space (Figure 1.5). Visual communications may include black and white or colored floor plans, **elevations** (drawings of walls), or perspectives. The presentation boards include samples of fabrics and finishes, and

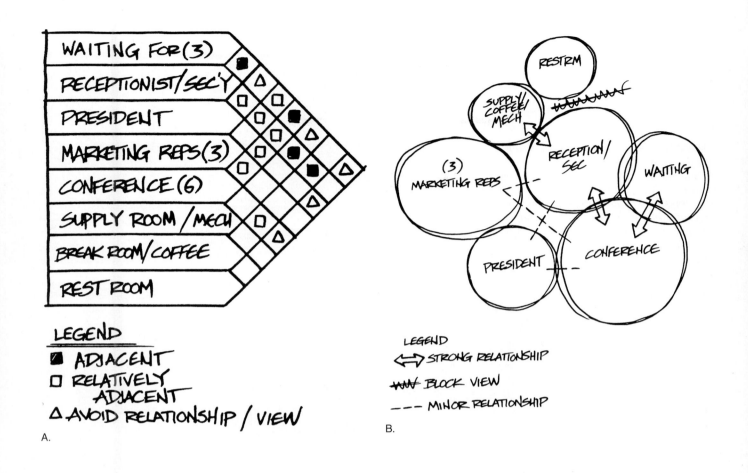

LEGEND
- ■ ADJACENT
- □ RELATIVELY ADJACENT
- △ AVOID RELATIONSHIP / VIEW

A.

LEGEND
- ⟷ STRONG RELATIONSHIP
- ⋙ BLOCK VIEW
- --- MINOR RELATIONSHIP

B.

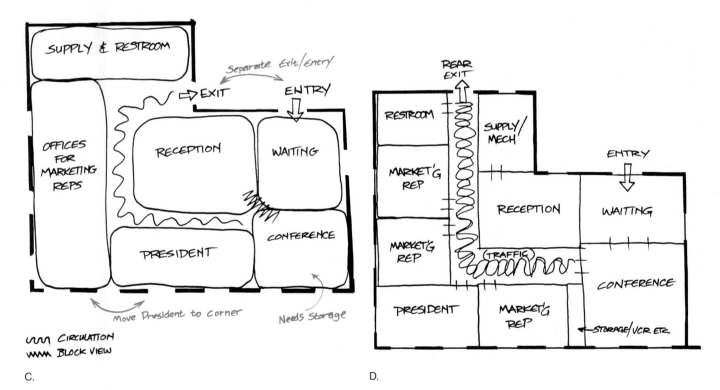

⌇⌇ CIRCULATION
⋙ BLOCK VIEW

C.

D.

Figure 1.4 *In this series of illustrations, a small commercial real estate office floor plan is developed through conceptual design: A, matrix; B, bubble diagram; C, blocking diagram—step 1; D, blocking diagram—step 2.*

Figure 1.5 *This commercial marketing firm's design development presentation included a series of boards. The designer illustrated the solution via floor plans, 3-D drawings, and actual samples of furniture, finishes, and fabric. Note how the shape of the exterior of the building is reflected in the space planning and finish applications. (Designer: Charlene Gabriel.)*

photographs of furniture, art, and accessories. Models are sometimes built to show unusual or dynamic spaces such as lobbies and entry halls or soaring ceiling designs. Current CAD technology can visually walk clients through a virtual interior (Figure 1.6).

As in the previous design phases, the designer is always aware of the budget and life safety and universal design requirements. None of the design recommendations are acted upon until the client has approved the design. This phase of design occupies 25 to 30% of the overall time in the design project.

Contract Documentation

The next phase of design, called **contract documentation,** allows the designer to document the design decisions made in the previous design phases. In collaboration with architects, designers prepare **construction** or **working drawings** (detailed plans, elevations, and sections). De-

signers also collaborate with allied professionals who determine architectural, mechanical, electrical, and structural requirements.

For a small residential project, the contract document (CD) phase may only include writing purchase orders for furniture, fabrics, and other items to be purchased for the client and installed by the vendors. For a large residential project or commercial project, the designer not only will be involved with the development of the working drawings but also may write **specifications.** The specification (or spec) book is a documentation of all the furniture and other items that are not attached to the building. The spec book or **furniture, furnishings, and equipment package (FF&E)** is then sent to several vendors for bidding.

The working drawings are also sent out to bid to qualified contractors. Once bids have been collected, reviewed, and awarded, the contract documents phase is complete. This tedious yet exacting phase of design may take 30 to 35% of the total design process time. If the budget preparation by the

A.

Figure 1.6 *A computer-generated view of the corporate office lobby is shown in A. B is a photo of the completed interior. (Architect: Thompson, Ventulett, Stainback & Associates Inc. Designer: TVS Interiors. Photograph by Brian Gassel.)*

B.

designer has proven effective, the bids meet the planned budget. Otherwise, the designer may need to select less expensive items, finishes, and alternative design solutions. Sometimes, however, the client may like the design enough to increase the budget to meet the higher cost.

Contract Administration

Contract administration is usually the most rewarding phase of the project. All of the design decisions become real as the walls are built, mechanical, lighting, and electrical sys-

tems are installed, finishes are applied, and the FF&E is placed according to the designer's plans. As the title implies, the designer is administering the contracts completed in contract documentation.

For a smaller residential project, the designer places orders, and continually monitors the status of the shipments and the installation of the items. For larger projects, the designer regularly visits the job site to verify that the working drawings are followed and the job is progressing as planned. The designer oversees the installation of the FF&E. At the end of this phase, which takes 5 to 15% of the design process time, the designer prepares a **punch list** indicating all the items not yet finished in the project. Final payments to vendors and contractors are withheld until the items are completed.

Evaluation

In this final phase of design, sometimes called **postoccupancy evaluation (POE),** the designer and client evaluate the effectiveness of the design decisions. The designer may interview selected individuals in the firm to determine their level of satisfaction with the new interior space. The designer may also photograph the space and visually analyze the design solutions.

According to NCIDQ's *Definition of Interior Design:* "The interior design process follows a systematic and coordinated methodology. Research, analysis, and integration of information into the creative process result in an appropriate interior environment." Utilizing these phases of the design process helps ensure that designers' solutions will not only satisfy their clients' needs but will also result in successful interior spaces.

The design process is a continuous flow of information through all phases. Certainly for billing and for educational purposes it is simpler to establish separate categories, although in practice the phases tend to merge. For example, in residential design a client may accompany a designer on a buying trip. On the trip, the selection, specification, and purchasing of goods (which correspond to the design development, contract documentation, and contract administration phases) may occur simultaneously. It is important to note in this situation that the designer completed the programming and conceptual phases (which correspond to the analysis and initial synthesis) prior to escorting the client on the buying trip. The Design Scenario at the end of this chapter illustrates a successful commercial design project.

Career Specializations in Interior Design

As the demand for quality housing, products, and commercial facilities rises, interior designers are finding more and more opportunities for creative design positions. When searching for a career path, a designer may choose from a variety of possibilities including residential design, contract or commercial design, product design, or other related design industries.

Residential Design

Residential design involves designing private living quarters or homes, including detached homes, condominiums, apartments, townhouses, and mobile homes (Figure 1.7). Designers may specialize in kitchen and bath design, residential lighting, designs for the elderly or disabled, children's rooms, vacation homes, remodeling, or additions. Residential designers usually work very closely with their clients, the **end users** of the space, to develop specific personalized solutions.

Figure 1.7 *A custom-designed mahogany door with onyx insets adds character to this interior space. The designer created an environment that accentuates the client's collection of paintings and decorative arts. (Designer: BRITO Design Studio. Photograph by Brian Gassel. As seen in* Atlanta Homes and Lifestyles.*)*

Contract or Commercial Design

The opportunities in commercial design are broad. Table 1.2 lists several of the options along with a brief explanation of each area. Commercial or contract designers work with a variety of clients who may or may not be the end user. For example, a designer working on a restaurant design may meet with the owner, the developer, and the chef to determine the desires of each for the new facility. Ultimately, however, the designer is designing for the client's client, the patrons who will be eating at the restaurant (Figure 1.8). Commercial as well as residential designers must follow strict fire and life safety codes, and must also meet universal design criteria. Surface materials, fabrics, and finishes must not endanger the health, safety, or welfare of the public.

Table 1.2 *Opportunities in Contract (Commercial) Design*

Major Specialty Areas

- Commercial office design   Involves extensive space planning and design of small to large corporate office environments.

- Healthcare design   Involves designs for hospitals, clinics, nursing homes, disabled and elderly care facilities, and doctors' offices.   The current trend in elderly care facilities blends this specialty with hospitality design.

- Hospitality design   Involves the design of hotels, motels, restaurants, casinos, resorts, clubs, and inns. Blends many aspects of residential design with contract design (see Figures 1.1 and 1.8).

- Institutional design   Involves the design of government buildings, such as courthouses, city halls, libraries, and museums as well as educational facilities such as public and private universities, colleges, and schools.

- Retail design   Involves the design of shopping malls, stores, boutiques, strip malls, and showrooms. Designers must be sensitive to the products to be displayed in the various areas.

Minor Specialty Areas

- Entertainment design   Involves the design of theaters, concert halls, auditoriums, and convention centers.

- Financial institutions   Involves the design of banks, stock exchanges, credit unions, and savings and loan facilities.

- Industrial design   Involves the design of warehouses, factories, laboratories, workshops, and manufacturing plants.

- Recreational design   Involves the design of health and spa centers, swimming pools, bowling alleys, and other sports facilities.

- Transportation design   Involves the design of airports, train stations, terminals, motor homes, boats and ships, and other transportation vehicles and facilities.

Related Design Professions

Designers may also choose to concentrate their efforts in one specific area or phase of design. Design specialty areas include communication (audio/video) design; exhibit design; model home design; solar design; and storage, cabinet, and closet design. Some designers may choose to specialize in selecting drapery and window treatment, or other finishes such as flooring or wall covering. Other designers may find that they have particularly strong selling skills and therefore may work as sales representatives.

Although many times overlooked, product design is an expansive field that requires creative minds. Product designers are responsible for the design of the furnishings, finishes, and fabrics in the interior environment. Textiles, wall and floor coverings, furniture, lighting, and hardware (to name

but a few) are items product designers create to be placed in the interior space.

Other challenging specialty opportunities are available in industry, manufacturing, transportation, communications, recreation, and in state and federal governments, where the diverse skills of design professionals are considered essential to long-range planning and product development. Table 1.3 lists additional design specialties.

Allied Professions

Interior designers must develop strong working relationships with other professionals in the construction and design industries. Allied professionals work closely with designers to form design teams and partnerships. This collaboration and networking enhances the communication skills required of interior designers.

Architects

The architect generally designs the exterior of the building. In small remodeling projects an architect may be contracted to advise on structural or mechanical systems. On larger residential and commercial facilities the architect works directly with the client designing the exterior as well as the structural components of the building. Architects and designers frequently collaborate on the building's interior construction of non-load-bearing walls. The architect may also oversee the construction of the space.

Engineers

Engineers work with architects and designers to produce the mechanical, electrical, plumbing, and structural drawings for a building. Proper communication is particularly critical when working with engineers to ensure that the design concept complies with engineering limitations. Designers should examine drawings produced by engineers.

General Contractor

The general contractor, or GC, administers the actual construction process. Generally, the GC oversees the process and subcontracts the work to others.

Graphic Designers

In commercial design, the graphic designer may assist in the development of appropriate signage for a building, brochure design, menu design, or a corporate identification and marketing package.

Landscape Architect

The landscape architect (LA) should be involved in the design process for the initial site selection. The LA can share crucial information with the architect and designer that may affect the shape and form of buildings. During contract documentation the LA provides important grading plans to prevent erosion

Figure 1.8 *The Old Well room in the Carolina Inn exhibits crisp cool colors, which create a comfortable environment for dining. The lobby (Figure 1.1) blends well with this dining room, creating a consistent flow of style. (Architect/Designer: The Glave Firm. Photograph by Robert Miller.)*

Table 1.3 *Related Opportunities in the Design Industry*

- Adaptive reuse designer   Works on the restoration or remodeling of historic buildings for a new function.
- Buyer   Purchases merchandise for furniture or department stores and studios.
- Color consultant   Aids clients in both residential and nonresidential design, with regard to color.
- Design journalist   Completes work for newspapers, magazines, or publishers on a variety of timely aspects of interior design.
- Drafter or CADD operator   Prepares precise mechanical drawings, often on the computer, for architects, designers, builders, and furnishing manufacturers.
- Educator   After seeking advanced degrees the educator instructs at a college or university.
- Facilities manager   Works with companies to determine the best use of their space and equipment.
- Fine art or accessory designer   Selects and purchases personal and corporate art and accessories.
- Green design consultant   Aids in the design and product selection of materials that ensure environmental sustainability.
- Historic preservation designer   Restores and preserves a historic structure as it was in the past.
- Lighting specialist   Designs lighting plans essential in the design process.
- Purchasing agent   Orders, coordinates, and installs FF&E per designer's specifications.
- Renderer   Prepares realistic, three-dimensional drawings and illustrations of a designer's concept for an interior.
- Set designer or stylist   Works on television, theater, and movie productions or creates complete room displays for department stores, furniture companies, and manufacturers for advertising.
- Universal designer   Specializes in the design of spaces for the elderly and disabled.

and future water problems, and provides planting and vegetation plans allowing the building to relate to its site.

Summary

From its beginnings in the 19th and 20th centuries, the profession of interior design has emerged into a multimillion-dollar industry. The profession has grown to encompass a broad scope of responsibilities, procedures, relationships, and opportunities, which NCIDQ synthesized into an established definition of the field of interior design. Professional design societies such as ASID and IIDA support NCIDQ by acknowledging the passage of the NCIDQ exam as one of their requirements for acceptance as a professional member.

In order to better analyze the abundance of information required in a design project and then synthesize that information into a cohesive design solution, the design process and scope of services were developed. Each phase of the process interlocks, ensuring creative design solutions that address the client's needs. These phases allow for the unique contributions of universal and green design solutions. Finally, allied design professionals collaborate to create the accurate communications necessary for successful interior environments

IMS HEALTH STRATEGIC TECHNOLOGIES

Project Description

Godwin Associates has been retained by IMS Health Strategic Technologies, Inc. (formerly Sales Technologies, Inc.) to help facilitate the company's move into a new corporate office facility and a customer service center. The new three-floor corporate office space will utilize approximately 60,000 square feet. The customer service center will result from combining two separate groups into one central 60,000-square-foot facility.

Programming: Figures DS1.1 through DS1.3 indicate space requirements for different areas of the firm. Note the important category called projected growth. Figure DS1.4 summarizes the square footage needs for the entire facility.

SALES TECHNOLOGIES
CORPORATE FACILITIES PROGRAM
30-Jan-97

DEPARTMENT/AREA	WORK AREA TYPE	CURRENT - 1997			PROJECTED GROWTH		
		QUANTITY	UNIT SQUARE FOOTAGE	TOTAL SQUARE FOOTAGE	QUANTITY	UNIT SQUARE FOOTAGE	TOTAL SQUARE FOOTAGE
RECEPTION/CONFERENCE							
Reception Area		1	600	600	0	600	0
Receptionist	WS	1	150	150	0	150	0
Conference		3	500	1500	0	500	0
A/V Storage		1	150	150	0	150	0
Subtotal:				2400			0
35% Circulation Factor:				840			0
DEPARTMENT TOTAL:				3240			0

NOTES:
1. All Conference Rooms to have the following: tackboards, whiteboards, recessed electric projection screens, variable lighting, and separate HVAC zone.
2. Conference Rooms to accommodate computer work area.
3. A/V Storage for slide/T.V. carts to be shared by all Conference Rooms.
4. Receptionist - 2 systems: Network PC with keyboard and Phone PC with keyboard
   - Would like to recess screens
   - Large Fax
   - Large Printer
   - Need wire management under desk
   - Currently no fax but will get one
   - Needs ticket drop-off areas
   - Transaction area needed for ticket pick-up

Figure DS1.1 *Programming requirements and estimated square footage needs for the reception/conference area. (Architect/Designer: Godwin Associates.)*

SALES TECHNOLOGIES
CORPORATE FACILITIES PROGRAM
30-Jan-97

DEPARTMENT/AREA	WORK AREA TYPE	CURRENT - 1997			PROJECTED GROWTH		
		QUANTITY	UNIT SQUARE FOOTAGE	TOTAL SQUARE FOOTAGE	QUANTITY	UNIT SQUARE FOOTAGE	TOTAL SQUARE FOOTAGE
PROFESSIONAL SERVICES/ IMPLEMENTATION							
Sr. Director	PO	1	150	150	0	150	0
Director	PO	2	150	300	0	150	0
Manager	PO	4	150	600	1	150	150
Customer Support Manager	WS	18	64	1152	4	64	256
Customer Support Specialists	WS	16	64	1024	3	64	192
Project Manager	WS	4	64	256	1	64	64
Intern	WS	1	64	64	0	64	0
Implementation Specialists	WS	8	64	512	2	64	128
Departmental Shared Areas							
File/Storage Room		1	120	120	0	120	0
Test Area		1	300	300	0	300	0
Subtotal:				4478			790
35% Circulation Factor:				1567			277
DEPARTMENT TOTAL:				6045			1067

NOTES:
1. Preferred department location is adjacent to Information Technology & Services, Customer Service and to Product Management/QA.
2. Implementation has total of (8) 36"W lateral files and (2) magazine racks.
3. Test area to be enclosed drywall area with glass sidelights and stereo/TV equipment.

Figure DS1.2 *Programming requirements and estimated square footage needs for the professional services area. (Architect/Designer: Godwin Associates.)*

SALES TECHNOLOGIES
CORPORATE FACILITIES PROGRAM
30-Jan-97

DEPARTMENT/AREA	WORK AREA TYPE	CURRENT - 1997			PROJECTED GROWTH		
		QUANTITY	UNIT SQUARE FOOTAGE	TOTAL SQUARE FOOTAGE	QUANTITY	UNIT SQUARE FOOTAGE	TOTAL SQUARE FOOTAGE
DEMO/TRAINING							
Manager of Customer Training	PO	1	150	150	0	150	0
Technical Training Coordinator	WS	1	64	64	0	64	0
Team Leader/Sr. Training Coordinator	WS	1	64	64	0	64	0
Sr. Training Coordinator	WS	2	64	128	0	64	0
Training Coordinator	WS	5	64	320	0	64	0
Team Leader Sr. Inst. Designer	WS	1	64	64	0	64	0
Sr. Instructional Designer	WS	1	64	64	0	64	0
Instructional Designer	WS	4	64	256	0	64	0
Departmental Shared Areas							
File/Storage and Demo Room		1	300	300	0	300	0
Test Area		1	300	300	0	300	0
Demo Room		1	800	800	0	800	0
Training Room		2	1200	2400	0	1200	0
Break Out Area		1	300	300	0	300	0
Telephone Area		4	25	100	0	25	0
Storage - Equipment		1	120	120	0	120	0
Subtotal:				5430			0
35% Circulation Factor:				1901			0
DEPARTMENT TOTAL:				7331			0

NOTES:
1. Test area to be enclosed drywall area not workstation area with sidelights and stereo/TV equipment.
2. Demo will require two entrances, one off of main reception area.
3. Training has total of (11) 36"W files and 40 L.F. of storage.
4. Training Room will have movable wall system to create (2) separate rooms.

Figure DS1.3 *Programming requirements and estimated square footage needs for the demo/training area. (Architect/Designer: Godwin Associates.)*

Godwin Associates' Project #96088   January 30, 1997

PROGRAM SUMMARY FOR SALES TECHNOLOGIES CORPORATE FACILITIES REVISION #1

DEPARTMENT AREA	EMPLOYEE TOTAL	CURRENT - 1997 S.F. (INCLUDING CIRCULATION)	CURRENT PLUS GROWTH EMPLOYEE TOTAL (*)	CURRENT PLUS GROWTH S. F. (INCLUDING CIRCULATION)
RECEPTION/CONFERENCE	1	3240	1	3240
EXECUTIVE	9	3274	10	3578
LEGAL	3	694	3	694
DEVELOPMENT	61	9480	69	10403
PRODUCT MANAGEMENT QUALITY ASSURANCE	11	1655	13	1828
SALES AND MARKETING	5	818	5	818
INFORMATION TECHNOLOGY & SERVICES	4	462	4	462
PROFESSIONAL SERVICES IMPLEMENTATION	54	6045	65	7112
INFORMATION SERVICES	10	6743	11	6829
FINANCE	7	1418	9	1591
VENDOR	4	346	4	346
TRAVEL SERVICES	5	743	5	743
DEMO/TRAINING	16	7331	16	7331
MAILROOM/COPY CENTER	1	918	1	918
SHARED AREAS - FLOOR A	0	2403	0	2403
SHARED AREAS - FLOOR B	0	1053	0	1053
SHARED AREAS - FLOOR C	0	1526	0	1526
TOTAL:	191	48,149	216	50,875

Figure DS1.4 *Summary of square footage requirements. (Architect/Designer: Godwin Associates.)*

Conceptual Design: After the programming information was analyzed, Godwin Associates developed a stacking diagram (Figure DS1.5). After generating bubble diagrams, blocking plans, and rough preliminary floor plans, the schematic furniture presentation plan was shown to the client (Figure DS1.6). Preliminary FF&E selections were also shared with the client.

Design Development: Based on the client's feedback and approval of the conceptual design, Godwin Associates continued to refine the design solution and select actual finishes and furnishings while defining custom details and elevations. The design development presentation had several components, including a computer-generated floor plan (Figure DS1.7) and several perspective renderings (Figures DS1.8 through DS1.10).

Figure DS1.5 *Stacking diagram. (Architect/Designer: Godwin Associates.)*

Figure DS1.6 *Schematic floor plan for the 14th floor. (Architect/Designer: Godwin Associates.)*

Figure DS1.7 *Design development: Computer-generated floor plan. (Architect/Designer: Godwin Associates.)*

Figure DS1.8 *Design development: Presentation perspective of the elevator lobby. (Architect/Designer: Godwin Associates.)*

Figure DS1.9 *Design development: Presentation perspective of the reception area. (Architect/Designer: Godwin Associates.)*

Figure DS1.10 *Design development: Presentation perspective of open office space. (Architect/Designer: Godwin Associates.)*

Figure DS1.11 *Construction drawing: Dimension partition plan for the 14th floor. (Architect/Designer: Godwin Associates.)*

Figure DS1.12 *Construction drawing: Reflected ceiling plan for the 14th floor. (Architect/Designer: Godwin Associates.)*

Figure DS1.13 *Construction drawing: Detail of the finish plan for the elevator lobby. (Architect/Designer: Godwin Associates.)*

Figure DS1.14 *Construction drawing: Furniture design of a typical open office workstation. (Architect/Designer: Godwin Associates.)*

Contract Documents: During the CD phase, Godwin Associates produced an extensive set of construction drawings and construction and furnishings specifications. Select examples are seen in the 14th floor Dimension Partition Plan (Figure DS1.11), the 14th floor Reflected Ceiling Plan (Figure DS1.12), and the Finish Plan for the Elevator Lobby (Figure DS1.13). Figure DS1.14 illustrates a furniture specification for an open office workstation.

Figure DS1.15 through DS1.17 show the completed elevator lobby and reception/waiting area.

Figure DS1.15 *Completed space: Elevator lobby. (Architect/Designer: Godwin Associates. Photograph by Brian Robbins Photography.)*

Figure DS1.16 *Completed space: Reception desk. (Architect/Designer: Godwin Associates. Photograph by Brian Robbins Photography.)*

Figure DS1.17 *Completed space: Reception area. (Architect/Designer: Godwin Associates. Photograph by Brian Robbins Photography.)*

History of **Style**

Throughout history, the diversity of cultures has found expression in many directions, including the way people have designed and furnished their built environment. Design is shaped by many factors, including environmental, religious, and political circumstances. As these factors change, design reflects these changes while building on previous design theories and philosophies. Styles of design, therefore, reflect these social surroundings and their foundations.

The term *style* generally refers to a segment of design history that is typical of an individual, a period, or a philosophy of design. Style may also refer to a particular culture or region. Style categories are developed by historians in an attempt to organize history. In reality, however, styles do not necessarily have sharp starting and stopping points. History is fluid. Designs from one region may influence others, and therefore styles intermingle.

Having a working knowledge of these styles is essential. Such understanding deepens the interior designer's aesthetic appreciation of design and serves as a basis to foster creative energies.

Designers study styles of the past and present to enrich current interior environments. This pictorial essay briefly outlines the major styles that have had an impact on architecture and interior design. The first section, Historical Styles and Their Evolution, reviews classical design styles and how these styles have been adapted through history. The pages on Ancient, Middle Ages, Renaissance, and Baroque eras define universal design styles based on time period classifications; the French, Hispanic, English, and American pages define styles that are more typically associated with their respective regions. The second section, Evolution of Modern Design, looks at the development of modern design and how these styles and philosophies have been applied.

Frank Lloyd Wright's modern residential design, Falling Water (1936), in Mill Run, PA, was built over a waterfall. It demonstrates the architect's philosophy: "A house should grow out of the land." (Courtesy of Western Pennyvania Conservancy.)

Historical Styles and THEIR EVOLUTION

Interior design and decoration dates back to the Upper Paleolithic era (30,000–10,000 B.C.). Drawings found in caves in Spain and France show evidence of wall decorations using grouping and spacing concepts as well as limited understanding of perspective. Sculptured figures of stone, ivory, and clay depicted the human form and often included enlarged reproductive organs, perhaps to influence fertility and thus the continuation of the species. These drawings and artifacts represent the following important concepts:

1. Creative expression is instinctive.

2. The art of interior design dates from early humankind and serves as an integral part of the human psyche.

Design evolved rapidly through the last several millenia. The Egyptians (circa 3000 B.C.), with their sophisticated art and architecture, made a lasting contribution to the interior design field.

Ancient

EGYPTIAN (4500–330 B.C.)

Egyptian chair with blocked feet

- Known for their pyramids built as tombs for kings and pharaohs

- Developed **trabeated** construction, in which vertical posts support a horizontal lintel.

- Used **hieroglyphics** (a system of writing using pictorial symbols) inscribed on walls

- Columns, perhaps originally made from papyrus reeds lashed together, created vertical lines, which lead to **fluting** on columns in later designs

- Utilized the mortise and tenon joint in their furniture

- Used straw for flooring, therefore furniture was raised on small blocks so animal-shaped legs could be seen

- Motifs included the lotus bud, reeds, papyrus, and lilies.

Trabeated construction

The Parthenon is located on the Acropolis in Athens, Greece. Completed in 438 B.C., the building was dedicated to the goddess Athena. Doric columns form a portico around the building. (Photograph from PhotoDisc.)

- Known for their order, proportion, and refinement of design

- Built temples to honor their gods, surrounded by open porticos (porches) and columns

- Developed the **truss** system, a triangulated load-bearing construction to allow for sloped roofs. The triangle formed by the truss is called a **pediment**

- Developed a system of naming the design and details of columns. These classical orders of architecture, still used today, include the Doric (plain square capital on top of column), Ionic (capital with spiral design called a volute), and Corinthian (capital with two rows of acanthus leaves)

- Mastered the art of carving marble into a human form. When used for support, the human form is called a **caryatid**

- Developed the klismos chair

Klismos chair

Pediment

Acanthus leaf

Fret

Doric

Ionic

Corinthian

- Known for their engineering expertise, particularly the development of roads and aqueducts

- Adapted Greek designs

- Vitruvius, a Roman architect, developed standard sizes and dimensions for the architectural orders (columns)

- Added two classical orders, the Tuscan (similar to Doric but without column fluting) and Composite (capital combines acanthus leaves and volutes)

- Developed concrete arch, barrel vault, and dome

- Developed **pilasters** (columns partially embedded in the walls)

- Motifs included dolphins, eagles, ribbons, swans, and **grotesques** (fanciful human/animal forms)

Roman bed

Roman marble table

Roman chair

The parts of the Tuscan order as defined by Vitruvius.

Tuscan

Composite

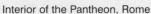

Interior of the Pantheon, Rome

Middle Ages

- Designs dominated by religion, particularly Christianity
- Four general divisions:

  1. Early Christian era (325–800): characterized by the development of the basilica church plan, rectangular, with side aisles and with **clerestory** windows lighting the central space

  2. Byzantine era (330–1450): church still the dominant building, with domed structures and elaborate mosaic designs

  3. Romanesque era (Norman in the British Isles) (800–1150): massive stone structures, including churches, monasteries, and castles, with round arches and heavy columns

  4. Gothic era (1150–1500): architectural features commonly associated with ecclesiastical design include the pointed arch and vault, tracery, slender columns in clusters, and buttresses or flying buttresses

The cathedral in Chartres, France, with its large stained-glass windows and soaring interior space, is considered an outstanding example of Gothic architecture. (Courtesy of the French Government Tourist Office.)

Early rose window

Linenfold motif

Gothic church plan

Renaissance

- Means "rebirth"
- Major influence came from Italy (1400–1580), although it spread throughout Europe
- Rejected Middle Ages design and returned to classic design motifs
- Included work by Andrea Palladio, Michelangelo, and Leonardo da Vinci

Plan, Villa Rotonda

Cassone

Cassapanca

Savonarola chair

The Villa Rotonda (1550) was designed by Andrea Palladio, who helped promote the rebirth of classic style. (Photograph from Art Resource, NY.)

Baroque

- Means "misshapen pearl"
- Major influence came from Italy and France
- Ornate, asymmetrical designs
- Flamboyant and heavy proportions

Baroque chair

St. Peter's in Rome was designed and built under the direction of a series of architects, including Donato Bramante and Michelangelo. The original design reflects the Italian Renaissance. In the interior, seen above, the immense altar canopy, designed by Gianlorenzo Bernini, incorporates Baroque characteristics. (Photograph from Art Resource, NY.)

Built during the reign of Louis XIV, Versailles became an immense complex of buildings housing 10,000 people. The designers included the painter Charles LeBrun and the architects Louis LeVau and, later, Jules Hardouin-Mansart. André LeNôtre's design for the surrounding landscape became a prototype for future town planning. (Photograph from Corbis LGI.)

- Coincides with reign of Louis XV
- Means "rock and shells"
- Related to interiors more than architecture
- Flowing, feminine design with delicate decorative details and free-form curves
- Pastel colors
- Gilded, painted, or **chinoiserie** lacquered surfaces on furniture
- Chinese influence introduced by Madame de Pompadour
- Motifs included fret designs, exotic flowers, birds, pagodas, monkeys, and mandarins (officials at the royal court)

Fauteuil

Console
and mirror

Tête-à-tête

Cabriole legs

Commode

Chinese black
lacquer and gilt
cabinet on stand

Lacquered
Chinese chair

Porcelain vase
on a stand

Chinese porcelain
garden seat

Chinese construction

Chinoiserie
motif

- Coincides with reign of Louis XVI and Marie Antoinette

- Similar to Rococo, but focused on straight lines, rectangular forms, and symmetrical balance

- Motifs and designs influenced by the discovery of Pompeii, an ancient Greco-Roman resort city in southern Italy, which had been buried by the eruption of Mt. Vesuvius in A.D. 79.

Fauteuil

Bergère

Chaise longue

Ormolu

Reeded legs

Bouillotte

- Coincides with reign of Napoleon

- Characterized by return of classic Greek, Roman, and Egyptian designs

- Massive, asymmetrical designs

Table support

Psyche mirror

Console with Egyptian heads

Fauteuil

French Empire bed

Lion's paw foot

Bergère

X-stool

- Designs for lesser nobility and merchants
- Copied or adapted Rococo and Neoclassic designs in simpler, unadorned styles

Stool

Open arm chair

Hutch

Salamander back

Long narrow table

1200–Present

Hispanic Styles

- Similar to Italian Renaissance but also included Moorish influence (1200–1600)
- Moorish interiors highly decorated and used the horseshoe arch
- Colored marbles, geometric patterns, tiled walls, and **wrought iron** (worked iron)
- Carved wood doors, window shutters, and ceilings called **artesonado**
- Influence in America called Colonial/Mission style

Ladderback

Shepherd's chair

Paneled door

Moorish arch

Spanish foot

Vargueno

English Styles

- Dominated by heavy, masculine designs
- Architecture characterized by **half-timbering** timbers are visible on the outside of the building) and oriel windows (projecting bay windows)
- Interiors characterized by plain, plastered walls or ornately carved panels
- Furniture frequently made of oak
- Elizabethan furniture had bulbous (melonlike) legs
- Jacobean furniture had turned legs

Tudor half-timber

Paneled hall

Tudor arch

Jacobean daybed

1612   1656
Chair legs

Linenfold motif

Jacobean wainscot chair

English Styles

- Prominent architects included Inigo Jones and Sir Christopher Wren
- Symmetrical designs exhibited dignity and formality, reflecting classic Greek and Roman architecture
- Queen Anne furniture based on cyma ("S") curve
- Most significant piece of furniture was splatback or fiddleback chair with **cabriole** (animal-like) leg and pad or club foot. Later chairs had ball and claw foot

Wren Georgian

Shell cupboard

c.1705   c.1710
Fiddleback/Splatback side chairs

Finial

Lowboy

Cupola on roof

Highboy

Gothic influence

Ladderback

Ribband back

Chinese Chippendale

Gothic back

Marlborough (left)

Claw and ball cabriole leg

Goddard foot

Camelback sofa

Pie-crust table

Breakfront

- Architecture still influenced by Wren

- Golden Age of great cabinet-makers, including Thomas Chippendale

- Chippendale wrote *The Gentleman and Cabinet-Makers Director* (1754)

- Chippendale chairs distinguished by yokebacks with Chinese, Queen Anne, Gothic, French, and Neoclassic influences

An American adaptation of Georgian design is seen in the Port Royal Parlor at the Winterthur Museum. Georgian features included Chippendale furniture with a few Queen Anne pieces, typical wood floors with Oriental rugs, dadoes, cornices with dentil trim, and a chimneypiece with the broken pediment design. (Courtesy of Winterthur Museum.)

English Styles

- Architecture influenced by Roman Palladian style; even more formal

- Coincided with French Neoclassic style and the discovery of Pompeii

- Robert Adams and his four sons designed classical interiors. Known for their sideboard designs. Utilized **paterae** (oval-shaped decorations)

- George Hepplewhite designed furniture with straight, square, tapered legs usually terminating with a spade foot. Known for his shield and heart-shaped chair backs

- Thomas Sheraton designed furniture with straight lines and classical motifs such as urns, festoons, and scrolls

Paterae

Longfellow House (1750), Cambridge, Massachusetts. Its classical detail with the triangular-topped pavilion reveals Gibbs's Palladianism. (Courtesy of National Park Service, Longfellow National Historic Site.)

Hepplewhite sideboard

Sheraton chair back

Sheraton armchair

Bellflower & eagle motifs

Tapered

Hepplewhite fluted leg with thimble foot

Tapered leg with thimble foot

Heart back

Shield back chair

Sheraton sofa

Serpentine front

Hepplewhite Pembroke table

Sheraton sideboard

Sheraton extension table

COLONIAL AMERICAN
(1600–1700)

- Influenced by Dutch, German, Swedish, English, French, and Hispanic styles

- Most common architectural styles true to American designs included:

1. Saltbox: front rooms with a lean-to on the back

2. Garrison (jetty): second floor extends over the first floor creating a **jetty**

3. Gambrel: a house with a double-pitched roof creating more headroom in the attic

4. Cape Cod: a house covered in wood with a sloped roof, central chimney, small paned windows, and plank door. Later features included dormers, Georgian details, and double-hung (sash) windows

Saltbox

Garrison or Jetty

Gambrel

Cape Cod

Half-house — 1650

Two-room or double house — 1675

Lean-to

Keeping room

Parlor

Entry

Lean-to or saltbox

The Oyster Bay Room at the Winterthur Museum reflects a typical 17th century interior: wood plank floors with an Oriental rug, plaster walls, a low beamed ceiling, a large fireplace, and simple wood furniture. (Courtesy of Winterthur Museum.)

- Most common Early American interiors included Tudor, Elizabethan, Jacobean, and Spanish Mission/Colonial style influences

- In southwest America, furniture designs were called the Santa Fe style and incorporated bold colors and geometric forms

Bannister back

Carver

Brewster

Indian pottery

Equipale leather and wood chair

Windsor

Hitchcock

Adobe house

Viga   Latillas
Niche
Adobe interior

Corbel bracket

Zapata
(double corbel bracket)

Lodge pole pine chair

Indian basket and wool rug

An interior reflecting the Santa Fe style features an architectural background of white plastered walls, recessed niches over the fireplace, Mexican tile, and dramatic lodgepole beams. The style is further expressed by the use of Mexican, Native American, Spanish, and contemporary furnishings and accessories. (Photograph by Pam Singleton.)

COLONIAL GEORGIAN
(1700–1790)

- Greatly influenced by English Georgian styles with variations in wood usage, specific ornamentation, and proportions

Wingback armchair

Desk

Martha Washington chair

Mirror

Grandfather clock

NEOCLASSIC
(1790–1845)

- Several distinctive designs including Federal, Greek Revival, Duncan Phyfe furniture, and Empire furniture

- Federal design emphasized Greek and Roman design, rejecting English influence. Thomas Jefferson was an advocate

- Greek Revival architecture particularly prominent in the South for plantation homes. Greatly influenced by early Greek designs

Monticello, home of Thomas Jefferson, was completed in 1809 in Charlottesville, Virginia. The Early Classic revival style was promoted as a "national" style by Jefferson. It reflects the Federal-Roman influence. (Photograph from PhotoDisc.)

American Styles

- Duncan Phyfe furniture characterized by fine proportions and simple lines

- Empire furniture was bold and monumental

- Industrial Revolution (circa 1830s–1900) brought about machine-made, mass-produced furnishings and a decline in the fine art of furniture making

Curule
form chair

American Empire
pier table

Duncan Phyfe sofa with
cornucopia legs

Girandole mirror
(Bull's eye)

Greek Revival
gondola chair

Greek Revival carved sofa

Farmers Hall, completed in 1826, in Pendleton, South Carolina, is an excellent example of Greek Revival architecture. (Courtesy of Lynn M. Jones.)

This parlor reflects the designs from the Greek Revival and Empire periods. (Courtesy of Winterthur Museum.)

A contemporary Greek Revival interior designed by Robert Metzger is reminiscent of this early nineteenth-century style, including the use of gold and blue, a patterned rug, torchères, and asymmetrical couches with the distinctive lion's paw foot. (Antique architectural Aubusson courtesy of F. J. Hakimian, Inc., N.Y,. and Robert Metzger Interiors. Photograph by Phillip Ennis.)

In the study of the history of design, a significant break in design occurs with the Industrial Revolution. The fine art of furniture making is overshadowed by the ease of mass-producing machine-made furniture. For this reason, the historical/classic eras end in the 1830s. It was also during this time that Americans first recognized the need to preserve our national heritage.

Green Design   AMERICAN CULTURAL HERITAGE

One of the finest examples of Green Design is the preservation and reuse of historic structures. The need to preserve America's cultural heritage began as a grassroots movement in the 1800s and continues to have its most effective results at the community level. One of the first architectural buildings to be preserved was George Washington's home, Mount Vernon. The Mount Vernon Ladies Association was formed and raised the funds to purchase and restore the home in the 1880s. The Mount Vernon Ladies Association is still responsible for the home and the tours.

Before the turn of the 20th century, America recognized the need to preserve its national treasures. Large areas of land were set aside as National Parks (a concept developed in America), National Monuments, and Historic Sites. In 1914 the National Park Service was formed to manage these and future acquisitions. Throughout the early 1900s many homes and buildings were preserved and restored to be used as museums to define America's heritage. Williamsburg, a reconstructed village, illustrates how an early American community lived and worked. The Historic American Buildings Survey, or HABS, was begun by the Park Service in 1933. The initial record produced 24,000 measured drawings of historic structures.

The National Trust for Historic Preservation in Washington, D.C., founded in 1949, is the largest organization in the country devoted to the preservation of historic buildings, districts, and neighborhoods. An organization sustained by both public and private contributions, the National Trust maintains the National Historic Register. The National Trust also administers historic buildings as museums, disseminates information about preservation to property owners and to the public at large, and assists in a variety of preservation, restoration, and rehabilitation efforts around the country. However, it is important to note that National Historic Register designation does not ensure the building's sustained preservation. The National Historic Register is a recognition status that requires only government-owned buildings to be subject to environmental review prior to proposed demolition. If a community is determined to maintain its local historic character, that community must invoke local ordinances and regulations to preserve their structures.

Through the 1950s, 60s, and 70s many national treasures were destroyed in the name of "progress." Of the structures surveyed by HABS in the 1930s, over half had been destroyed. Recognizing the need to reaffirm America's historical heritage, the grassroots movement lobbied Congress, and the national Historic Preservation Act was greatly enhanced in 1980. Tax relief and grants-in-aid (among other important legislative actions) were established to promote preservation. Downtown communities were granted funding through the Mainstreet Program to save their historic downtown character. Businesses that renovated historic homes, public buildings, and even factories helped to create the design specialty of adaptive use.

Through the grassroots efforts of many individuals and organizations, America's cultural heritage before and after European occupancy can be observed through buildings, historic sites, and communities, as well as in the open spaces of National Parks and Monuments. Americans have recognized the need to preserve a *sense of space*. They also recognize that natural resources, elaborate architecture, and unique details are costly to replace once destroyed. In fact, many are irreplaceable.

Old Faithful Inn (1901) in Yellowstone National Park, designed by architect Robert Reamer, is listed on the National Historic Register. Reamer created the rustic lodge to serve as a safe refuge from the wild. Victorian, Arts & Crafts, and Swedish details are prevalent. Photographs courtesy of Lynn M. Jones.

Historical Styles SUMMARY

The cyclical nature of design is seen in the shift from the clarity of the Egyptian and early Greek designs to the eventual heavy embellishment of the more ornate Roman designs. The cycle was repeated in the early simple English Queen Anne style that led to the Georgian and Federal styles, which eventually led to the heavy, ornate furniture of the Empire era. It is the nature of design to start with the purest and cleanest forms and then to embellish those forms again and again until the next generation must once more break free (or "rebirth") to new classics. The following section begins with yet another heavily decorated era, that of the Victorian period. From this ornately decorated state, designers once again rebelled against the elaborate motifs and designs; architecture and interior design evolved into the Modern Era.

Evolution of Modern Design

The roots of modernism are primarily traced to the Industrial Revolution, a period that continued from the early 1800s until the early 20th century. This era introduced machines for manufacturing furniture and other modern conveniences, changing the way people lived. Advancements in technology and the development of new materials led to extraordinary architectural innovations. For example, iron grid construction allowed the architect to enclose vast spaces for railroad stations, exhibition halls, libraries, stock exchanges, theaters, and other public buildings.

The first World's Fair and Exhibition, held in London in 1851, is a fundamental starting point for modern designs. The Fair's Crystal Palace, designed by Joseph Paxton, was over 1600 feet long and resulted from technical advances in the use of glass and iron. The Exhibition serves as a transition between historic and modern design, for although the structure and modern machines housed within spoke to the 20th century, the furnishings and architectural details produced by the machines were rooted in the past.

Victorian Era (circa 1840–1920)

- Coincided with reign of Queen Victoria

- Nostalgia for past styles prevailed with machinery producing intricate designs, details, and carvings referred to as gingerbread

- Four major architectural styles in America included:

  1. Gothic Revival: Andrew Jackson Downing main proponent

  2. Italianate: modified Italian villa

  3. Mansard or Second Empire: style delineated by sloping mansard roof defining the top floor

  4. Queen Anne: most whimsical of all Victorian era eclectic styles (not related to Queen Anne furniture styles previously discussed)

Carpenter Gothic

Mansard Victorian

Italianate Victorian

Queen Anne

- Other Victorian styles included Exotic Revivals, Octagonal, Stick, Shingle, and Romanesque

- Interiors were profusely decorated with patterned wallpaper, fabrics, and rugs

- Elaborate furnishings were adapted from French Rococo, Neoclassic, Gothic, Renaissance, Oriental, and Elizabethan/Jacobean eras

- Prominent designers included John Belter (who developed a wood laminating technique that allowed for ornate rosewood carvings) and Charles Eastlake.

A contemporary Victorian interior, designed by Michael R. LaRocca, demonstrates the eclectic look. Tudor, Moorish, French, and Greek Revival are the principal styles employed. The patterned rug and numerous accessories further convey the Victorian feeling. (Antique French needlepoint courtesy of F. J. Hakimian, Inc., N.Y., and Michael R. LaRocca, Ltd. Photograph by Phillip Ennis.)

Eastlake chair

Belter carved rosewood sofa

Traditional Revivals

(circa 1880–1920)

- Revival of Old World styles
- World famous design school L'École des Beaux Arts in Paris promoted these styles
- Opulent designs by Richard Morris Hunt and McKim, Mead & White (architectural firm)
- Included Beaux Arts, Châteauesque, Georgian Revival, Spanish Colonial, Neoclassical, Tudor, Colonial Revival, French Eclectic, and Italian Renaissance

Biltmore House (1888–1895), the Châteauesque mansion built by architect Richard Morris Hunt for George W. Vanderbilt and patterned after a French Renaissance château. (Courtesy of Biltmore House and Gardens.)

Lavishly decorated dining room at The Breakers, the summer "cottage" of the Vanderbilt family in Newport, Rhode Island. (Courtesy of The Preservation Society of Newport County, Newport, R.I. Photograph by John T. Hopf.)

Early Modernism

- Coincided with Victorian Era and Traditional Revivals

- Pioneering designers rebelled against historical eclecticism

- Utilized technological advances in iron frame construction, laminated wood, and plate glass windows

- Bridged art and technology

- Earliest designs came from the Shakers, a religious order who believed beauty resides in utility and simplicity

- Austrian designer Michael Thonet (1830–1870s) developed process for bending wood into gentle curves

- Thonet's designs still used today, including the famous bentwood rocker and café chair

Bentwood rocker
Michael Thonet

Vienna café chair
Michael Thonet

ARTS AND CRAFTS MOVEMENT
(1860s–1920s)

The Gamble House in Pasadena, California, now the headquarters for the Greene & Greene Foundation, remains the finest example of their craftsman approach to architecture. (Photograph ©Peter Aaron/ESTO.)

This interior view of the Gamble House reveals exquisitely handcrafted wooden architectural members and handcrafted furnishings. (Photograph ©Peter Aaron/ESTO.)

- Revolted against machine-made products

- Advocated hand-crafted furnishings

- Prominent English architects and designers included William Morris, Charles Eastlake, Edward W. Godwin, Philip Webb, Ernest Gimson, and Charles F. A. Voysey

- Prominent American architects and designers included Gustav Stickley, Frank Lloyd Wright, Henry Hobson Richardson, and Charles and Henry Greene

- Greene brothers developed the bungalow

Voysey chair

Stickley chair

- Although the first metal frame buildings were in New York, the skyscraper is credited to Chicago architects

- Louis Sullivan, father of the skyscraper, is credited with coining the phrase "Form follows function"

- Many skyscrapers reflect the three parts of a column: the base, the shaft, and the capital

The Home Insurance Company Building (1883–1885), Chicago, by William LeBaron Jenney, was the first fully steel-frame building. Jenney studied in Paris at L'École Centrale des Arts et Manufactures. Unfortunately, the building was demolished in 1931. (Courtesy of Chicago Historical Society.)

ART NOUVEAU
(circa 1890–1910)

- Style based on nature, employing organic flowing forms

- Prominent proponents included Victor Horta, Henri van de Velde, Hector Guimard, and Antonio Gaudi

- Called *Jugendstil* in Austria and Germany

- Charles Rennie Mackintosh combined aspects of Art Nouveau with strong geometric forms

- Louis Comfort Tiffany is best known for Art Nouveau stained-glass designs

Art Nouveau chair
Hector Guimard

Art Nouveau chair
Antonio Gaudi

Argyle chair
C.R. Mackintosh

The Tassel House (1892–1893) in Brussels, Belgium, is one of Victor Horta's best-known town houses and one of the earliest private residences designed in the Art Nouveau style. Swirling organic forms decorate the entry. The graceful stair railings and supports are fashioned in iron. (Photograph courtesy of the Museum of Modern Art, New York.)

Early Modernism

* Influenced Wright, Mackintosh, the Greene brothers, and Godwin, among others

* Emphasized simplicity, horizontal line, and non-formal balance

Cocktail table "monkey paw" leg

Chest with brass fret hardware and "monkey paw" leg

Wood armchair

Rattan armchair

Japanese house

Modern Styles

• Characterized by a building that appears to "grow out of the land"

• Greatest proponent was Frank Lloyd Wright

• Wright developed *prairie style* house (see Figure 1.3)

• Style based on functionalism and purity of line

• Term coined by American architect Philip Johnson

• Common materials included reinforced concrete, stucco, steel, and glass

• Stark white finishes

• Open floor plan and large expanses of glass

• International design movements leading to the fully developed style included:

1. The Secession—an artistic movement in Austria led by Otto Wagner, Adolf Loos, and Josef Hoffmann. Hoffmann also led the Wiener Werkstätte (studio), a more geometric offshoot

2. De Stijl—a movement in Holland that reduced design to its basic elements, including the use of only red, blue, yellow, black, gray, and white. Most famous proponent was Gerrit Reitveld

Fledermaus chair
Josef Hoffmann

Prague chair
Josef Hoffmann

Haus Koller chair
Josef Hoffmann

3. Bauhaus–an experimental design school in Germany formed to simplify design to its purest state, incorporating machine-age manufacturing. School was closed by the Nazis in 1933, and designers fled to America. Most famous proponents included Walter Gropius, Marcel Breuer, and Ludwig Mies van der Rohe. Mies coined the phrase "Less is more."

4. Le Corbusier (Charles-Edouard Jeanneret-Gris)–a giant of modern architecture; studio was in Paris. Designed the Villa Savoye, the chapel at Ronchamp, and classic furniture pieces

One of the finest examples of furniture from De Stijl is the Red/Blue chair (1918), designed in Holland by Gerrit Reitveld. It is constructed of wood in an abstract arrangement and painted red, blue, yellow, and black. (Courtesy of Cassina USA Inc.)

Secession stool
Otto Wagner

Barcelona chair
Mies van der Rohe

Grand Confort chair
Le Corbusier

Classic Bauhaus furniture designed by master architect and furniture designer Marcel Breuer. From left to right, the Cesca chairs, Laccio table and Wassily lounge, designed by Breuer while he taught at the Bauhaus. The Isokon lounge, far right, was designed in 1935 in England. (Courtesy of Knoll.)

Zig-Zag chair
Gerrit Reitveld

The Villa Savoye, designed by Le Corbusier, comprises three floors. The main living level is on the second floor, which opens to a terrace and the third-floor roof garden. Le Corbusier wrote "The house is a machine to live in." (Photograph from Art Resource, NY. ©2000 Artists Rights Society (ARS), New York/ADAGP, Paris/FLC.)

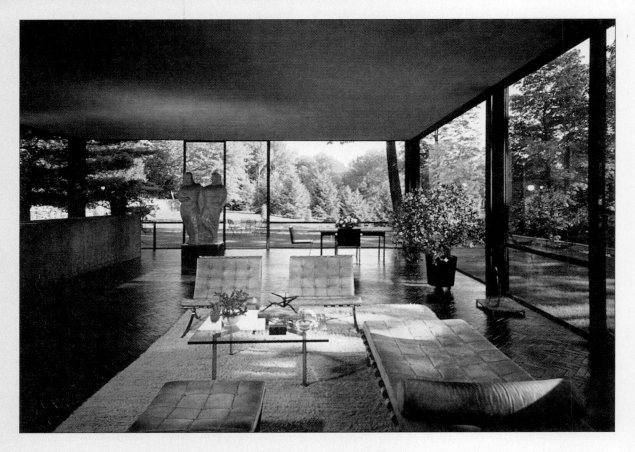

Architect Philip Johnson's "Glass House" in New Canaan, Connecticut (1949), with glass walls and Barcelona furniture by Ludwig Mies van der Rohe. Johnson was an early follower of Mies van der Rohe. (Photograph by Bill Harris, ©ESTO.)

ART DECO
(circa 1909–1940)

- Decorative style advocating strong geometric forms including the pyramid, ziggurat (stepped pyramid), zigzag, and sunburst

- Inspired by the glamour of movies and stage, jazz music, African art, and new technology

- Prominent designers included Paul Frankl and Donald Deskey

- Eliel Saarinen, a Finnish-born designer, started the prestigious Cranbrook Academy in Michigan

Paul Frankl helped promote modern American furniture during the 1920s and 1930s and was inspired in his own approach to furniture design by the uniquely American skyscraper—an Art Deco theme he employed for numerous pieces.

Eliel Saarinen designed the Blue Chair in 1929, at the Cranbrook Academy of Art. The Art Deco piece has a blue lacquered frame accented with gold leaf. (Courtesy of ICF.)

- New architectural directions emerge

- New technologies included air-conditioning, suspended ceilings, synthetic fibers, and plastics

- Scandinavian designers included Alvar Aalto, Eero Aarnio, and Hans Wegner

- Italian designers in particular exploited the use of plastics; designers included Joe Columbo and Vico Magistretti

- American designers included:

  1. Charles and Ray Eames—pioneered chairs constructed of molded plywood and fiberglass

  2. Eero Saarinen—came to the U.S. with his father Eliel; known for his womb and tulip chairs

  3. Buckminster Fuller—known for his geodesic domes

- Brutalism develops as a reaction to the International style. Massive, sculptural structures of raw concrete were designed by noted architects such as Paul Rudolph and Louis Kahn

Palmio (Scroll) chair
Alvar Aalto

"The Chair"
Hans Wegner
Scandinavia

Tulip/pedestal chair
Eero Saarinen
U.S.A.

Peacock chair
Hans Wegner
Scandinavia

Eames lounge
Charles Eames, U.S.A.

The spherelike U.S. Pavilion at the Montreal World's Fair Expo '67, designed by Buckminster Fuller, is a good example of the architect's patented method of construction known as the geodesic dome. (Courtesy of Miriam Stimpson.)

Finnish designer Alvar Aalto designed the cantilevered Pension chair in 1946 using laminated birch with a seat and back of webbing. The birch table is also by Aalto. They are excellent examples of Scandinavian modern furniture design. (Courtesy of ICF.)

Modern Styles

- The style borrows from the past but in extremely contemporary terms

- Major exponents include Michael Graves, Robert Venturi, Robert Stern, and Philip Johnson

- Furniture styles include the Craft Revival, Art Furniture, Ergonomic Furniture, and most recently furniture to meet the needs of a mobile work force

- Other design trends during the Post-Modern era are generally divided into four categories:

  1. High Tech Style—utilizes exposed industrial and construction elements; started by the Eames

  2. Memphis Style—advocates freedom of expression in style, color, and form

  3. Classic Modernism—advocates classical, simplified elegance; influenced by ancient Greek designs

  4. Deconstructivism—an extreme reaction to the negative aspects of current society; leading proponent is Frank O. Gehry

Graves chair
Post-Modern

Venturi chair
Post-Modern

Grande Flute
Angelo Donghia
Classic Modern

Horses bench
Judy K. McKie
Craft Revival

Queen Anne, Queen Anne
Terence & Laura Main
Art Furniture

Seconda chair
Marlo Botta
Italy

Dakota Jackson has designed many detailed functional pieces of furniture, including his Calliope Chaise (1995). (Also see Figure 8.20.) (Courtesy of and design by Dakota Jackson.)

Michael Graves designed this Post-Modern residence in New Jersey in 1986. In the entry, tall lighting fixtures are capped with Egyptian-like capitals. In the living room beyond, the fireplace wall dominates the space. See Figure 12.36. (Photograph by William Taylor.)

This unique modern sofa upholstered in bright-colored fabrics reflects the Memphis style, a style originated by Austrian-born Italian designer Ettore Sottsass in 1981, advocating freedom of expression, especially when combining color and form. (Courtesy of Thayer Coggin, Inc. and designer Milo Baughman.)

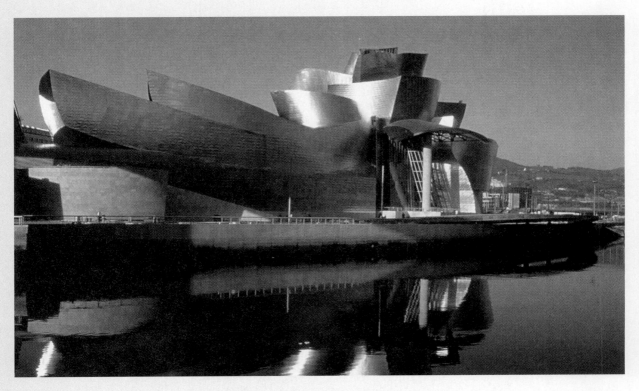

Completed in late 1997, the Guggenheim Bilbao in Spain was designed by Frank Gehry. The fragmented volumes and curved forms are covered with titanium. A central axis and curved interior forms reflect the influence of the Guggenheim Museum in New York by Frank Lloyd Wright. (Photograph from Liaison Agency.)

Modern Design SUMMARY

Historians cannot define what will be considered classic 100 years from now. Current design trends may be remembered only as passing fads, or they may start a definitive movement in history. Note that once again design seems to have reached the end of a cycle. Whereas design was formerly clean, crisp, and uncomplicated (as promoted by organic architecture and the Bauhaus purism), the current images of the avant-garde Memphis-styled expression, the re-inventing of the classic Queen Anne chair in style and color, and the radical nature of Deconstructivism suggest that the next movement may be to a new cycle of simplicity.

Style Selection

After studying these design styles, you should consider how these historical styles could be adapted and applied in current interiors. When selecting a style for a client, it is important to understand the overall feeling that the client desires. Generally, five basic style categories are used to help guide the client. They are formal traditional, formal modern, informal provincial, informal modern, and eclectic.

FORMAL TRADITIONAL

The term formal traditional refers to interior furnishings, finishes, and backgrounds from historical styles that are of the more refined or court types. Many of the traditional designs come from the 18th and early 19th centuries, an age of great prosperity during which the arts flourished in the Western world. French and English furniture styles of this period exemplify this warmth, grace, and elegance. Some of these styles have been adapted and scaled to meet present-day requirements without losing their character (see Figures VI.1 and VI.2). Styles appropriate for a formal traditional look include English designs (Queen Anne, Chippendale, Adam, Hepplewhite, and Sheraton), Court French (Louis XV, Louis XVI, Empire), and America's Federal.

FORMAL MODERN

A formal modern environment can be created by employing modern furnishings, finishes, and backgrounds that are elegant and sophisticated. Art Nouveau, Art Deco, Classic Modern, and Post-Modern furniture are particularly well suited for a formal setting (see Figure VI.3). Italian, Secession, Wiener Werkstätte, De Stijl, Bauhaus, and International Style furniture may be very formal and sophisticated, depending on supportive elements. Modern Oriental is often used in a formal manner.

INFORMAL PROVINCIAL

Historically, provincial furniture was produced in rural areas. Provincial furniture used native woods and techniques that imitated finer, more expensive finishes. The provincial interior is generally handcrafted, simple, and casual, appearing unpretentious. The look is cloistered, comfortable, and rustic; it may incorporate furniture from a number of countries as long as designs are rooted in the past and have an aura of charm and informality (see Figure 13.6). Styles most commonly employed that provide this feeling are Colonial American, Medieval English (as well as simplified Georgian), French Provincial, and Spanish. Also appropriate are Dutch, Swedish, and German furnishings.

INFORMAL MODERN

Numerous types and styles of modern furniture are available on the market, drawing principally from European, Oriental, and American designers. When an informal modern setting is preferred, generally casual fabrics with a matte finish, simple materials, and unpretentious accessories are used (see Figure 13.1). Informal modern can also use fun, "funky" designs. Plastics and disposable furniture work in this style. Informal modern furniture styles particularly suitable for this direction include Scandinavian and modern furniture inspired by Japanese prototypes and the Craft Revival. Other modern styles including Secession, De Stijl, Bauhaus and International Style, Post-Modern, and Italian can generally be designed in either an informal or formal manner, depending on the supportive treatment.

ECLECTIC

The **eclectic** look—which is a mixing rather than a matching one—is common; however, eclectic does not mean hodgepodge. Furnishings should be related in scale and chosen with a final goal in mind. There should be a common theme—some element that ties the pieces together. For example, to achieve the provincial look, informality may be the key, and all country furniture, regardless of the source, is generally compatible. For a formal traditional look, dignity may be the key, and refined pieces of almost any style can be combined with pleasant results. The eclectic look often allows for more daring and imaginative interiors (see Figure 13.3).

Whatever the general theme of a room, it should not dominate and thereby create a feeling of monotony. Interest is aroused by the unexpected. For example, a pair of Victorian chairs placed in a modern setting brings something special to a room. A modern sofa gives a period room a fresh, updated look. The clean sweep of contemporary decor may serve as the most effective background for a highly prized antique.

PART II

Design Fundamentals

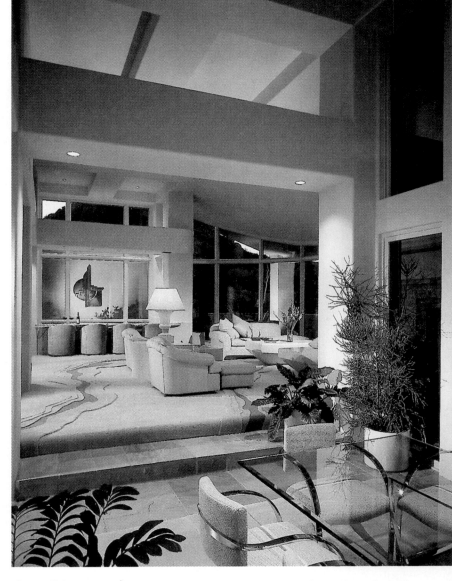

Figure II.1 *Efficient open planning allows space to flow freely throughout the interior of this contemporary home. Spaces for various functions are defined by the arrangement of furniture and by a change in floor level rather than by walls. (Photograph by Mark Boisclair.)*

Designers are aware of the impact of the physical interior environment on the occupants' lives. The need for adequate shelter is only the beginning. The environment must promote the comfort and convenience of the end users, both physically and psychologically, while taking into account economic realities. Meeting human needs in specific environments, whether residential or commercial, requires a balance of technical knowledge and an appreciation of quality aesthetics.

	in	cm
A	54	137.2
B	12	30.5
C	30	76.2
D	48	121.9
E	18	45.7
F	42	106.7
G	9	22.9
H	24	61.0
I	40	101.6
J	16	40.6
K	10	25.4
L	116–128	294.6–325.1
M	18–24	45.7–61.0
N	80	203.2
O	78–90	198.1–228.6

Figure II.2 *This drawing illustrates the minimum dimensions needed to seat six individuals around a table. (From* Human Dimension & Interior Space *by Panero and Zelnik © 1979 Whitney Library of Design)*

Goals of Interior Design

The designer's ultimate goal when planning a residence or commercial structure should be the integration of the basic requirements for an efficient and aesthetically pleasing space. If the interior space satisfies the *function* requested by the client, meets the *aesthetic* criteria of the design, and is completed within the client's *economic* directives, the project is a success (Figure II.1).

Function and the Human Factor

To be livable, an interior first should fulfill its intended function of satisfying the needs of the people for whom it is designed. Careful consideration of functional space begins in the programming phase. Specific design requirements may be necessary for the special needs of users such as children, the elderly, or the physically challenged. The human factor is a primary concern when determining the function of the space (Figure II.2). This is obvious when one considers the needs of a day care or elementary school in contrast to a care center for the elderly or a university classroom building.

From a psychological viewpoint, humans must feel comfortable in relation to the scale and proportion of the architecture. The three-dimensional aspects of ceiling height, wall length, and cubic feet should be considered, because if the space is too vast or too small, the occupants may feel uncomfortable or out of place. Satisfying human psychology entails many other design criteria as well, including selection and arrangement of line, color, form, lighting, and texture to create a sense of balance and harmony.

Interior spaces and fixtures need to be scaled to meet the proportions of the users, while also meeting their physical needs. Furniture should be suitably scaled and arranged for purpose and efficiency. For example, a chair for relaxing should be comfortable and should fit the size of the occupant, with a table at the appropriate height close by to accommodate a lamp that produces adequate lighting with no glare.

The designer should create an environment that not only meets the client's needs, but is also a safe environment in which to live. Life safety and building codes must be followed. No matter how wonderful an interior space looks, if the users cannot efficiently complete the activities and functions required in the space, the design has failed.

Aesthetics

The second goal of an interior space should be to create a pleasant and appealing environment. It is essential that students of design develop awareness and sensitivity to the aesthetics of all interior environments, including private dwellings, financial or educational institutions, offices, retail and hospitality spaces, health care centers, and other nonresidential interiors.

Anyone can express personal preference, but developing good aesthetic judgment requires a high level of *discernment* that is acquired through years of experience and observation. Good design has no absolute formula; however, the successful use of aesthetic principles—scale and proportion, rhythm, balance, emphasis, and harmony—aids in decision making and enhances the designer's results. Integrity and simplicity are important ingredients in good design, along with consideration for the design's function and its relationship to the environment and to people.

Radial balance

Asymmetrical balance

Symmetrical balance

Figure II.3 *Objects in nature demonstrate the various types of balance. A spider's web indicates radial balance. This tree exhibits asymmetrical balance, whereas a butterfly is an example of symmetrical balance.*

The following guidelines can help the beginning designer develop a discriminating eye for quality design:

- The elements and principles of design (discussed in Chapter 2) must be understood and applied.
- Objects in nature should be carefully observed. Their play of light and shadow, their shape, texture, pattern, and color are fine examples of design (Figure II.3).
- Historical and contemporary eras of design serve as a foundation for current design solutions.
- Professional design periodicals provide valuable ideas. (A listing of selected periodicals appears at the end of the reference list.)
- Fashion is not a criterion of good design. Like fashion in clothes, fashion in home furnishings often becomes outdated. National trends, events, and celebrities can influence individual taste, but do not necessarily relate to good design.
- *Simplicity* is key to quality design. The famous architect Ludwig Mies van der Rohe coined the phrase, "Less is more."
- All design decisions and selections should possess *integrity*. Furnishings with integrity exhibit their true identity. For example, a plastic laminate surface should look like plastic, not like cheap wood grain.
- Quality design is not "cute."
- Quality design is timeless.

Knowledge of what constitutes good design enables designers to guide their clients toward wise design decisions. This may mean educating the client. Good design is a long-term investment, and although at times expensive, it is worth the cost.

Economics and Ecology

The third goal of interior design is to work within the proposed budget. Designers work to satisfy the client's needs and desires within a reasonable budget to which both parties agree. If during the planning stages it becomes apparent to the designer that the project is exceeding the cost of the original projection, the designer has an ethical obligation to inform the client. Changes in the project scope or budget need to be addressed immediately.

Value becomes an important factor when designing and selecting interior components. Long-term upkeep and **life-cycle costing** (the total manufacturing and operating cost for the life of the product) are important factors when considering which items to recommend to a client. For instance, a desk chair for a client's office may be available at a local office supply store for around $100; however, if the casters easily fall off or the chair is not ergonomically designed to fit the client, the value of the chair is low. Conversely, a more expensive office chair with a five-star base, adjustable arms, back, and seat would prove to be the better long-term investment, and therefore is a better value to the client.

Economic considerations also relate to ecological and environmental concerns, or green design. Designers must not compromise their client's health by specifying potentially harmful materials to save on costs. For example, some inexpensive carpet padding may serve its intended purpose, but the gasses released from the padding could harm the building's inhabitants.

Similarly, designers should consider long-term environmental costs before specifying the use of any product that may be rare or endangered, or that through its production may harm the environment. For instance, rare woods may look appealing, yet by specifying them the designer may be encouraging the harvesting of threatened forests. Effective environmental design decisions produce interiors that utilize materials and products that ensure environmental sustainability for future generations (Figure II.4). Green design solutions are discussed in various chapters throughout the text.

Creating interiors based on the goals of function and the human factor, aesthetics, and economics and ecology allows the designer to address all aspects of a successful interior environment. Part II reviews necessary foundation information that will assist the beginning designer in more thoroughly understanding the aesthetic nature of design. Chapter 2 begins with a review of the two basic design directions, structural and decorative design, followed by a detailed discussion of the elements and principles of design. Chapter 3 is dedicated to the study of color.

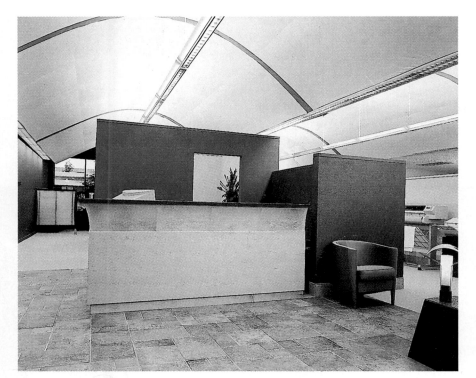

Figure II.4 *This industrial and mechanical engineering firm's office is designed to bring the feeling of natural light into the building. With only one side of the building open to natural sunlight, a product called Tyvek (normally used in overnight express mail packages) was suspended from the ceiling. The translucent canopy allows light to filter into the room much like sunlight. (Architect/Designer: Lippert & Lippert Design, Palo Alto, CA. Photograph by Don Roper Photography.)*

CONSTRUCTION/
FURNITURE PLAN

2

Elements and Principles of Design

Figure 2.1 *This dramatic and visually pleasing environment is the result of understanding the function, aesthetics, and economic requirements of the interior. Knowledge of the elements and principles of design and the ability to apply them are also essential for solving design problems. (Photograph by Mark Boisclair.)*

Design is the planned arrangement of basic elements and principles that work together to create an image, object, or environment (Figure 2.1). The creator of a well-planned and well-executed design—whether for a brass candlestick, a bedroom, or an entire office building—has carefully analyzed the use of space, line, shape and mass, texture, light, color, and pattern. The creator synthesizes these elements to ensure that the unity and variety of the design encompasses appropriate scale, proportion, balance, rhythm, and emphasis.

Two Basic Types of Design

Becoming familiar with the two basic types of design, *structural* and *decorative,* is a helpful introduction to the principles and elements of design (Figure 2.2).

Structural Design

Structural design relates to the size and shape of an object reflected in the materials. In other words, the design is an integral part of the structure itself. For example, the ancient pyramids of Egypt are structural designs because they expose the stone blocks from which they were made. Contemporary architecture, both inside and out, reveals the materials that make up the basic structure, such as wood or metal beams, brick, stone, and concrete (Figure 2.3). In modern furniture, the form itself (such as the metal frame of the Barcelona chair shown in Figure 2.14) is an integral part of the design statement. Successful structural design depends upon *simplicity* and *appropriateness of materials used.*

Figure 2.2 *Structural design and applied ornamentation or decorative design.*

Simplicity

A structure, whether serving as the finished product itself or as the supporting element of a design, should be kept simple. For example, a room with too many or poorly placed openings, arches, and niches is seldom pleasing.

Appropriateness of Materials

Various objects use different materials and require different methods of construction. Glass is blown and can be intricately decorated by skilled craftspeople; molded plastic chairs may be turned out on an assembly line. Interchanging procedures and materials when producing an object may not be feasible or may not achieve the desired result. Materials selected for a structural design should be appropriate for the intended purpose.

Applied Ornamentation or Decorative Design

Decorative design relates to the ornamentation of the basic structure with color, line, texture, and pattern. For example, the exterior surfaces of East Indian temples are completely

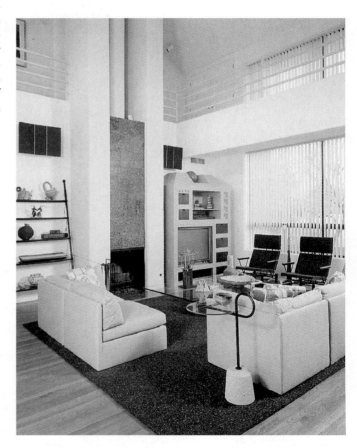

Figure 2.3 *In this living room designed by Laurence Lake, both the architectural background and the furnishings demonstrate clean structural design. Pillows and other accessories soften the geometric effect and add a decorative quality. (Photograph by Pam Singleton.)*

Figure 2.4 *Applied pattern, or ornamentation, is found on virtually every surface in this elegant bedroom, from the patterned rug and the brocade spread to the delicate carving on the chairs, paneled walls, and fireplace. (Antique Oushak courtesy of F. J. Hakimian, Inc., N.Y. Design by Ron Grimaldi for Rose Cumming, Inc. Photograph by Phillip Ennis.)*

covered with embellishment in color, line, and texture. Victorian-style houses often couple fanciful decoration and bright color schemes with unique structural elements. Furniture may be handsomely carved to add charm and dignity. Fabrics, wallpapers, rugs, accessories, and other furnishings can be attractively enhanced with decorative design (Figure 2.4).

Four classifications (as seen in Figure 2.5) apply to applied ornamentation or decorative design: *naturalistic, stylized, abstract,* and *geometric.*

1. Naturalistic, realistic, or photographic design reproduces a motif from nature in its natural form. In naturalistic design, flowers look like flowers as they are seen in the garden or growing wild.
2. Stylized design creates a motif taken from nature but adapted to suit the shape or purpose of the object to be decorated. In this case, flowers are recognizable but are modified or slightly changed. This type of design is often used for interior furnishings.
3. Abstract design departs from nature. The elements, which may or may not be recognizable, are transformed into nonrepresentational design.
4. Geometric design is made up of geometric motifs such as stripes, plaids, chevron patterns, and zigzags.

Successful decorative design depends on *suitability and placement* and *appropriateness.*

Suitability and Placement

An item's purpose should be immediately recognizable. Additionally, the embellishment on any item should not interfere with the item's comfort or functionality. **Bas-relief** on a wall plaque is attractive and suitable, although such carving on the seat of a chair would be very uncomfortable to the occupant!

Naturalistic

Stylized

Abstract

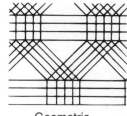
Geometric

Figure 2.5 *Types of applied ornamentation.*

A.   B.

Figure 2.6 *These successful corridor designs illustrate structural and decorative design solutions. Structural design is stressed in A. Vertical and horizontal lines emphasize the angles of the building. Applied design is limited. (Resurgens Orthopedics, Atlanta, Georgia. Design Firm: Farrington Design Group. Hiro Isogai, Design Director. Photograph by Hedrich-Blessing.) B emphasizes decorative design. Applied ornamentation results in colorful walls and decorative carpet treatments. (MTV Network, Atlanta, Georgia. Design Firm: studio epic 5, Hiro Isogai, Principal. Photography by Hedrich-Blessing.)*

Appropriateness

Appropriate decoration should accent the shape and beauty of the object. For example, vertical fluting on a supporting column makes it seem higher, but crossbars appear to reduce its height and detract from its dignity. Classic figures on a Wedgwood vase emphasize its rounded contour, whereas harsh lines would destroy its beauty.

The amount and type of surface decoration should be chosen with great care, while keeping the basic structure in mind. Figure 2.6 illustrates contrasting examples of structural and decorative design.

Elements of Design

The **elements of design** are space, line, shape and mass, texture, light, color, and pattern. These elements aid the designer when creating a visual environment and are often referred to as *tools*. The organization and arrangement of these elements or tools are closely allied to the principles of design, which are explained later in this chapter.

Space

Space is best explained as the area found within an enclosure, either real or perceived. This may include one's personal space, the walls and ceilings of a room, a fence around a yard, or even the boundary lines that define nations. Space is the area in which people live. Line, shape or mass, texture, and so on, are elements working together in space to form dynamic negative-positive interactions (Figure 2.7). In design, walkways or **traffic lanes** define some of the negative space; furnishings define the positive. Well-planned and well-organized space produces a functional and comfortable interior.

The challenge of many residential interiors is that they may simply lack the adequate space required to complete necessary tasks. Many individuals have acquired more "stuff" than is needed; in some situations, in order to provide enough space, the designer must gently persuade the client to remove some of their "precious cargo." In design, less is more. On the other hand, an accumulation of memorabilia may be important for the elderly. As always, designers must be sensitive to their client's needs.

Figure 2.7 *In this study the artist illustrates a variety of forms that delineate negative and positive space. The design illustrates the diversity of reverse imagery. (Artist: Elizabeth McKay.)*

In commercial environments, the quantity of space is equally as important, especially when clients are leasing the interior and paying for it based on the quantity of square feet. A designer who understands how to utilize the premium commodity of space cleverly and efficiently will be rehired on future projects. Part IV, "Space," reviews layout and space requirements for furniture arranging as well as space planning for a variety of rooms.

Line

Line forms the direction or feeling of a design and is particularly dominant in contemporary art and interiors. The composition of a room is established by the lines that give it motion or repose. Skillful use of line is therefore of utmost importance (Figure 2.8).

Line can seemingly alter the proportion of an object or an entire room. For example, in Figure 2.9, two identical rectangles are divided, one vertically and the other horizontally. As the eye travels upward along the vertical line, the rectangle seems higher. Along the horizontally divided area the eye is directed across, making the rectangle appear wider. Each kind of line has a particular psychological effect on a room. To achieve the desired result, the interior designer should keep in mind the distinct effects of each line.

Vertical lines tend to provide a feeling of height, strength, and dignity. These lines are particularly evident on the exterior of a building where columns are used, in the interior where upright architectural members are conspicuous, in tall pieces of furniture, and in the long straight lines of vertical louvers or folds of drapery.

Horizontal lines create a feeling of repose and solidity, and like vertical lines also provide strength. These lines are often seen in **cornices, dadoes,** bookshelves, and long, low pieces of straight-lined furniture. Falling Water, a famous Frank Lloyd Wright house, is an excellent example of horizontal architecture (see page 23).

Figure 2.8 *Soaring verticals and intersecting diagonals silhouetted against the sky carry the eyes, and spirit, upward in the Thorncrown Wayfarer's chapel in Arkansas, designed by E. Fay Jones. (Courtesy of E. Fay Jones, FAIA, Maurice J. Jennings, AIA, and David W. McKee, AIA.)*

Diagonal lines give a room a feeling of action and movement. They are evident in slanting ceilings, staircases, Gothic arches, and sloping furniture. Too many diagonals in a room, however, may create a feeling of unrest.

Curved lines have a graceful and delicate effect on a room. They are found in arches and other curved architectural treatments, drapery **swags,** rounded and curved furniture, and rounded accessories. The Taj Mahal is a supreme example of graceful architecture primarily employing curved lines (Figure 2.10).

Curved lines fall into the following four general categories:

1. Large convex (upward) curves tend to provide an uplifting feeling, such as a curved staircase opening from a foyer.
2. Large concave (downward) curves often give a feeling of solidity, and in art, even sadness. (Artists have used this line to evoke a feeling of mourning or unhappiness.) Downward curves such as a domed ceiling or series of arches may also be very dramatic.
3. Long, flowing horizontal curves (like those seen on a shoreline or gently curving mountain road) can imply restfulness.
4. Small curves such as those commonly found in patterned carpets, rugs, and fabrics often express lightness and merriment. They add life and character to a space.

Figure 2.9 *The use of line.*

When two identical rectangles are divided differently—one horizontally and one vertically—the proportion seems to change.

Horizontal lines give a feeling of repose.

Diagonal lines are lines of movement.

Vertical lines add height and dignity.

Vertical lines emphasize and enhance the basic structure.

Zigzag lines detract from the basic structure.

The curved line was used by Eero Saarinen to create the classic pedestal chair.

Too much line movement in a room may evoke a feeling of instability. A careful balance of line is essential to the feeling of comfort and harmony in a room. A designer can use line to create a mood or feeling, give direction to a room, create an optical illusion, achieve a feeling of balance and rhythm, support a room's focal point by directing the eye toward that feature, and give variety and unity to a room through the skillful blending of the various line types.

Shape and Mass

The terms form, shape, and mass are frequently used interchangeably in the profession. Technically, however, *form* de-

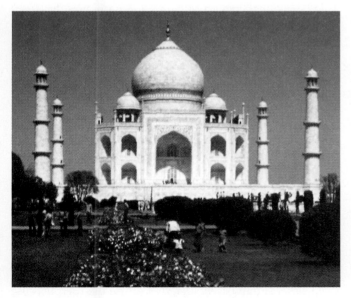

Figure 2.10 *The Taj Mahal incorporates graceful curved lines. (Photograph from Prentice Hall.)*

fines the essential nature of the design that distinguishes it; a piano looks like a piano because of its form. The contour of an object is represented by its *shape,* which is made up of lines. When a two-dimensional shape takes on a third dimension, it becomes a *mass* made up of a volume outlined by the shape. In the planning of interiors, mass is perceived as objects (e.g., furniture) that require space and may be moved to various locations. The arrangement of mass within a room—furniture arrangement—is discussed in Chapter 6. Basic masses (or forms as used below) or shapes fall into the following three categories:

1. Rectangles and squares are the most dominant shapes used in architecture and interior design. They provide a sense of unity and stability, are easy to work with, and may be arranged to conserve space. Too many rectangular and square forms may produce monotony; however, introducing circular and angular forms into the space alters this effect.

2. Diagonal forms frequently begin with triangle shapes. The diamond shape results when triangles are arranged base to base. A variety of other shapes using the diagonal line may be created. These forms are often seen in sloping ceilings and motifs applied to fabrics and wallpapers. Triangular, diamond, and other diagonal shapes may be used for flooring materials, furniture, and accessories, providing a dynamic effect.

3. Curved forms include spheres, circles, cones, and cylinders. Curved forms are found everywhere in nature. (The shape of the human body is curved.) Curved forms are constant, unifying, and pleasing. When used in the interior environment, curved forms may be dramatic, like a sweeping staircase or domed ceiling; curved forms are also used for accessories like pieces of pottery, plates, lamps, round tables, or sculptures. Curves may give relief and variety to a room with a predominance of angular and rectilinear forms.

Very few interiors employ only one shape or form. The environment is most often enhanced by skillfully combining the three basic forms for architecture and furnishings. However, too much variety of form and shape may produce a room with a feeling of confusion. The visual transition from one object to another should be easy and pleasurable. The emphasis created when a curved form is placed against a rectangular panel may provide unexpected and agreeable relief to a room's otherwise severe lines. For example, a curved floor plan, when used with rectangular rooms, as seen in Figure 2.11, creates such an effect. The sophisticated combination of forms is evident today in both modern and traditional styles.

Texture

Texture refers to the surface quality of objects—the quality that can be not only touched but also sensed in memory. The roughness of sandstone, the softness of a deep-pile rug, the smoothness of glass, and the shininess of growing leaves all produce a particular sensation because of previous associations with these textures.

Basically, textures fall into the following categories: soft or hard, smooth or rough, and shiny or dull. Throughout history, smooth, highly polished surfaces, lustrous metals, and fabrics of satin, silk, and fine linen have been symbolic of wealth and high status, whereas rough, handhewn textures and homespun fabrics have characterized lower economic classes. This is no longer the case. Many wealthy individuals prefer a handcrafted look, which may well cost as much as the most refined look. Additionally, smooth and shiny surfaces have been reserved for formal interiors, while dull and rough textures have been associated with informal treatments. Regardless of style, a knowledgeable use of texture is a sure way to bring character to a room. Textures in the interior environment often combine several characteristics. For example, a wool carpet can have a soft and dull texture. Properties and considerations regarding texture are discussed below.

Visual Interest, Beauty, and Character

Texture adds much visual interest in the environment. The early Greeks delighted in the smoothness and beauty of marble floors. The people of Iran take pride in the fine texture of their hand-knotted rugs, and the Japanese enjoy the woven texture and look of grass mats called **tatami.** Modern interiors depend on the physical impression of texture to create variety and interest. The texture of a surface reflects a particular character and unique beauty that makes a lasting physical or psychological impression.

Light Reflection

Each texture has a surface quality that affects light reflection. Smooth, shiny surfaces like glass, mirrors, satin, porcelain, and highly polished wood reflect more light than rough and dull textures like brick, concrete, stone, and coarse wood.

Maintenance

The choice of a particular texture determines the amount of maintenance a surface requires. Smooth textures may show fingerprints. Shiny textures may scratch easily. Rough textures, while more durable, may collect dirt in crevices. A shiny glossy paint will hold up longer but will highlight imperfections in the wall. A matte finish paint may not wash as well, but it hides imperfections in the wall.

Acoustics

Textures can absorb or reflect sound. Smooth and hard surfaces tend to magnify sound, while soft and rough textures have a tendency to absorb sound. Walking through an unfurnished room with a hard floor produces a high level of sound. When the same room is furnished with rugs, fabrics, draperies, and furniture, the sound is greatly muffled. Designers can control the acoustics of a particular space with wise textural combinations.

A Combination of Textures

Formal textures like satin and polished marble and informal textures like burlap and stone generally are not mixed in the same environment unless a specific effect is desired. The dominant texture of a room is often established by the architectural background. For example, a room paneled in fine-grained and polished wood or papered in a traditional formal wallcovering generally requires furniture woods and fabrics with a smoother and shinier texture than that required of a room paneled with natural course-grained wood or constructed of masonry. Contemporary use of texture may break these traditional rules, providing an element of surprise. A combination of textures, whether employed for an avant-garde or conservative environment, enhances the total visual experience (Figure 2.12).

Light

The element of *light* combines the creativity of the arts and the technology of science. Light affects the physical as well as the emotional comfort of the user. A room must have sufficient light; however, too much light or the inappropriate use of light can cause headaches and inhibit productivity.

The mood and appearance of a room can be greatly altered through the use of light. Uniform light (light lacking in contrast) can lead to boredom and a lack of energy. The quantity as well as the quality of light is critical in a well-designed room. Light variations create interest in a room, but can also affect the perceived color of the interior. Without light, no visual elements can be experienced. Light, its effect on the user, and its proper placement and selection are discussed briefly in Chapter 3 and in detail in Chapter 4.

Color

Color is dependent on light. Color can alter the perceived shape, size, and location of an object. It can create the illusion of texture, stimulate interest, or calm a busy environment. Color has a strong psychological effect on the user. Because of its central role in design, color is discussed in greater detail in Chapter 3.

Figure 2.11 *In this curved office environment, the designers created a sweeping curve opposite the library. The circular balcony pierces the rectangularly shaped trade floor. The ceiling and furniture also employ the familiar curves. (Architect/Designer: Alan J. Feltoon & Associates, Inc. Photograph ©Peter Aaron/ESTO.)*

0 4' 8' 16'
5m

Figure 2.12 *An unusual 5600-square-foot carriage house was converted into a development center. This upstairs break-out room combines the rough texture of limestone walls and sisal mats with sleek furniture and wall panels. (Architect/Designer: HOK. Photographer: Steve Hall/Hedrich-Blessing.)*

Pattern

Pattern is a decorative design, figure, or motif created through the use of space, line, shape, light, and color. Pattern can be effectively employed to create interest (see Figure 2.4), although too much pattern can make a room too "busy" and uncomfortable. In contrast, a room devoid of pattern may be stark and uninviting. The total arrangement of the components of a room creates an overall pattern, but more obvious patterns are seen in fabric and wallpaper. The use of pattern and pattern combinations is more thoroughly covered in Chapter 9, "Textiles."

Principles of Design

Through the centuries certain **principles of design** have evolved through careful observation of both nature and art. When these principles of design (scale and proportion, balance, rhythm, emphasis, and harmony) are thoughtfully considered and sensitively applied, they contribute to achieving the goals of design. The elements of design discussed in the first part of this chapter (space, line, shape and mass, texture, light, color, and pattern) can be manipulated to achieve the desired principles of design.

Although there are no absolute rules when creating a design project, most interiors are enhanced by adhering to these basic guidelines. Although some successful contemporary designs violate these time-tested principles, understanding them is central to the interior designer's creativity and is essential to the beginning designer.

Scale and Proportion

The elements of *scale* and *proportion* are both dependent on size and the relationships between objects. Scale compares an item or space to *something of a known size*. For instance, in order to understand the meaning of a small-scale (or sized) living room, one must know the standard scale or size of a living room. Children's rooms or furniture in elementary schools are *scaled down* or reduced in scale to fit the needs of the occupants.

In interior design, human scale is the most common source of a known reference. Interior design deals with size relationships geared to human scale (Figures 2.13 and 2.14). Considering that human beings usually weigh between 100 and 200 pounds and are between 5 and 6 ft in height, an interior environment can be planned and scaled accordingly. Successfully scaled rooms and furnishings make both adults and children feel comfortable—the rooms are not too large or too small, but well suited to the occupants.

Furniture should be scaled to fit a room. Because an object is perceived in relation to the area around it (Figure 2.15), objects that are too large crowd a small room and make it appear smaller, while furniture that is too small seems even smaller in an oversized room. Large overstuffed furniture should not be placed in a small living room (Figure 2.16). When surrounded by small-scaled furniture, a large piece of furniture appears larger than when surrounded by

Figure 2.13 *Le Corbusier planned his architectural projects to be consistent with the proportions of this human Modular (left). The same ideal proportions can be applied to the famous statue of the Apollo Belvedere (right), probably a 1st century B.C. Roman copy in marble of a 4th century B.C. Greek original.*

Figure 2.14 *The beautiful lines and proportions of the highly acclaimed Barcelona chair, designed by Ludwig Mies van der Rohe in 1929 for the Barcelona Exhibition, have made it a timeless classic. (Courtesy of Knoll.)*

Figure 2.17 *In this presentation floor plan of a garage conversion, the designer arranged the furniture and floor coverings to allow the seating arrangement to more closely reflect the proportions of the golden rectangle.*

large-scaled pieces. A small table with spindly legs placed at the end of a heavy sofa or chair looks out of place, and a large-scaled table placed near a dainty chair is not enhanced.

Accessories such as mirrors, pictures, and lamps need to be scaled for the items with which they are to be used. A lamp generally must not overpower a table, nor should it be so small that it looks ridiculous. Both the lampshade and base must be suitably scaled.

Scale is a relative issue, dependent on the known size of another object. *Proportion* is also a relative issue, but it does

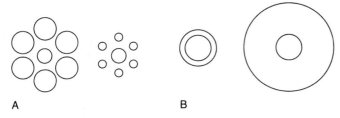

Figure 2.15 *Perception: The center circles in each of the diagrams are identical. The apparent change in size is due to the difference in size of the surrounding circles.*

Poor   Better

Figure 2.16 *These plan views indicate inappropriate and appropriately scaled furniture.*

not depend on a known size. Proportion encompasses both the relationship of one part of an object to its other parts or to the whole, as well as the relationship of one object to another. Both aspects of proportion involve shape or form.

Proportion has been a major concern of creative minds through the ages. Although no absolute formula for good proportion works in all design projects, the Greeks discovered some secrets of good proportion over 2,000 years ago and set down rules that have been incorporated into compositions for centuries. For instance, a square room has been considered the most difficult room to design and is also the least pleasing to the eye. Recognizing this, the Greeks developed the **golden rectangle,** which is a rectangle whose proportion of width to length is 2:3. This proportion is considered the most pleasing. A common use of the golden rectangle is in the residential conversion of a 24 ft by 24 ft garage. Designers must artfully place furniture and interior components to give the square room the illusion of a rectangular space (Figure 2.17).

The **golden section,** also developed by the Greeks, involves the division of a line or form in such a way that the ratio of the smaller portion to the larger is the same as that of the larger portion to the whole (Figure 2.18). The progression

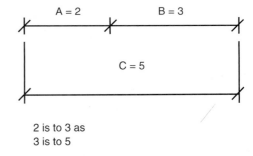

2 is to 3 as
3 is to 5

Figure 2.18 *In the golden section the ratio of A to B is the same as the ratio of B to C. In other words, 2/3 is approximately equal to 3/5.*

The Parthenon at Athens—based on a mathematical ratio of 1:1.6—fits almost precisely into a golden rectangle. Because of the frequency with which it occurs in the arts, the golden rectangle has mystified experts for centuries.

4:7 is a pleasing proportion.

The golden mean. The division of a line somewhere between one half and one third is the most pleasing.

Figure 2.19 *The use of Greek proportions.*

2, 3, 5, 8, 13, 21, 34, and so on, in which each number is the sum of the two preceding numbers, provides a close approximation to this relationship. For example, 2:3 is roughly the same as 3:5, and 5:8 is roughly the same as 8:13, and so forth. Another pleasing ratio is 4:7. These ratios can help designers decide room sizes and shapes, as well as the most pleasing proportions for windows and fireplace moldings and openings.

Perhaps the most important application of these proportions in planning and furnishing lies in the relationship of sizes or areas. For example, if the length of a room measures 25 ft, a desirable width would be 15 ft. This measurement is determined by the following process. Because the length of the living room (25 ft) is divisible by 5, the 3:5 ratio may be used.

$$\frac{3}{5} = \frac{x}{25}$$

To solve for *x,* cross multiple 3×25 to get 75. Now divide 75 by 5 to get 15.

In another example, a piece of furniture 4 ft long would be a good size to place against a 7-ft wall space. These dimensions have the desirable ratios of 4:7 (Figure 2.19).

Another Greek discovery was that the division of a line somewhere between one-half and one-third its length is the most desirable. This division, called the **golden mean,** can be applied when planning any wall composition, such as determining the height for a mantel, tying back drapery, or hanging pictures, mirrors, or wall sconces.

The Greeks also observed that odd numbers are preferable to even ones. A group of three objects is more pleasing than two or four. These guidelines might be applied, for example, when selecting the quantity of pillows for a sofa or when arranging pictures on a wall.

In addition to form, the elements of color, texture, and pattern are also important in the consideration of scale and proportion. Whatever attracts the eye seems larger. Coarse textures, large patterns, and bold colors cause the object on which they are used to appear larger than an object with smooth textures, small patterns, and soft, light colors. Through the skillful use of these principles, the apparent size and proportion of rooms and objects may be altered.

Balance

Balance is that quality in a room that establishes a sense of equilibrium and repose. It is a sense of weight as the eye perceives it. Generally, humans have a need for balance in many aspects of their lives (review Figure II.3). In the interior environment, balance is necessary to achieve a comfortable atmosphere.

The architectural background of rooms including doors, windows, paneling, and fireplaces, along with accompanying furnishings, can be effectively arranged to provide a feeling of equilibrium. Some considerations include the following:

- Opposite walls and interior spaces and objects should have a comfortable feeling of balance through the distribution of high and low, as well as large and small objects.
- When furnishings are positioned above eye level, they appear heavier than items positioned below.
- Bright colors, heavy textures, unusual shapes, bold patterns, and strong lighting readily attract attention and can be manipulated to achieve balance within a space.
- Large furnishings in a space can be complemented by placing them next to groups of small items, and vice versa, creating a refreshing contrast.

The three types of balance used to provide this equilibrium are symmetrical, asymmetrical, and radial (Figure 2.20).

Symmetrical, or Formal, Balance

In **symmetrical balance** identical objects are arranged equally on each side of an imaginary line. This type of bal-

Symmetrical   Asymmetrical   Radial

Figure 2.20 *Three types of balance.*

Figure 2.21 *The Scandinavian influence in the American home shows a congenial combination of the Organic and International styles. Clean white walls with wood detailing are typical. The classic modern Scandinavian chairs on the right were designed by Poul Kjaerholm of Denmark in 1956. The expanse of windows is balanced by the artwork. (Photograph by Ezra Stoller/© ESTO.)*

ance is often employed in traditional and formal environments and adds a feeling of dignity to the interior. Formal balance usually conveys a restful and peaceful sensation, because this type of balance is easily perceived and appreciated; however, too much symmetry can create a dull interior.

Asymmetrical Balance

Asymmetrical balance is more subtle than symmetrical balance. It requires more thought and imagination, but once achieved, remains interesting for a longer time (Figure 2.21). In this type of balance objects of different sizes, shapes, and colors may be used in an infinite number of ways. Two small objects may balance one large item, a small shiny object may balance a larger dull one, a spot of bright color may balance a large area of neutral color, and a large object

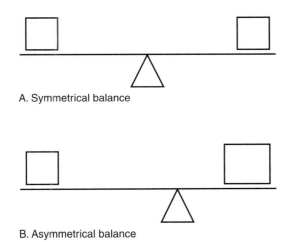

A. Symmetrical balance

B. Asymmetrical balance

Figure 2.22 *In asymmetrical balance, the triangular balance point must be moved to the right in order to keep the seesaw level.*

moved closer to a central point may balance a smaller one pushed farther away (Figure 2.22). No measurement indicates at what point these different items must be placed; the point at which balance is achieved must be sensed. Asymmetrical balance

- Tends to shift the focus from the center and achieves balance by visual tension created between dissimilar objects
- Is predominant in contemporary interiors
- Tends to be informal
- Is generally more active than symmetrical balance
- Provides a more spacious appearance.

Radial Balance

In **radial balance** all elements of the design radiate from a central point like the spokes of a wheel radiating out from the hub. This balance can be seen in a room where chairs surround a round table, in flower arrangements, and in chandeliers. Radial balance is often used in large congregating areas such as hotel and office lobbies (Figure 2.23) and central areas in shopping malls. Radial balance is often a visually pleasing alternative and combines effectively with the other two types of balance.

All rooms require balance, and most rooms combine symmetrical, asymmetrical, and radial balance in different proportions. The combination of all three will create a pleasing effect that will remain interesting over time.

Rhythm

Rhythm assists the eye in moving easily about a room from one area to another, creating a flowing quality. Rhythm can be achieved through repetition, transition, and gradation or progression (Figure 2.24). The effective application of rhythm creates continuity and interest.

Repetition is rhythm established by repeating color, pattern, texture, line, light, or form. For example, a color in the

Figure 2.23 *The domed ceiling, floor pattern, and furniture arrangement in this investment office lobby indicate the use of radial design. (Architect/Designer: VOA Associates, Inc. Photographer: Steven Hall/Hedrich-Blessing.)*

Figure 2.25 *In this commercial interior, the designer repeated a square motif from the architecture into the interior lobby. Grids demarcate columns and floor tiles, and are repeated through the use of contrasting woods on the desk. (Designer: Godwin Associates. Photograph by Gabe Benzur.)*

upholstery fabric of a sofa can be repeated on a chair, the drapery, and a pillow, thus introducing rhythm. The repetition may also include alternating an object or pattern in a sequence (Figure 2.25). Repetition is a common means of achieving rhythm in a room because it is a relatively easy approach, although too much repetition can produce confusion, monotony, or lack of stability.

Transition, another type of repetition, is rhythm found in a curved line that carries the eye easily over an architectural element, such as an arched window, or around items of furnishings, like drapery swags. A curved chair placed in the

corner of a room beside a round table will soften the sharp angle of the merging wall planes, allowing the eye to flow through the space. In Figure 2.26, the curved window softens the corner of the room, thereby providing a transition.

Gradation or *progression* is rhythm produced by the succession of the size of an object from large to small or of a color from dark to light. Radiating lines are not only a form of balance (as previously discussed), but may also be a form of gradation (note the ceiling recesses in Figure 2.23). Other examples include the progression of one step up to another step, the gradation of a small salt container to a medium-

Figure 2.24 *Types of rhythm: Gradation, repetition, and transition.*

Gradation

Repetition

Transition

Figure 2.26 *In this large room, the curved window bay and large sofa soften the edges of the converging architectural planes. The focal point of the architecture is the fireplace wall. The stunning painting by J. D. Challenger commands attention as a result of its location and the elements of design used to draw the eye to this feature from any area in the room. (Photograph by Mark Boisclair. Interior Designer: Carol Conway. Architect: Kevin Bain.)*

sized sugar container up to a large flour container, and a rug that might have a dark border, a lighter inner border, and a very light interior area.

Emphasis

Emphasis in a room refers to the focal point and supportive furnishings that create the center of attention. In every well-planned room, it is effective to have one feature repeatedly draw the eye. This emphasis or focal point can bring a feeling of order and unity into a room, with all other groupings subordinated to it. When there is a lack of emphasis in a room, boredom due to a visually uninteresting space can result. Too much emphasis (i.e., more than one or several centers of interest) can produce chaos and unrest. Analyzing a room and determining what components to emphasize and subordinate can be a challenging task. A general approach includes viewing the room on four basic levels of emphasis and then determining what components will be featured.

1. *Emphatic.* These features may include a dramatic view, fireplace, or architectural feature. For example, if a fireplace is prominently placed and designed, it naturally becomes a focal point; in addition, a burning fire radiates warmth, movement, color, and hospitality—a natural site for a main seating arrangement. Many rooms, however, may not have an emphatic feature.
2. *Dominant.* In many instances this is the level where most designers begin. In the absence of dramatic features in a

room, a dominant focal point may exist or be created. A fireplace in this case may not be an architecturally dramatic feature, but it certainly can be played up and designed to dominate a room. Other dominant features might include a wall of books, a composition of paintings, a beautiful piece of furniture, or a garden view.
3. *Subdominant.* This category includes the level of furnishings that support the focal point and may include large pieces of furniture or the window, ceiling, and floor treatments. This might include the arrangement of furniture in front of a fireplace supporting the dominant focal point of the fireplace (see Figure 2.26).
4. *Subordinate.* This level most often includes accessories like lamps, plants, art objects, and small furnishings.

This method of analyzing a room and breaking it down into various levels of importance can aid the designer. Furnishings and architectural features can be rearranged within this framework depending on the desired outcome. The emphasis of the room may be planned or manipulated by the use of the elements and principles of design, such as the following:

- *Color* is probably the most important element by which a grouping may be brought into immediate focus. Color can be used artfully to achieve the desired amount of emphasis.
- *Form* usually involves arranging furniture within the space—placing furnishings so they focus on the point of emphasis. Unusual or strong form used for furnishings

Figure 2.27 *In this hotel lobby, color, form, texture, light, and pattern all creatively support the central focus. Plants soften architectural edges and a custom carpet defines the seating area and grand staircase. (Designer: Marcia Davis & Associates, Inc. Photographer: Peter Paige. Courtesy: Lacey-Champion, Inc.)*

or architectural background can be dominant or even dramatic.

- *Texture*, whether rough, smooth, shiny, or dull, can help draw the eye to a particular item. The designer can use this tool to create dominance or to allow a component in the room to blend into the background.
- *Lighting* can be used creatively to tie the group together, dramatize, attract attention, or create a focal point.
- *Pattern*, especially a distinctive design with strong color or value contrast, can attract the eye to a desired focal point.

Because emphasis in a room is planned and even manipulated through the use of the elements of design, it is essential that all parts relate to and support each other (Figure 2.27).

Harmony

All the other elements and principles work together to promote *harmony*. Harmony is the unique blend of *unity* and *variety*. A unifying theme or common denominator should run through all component parts and blend them together. Exteriors and interiors are attractive when there

is a pleasant relationship that provides unity, yet the aspect of variety is essential to provide interest. Variety can create the focal point or add the spark that enlivens the room. Following are some of the most common and important considerations when seeking a harmonious living environment:

- In every room, the *interior architecture* is a determining factor. Just as the exterior and interior architecture should be consistent, the furnishings of a room must also be in harmony with the background. For example, molded plastic chairs do not belong against formal 18th-century paneling, nor is a classic Louis XVI chair desirable against a heavy concrete block wall. A surprising juxtaposition of seemingly unrelated objects may occasionally add relief, but this practice requires sophisticated judgment.
- *Furniture* in the room should appear to belong there. Whether the room is large or small, furniture should be scaled accordingly. For example, if the architectural background is strong—perhaps with exposed beams and masonry construction—the furniture should reflect the same feeling.

Figure 2.28 *All the elements and principles of design are effectively used in this exquisite private residence in Georgia, designed by C. Smith Grubbs. The eclectic room combines 18th-century English and French styles in a fresh contemporary interpretation. Final accessorizing touches add individuality and character. (Photograph by David Schilling/Atlanta.)*

- *Colors* appropriate to the style and scale of furnishings should be considered; however, today's interiors often show great flexibility in color usage. A sensitive approach to color harmonies in relationship to furnishings, background, and style is important in achieving an appealing result.
- The *textures* of surfaces (i.e., smooth, rough, shiny, or dull) help determine the success of a room's harmony. Textures should be compatible with the design and style of all furnishings. For instance, a heavy homespun fabric is generally not suitable on a formal Hepplewhite chair, nor is delicate silk damask usually at home on a rough-hewn ranch oak chair.
- A *window treatment* can contribute to the room's total harmony; planning a hard or soft line treatment suitable for the theme and style is essential. For example, ruffled cottage curtains are out of place in an Oriental-style house, and elegant damask swags are inappropriate for a country cottage.
- Carefully selected *floor coverings* help unify the scheme. Hard floor surfaces like wood, tile, and stone are extremely versatile and enhance most living areas. Area rugs, such as a Persian Oriental, are appropriate in any decor, and wall-to-wall carpeting can tie an entire room together.
- Consistency or harmony is best achieved by carrying out a basic *theme* or *style*. The basic style need not be followed slavishly, but a general feeling of unity should be maintained throughout (see the pictorial essay on "History of Style"). This allows the designer to combine good design from many periods with one theme dominating.

Within this overall theme, an occasional surprise to give variety and interest can provide charm and individuality.
- *Accessories* can enhance a room or completely destroy the desired effect. If an accessory is not beautiful, useful, or meaningful to the person using it, it does not belong. The final touches added to a room reveal individual personality more readily than any other items of furnishing and cannot be overlooked in creating rooms of beauty and interest (Figure 2.28). Items that are essentially attractive and well designed, however, can lose their charm when not well used. For example, a gracefully scrolled wrought-iron wall sconce can add much to a room of Spanish or Mediterranean styling but would look heavy and out of place in a pastel room with delicate furnishings. (Chapter 8 discusses accessorizing in greater detail.)

Summary

The elements of design (space, line, shape and mass, texture, light, color, and pattern) and the principles of design (scale and proportion, balance, rhythm, emphasis, and harmony) form the foundation for all design. The organization of these elements and principles, along with the design process discussed in Chapter 1, helps to ensure a quality design that satisfies the needs and desires of the client. All of these elements and principles, including color and light (which are discussed in following chapters), help the designer create an interior that is physically and psychologically comfortable, as well as uniquely attractive.

3

Color

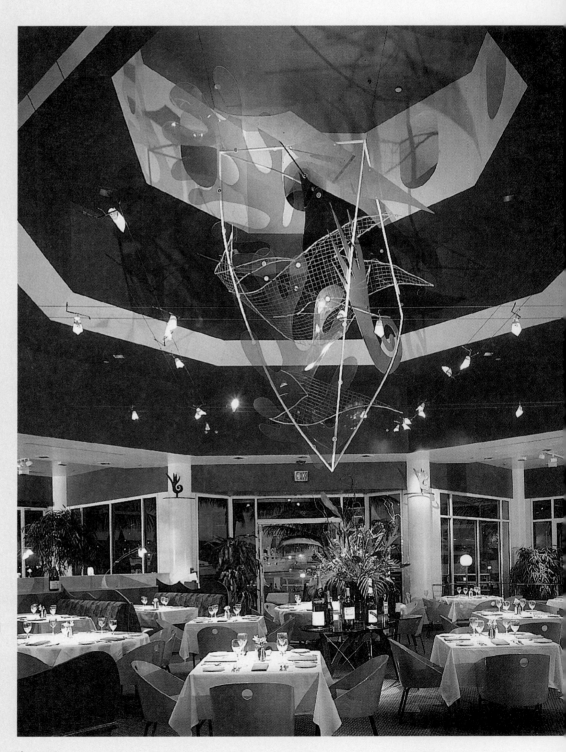

Figure 3.1 *This vibrant restaurant uses brilliant colors of intense chromas. Color defines this interior space. (Architect/Designer: Engstrom Design Group & To Design. Photograph by Dennis Anderson ©.)*

The great 19th-century writer and critic John Ruskin said, "Color is the most sacred element in all visual things." Designers agree that color is the most vital and expressive of the elements of design, as demonstrated in Figure 3.1. Therefore, it is essential that designers have a thorough knowledge of the properties and character of various colors, color theory, color schemes, color associations, and other considerations of color for use in planning both residential and commercial interiors.

Color can have psychological effects; it can enliven a room or create a subdued mood. Color's elemental partner—light—can do the same thing. Light affects the colors we see. In bright afternoon sun, colors are crisp and clear. But in evening sunsets, red and orange tones cast a warm glow. In candlelight or moonlight, colors are muted and dulled. It is essential when studying about color first to understand that the source of color is light.

Light in Color

Light is a form of energy that is part of the electromagnetic spectrum. Daylight, or the light that humans are able to see in the *visible spectrum,* is a mixture of wavelengths in a narrow band of this field. Infrared waves, X-rays, and even radio waves are also forms of energy in this spectrum, but are not visible to the human eye. Color is light broken down into electromagnetic vibrations of varying wavelengths. The longest wavelengths form the reds, followed by oranges, yellows, greens, blues, and violets. This effect can be seen in a rainbow or when light is shown through a prism, which separates or splits the spectrum (Figure 3.2). Artificial lighting that is designed to mimic the sun's light is called white light. Other types of artificial lighting create different combinations of wavelengths that change the color or *look* of an object. Lighting is discussed in greater detail in Chapter 5; however, it is important to realize that without light, color would not exist.

The color that we actually see in an object is the color of light that is not absorbed by the object, but reflected into the eye from the object's surface. A particular surface absorbs or reflects a color of the spectrum depending on its composition. This is referred to as **subtractive color,** because the objects *subtract* all the wavelengths except those that are seen. For instance, a teal rug subtracts all the wave-

lengths except for some of the blue and green wavelengths, which it reflects back. A black tiled wall subtracts all the wavelengths.

The colors in objects are referred to as pigment colors. Pigments are various substances that can be ground into fine powder and used for coloring dyes and paints. Pigments are combined to produce certain colors, such as when red and yellow are mixed to obtain orange. Pigments may be naturally occurring (as discussed in the feature on green design), artificially created, or a combination of both.

Warm, Cool, and Neutral Colors

Colors are grouped into categories. The simplest division categorizes all colors as warm, cool, or neutral.

GREENDESIGN

Natural Earth Colors

Natural earth colors are inorganic pigments found in minerals, principally iron oxides, from the soil. They are washed and ground, then mixed with other substances to create paints or dyes. Earth colors usually include ocher (yellow), sienna, red oxide (red), umber (brown), and terra verde (green).

Earth colors have been used for millennia. For example, these pigments were used by the ancient Egyptians to paint the walls of their tombs, and by the artists of the Middle Ages and Renaissance in their paintings.

Earth colors are still used today for many purposes, especially to help protect items from corrosion. Earth colors are the most permanent colors available, are usually nontoxic, and are not affected by atmospheric conditions.

Figure 3.2 *A ray of white light passed through a prism separates into distinct bands of color. The longest wavelength in the visible spectrum is red, followed by orange, yellow, green, blue, and violet, the shortest visible wavelength.*

White light

Prism

Red
Orange
Yellow
Green
Blue
Violet

Warm Colors

The *warm colors* of the spectrum include red, red-orange, orange, yellow-orange, and yellow. Generally, these warm colors are considered engaging, active, positive, cheery, cozy, and stimulating. Warm colors tend to advance and can enclose space. If used in strong intensity in large areas, warm colors may cause individuals to feel irritable.

Cool Colors

The *cool colors* are blue, blue-green, green, violet, and blue-violet. Cool colors are generally felt to be relaxing, restful, and soothing. Cool colors recede and tend to expand space. Cool-colored rooms may be perceived as cold and unfriendly, and may lack variety.

Neutral and Neutralized Colors

Technically, *neutral colors* are gray, white, and black because they are without an identifiable **hue** (another word for a color). These neutral colors are often called "achromatic," which in Greek means "without color."

Colors falling midway between the warm and cool color groups, such as beige, brown, taupe, cream, ivory, off-black, and off-white (white with any small amount of a color added), are called *neutralized colors*. Neutralized colors are generally important to every color scheme. They tend to be restful, tranquil, livable, unobtrusive, and supportive. However, if not used effectively, neutral and neutralized colors can produce feelings of boredom and weariness.

The Standard Color Wheel

Warm and cool colors can be distinguished most easily using the standard color wheel (Figure 3.3). This theory of color is known as the Palette theory, the Prang theory, or the Brewster color theory; it is the simplest and best known of the color theories or systems. The standard color wheel system is based on three *primary colors:* yellow, red, and blue (Figure 3.4). Primary means the colors cannot be mixed from other pigments, nor can they be broken down into component colors. Theoretically, with five tubes of paint—the three primaries plus black and white—one could produce the entire range of colors, although the degree of precision needed makes this almost impossible. By using the three primaries, however, the twelve colors of the complete wheel can be derived.

Equal amounts of any two of the primary colors result in a *secondary color* (Figure 3.5). The wheel has three such colors: green, which is produced by mixing yellow and blue; violet, by mixing blue and red; and orange, by mixing red and yellow. The secondary color lies midway between the primary colors from which it is formed.

In similar fashion, a *tertiary color* or intermediary color is created by mixing equal amounts of a primary color and a secondary color (Figure 3.6). These hues are also situated midway between the two hues that produced them and are identified by hyphenated names such as blue-green, red-orange, and red-violet.

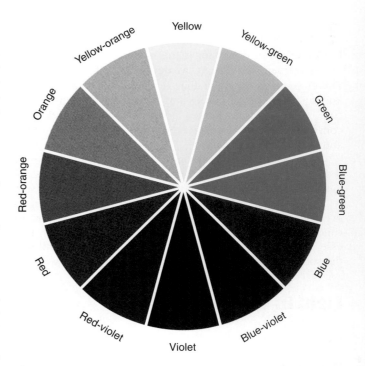

Figure 3.3 *The standard color wheel. It is often referred to as the Prang color wheel, but was originally developed by David Brewster for the Brewster color theory.*

Figure 3.4 *Primary colors.*

Figure 3.5 *Secondary colors.*

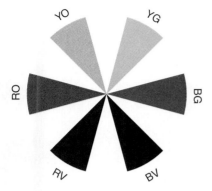

Figure 3.6 *Tertiary or intermediate colors.*

Color's Three Dimensions

The three dimensions of color (hue, value, and intensity or chroma) can be accurately measured and are essential in visualizing and describing any color.

Hue

Hue, or the color name, is a singular characteristic that sets each color apart from all the others. A color may be lightened or darkened, made more intense or less intense. If blue is the hue used, the result will be light blue, dark blue, bright blue, or gray-blue, but each will be of a blue hue. In all, about 150 variations of full chroma of hue exist, of which only 24 basic hues of full chroma have enough variation to be of practical use.

Value

Value is the degree of *luminosity,* or *lightness or darkness* of a hue in relation to black and white. Nine such gradations are easily visible to the eye (Figure 3.7). The value of any hue can be raised by adding white; this forms a **tint.** The value is lowered when black or another darkening agent is added; this is called a **shade.** For example, a tint of red is pink; a shade of red is burgundy.

In addition to shades and tints, a third classification is **tone.** A tone is formed by adding both black and white to the hue. These grayed hues are extremely useful in working out color schemes in which muted colors are necessary to tone down the brighter hues (Figure 3.8).

Intensity or Chroma

Intensity or **chroma** is the *degree of saturation* of pure color. It describes the brightness or dullness and strength or weakness of the pure color that a hue contains. Just as any color may be raised and lowered in value by the addition of white or black, its intensity may be strengthened by the addition of pure chroma or lessened by the addition of its complement (the color directly across from it on the standard color wheel). The more of the color's complement that is

Figure 3.7 *In the nine gradations of value from white to black, the small circles are identical in shade, demonstrating that the eye perceives color not in itself but in relation to its environment.*

added, the less pure color the original hue contains. Two colors may have the same hue and the same value, yet may be markedly different because of the different color strength or intensity (Figure 3.9). Strong chroma visually enlarges objects. Furniture seems more dominant if intense colors are used (Figure 3.10).

The skillful application of color, value, and intensity can play a vital role in creating exciting and livable interiors.

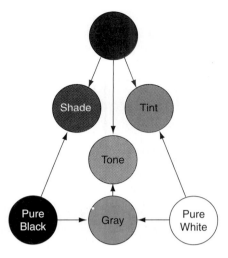

Figure 3.8 *Although black and white pigments are not considered true colors, their addition to colored pigments produces tints, shades, and tones. Adding black to a pigment color produces a shade; adding white produces a tint. Adding gray (a mixture of black and white pigments) to a color produces a tone.*

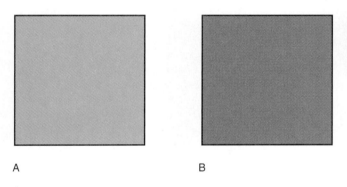

A   B

Figure 3.9 *In this example the green on the left exhibits a high intensity, but when green's complementary color red is added, the intensity is lessened.*

Figure 3.10 *Bright chroma in red, blue, yellow, green, and purple are creatively combined for this bookcase, mirror, and table. Because of the strong chroma, these pieces attract the eye first, seem to advance, make the furniture seem larger in comparison to neutral surfaces, and make a lasting visual impression. (Courtesy of The Naturalist.)*

Even when all the hues in a room are correct, it may lack interest. Adding a contrasting value or intensity to the color harmony can provide interest and variety.

Color Theorists and Color Theories

A number of color theories, or color systems, have been developed and are used by interior designers. Some incorporate psychological as well as physical factors. Johannes Itten (1889–1967) originated his ideas on color while a teacher at the Bauhaus in Germany during the 1920s. One of his theories is the popular "Four Seasons—Personal Color Analysis" based on color palettes associated with the four seasons of the year. Josef Albers (1888–1976) was a pi-

oneer of modern design and a teacher and color theorist at the Bauhaus in Germany and later at Yale University. He is particularly known for his theories on color perception. Albers's series of paintings entitled "Homage to the Square" demonstrate how one color reacts when placed next to another color. He found that color changes greatly as a result of its environment.

A variety of color systems have been produced, each based on a different group of basic colors. The three most common are:

- **The Brewster, Prang, or Palette system** (which has already been discussed), based on the three primaries: yellow, red, and blue.
- **The Ostwald system,** based on four principal hues: yellow, red, blue, and green, plus black and white.
- **The Munsell system,** which begins with five hues: yellow, red, blue, green, and purple.

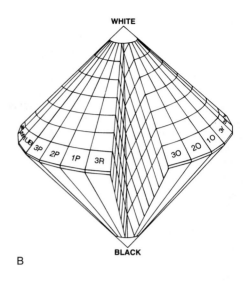

Figure 3.11 *The Ostwald color system. (A) The Ostwald color wheel is based on 24 hues that are either a pure hue or mixed with a pure hue plus white and black. The principal hues are yellow, orange, red, purple, ultramarine blue, turquoise, sea green, and leaf green. The other 16 hues are intermediate hues of these colors. (B) The hues and their ranges of value and chroma are arranged to form a three-dimensional double cone.*

A

B

The Ostwald System

The Ostwald system was named after its creator, German scientist Friedrich Wilhelm Ostwald (1853–1932). The Ostwald color wheel, which uses yellow, orange, red, purple, blue, turquoise, sea green, and leaf green, is based on hue plus the white content and the black content of the hue. Theoretically, 24 hues can be derived from mixing these hues plus pure white and black. There are 28 variations of these 24 hues, resulting in a total of 672 hues and 8 neutrals. The cool group of hues is on one half of the circle and the warm group of hues on the other half of the circle. Ostwald arranged the hues in a conical configuration with a value and chroma scale similar to Munsell's system, discussed next (Figure 3.11).

The Munsell System

The Munsell system of color notation is essentially a scientific concept of describing and analyzing color in terms of three dimensions of hue, value, and chroma. The designation of each color is written as H v/c (Figure 3.12). Hue is indicated by the capital letter H, followed by a fraction in which the numerator represents the value and the denominator indicates the chroma. In the figure, hue is indicated by the circular band.

Value is indicated by the central axis, which shows nine visible steps from darkest value at the bottom to lightest value at the top, with 5/ for middle gray. Pure black would be designated as 0/ and pure white as 10/.

In the Munsell system, chroma, the Greek word for color, is used instead of intensity. The chroma notation is shown by the horizontal band extending outward from the value axis. It indicates the degree of departure of a given hue from a neutral gray of the same value.

Related Color Systems

No one color system is universally accepted. Most industrial nations have their own systems of color classification and, regrettably, these systems are not interchangeable. Those working with color generally use the type of color system that best suits the needs of a particular project. In addition to the Brewster, Ostwald, and Munsell systems, other color systems are available to the designer. Two of the best known are the *Gerritsen color system,* based on color perception and six primary colors, and the *Kuppers color system,* based on six primary colors: blue, green, yellow, red, cyan (a blue-green), and magenta.

In addition, many major paint manufacturers have made available convenient color systems, color keys, and color codes that coordinate colors in particular ways with their products. The colors usually are coded according to cool, warm, and neutral harmonies.

Computer Applications

The computer is capable of performing many design-related tasks including color analysis and color matching. Currently a number of corporations offer designers and other clients color matching based on the latest computerized matching technology. These systems contain thousands of color samples for project specifications. Computerized colorant formulation systems can reproduce and record approximately 16 million colors. Furthermore, they can accurately combine and reproduce these colors, showing such criteria as light reflection and textural effects, and can even deal with **metamerism**—the tendency of samples that match under one light to appear mismatched under a different light. Printouts can show how the specified colors will appear in a particular setting—a valuable tool for the designer.

Figure 3.12 *The Munsell color system, including hue, value, and chroma relationships. (A) The circular band represents the hues in their proper sequences. The upright, center axis is the scale of value. The paths pointing outward from the center show the steps of chroma increasing in strength, as indicated by the numerals. (B) Hue notations of the five principal and the five intermediate hue families are encircled. A breakdown into 100 hues is indicated by the outer circle of markings, and the breakdown of each hue family into four parts (2.5, 5, 7.5, and 10) indicates the 40 constant-hue charts appearing in the* Munsell Book of Color. *(C) Hue, value, and chroma are shown in relation to one another. The circular band represents the hues in their proper sequences. The upright center axis is the scale of value. The paths pointing outward from the center show the steps of chroma, increasing in strength as indicated by the numerals. (Courtesy of Munsell Color Company, Inc.)*

White

VALUE

9/
8/
7/
6/
5/
4/
3/
2/
1/

Black

A

HUE

5R 5YR 5RP 5P 5Y 5PB 5GY 5B 5BG 5G

Ten Hues at Strong Chroma

/2 /4 /6 /8 /10 /12

CHROMA

Six Reds from Gray to Strong

B

C

Creating Color Schemes

Planning and organizing color schemes can be a challenging and satisfying task. Endless color possibilities are available. Individual color preferences are naturally a consideration. Harmonizing colors from the standard color wheel is a popular approach.

The basic color schemes are achromatic, monotone, monochromatic, analogous, and complementary. Color schemes may also emphasize international influences, as seen in the shibui and feng shui color palettes. Although professional interiors seldom fit a specific scheme perfectly, most rooms can be classified into one of these categories.

Achromatic

An **achromatic** color scheme is created by utilizing black, white, or variations of gray. It contains no identifiable hue, only values (Figure 3.13). Accent colors in art or foliage may enhance these interiors, but do not affect the color scheme.

Monotone

Monotone color schemes are created from a color with low chroma. In other words, they contain some chroma as opposed to the achromatic or no-chroma scheme. Neutralized colors fall halfway between warm and cool colors and can be employed as tints, tones, or shades. The most typical neutralized or monotone colors include off-white (white with a small amount of any hue), off-black (a rich brown-black), beige, cream, tan, and brown. Accents of stronger chroma may be used for smaller furnishings and accessories without changing the neutral scheme and can add visual interest.

Monochromatic

Monochromatic color schemes are developed from a *single hue,* but with a range of values and different degrees of intensity. Unity is probably the most notable element in this type of scheme, and if light values predominate, space will appear to be expanded. A danger in the one-color scheme may be monotony; however, looking to nature, where monotony is never present, the guidelines are clearly apparent. When examining the petals of a rose, one may see shadings from soft, delicate pink to deep red. The variety of tones, tints, and chroma of the green leaf can be combined in a room using the subtle neutralized tones for large wall areas, slightly deeper tones for the carpet, medium tones for large furniture, and vivid chroma for accents.

Monochromatic schemes are often further enhanced by the use of textures such as fabric, wood, stone, metal, and glass. Pattern can also add variety and character to the one-color scheme. Black and white can be used without changing the character and, in fact, may sharpen the scheme and add interest.

Analogous

Analogous color schemes are produced from any segment of colors that are side by side but contain no more than half the colors on the standard color wheel, as seen in Fig-

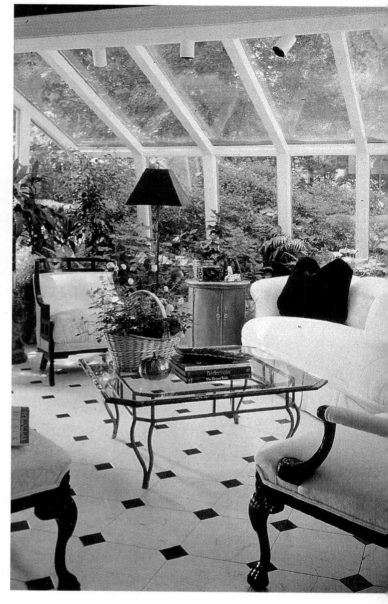

Figure 3.13 *The achromatic color scheme is an effective choice in this sunroom where brightly hued flowers change with the season. (Courtesy of Century Furniture Company.)*

ure 3.14. Harmony is easily established with analogous colors because generally one dominant color should be present. Yellow, for example, is the common factor in orange and green, and by using the intermediate colors of yellow-orange and yellow-green, an interior designer can achieve a close relationship with a great variety of values and intensities.

Complementary

Complementary or contrasting color schemes are also widely used because they offer variety. Values and intensities may vary depending on the use and the amount of area to be covered. All contrasting hues placed side by side enhance each other, and if they are of similar intensity, each

Figure 3.14 *An analogous color scheme achieves harmony by employing hues close together on the color wheel. In this room orange, red, and gold, neighbors on the color wheel, have been used for the principal furnishings and background. A small amount of blue provides contrast. (Courtesy of Bill E. Coleman and J. H. Armer Company.)*

makes the other seem more intense. Complementary schemes always contain warm and cool colors because they are opposite on the color wheel. In strong chroma they are lively and vigorous; in grayed tones they may be subtle and restful. One dominant hue usually sets the mood.

Six types of complementary schemes are direct complement, split complement, triad, double complement, alternate complement, and tetrad, as illustrated in Figure 3.15. The most commonly used ones are defined below.

Direct Complement

The *direct complement,* the simplest of the contrasting color schemes, is formed by using any two colors that lie directly opposite each other on the color wheel. One of the hues should dominate. Used in equal amounts and in strong intensity, complementary colors clash, thus creating an unpleasant element in a room. The secondary color, therefore, works best when neutralized or used in small areas (Figure 3.16).

Split Complement

The *split complement* is a three-color scheme composed of any hue plus the two hues next to its complement. For example, if yellow is selected as the dominant color, red-violet and blue-violet are the complementary colors. These colors contrast less than the direct complement, which is violet. Red has been added to one and blue to the other,

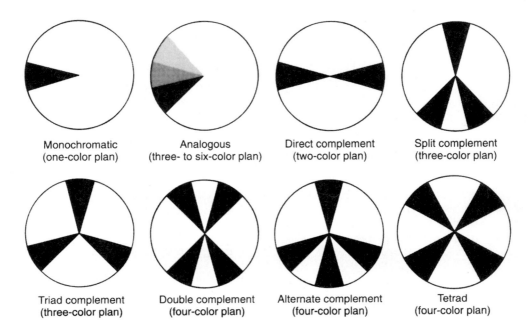

Monochromatic (one-color plan)   Analogous (three- to six-color plan)   Direct complement (two-color plan)   Split complement (three-color plan)

Triad complement (three-color plan)   Double complement (four-color plan)   Alternate complement (four-color plan)   Tetrad (four-color plan)

Figure 3.15 *Basic color schemes derived from the color wheel.*

Figure 3.16 *In this traditional interior, green and a tint of its direct complement, pink, are used to create a comfortable interior. Black and white add additional contrast to the enhanced palette. (Photograph by Alex Groves.)*

giving softness to the scheme and at the same time adding variety.

Triad Complement

The *triad complement* is another three-color contrasting scheme. The triad is made up of any three colors that are equidistant on the color wheel. These colors may be sharp in contrast, using strong chroma such as the three primaries—red, yellow, and blue, or red-orange, yellow-green, and blue-violet—or they may be neutralized, raised, or lowered in value to produce a tranquil scheme.

Shibui

Shibui (pronounced shih BOO ee) or **shibusa** expresses in one word the Japanese approach to beauty as well as the intrinsic nature of Japanese culture. No single word in the English language precisely describes shibui. It suggests an appreciation of *serenity* and a protest against ostentation. Belief in the power of the *understated and unobtrusive* dominates this sophisticated philosophy.

To produce a shibui effect, colors are brought together to enhance each other in a harmonious whole that will be deeply satisfying to live with for a long time. Schemes must have depth and complexity, or they will soon become tiresome. The following ideas are incorporated in achieving a shibui effect (Figure 3.17):

- The shibui concept of color is based on nature. Colors found in the largest areas are quiet and undemanding (neutralized). Bright, vibrant colors are found in a small proportion.
- Nature has thousands of colors, but none of them match or are uniform. In nature the darker, more solid colors

occur underfoot. As one looks upward, colors become lighter and more delicate.
- Most of the natural landscape shows a matte finish with little shininess or glitter, such as the sun sparkling on a ripple in a stream.
- Pattern and texture in nature are everywhere, but they have to be discovered through close examination.
- No two patterns are identical, yet unity prevails. Although natural colors, textures, and patterns appear simple, on close scrutiny they prove highly complex.

American architect Frank Lloyd Wright greatly admired the shibui design philosophy and incorporated its concepts into many of his works.

Feng Shui

The feng shui (pronounced fung shway) color scheme is based on several ancient Chinese philosophies and practices. One such system, the compass mythology, is rooted in the Pa Kua (pa gwa), an eight-sided symbol that corresponds to the four compass directions and their subdirections.

Feng shui color schemes are interpreted differently for each individual based on the birth year, which also relates to the person's basic elements of earth, water, wood, fire, and metal. For instance, green represents wood; therefore, someone born in the year of wood might use green as a color scheme. The person would avoid red, which is associated with fire, because fire destroys wood.

In a feng shui color scheme, white is highly valued because it is associated with light. Black is used selectively. Because it represents water and money, black is valuable, but it is also the opposite of light and therefore should be applied carefully.

Figure 3.17 *The shibui concept of color scheming is translated into an American interior by Jack Lenor Larsen, with an emphasis on texture and simple colors. Flowers provide touches of brightness. The effect is subtle and unpretentious. (Photograph © Norman McGrath.)*

Another overlying principle of feng shui is the appropriate balance of the yin and the yang, which represent a balance of complements or dualisms. Successful feng shui color schemes create a harmony of these balances.

Psychological and Physiological Effects of Individual Colors

Color creates powerful psychological and physiological (or physical) effects. Psychological effects are sensed in the mind; physiological effects actually cause a change in the body. It is important to note that people may react differently to the same color, based on their previous experiences or learned behavior. Research studies have shown that:

- Color affects an individual's moods or feelings in regard to space. Light and cool colors seem to expand space; dark and warm colors seem to enclose space.
- Color affects the eye's perception of weight and size. Dark and bright colors seem heavier than light and cool colors. However, it is interesting that the opposite effect is true in fashion design. Dark colors tend to slim the figure, whereas light colors are usually thought to make one look heavier.
- Color affects a person's perception of temperature. Studies have indicated that body temperature actually fluctuates in response to various colors. For example, red, orange, and yellow can raise one's temperature; cool colors have the opposite reaction.
- Color can cause feelings of boredom and calmness, or stimulation and liveliness. Colors may cause the nervous system to become agitated, and the body reacts in negative ways to this stimulus.
- Colors can affect one's reaction to sounds, taste, odors, and time perception.
- Colors can improve the rate of recovery of sick patients.

Feelings and Reactions to Color

Emotional reactions associated with color are spontaneous. The reaction, often due to the perception of a color rather than to the color itself, may be positive or negative. The following section discusses typical feelings and reactions that may be created by colors; however, remember that clients may react differently to the same color.

Red (Warm Group—Primary Color)

Psychological and physiological associations Courage, passion, love, excitement, danger, martyrdom, anger, fire, strength.

Application Red is conspicuous wherever it appears, and because it is lively and stimulating, it should be used with care. Red mixes well and most rooms are enhanced by a touch of one of its tones. A variety of popular colors are derived from red when it is lightened, darkened, brightened, or dulled. For example, when red is darkened and muted it becomes maroon, and when it is lightened it becomes pink. Pink, a delicate and flattering color, is often enhanced by a stronger contrasting color and blends especially well with grays, browns, greens, blues, and purples.

Yellow (Warm Group—Primary Color)

Psychological and physiological associations Cowardice, deceit, sunlight, optimism, warmth, enlightenment, and communication.

Application High-noon yellows are the most revealing and demanding and merit careful attention. Gray-yellows of early dawn are foils for more fragile colors—pinks, blues, and pale greens. Warm afternoon yellow is a foil for rich, warm woods. The burnished yellows of brass give a cast of copper gilt and bring life to a room. Gold provides an elegant and luxurious touch, especially for accents or accessories. All yellows are reflective, take on tones of other colors, and add flattering highlights.

Orange (Warm Group—Secondary Color)

Psychological and physiological associations Cheerfulness, stimulation, sunset, excitement. When lightened and muted, the peach tone may appear cool or refreshing.

Application Like red, orange has stimulating properties but is not as demanding. Peach tones enhance human skin tones. Peach also serves as a cross between a warm and cool color, partly due to the association with the fruit.

Blue (Cool Group—Primary Color)

Psychological and physiological associations Honesty, truth, loyalty, masculinity, formality, repose, tranquility, sobriety, sky, depth of sea.

Application Blue is cool and soothing, recalling sky, water, and ice. It is difficult to mix and varies greatly under different lighting. More than any other color, blue is affected by the different materials it colors. Lacquer and glass, for example, have a reflective quality that intensifies blue. In deep-pile carpet, blue has great depth. Nubby fabrics soften blue. Shiny materials make blue look frosted. Light blue can give a ceiling a cool and celestial appearance. Blue can be somber, cold, and even depressing if not used effectively.

Green (Cool Group—Secondary Color)

Psychological and physiological associations Nature, serenity, hope, envy, safety, peace, passivity, security.

Application Fresh and friendly, green is nature's color and is a good mixer, especially yellow-green and spruce or forest green. White brings out green's best qualities. When grayed, warmed, or cooled, green makes an excellent background. When lightened, it is retiring and restful. Green is particularly pleasing in food areas. Deep dark green is a favorite color for floor coverings.

Violet (Cool Group—Secondary Color)

Psychological and physiological associations Royalty, nobility, snobbery, power, drama, opulence, mystery, worship, dignity.

Application Naturally a dark value, violet is a blend of blue and red. When pink is added, it becomes warm, and a touch of blue makes it cool. It combines well with both pink and blue. A light value of violet produces lavender. Other violet hues are plum, eggplant, and lilac. Often violet is used in small amounts as accents. It can be dramatic or even disturbing when used on large surfaces.

White (Neutral Color—Achromatic) and Off-White (Neutralized Color)

Psychological and physiological associations Purity, cleanliness, sterility, sophistication, and freshness.

Application White and off-white have the quality of making all colors in a room look cleaner and livelier. Warm off-white is considered unequaled as a mellow background color and works wonders in blending furniture of different woods and styles. Changes of light from day to night are kind to off-white and give it quiet vitality. White and off-white can give a mood of sterility and emptiness if used alone.

Black (Neutral Color—Achromatic) and Off-Black (Black-Brown—Neutralized Color)

Psychological and physiological associations Mourning, sorrow, depression, sophistication, mystery, magic, night.

Application Black and off-black (a rich black-brown) in furniture finishes, small areas of fabric, or accessories add an important accent that makes other colors crisp and clear. When used for larger areas, black can be extremely dramatic but can also be oppressive and claustrophobic.

Gray (Neutral Color—Achromatic)

Psychological and physiological associations Penance, gloom, storm, fog, depression, wisdom, intelligence, business, high-tech, sophistication.

Application Gray is used when a neutral appearance is desired. It may be tiring or monotonous without colorful accents for other furnishings. Gray is a good mixer with other colors, especially pinks, purples, and blues. Dark gray on large areas may be depressing. Light gray provides a pleasant background color.

Brown (Neutralized Color)

Psychological and physiological associations Earth, wood, warmth, comfort, security, support, and stability.

Application The homeyness of brown tones makes them universal favorites, especially for furnishings made of wood. Ranging from pale cream beige to deeper chocolate brown, these tones, tints, and shades can be used together in a room to give infinite variety. Light browns, such as beige, make excellent supportive backgrounds.

Knowledge of the psychological and physiological effects of color is immensely valuable to the designer when planning both residential and nonresidential spaces. For example, responding to the generally accepted notion that red will excite one to action and blue will calm one's nerves, some athletic directors have painted their players' dressing rooms in bright reds and oranges and visitors' dressing rooms in pale blues. The directors claim that it works.

In another example, a *Los Angeles Times* article by John Dreyfuss reported that a meat market in Chicago lost business when the walls were painted a bright, cheerful yellow. A color consultant quickly informed the owner that the yellow walls caused a blue afterimage. It gave meat a purplish cast, making it appear old and spoiled. The walls were repainted bluish green, creating a red afterimage that enhanced the appearance of meat, and sales zoomed.

Some color studies have found that:

- Workers function more efficiently in surroundings painted pleasant colors than they do in drab environments.
- Young people in detention homes responded more positively when dull-colored walls were repainted in a bright color.
- Most people prefer to eat from a white dinner plate rather than a colored one.
- Doctors' offices painted in soft, calming colors, as opposed to stark white, make patients feel more comfortable.
- Fast-food restaurants tend to use bright warm colors for interior surfaces in order to stimulate the appetite and hurry patrons through their meals.
- Warm color tones are best in hospitals and nursing homes; cool, calming colors are more appropriate in intensive care facilities.
- After factory workers complained how heavy their black boxes were to carry, a color expert painted the boxes light blue. The workers then congratulated management on making the boxes lighter.

The knowledge on which popular assumptions about color are based is often superficial. But color and emotion are closely related, people react differently to color, and individuals have definite color preferences. Authorities do not agree on the emotional effects of color, nor do they know whether emotional reactions to colors are inherent or learned.

Multiculturalism and Color

Color, like music, is an international language. Throughout the world, many objects are identified by their coloring. However, colors may have different meanings. Green is universally accepted as sign of nature, freshness, or ecology. Green Day in Japan is celebrated for the Emperor Hirohito because he loved gardens. To Muslims green is a sacred color, and to the Celtics green was associated with fertility.

According to *The Indian Tipi* by Reginald and Gladys Laubin, to Native Americans, white used during one ceremony may symbolize the north, yet in the next ceremony the north may be represented by blue; the significance of color originates in the visions of the individual.

In Western culture, white is associated with purity and piety; however, in many Asian cultures white is the color of mourning. This is true in China, but white is also symbolic of light, and therefore very auspicious in that country. Red symbolizes happiness and is used at weddings.

In ancient China, yellow had religious significance. In ancient Greece and Rome, red was believed to have protective powers. Purple was the imperial color of the ancients and was restricted for the use of the nobility—hence the term "royal purple." When the remains of Charlemagne (742–814) were disinterred in the middle of the 12th century, the coffin was found to contain robes of sumptuous purple velvet.

Designers working with clients from different cultures need to be sensitive to cultural color associations. Careful observation, thorough research, and comprehensive programming will help prevent cultural color mistakes.

Figure 3.18 *The opulent Palm Court establishes an art deco theme for the historic Omni Netherlands Plaza Hotel in Cincinnati. (Courtesy of White House Publishing Co., Cincinnati.)*

Reflecting Personality

Color is a valuable design tool for reflecting personality. Obviously, the problem of selecting colors that reflect personality is compounded when a number of individuals are to use the same interior space. The opinions of all occupants should be considered before final color decisions are made. Current trends may be taken into account but need not be the determining factor. Regardless of what colors are in fashion, the personal preferences of the occupants should always be the main consideration.

Reflecting the Mood of the Room

More than any other element, color is capable of setting the general mood of a room. Strong chroma tends to create a feeling of informality; soft neutralized hues are generally reserved for a more formal atmosphere. Because rooms are backgrounds for people, color is generally most pleasing when not too demanding. The psychological effect of large areas of intense color can be irritating, so it may be wise to select colors in softly neutralized tones for large background areas in rooms where the occupants spend considerable time. General color moods can be evoked for specific areas of the home or office.

The *entrance hall* introduces the home, the same way a *reception area* introduces an office space or hotel lobby (Figure 3.18). The entrance area can effectively set the tone for the space.

Living areas, boardrooms, or conference rooms used for more formal purposes generally have neutralized color schemes that tend to produce an atmosphere of tranquility.

Dining areas are at their best when the color schemes are unobtrusive, permitting a variety of table decorations as well as a serene dining atmosphere. In theme restaurants, color schemes vary greatly.

Informal living areas such as *family* and *recreation rooms* are often treated with stimulating color schemes that create a cheerful and casual environment. *Kitchens* and *break rooms* are usually more desirable when large areas of color are light, fresh, and clean looking.

Bedrooms are private areas, and personal preference should be the determining factor in the choice of colors. As a general rule, the master bedroom should be completed in restful tones pleasing to the occupants. Children can be given the opportunity to select colors for their own rooms (Figure 3.19).

Figure 3.19 *In these children's rooms, a faux artist depicted scenes selected by the children. Furnishings remain neutral in order to grow with the child. Note the clever continuation of the mural onto the ceiling to increase the apparent room height. (Designer/Artist: Shannon Pable. Photographs by John Orth.)*

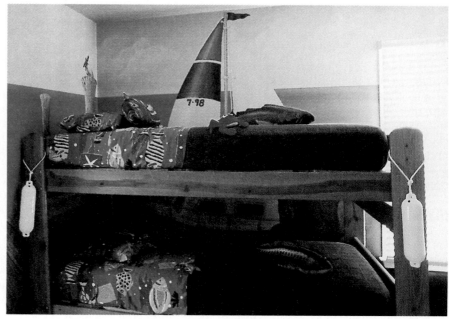

Private offices are like bedrooms and personal preferences should be the deciding factor; however, bays or groups of offices should relate to one another. *Examination rooms* in doctors' offices should be comfortable. Colors should be warm and inviting.

Color schemes for *bathrooms* usually reflect the style and mood of adjoining rooms. Warm colors in muted tones enhance skin tones. Bathroom fixtures, sinks, toilets, bidets, and showers are difficult and costly to replace when trends in colors change, so select these fixtures in light neutrals. (Dark neutrals are difficult to maintain and require daily cleaning.) Add the color in the walls, rugs, and other finishes and decorative elements.

Color also interacts with the elements and principles of design. The next section discusses the relationships between color and these design guidelines.

Interactions Between Color and the Elements and Principles of Design

Space

Colors look different depending on space and distance. Near colors appear darker and more brilliant than the same colors at a greater distance. Brighter and darker colors used in large rooms therefore seem less demanding than the same colors used in small rooms. Colors appear stronger in chroma when covering large areas. For example, a small color chip may be the exact color tone preferred for a room, but when that tone is painted on four walls, it looks much darker and brighter because the area of that color chip has been multiplied many thousands of times. When selecting a wall color from a small color chip, it is best to choose a color several tints lighter than the color desired for the completed room. A good approach is to paint a sizable area of color on walls in opposite corners of the room and observe them at different times of the day and night before completing the application.

Texture

Color appears different when the texture is varied. Smooth surfaces reflect light. Fabrics with a deep, textured surface, such as pile carpet, velvet, and all manner of nubby weaves, cast tiny shadows. These materials appear darker than a smooth fabric dyed with the same hue, in the same value and chroma. A rough-textured wall may appear grayed or soiled under artificial light because of shadows cast from the uneven surface. A dull or matte surface absorbs color, and if it is also dark, may absorb much of the light.

Size and Proportion

An object that attracts the eye usually seems larger; therefore, furniture may appear larger if painted or upholstered with colors in strong chroma. A small room may seem even smaller if demanding colors, which fill space, are used on backgrounds and furniture. Light, cool colors expand a room and seem to create more space. Through the skillful appli-

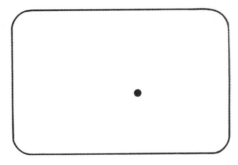

Figure 3.20 *Complementary afterimage. Stare at the black dot just below center in the image at top for 30 seconds, then look at the black dot in the white space below. Prolonged concentration on any color reduces eye sensitivity to it, and the reverse (complementary) color, remaining unaffected, dominates the afterimage for a brief period until balance is restored.*

cation of color a room's dimensions may be altered significantly, and architectural features and furnishings can be highlighted or minimized.

Balance

Because that which attracts the eye seems larger and therefore appears heavier, a small area of bright color balances a large area of softly muted color, and a small area of dark color balances a larger area of light color. For example, a small bouquet of bright flowers placed near one end of a long console table balances a large lamp of soft color placed near the other end. A small bright blue chair balances a much larger gray-blue sofa. Entire areas of rooms may also be balanced through the use of color. A large end wall treated with bright or dark colors may be balanced on the other side of the room with a dark, massive piece of furniture.

The Juxtaposition of Colors

Color is not important in itself. What is important is what happens when different colors are brought together. The eye perceives color in relation to its environment. Physiologists have shown that people are not color blind to one color only but to two or four; the eye is sensitive to colors not singly but in pairs. The familiar afterimage effect demonstrates this perception. If a person looks at any one color for about 30 seconds, then looks at a white page, the complement of that color appears (Figure 3.20). Also, when the eye sees a colored object, it induces the color's complement in the environment. For example, when a green chair is placed against a light neutralized background, the eye sees a tinge of red in that background.

When two primary colors are placed side by side, they appear tinted with the omitted primary; for example, when placed near blue, red takes on a yellow tinge. When contrasting or complementary colors in strong chroma with the same value are used against each other, they clash, producing a vibration that is fatiguing (Figure 3.21). When contrasting colors with strong differences in value are used side by side or one against the other, the colors stand out but do not clash. For example, a painting with predominantly orange hues seems more orange if hung against a blue wall. Harmoniously blended colors of middle value used against each other tend to blend together, and at a distance the difference

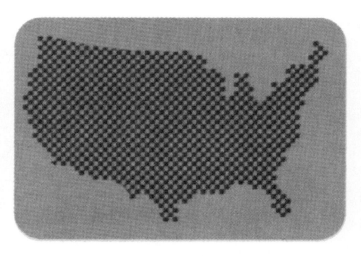

Figure 3.22 *Additive spatial fusion. The green dot pattern in the shape of the United States merges into solid gray when viewed from a distance of 6 to 8 ft. At that distance the eye no longer distinguishes the individual colors. (Courtesy of Large Lamp Department, General Electric Company.)*

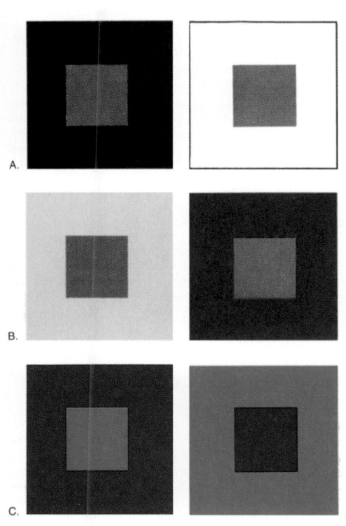

Figure 3.21 *These diagrams illustrate the effect of adjacent colors: (A) Gray looks much darker against white than it does against black; (B) A gray or neutral against a colored background appears to be tinted with the complement of the color; (C) When placed side by side, complements of equal intensity create visual conflict. Complements of varying intensities enhance each other. (Courtesy of Large Lamp Department, General Electric Company.)*

becomes almost indiscernible (Figure 3.22). The latter combination is the basis for most shibui color schemes.

Black and white have a strong visible effect on other colors when brought together. Black tends to make adjacent colors look richer. White reflects light into adjacent colors. Rooms that seem lifeless may be given sparkle and interest by the addition of black, white, or both.

The juxtaposition of colors affects not only hue but also value. The change of value may be seen when a gray circle is placed on a white background. As black is added to the background, which becomes progressively darker, the gray circle appears progressively lighter, showing that colors may be made to appear either lighter or darker according to the tonal value of the adjoining or background color. The use of sharp value contrast emphasizes an object. When black and white are placed side by side, the white looks whiter and the black looks blacker. For example, the fine lines of a dark piece of furniture are accentuated if placed against a light background. Colors closely blended conceal an object; contrasting colors emphasize an object. A piece of furniture seems unobtrusive if it is the same value as the background (Figure 3.23).

Value may be applied in many ways when designing and furnishing a room. As an object is raised in value, its apparent size increases. A fabric colored in low value makes a chair seem smaller than one in high value. Because light colors recede and dark colors advance, one may, with skill, alter the apparent size and proportion of individual items or of an entire room. In small rooms, light values expand walls and ceilings. In long narrow rooms, colors in darker value pull in end walls and make the room appear shorter.

The apparent size and proportion of a room or object may also be altered through the use of chroma. Color in strong chroma visually enlarges an object; walls in strong chroma, as with dark value, seem to advance and make a room appear smaller (see Figure 3.10).

A chair in light value blends into a similar background.

A chair in dark value placed against a light background produces a contrast.

A chair in light value placed against a dark background creates a more pronounced contrast.

Figure 3.23 *Value effects—three treatments.*

Light

As previously discussed, without light color does not exist. Because light is so closely tied to color, a brief discussion on light's interaction with color is in order. (Chapter 5 elaborates on lighting.) A major consideration in planning the color scheme for a room is the study of the quantity and quality of light and the method of lighting.

The level of illumination affects the appearance of color. When the light is bright the color can be stimulating; low light can produce a relaxing feeling. Color may become dull, lifeless, and dreary with insufficient light, however, and too much light can wash out a color. In general, as illumination increases, color becomes more vibrant. A room with low light levels is enhanced by light-reflecting colors. A room with high light levels may be more pleasant with a predominance of darker light-absorbing colors.

One concern for the designer is how various qualities of natural and artificial light can change the visual perception of a surface, the phenomenon known as metamerism. For example, two fabrics that match in color during daylight may not match under artificial light at night. All types of lighting (natural lighting and artificial lighting such as incandescent, fluorescent, halogen, etc.) produce unique effects. The quality of natural light depends on the direction from which it comes and the time of day. The color of artificial light is determined by the type of light and fixture used. Therefore, it is important when selecting colors for backgrounds and furnishings to view each surface under all types of lighting conditions to ensure that the colors will match or be harmonious.

Review of the color wheel demonstrates that to gray or neutralize a color, some of its complement must be added; to intensify a color, more of the basic hue must be added. Light produces the same effect. Warm light accentuates warm colors and neutralizes cool colors. Cool light intensifies cool colors and deadens warm colors. For example, a yellowish light brings out the yellow in yellow-green and yellow-orange. A cool light brings out the blue in blue-green and blue-violet. Warm light is friendly and tends to unify objects. Cool light expands space, produces a crisp atmosphere, and tends to make individual objects stand out.

Color is also affected by the method of lighting. Light rays that fall directly from the source onto a surface can create a warm glow over an area. An indirect light reflecting from a cove onto the ceiling produces an overall light resembling the light of midday.

When understood and used with skill, light may alter, subdue, highlight, or dramatize the colors of a room in a way that no other decorative medium can. Because any situation has many variables, it is impractical to set down definite rules for the use of light and color. Therefore, before making a final choice, try each color in the environment in which it will be used and observe it during different hours of the day and after dark.

Application of Color to Interior Backgrounds

Applying color to a room's architectural backgrounds requires careful consideration. For instance, a common notion is that off-white in itself is a specific color and complements any decor. This concept needs refinement. Off-white is white tinted with a hue—any hue. To be compatible, however, off-whites must contain only the same or a similar hue as used in other areas of the room. Warm off-whites are more easily blended than cool off-whites, recalling a basic characteristic of warm and cool colors.

Ceilings

The ceiling is the largest unused area of a room, and its color is important to the general feeling. If the objective is

Figure 3.24 *In this dining room the designer painted the ceiling a pale yellow-green (a tint of the wall color). The cool color helps make the ceiling recede. (Designer: Kimberly Latham Interior Design. Photograph by Dominique Vorillon. Courtesy of American Homestyle & Gardening.)*

to have the wall and ceiling look the same, the ceiling should be a tint of the wall, because the reflection from the walls and floor tends to make the ceiling look several shades darker than it actually is. If the walls are papered, the ceiling may be a tint of the background or the lightest color in the paper. Where walls are paneled in dark wood, the ceiling can be effective when painted white or a light tint of the wood color. If the wood trim is painted white, a white ceiling can work well. When the ceiling is too high, a darker shade or brighter hue makes it appear lower. For a low ceiling, the opposite treatment can help make it appear higher (Figure 3.24).

Paneled Walls

In a room with dark wood paneling, colors of intense chroma can be used because deep wood tones tend to absorb color. If paneled wood walls are light and a blended effect is desired, colors may be light and less intense. More formal wood paneling calls for a more formal color scheme; if wood paneling is informal, colors should enhance that casual effect.

Window Treatments

The success of any room largely depends on the window treatment and the color used for draperies, curtains, blinds, screens, shades, shutters, or other window decor. If the objective is to have a completely blended background, the window treatment should be the same hue, value, and intensity as the wall. If a contrasting effect is desirable, a color that con-

trasts with the wall can be used, but it must relate well with other colors throughout the room. Remember to consider how the drapery lining or sheers will look from the outside. Sheers are usually more pleasing when white or off-white.

Wood Trim

The color of wood trim around doors, ceilings, floors, and other architectural features is important to the general color scheme of the room. When painted, trim may be (1) the same hue, value, and intensity as the wall (which tends to cause molding to disappear into the wall); (2) a darker shade of the wall hue (which allows the molding to stand out); or (3) a color that contrasts with the wall (which accentuates the molding). Many professional designers maintain the same wood trim color throughout the interior environment for an effective color transition from room to room.

Color in Wood

Because wood has color and each type of wood has a particular beauty, wood should not be overlooked when planning a color scheme. Heavily grained woods generally call for heavier textures and stronger colors than do fine-grained woods, as seen in Figure 3.25. Mixing woods can add interest to a room, but it is wise to use woods in close proximity that are similar in feeling. For example, rough-grained golden oak and formal reddish-brown mahogany are not particularly good companions, but finely grained light-brown maple and brownish walnut usually combine well.

All of these items should be taken into consideration when planning the colors for an interior environment. The next section should help the beginning designer start the process of choosing a color scheme.

The Selection of a Color Scheme

When deciding on a color scheme, designers must first consider the needs and desires of the client. Many times clients select a specific color on which to base the interior environment. Other starting points for color schemes may include an attractive fabric or wallpaper, an area rug, or a prized painting or work of art. Commercial office or hospitality environments may also begin color schemes based on a corporate logo or patterned carpet. No matter where the designer begins, the color selections for the room must also allow for the appropriate distribution of color and a transition from one room to another.

Distribution of Color

Color is the most unifying element available to the interior designer, and its skillful distribution is essential to a feeling of unity. Color distribution can be achieved in two major ways:

1. Planned value distribution is a necessary step. Each room can be enhanced with some light, some dark, and some medium tones used in varying amounts according to the effect desired. In most cases the darkest tones are used in the smallest amounts, although in special rooms the reverse may be employed with dramatic results (Figure 3.26). Intense colors can work well when reserved for small areas

and accents. This concept of using less intense or more neutralized hues for the large areas and proportionately stronger chromas as the areas or objects get smaller is called **the law of chromatic distribution.** When applying the law of chromatic distribution to a room, backgrounds will be in the most neutralized tones, large pieces of furniture will have more intensity, and accents such as small chairs and accessories will be in the strongest chroma.

2. Many successful rooms are planned around one dominant hue. This color need not be used on all major pieces of furniture, but it should be repeated at least once to give a feeling of unity. Unity may also be achieved by using colors containing one hue common to all. For example, hues on the color wheel going clockwise from red-orange to blue-green all contain yellow and combine well together. The color that is common to all—yellow—recedes and the other colors stand out.

Although the preceding guidelines describe the safest way to color scheme a room, deviating from them is possible and sometimes desirable. For example, dark walls can create a feeling of comfort, warmth, and security and unify the room's furnishings. A light floor visually expands space, and when adjacent to dark walls creates a dramatic effect. Under most conditions dark ceilings decrease the feeling of space and are oppressive. On the other hand, depending on the architecture, a ceiling may be painted in a dark value to give the illusion of viewing the infinity of the night sky. In commercial design, dark ceilings are frequently used in restaurants and retail establishments to conceal the network of **HVAC** (heating, ventilating, and air conditioning), plumbing pipes, and electrical cables.

Figure 3.25 *Fine-grain woods, shown in this custom interior office space, blend with warm, refined fabrics creating an upscale interior. (Designer: Martha Burns. Photograph by Peter Paige.)*

Figure 3.26 *Predominantly dark and medium values have been used in this masculine retreat, establishing a cozy effect. Light values such as the pictures and coffee table accessories function as accents. The entire room is dramatized with pools of artificial light. (Antique sarouk faraghan courtesy of F. J. Hakimian, Inc. Design by Renny B. Saltzman, Inc. Photograph by Phillip Ennis.)*

Color Transitions from One Room to Another

Whenever two rooms adjoin, their colors should relate. One or more colors carried from one room to the other—but not necessarily used in the same manner—will make a pleasing transition. For example, the accent color in the wallpaper of an entrance hall may be neutralized and used on the walls of the adjoining living room or may be emphasized in a piece of upholstery fabric.

Where one room may be seen from another, as in conference rooms and reception areas, closely related colors establish color unity. Following are some of the most common and successful methods of achieving color transition.

- Many professional designers keep the floor covering consistent from room to room. For example, a gray carpet might be used for all rooms with the exception of hard floor surfaces for entries, conference rooms, or utility areas.
- Similar or matching wall and ceiling colors from room to room create a continuity of color transition.
- The consistent use of moldings and architectural trim throughout the home helps provide unity.
- Related colors employed on various pieces of furniture and for window treatments should be considered for effective color transition.
- Accessories carry colors from one interior space to another and aid in creating an effective flow of colors.

Developing the skills to bring a color scheme together while thoughtfully employing the law of chromatic distribution and considering the transitions required from room to room takes time and patience. The goal of all designers is to develop the skill to visualize the room before it is completed.

Visual Communication

Forming a mental picture of how colors appear when juxtaposed is not easy, and students and clients may need visual aids. Visual communication skills help the designer prepare presentation boards, charts, and plans that help the client, as well as the designer, visualize the completed space. Following are three methods used for visual communication of a color scheme. They are usually completed during the conceptual design and design development phases discussed in Chapter 1.

1. A chart using approximate proportions of various elements such as walls, floor, ceiling, furniture, and accents is developed. Fabric, paint, and hard material samples are attached to the chart. This method does not show exactly how the completed project will appear, but it is helpful.
2. A setup with actual samples of all items to be used, in approximate proportions, is assembled. This method more closely approximates the look of the completed room.

3. Many professional designers develop presentation boards that include rendered floor plans, elevations, and perspectives of the interior. The boards also include pictures of the furniture with samples of fabrics. Additionally, finishes are shown for all walls, floors, and other surfaces (see Design Scenario: Universal Design).

Other color tools are also available to designers. Paint companies have interior and architectural sample kits, with paint samples that are 2″ × 5″ or larger. Pantone, a standard in commercial color identification, also produces color sample books that may assist designers in communicating colors to clients. Whatever method is used, it is important to remember that the goal is to visually explain to the client the final appearance of the color scheme.

Color Forecasting

Organizations that help determine color preferences for American residential and nonresidential design include the Color Marketing Group, the Color Association of the United States, the Home Fashions League, the International Colour Authority, the National Decorating Products Association, and Colorcast. Color forecasts are drawn from the latest research conducted by color stylists and authorities, and they provide annual predictions that help consumers, professional designers, and merchandising experts.

Ken Charbonneau, Industry Partner of ASID, is a frequent speaker and presenter of color marketing forecasts. In *the GRID,* published by InPro Corporation, he notes that the forecast palette for the new millennium will be "more sophisticated, wider in scope and will allow for more individuality in color selection." Clients want lasting classic designs that won't look trendy or outdated in four or five years. According to Charbonneau, "Too many consumers out there were led down the 'rose, mauve, and touch of teal' (colors of the late '80s and '90s) path and now hate these colors. . . ." Colors are often enhanced by a touch of metallics, pearlescents, and layering. Classic colors that will remain in style include "navy blues, hunter or forest greens, burgundy, terra cotta, black, and white. These great, reliable, dependable, and pleasing colors will always be there."

Figure 3.27 *Variations in texture and light play a significant role in the warmth and richness of this interior living environment. The designers were particularly observant of the effects of light as it changes throughout the day. Reflective surfaces on the floor and ceiling add to the character of the space and contrast with the rough stone walls. (Designer: Gandy/Peace, Inc. Photograph by Chris A. Little.)*

When reviewing color forecasts made by various professional sources, it is important to remember that there are no absolute color rules that can be applied at any particular time. It is good to be aware of color trends, but, ultimately, personal preferences for comfortable and pleasing colors are the most valuable consideration. The interior designer's responsibility is to help the client select colors that are right for a personal environment.

Summary

The interaction between light and color creates great opportunities for designers as well as unique challenges (Figure 3.27). Planning and accurate programming are required to determine a client's personal tastes relating to a color scheme. Color schemes can be developed based on the mixing or blending of colors from the color wheel, from nature, or from another color source such as a work of art or a patterned rug. The final development of the color scheme must also take into account the juxtaposition of different colors to each other, the desired effects from the elements and principles of design, and the appropriate distribution of color. Ultimately, the greatest challenge to any designer (and possibly the most satisfying reward) is to achieve beautiful and livable schemes that meet the client's needs.

Project Description

This residential design project for an elderly woman with rheumatoid arthritis was developed by the IIDA Georgia chapter. Final presentation drawings were required to visually explain the design solution for the renovation of an existing brick home.

Programming: A 65-year-old widowed woman, who lives with her son, requires renovations to her home that will allow for accessible living. The design solution must incorporate retrofitting the bedroom, kitchen, and bathroom. Exterior doors and windows may not be altered. Specific requirements of these areas follow.

Bedroom:

- Hospital bed
- TV with remote
- Dresser, bedside table, and comfortable seating for one visitor

Bathroom:

- Handicap toilet and sink
- Roll-in shower
- Utility sink and linen storage
- Grab bars

Kitchen:

- Dishwasher, microwave, side-by-side refrigerator, drop-in range, double sink, and cabinets

Conceptual/Schematic Design Solution: This design solution incorporates the requirements as listed above and presents them to the client in a concise and aesthetically pleasing manner. The floor plan (Figure DS3.1) illustrates the layout for the home. The area to be renovated is shaded to draw the client's eye toward this area. Dotted circles, which represent areas five feet in diameter, indicate areas large enough to accommodate a turn-around for a wheelchair.

The designer selected a warm color palette and emphasized the client's bedroom using an axonometric drawing (Figure DS3.2). Fabric samples are neatly folded and wrapped and appear across the bottom of the presentation board. Because the client was also concerned about the accessibility of the bathroom, elevations illustrate the grab bars and hand-held showerhead that enable the client to be independent. During the presentation (and contradictory to the programming requirements), the designer suggested that the front door hinge be moved to allow for more efficient traffic flow.

Presentation boards such as these allow the designer to visually understand the relationships of the colors in the space and create a medium in which to explain these colors and design concepts to the client.

Figure DS3.1 *This presentation floor plan illustrates the layout of the furniture and rooms throughout the home. The designer added finish information to the plan, indicating hardwood floors, wood furniture, and tile. (Design by Shoko Nishimura.)*

Figure DS3.2 *The second presentation board shows an axonometric drawing of the bedroom, which is very beneficial in helping the client visualize the space to be created. It also includes elevations (drawings of the vertical surfaces) of the bathroom. All drawings were color rendered to emphasize the color scheme. Actual fabric samples were added across the bottom of the board. (Design by Shoko Nishimura.)*

> *Communication,*
>
> *collaboration, and*
>
> *cooperation: These*
>
> *three C's are essential*
>
> *among design team*
>
> *members in order to*
>
> *create successful*
>
> *environments.*
>
> *Anonymous designer*

Figure III.1 *This two-story framing diagram illustrates platform or western frame construction. Note the various terms for the different construction components.*

The building system components that are usually hidden in the walls, ceilings, or floors form the basis for human comfort in interior environments. The heating, ventilating, and air conditioning (HVAC), electrical, lighting, communication, and plumbing systems (to name a few) are integrated into the construction of a building. Knowledge of how these systems work together and an understanding of when they are installed during the construction process allow the designer to accurately guide the client during construction or remodeling.

The interior designer is a member of a design team. Although the designer should be familiar with the construction process, he or she is actively working with (and in many cases relying on the expertise of) the allied design professionals (see Chapter 1). Understanding system terminology and recognizing standard architectural symbols enhances the designer's ability to communicate effectively with colleagues and clients.

The Construction Process

The process of building or remodeling a structure requires several steps. The **critical path** is a timetable (or schedule) that charts this process. For example, a small remodeling job may require only four or five weeks to complete, whereas a typical residence may take four or five months; a large commercial building may take one to three years to finish.

For almost all projects, the order of the steps is similar; steps that are not required are simply skipped. The scheduling of the project usually becomes the responsibility of the general contractor. The following explains the construction process for a residential project using wood frame construction. Refer to the figures for further understanding.

Site Selection and Development

Site selection is the first step in the construction process. The site frequently dictates the style of house to be built. Site work also contributes significantly to the flow of traffic and physical location of the building. Once a site has been selected and an appropriate house designed to fit it, the site must be prepared. Utility lines are buried (or strung) to meet local codes. Vegetation is removed or protected from large earth-moving machines and a hole is excavated for the footings, foundation walls, and basement or crawl space. Site work continues throughout the entire construction process and does not end until drains, lawns, shrubs, trees, driveways, sidewalks, decks, patios, and parking areas are installed.

Footings and Foundations

After the initial site work is complete and the initial hole is dug, careful measurements are made and forms

Figure III.2 *Left, a poured footing and foundation wall. Right, also a poured footing, but its foundation wall is formed using concrete masonry units (CMU), commonly called concrete blocks.*

are placed to hold the concrete that will be poured to form the footings. **Footings** are the structural foundation of the building. In colder climates, footings must be placed below the frost line.

Foundation walls are built on top of the footings. The walls may be poured concrete or concrete block (Figure III.2). (Note: *Cement* is a dry ingredient of concrete. Concrete is a mixture of cement, composed of lime, silica, and other materials, along with gravel and water.) Space must be allowed for basement windows (which must meet fire egress codes) or crawl space air vents in the foundation walls.

Some buildings have concrete slab floors. The floors are reinforced with rebar (strong steel rods) or wire mesh. In a building with a concrete slab, all plumbing, electrical, or mechanical ductwork that will penetrate the floor must be in place prior to pouring the concrete slab floor. It is wise for the architect or designer to make a site visit during this time to ensure that electrical and plumbing components are installed as noted on the blueprints. Chiseling or coring a slab for ductwork after the concrete slab has

set is possible, but costly. In remodeling jobs, however, this may be the only solution.

Once the concrete has set and the forms are removed, the holes are backfilled with dirt and compacted. The building is ready to be framed.

Framing

In wood frame construction, the first item to be framed is the floor. A **sillplate** secures the floor to the foundation (Figure III.1). Horizontal wood members are attached to the sillplate and a subfloor is laid over the top. The vertical load-bearing walls are added to support the weight of the roof, transferring the load to the foundation walls, which transfer it to the footings. Not all walls are load bearing. In a remodeling job, before specifying the removal of a wall, the designer must consult with an architect or engineer to determine which walls are load bearing. Load-bearing walls can be moved after proper alternative structural support is in place; however, the work must first be documented by the licensed architect, engineer, or builder.

The vertical walls are formed by 2″ × 4″ or 2″ × 6″ studs. Rough openings in the wall are made for doors and windows (Figure III.3). A **header** is placed over the opening to transfer the load to a supporting stud. Again, the architect or interior designer should carefully survey the construction as walls are being built. Improperly located doors, windows, and walls are easier to move the sooner the mistake is noticed. Check the blueprints to make sure they are followed.

Next, the roof is framed and attached to the vertical stud walls (Figure III.4). The angular wood pieces are called rafters. Many wood-framed roofs are made from prefabricated truss systems constructed off-site (Figure III.5). Although more economical, truss systems do not allow for attic use.

Sheathing, Roofing, and Interior Building Systems

As the framing is completed, *sheathing* (rigid wallboard, plywood, or similar material) is added around the perimeter of the building and to the roof. The sheathing (sometimes called decking on the roof) adds structural support and insulating qualities. It also may serve as a nailer for the finish materials (see Figure III.6 and Figure 4.1).

As the roofing material is placed on the decking, windows and doors are installed and rough plumbing (sometimes called top-out plumbing), HVAC, and electrical lines are run in the walls and basement (if applicable). Shower stalls and tubs are installed so that interior finishes cover the seams. Central vacuum units, security systems, and intercom systems also are installed at this point. Once again the location of the outlets, switches, overhead lighting, HVAC vents, intercom systems, and other specified components should be carefully checked. After wall material is applied over the studs, it is more costly and difficult to make changes. Last, insulation is added to the walls and ceilings.

Finish Materials

The exterior of the building receives its final material, such as wood clapboard, brick, or siding, and it is fin-

Figure III.3 *Additional support in the form of double studs and a header strengthen the rough opening that will eventually house a window.*

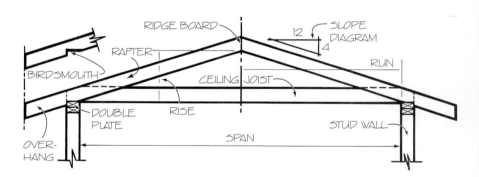

Figure III.4 *Framing components and associated terminology. Note that the slope of this roof is a 4/12.*

ished appropriately. **Soffits** (the area below the eaves) and **fascia** (the front of the eaves) are completed (Figure III.6). Trim is installed around windows and doors. Concrete porches and walks, wood decks, and railings complete the site work. Exterior hardware is installed.

Interior finish materials are applied to the walls. (These options are discussed in Chapter 11.) Other construction components such as trim, bookshelves, closet systems, and doors are installed. Painting and staining are completed. Cabinets, countertops, tile floors, and backsplashes are

Figure III.5 *A prefabricated truss system.*

Figure III.6 *This cut-away section illustrates the construction components where the roof meets the walls. Finish materials such as shingles are applied over the roofing felt and decking.*

installed. Wallcovering is hung and plumbing and lighting fixtures are placed. The interior door hardware, appliances, carpets, and window treatments are installed. Finally, the furniture is delivered. Artwork and accessories are arranged.

The last step is the final walk through, and noting tasks yet to be completed on a punch list. Inevitably, the movers will dent a doorframe or the carpet installers will mar a wall. Electrical outlet covers and heater vents will be misplaced. Light bulbs will burn out or break. The architect or interior designer needs to ensure that all items are fixed prior to approving the final payment to the contractor.

The construction process is complex and it is only through proper planning that a building is completed in a given time frame. Attention to detail and a collaborative effort by all allied professionals ensure a space that meets the needs and desires of the client.

The following two chapters provide more detailed information on building systems. Recognition of building symbols and an understanding of each system's components and requirements will assist designers in working with clients and communicating with construction professionals.

4

Construction, Systems, and Codes

Figure 4.1 *Construction site. (Photograph from Photo Disc.)*

The technical aspects of interiors help to define design possibilities. Understanding how construction systems fit together and developing a working knowledge of how these systems are visually communicated help the designer achieve the desired outcome (Figure 4.1). This chapter reviews the visual components in a set of construction drawings, defines and illustrates various systems in the built environments, and outlines the various codes and federal regulations relating to interior design.

Contract Documents

Contract documents consist of construction drawings and a set of written specifications defining the quality of materials and craftsmanship. Construction drawings (which are explained throughout this chapter) generally include the following information:

- Cover sheet, used as a table of contents
- Site and grading plans
- Landscape plans
- Foundation plans
- Floor plans, generally starting with the lowest floor and rising
- Lighting location plans
- Electrical and communication location plans
- Finish plans
- Exterior elevations
- Interior elevations
- Sections
- Schedules
- Details and custom cabinetry
- Roofing plans
- Engineering drawings, including lighting, electrical and communications, plumbing, HVAC, fire protection, and security

Drawings are deleted or inserted as required for the specific project. The written specifications (developed into a complex booklet) include requirements for each area listed above. For example, the specifications may list the acceptable tolerances (or gaps) between parts in wood construction.

Furniture, finish, and equipment specifications also may be developed and are considered part of the contract documents (see Chapter 1). The following section describes these various drawings. Appendix C illustrates a small set of construction drawings.

Plans

Plan drawings show the layout of a site or building when viewed from above, looking into the various floors of the building. Plans are generally drawn to 1/8" = 1'-0" scale or 1/4" = 1'-0". (This means that 1/8" or 1/4" respectively on the drawing is equal to 1'-0" in real-life dimensions.) Designers need to be able to interpret the standard symbols used in plan drawings. Figures 4.2 through 4.4 indicate typical architectural symbols. (Chapter 12 also illustrates standard symbols for doors and windows.)

Site, Grading, Landscape, and Foundation Plans

Site and grading plans and landscape plans, although rarely used by the designer, are helpful in orienting the design to the landscape and the direction of the sun. Foundation plans show the location of HVAC and plumbing lines.

Floor Plans

Floor plans are critical to the designer. These plans define locations of walls, doors, windows, and other built-in components such as bathroom fixtures, cabinets, and stairways.

Stairways can be bold and dramatic or simply functional. Often the stairway functions as a focal point and can be aesthetically stimulating as well as serviceable, as demonstrated in Figure 4.5.

The stairway consists of the horizontal portion, called the **tread,** and the vertical portion, called the **riser.** The depth of a tread should accommodate the entire length of the foot (11 in. is generally used).

In a residence, the tread is often carpeted for additional safety. The riser should be no more than 7 in. high. Treads and risers should be consistent in size. A person expects and needs each step to be the same height and depth (Figure 4.6). Headroom clearance should be planned for the top and bottom of the staircase; 6 ft. 8 in. is considered a minimum clearance.

A handrail (or **banister**) is usually mounted at 34" above the steps. The upright supports for the handrail are called **balusters;** they must be spaced close enough to prevent toddlers from falling though the supports. A **balustrade** is the handrail together with its balusters.

Designers may produce the floor plan on their own, but must collaborate with an architect or builder on structural components. Furniture plans, although not part of the formal construction drawings, are generated from the floor plans.

Lighting Plans

Lighting plans may be produced by designers in collaboration with engineers. Lighting plans are slightly different from the other plans because they are drawn as if looking up at the ceiling instead of down at the floor. In residential design, lighting plans are commonly combined with electrical and communication (telephone) plans. In commercial design, lighting plans may be called **reflected ceiling plans** and may include HVAC and sprinkler information. Chapter 5 discusses lighting fixtures and design, along with electrical and communication systems.

Finish Plans

Finish plans, drawn by designers, define what as well as where finishes are placed on floors, walls, and ceilings. Some designers use finish schedules instead of plans. The schedule is a chart indicating the finish and its location on each surface.

PLAN/SECTION SYMBOLS

WOOD
- INTERRUPTED BLOCKING
- PLYWOOD (LARGE SCALE)
- PLYWOOD (SMALL SCALE)
- ROUGH (FRAMING)
- FINISH WOOD

EARTH WORK
- EARTH
- POROUS FILL (GRAVEL/STONE)
- ROCK
- RUBBLE STONE
- SAND

METAL
- ALUMINUM
- STEEL
- STRUCTURAL STEEL

MATERIAL SYMBOLS

CONCRETE
- BLOCK
- LIGHTWEIGHT
- STRUCTURAL

MASONRY
- BRICK
- CUT STONE

FINISHES
- ACOUSTICAL TILE
- CARPET AND PAD
- MARBLE
- PLASTER/STUCCO
- TERRAZZO

INSULATION
- LOOSE BATT
- RIGID

ELEVATION SYMBOLS
- BRICK
- CERAMIC TILE
- CONCRETE, PLASTER, STUCCO
- GLASS
- RUNNING BOND MASONRY
- STACK BOND MASONRY
- SHEET METAL (FLASHER)
- SQUARED STONE
- RUBBLE STONE

TYPES OF LINES
- BOUNDARY LINES
- BREAK LINES
- CENTER LINES
- CUTTING-PLANE LINES
- DIMENSION/EXTENSION LINES
- HIDDEN LINES
- OBJECT LINES

CONSTRUCTION DRAWING SYMBOLS

- BUILDING SECTION
  - INDICATES SECTION NO.
  - INDICATES PAGE WHERE SECTION IS FOUND
- DOOR NUMBER
- REVISION NUMBER
- WINDOW REFERENCE
- WALL SECTION/ELEVATION REFERENCE NUMBER

Figure 4.2 *Material symbols in plan/section/elevation, and line and graphic symbols.*

TYPICAL WALL

EXTERIOR WALL WITH MASONRY FACE

WALLS TO BE DEMOLISHED

CONCRETE WALL

WALL WITH WINDOW

FIREPLACE IN WALL

Figure 4.3 *Wall symbols.*

Figure 4.5 *The Arts and Crafts movement (see p. 44) inspired this spiral staircase designed for the American Forest & Paper Association. (Architect/Designer: Greenwell Goetz Architects. Photograph by David Patterson.)*

SINK

TRASH COMPACTOR

DISHWASHER

DROP IN RANGE

BUILT-IN MIX CENTER

COOK TOP

FREE-STANDING UNIT RANGE

OVEN

CORNER REVOLVING SHELVES

FREEZER

WALL CABINET

BASE CABINET

DRYER

REFRIGERATOR

WASHER

Figure 4.4 *Kitchen symbols.*

View down

Stair width 44" min.

Baluster

Banister

Stairwell

Treads 11"

Headroom 6'8" clearance min.

Risers 7"

Face

rise height

Stringer

Wall stringer

Railing height 34"

Nozing

run length

Figure 4.6 *Stairway terminology.*

Figure 4.7 *Typical elevation of a fireplace wall.*

KIRK BARRON 3-99

Figure 4.8 *Transverse section of a three-story building.*

Elevations

Elevations are drawings of the walls. Exterior elevations delineate the outside of the building and define finish materials, as well as heights and locations of exterior components. Interior elevations are necessary to show custom cabinet or wall designs (Figure 4.7).

Sections

A **section** is a cut-through view of a building indicating appropriate framing and construction (Figure 4.8). Sections also may be cut-through interior walls or cabinets (Figures 4.9 and 4.10).

Figure 4.9 *Typical wall section. Note the terminology and use of construction symbols.*

Figure 4.9 labels:
SHINGLES
BUILDING PAPER
PLY. ROOF DECK
GALV. ROOF EDGE
RAFTER/16" O.C.
CEILING JOIST/16' O.C.
DRYWALL
TOP PLATES
VENT
PLY. SOFFIT
SUB FASCIA
FASCIA
DRYWALL
WALL STUDS/16'00"
PLYWOOD SIDING
FIBERBOARD SHEATHING
FIBERGLASS INSULATION
BASE TRIM
CARPET AND PAD
PLYWOOD FLOOR DECKING
SOLE PLATE
SILL HEADER
SILL PLATE
FLOOR JOIST/16'00"
TERMITE SHIELD
GRADE LINE
SILL ANCHOR BOLT
CONC. BLOCK FOUNDATION WALL
POROUS GRAVEL FILL
DRAIN TUBE
CONC. FOOTING
REBAR
GRADE

Figure 4.10 labels:
12"
1" X 3 1/2" BLOCKING AS REQ'D
OAK NOSE
3/8" HARD BOARD BACKING
3/4" PAINTED PLY
1" X 3 1/2" BLOCKING AS REQ'D
1" X 1 1/2" OAK FACE FRAME
30"
1" OAK PANEL
1" X 1 1/2" OAK DOOR FRAME
18" +/-
24"
PREFORMED LAMINATE COUNTERTOP
1" BLOCKING AS REQ'D
1/2" PAINTED PLY.
DRAWER RUNNER
3/8" HARD BOARD BACKING
OAK NOSE
3/4" PAINTED PLY.
1" X 6" BLOCKING AS REQ'D
1" X 5" BLOCKING
1" OAK PANEL
1" X 1 1/2" OAK DRAWER FRAME
1" X 1 1/2" OAK DOOR FRAME
1" OAK PANEL
1" X 1 1/2" OAK FACE FRAME
36"
3/4" SHOE

Figure 4.10 *Typical cabinet section. Designers frequently create custom cabinetry not only for kitchens, but also for media rooms, libraries, and family rooms.*

Key	Quan	Rough Opng.	Type	Mfg. No.	Mullion	Remarks
W-1	3	2'-11" × 2'-6"	SASH	3W 1748	NONE	Painted
W-2	8	3'-10" × 2'-6"	"	3W 1783B	1'-3$\frac{1}{3}$"	Stained
W-3	7	3'-9" × 2'-6"	"	3W 1785	2'-3$\frac{1}{3}$"	Stained
W-4	2	4'-11" × 3'-2"	CASEMENT	3W 1880	NONE	See Detail
W-5	4	4'-5" × 2'-3$\frac{7}{8}$"	CASEMENT	AA6 1440	NONE	Stained

Figure 4.11 *Window schedule.*

Schedules

A schedule is a table that indicates the material to be used in a specific building process, such as a chart indicating window and door information (Figure 4.11). Schedules also may be used to list hardware for windows and doors, as well as finish materials for floors, ceilings, and walls.

Details

Details are enlarged drawings indicating how components are to be constructed. Interior designers may design particular furniture pieces and wall moldings or trim. The most common interior details relate to the design of custom cabinetry such as bookshelves, media centers, built-in computer desks, and custom storage and kitchen units.

One of the key design elements true to all cabinet construction involves construction style. The two broad divisions are *faceframe construction* and *frameless construction*.

1. Faceframe construction allows the doors and drawers of the cabinets to be flush (in the same plane). The frame of the cabinet is recessed forming a reveal, and may be made of the same or contrasting materials (Figures 4.12 and 4.13).
2. Frameless construction is a cleaner, contemporary style of construction. Only doors and drawer fronts are visible. Wood grains can be matched between door and drawer fronts. Plastic laminates are well suited for this style (Figures 4.14 and 4.15).

Figure 4.13 *In this interior, faceframe cabinet construction was used to give a warm traditional look. (Courtesy Quality Cabinets, Division of Tekwood Industries Inc.)*

Figure 4.12 *Section looking down on two cabinet doors. Note recessed faceframe in construction.*

Figure 4.14 *Section looking down on two cabinet doors. Note flush front appearance in frameless construction.*

Roofing Plans and Engineering Drawings

Roofing plans and engineering drawings provide designers with an insight into building systems. In general, designers should check that electrical, lighting, communication, and emergency lighting systems are placed where specified by the engineers. Where possible, emergency lighting and alarms should be selected and placed to blend with the interior finishes.

Interior designers must be able to read, interpret, and in many instances assist in preparing construction drawings for non-load-bearing walls. Terminology and specific processes in building systems follow.

Heating, Ventilating, and Air Conditioning (HVAC) Systems

HVAC systems are designed to maintain human comfort. In addition to controlling temperature, HVAC systems should also regulate the humidity, air quality, and air movement through a space. The most common heating systems are forced air heat, radiant heat, and solar energy. (Also see "Green Design: Solar Energy.")

Forced Air Heat

Forced air heaters require a furnace and ductwork. The furnace heats air, which is then forced through the ductwork by a fan. Return vents draw cool air back into the furnace for recirculation (Figure 4.16). A heat pump works in conjunction with a furnace by extracting heat from the outside air.

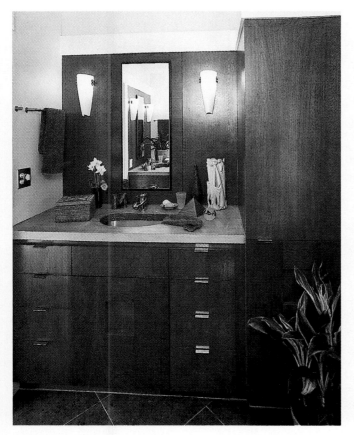

Figure 4.15 *This bathroom cabinet utilizes frameless construction to achieve its sleek, clean appearance. Cherry wood with chrome drawer pulls accentuates the image. (Architect/Designer: Lippert & Lippert Design, Palo Alto, CA. Photograph by Don Roper Photography.)*

Figure 4.16 *In this HVAC plan, numbers indicate pipe sizes. Boxes with X's indicate registers. Dotted lines indicate the return air flow system.*

GREEN DESIGN

Solar Energy

Solar buildings are built to capture the sun's energy and conserve conventional fuel.

The passive solar system The **passive solar system** is a nonmechanical method relying on the building itself to absorb and store the sun's heat. (Note: All compass directions are given relative to the northern hemisphere; for southern hemisphere applications, substitute north for south.)

- Buildings are space planned so that frequently used spaces are on the south side.
- Windows are generally limited to the south wall, with occasional east and west wall use.
- The north side of the building is slightly **bermed,** or buried under dirt.
- Evergreen trees are planted to the northwest of the building to block cold winter winds.
- Deciduous trees (those that lose their leaves in winter) are placed to the south to block the hot summer sun, yet allow winter sun to reach the building.
- Overhanging eaves are designed in accordance with the angle of the sun to allow winter sun to enter a building, while blocking summer sun.
- Thermal storage units, such as masonry walls, fireplaces, stone floors, or large water containers (such as an indoor pool), are located to absorb solar energy during the day. At night the stored heat is released into the building.
- Exterior doors enter into small passageways that serve as an air lock.
- Highly efficient stoves may function as auxiliary heating devices.
- In the summer, lower windows may be opened to draw in cooler air, while skylights, ceiling fans, and upper windows are used to draw the warmer air up and out of the building.
- Low-growing vines and shrubs are planted on the south side of the building to prevent glare.

The active solar system The **active solar system** relies on mechanical means—photovoltaic (or solar) panels, fans, and pumps—in addition to the principles of passive solar design to trap and use energy from the sun.

Active solar systems can also provide electricity for the building. Photovoltaic panels convert sunlight into DC electricity, which is stored in a series of batteries. An inverter changes the electricity from DC to AC, the type used in conventional building designs. Batteries are generally housed in a utility room with a small vent to the outside for gases to escape.

A solar batch water heater can be used in sunbelt areas. This type of water heater provides hot water by mid-morning on sunny days, and keeps it hot until well after sunset.

Radiant Heat

Radiant heat is available through steam heating systems, electric baseboards, portable space heaters, and wood stoves.

In a steam heating system, water is heated in a furnace or boiler and then carried by a water pump through pipes. Thin metal fins surrounding the pipes radiate the heat into the room. Electric or gas baseboard heaters and portable heaters work in similar fashion by heating strips or coils, which in turn radiate the heat into the surrounding space. Wood stoves are discussed in Chapter 12.

Both forced air and radiant heating systems may require the use of a separate humidifier to control the level of humidity.

Ventilation

Ventilation refers to the exchange of air inside a room. Natural ventilation occurs when windows and doors are left open to allow breezes to enter the building.

Hot, stale air rises in a room and should be vented via skylights, high windows, or exhaust fans. Ceiling fans also help to circulate air. Cooler, cleaner air is drawn in from windows and doors as hot air is eliminated. Cross-ventilation is also helpful wherever possible.

When fresh air is not brought into buildings, stale air and toxins emitted from plastics, chemical finishes, smoke, and other airborne pollutants can lead to **sick building syndrome.** (See "Green Design: Indoor Air Quality.")

A ventilation standard has been set by the American Society of Heating, Refrigeration, and Air Conditioning Engineers. The standard, called ASHRAE #62-1989, although primarily applied by HVAC engineers, establishes airflow minimums for interiors.

Air Conditioning

Air conditioning refers to the cooling of a building. With central air conditioning, a forced air heating system's ductwork

GREEN DESIGN

Indoor Air Quality

Most people are familiar with the detrimental effects of outdoor air pollution, but indoor air pollution may be equally (if not more) hazardous to one's health. Indoor air quality, or **IAQ,** has come under close scrutiny because it is estimated that Americans spend 90% of their time indoors.

In general, indoor air pollution results in what has been termed *sick building syndrome* or SBS. SBS defines a building where inhabitants complain of health problems, such as respiratory, sinus, and digestive problems, irritability, and fatigue. The sources of indoor air pollution are complex but can be divided into three general types of pollutants:

1. Biological—organic toxins such as bacteria, molds, dust mites, and insects.
2. Earth elements—harmful naturally occurring materials such as sheetrock dust, asbestos, and radon.
3. Volatile organic chemicals (VOCs)—chemicals that are emitted into the air from building materials, furniture, fabrics or finishes, and other building processes. Typical VOCs include formaldehyde, styrene, and benzene.

According to the American Society of Interior Designers' *Indoor Air Quality Two-Part Program,* pollutants may stem from a variety of sources throughout a building, including:

- Construction products such as sealers, insulation, paint, caulks, and adhesives.
- Fixtures and furnishings such as carpet, carpet pads and adhesives, furniture, finishes, and chipboard.
- Waxes, polishes, solvents, and insect repellents.
- Machines and electronics such as computer screens, printers, and lasers, which may emit electromagnetic fields.
- Photographic processes, perfumes, and sprays.
- Operational equipment, inadequate air filtering, poorly designed HVAC systems, or standing water.

As a member of the construction team, a designer should be familiar with IAQ issues and products. For instance, the Carpet and Rug Institute (CRI) has developed a testing program for carpet, cushions, and adhesives. Products that meet low levels of emissions of VOCs are allowed to carry their label. CRI also makes the following installation recommendations.

- Carefully plan the carpet installation using the manufacturer's installation guidelines and/or the *CRI 104 Standard for Installation of Commercial Textile Floorcovering Materials.*
- Ensure adequate fresh air ventilation during the entire installation process and for 48–72 hours afterwards.
- Vacuum the old carpet prior to removal to minimize airborne dust.
- Vacuum the subfloors prior to carpet installation.
- Use low-VOC adhesive in glue-down installations.
- Use low-emitting carpet cushion.
- Vacuum the new carpet with a high-efficiency vacuum, using a high-efficiency particulate filter bag to minimize airborne particles. Make sure all moisture and cleaning agents are removed with each cleaning.

In addition to the proper selection of products, designers should remember the following:

- Avoid blocking air intakes and vents with window treatments or furnishings.
- Install exhaust fans in smoking areas, bathrooms, kitchens, and other areas where chemicals or sprays may be used.
- Provide humidity controls.
- Encourage proper maintenance.
- When installing open office systems, allow airflow at the base of the partition (1″–6″).*
- Arrange computer terminals so that users are seated 30″ away from the computer screen to avoid the electromagnetic fields.*

One part of an IAQ program is the installation of live plants, which act as air filters by absorbing indoor air pollutants. For example, the philodendron and the spider plant absorb formaldehyde, and the common peace lily absorbs benzene. Through the process of photosynthesis, plants trap airborne contaminants, as well as regenerate the air with oxygen. However, plants are not a quick fix for a sick building. They do require maintenance and proper light.

Finally, designers should monitor the market for advances in IAQ research and should maintain documents regarding IAQ design decisions.

*From Grazyna Pilatowicz, in *Eco-Interiors.*

is used in conjunction with a separate cooling unit. Individual units may be installed in the wall or window to cool separate rooms or areas. In humid climates, a dehumidifier should also be installed.

In dryer climates, evaporative coolers, called swamp coolers, force air through moistened filters and pads, thereby removing heat and providing cooled air.

With all HVAC systems, designers must avoid blocking supply and return air vents; otherwise, the systems will not function as designed. In new construction, designers should work with engineers to place vents away from possible furniture arrangements and window treatments.

Plumbing

Plumbing systems include the supply system for bringing water to the building, the system for heating the water, the fixtures involved in distributing the water, the removal of wastewater (black water from commodes and gray water from all other sources), and the required venting of the system. Plumbing also may include sprinkler systems in high-rise buildings and public places. Typical plumbing symbols are shown in Figure 4.17.

Supply Systems

Water may be supplied via a county or city water system, or it may be received from a well. In remote arid regions, rainfall may be collected in a large reservoir and piped to a house. No matter what system is used, water must be pressurized to flow from the faucet.

Water containing a high concentration of minerals may need to be softened or purified to prevent laundry problems and accumulated deposits in pipes. Minerals also may add a particular taste to water.

Heating Systems

Water may be heated via a gas, electric, wood, or solar water heater. (Gas and electric are the most common.) Water heaters should be reasonably close to their source of use. On-demand water heaters are placed immediately next to their source of use; they have no holding tank. These small units fit in walls or under sinks and heat water only as needed.

Plumbing Fixtures

Fixtures for commodes, bidets, and lavatories are available from many manufacturers. Porcelain fixtures are the most common, and are available in many different colors. White or neutral colors serve clients best, because black and other dark-colored fixtures show soap rings easily. As color preferences change, paint and wallcoverings can be adapted to coordinate with white or neutral fixtures.

Shower stalls and bathtubs are commonly made from fiberglass. These fixtures should have smooth corners and no

Figure 4.17 *Plumbing and heating symbols.*

crevices where dirt can collect. As with the commode and lavatory fixtures, white or light neutral colors are usually the wisest choice (Figure 4.18).

Waste Removal

The removal of wastewater involves three important concepts:

1. Wastewater from commodes (called black water) requires a minimum 4″ pipe, which will not fit in a standard 2″ × 4″ stud wall. Wastewater plumbing on upper floors must be routed through a wider 2″ × 6″ stud wall, or carried down a **chase** (a concealed column usually located in the corner of a room).
2. All waste lines (both black and gray water) must tie into air vents that allow fumes to escape through the roof of the building.

Figure 4.18 *In this renovated bathroom, the designer provided a variety of lighting accents and classical details to create a functional and elegant space. (Design by Jackie Naylor Interiors. Photograph ©Robert Thien. As seen in:* Atlanta Homes & Lifestyles.*)*

3. Wastewater relies on gravity to flow to the septic tank or municipal sewer system. Consequently, all wastewater pipes must have a downward slope of 1/4″ for every horizontal foot of length. In high-rise buildings and commercial spaces with poured concrete floors, commodes must be located near predetermined sanitary lines and wet columns (columns with hidden supply and sanitary water lines). If a drain is located in a basement that is below the level of the septic tank or municipal sewer system, a sump pump is installed in the floor of the basement to pump the waste water up and out of the building.

Figure 4-19 illustrates a typical residential drainage system.

Figure 4.19 *Multistory residential wastewater system.*

Acoustics

Sound can travel directly through the air and also may be transmitted through objects. Designers can assist in controlling sound through proper space planning and material usage.

Sound is measured in **decibels** (dB). Zero dB is the quietest sound an average human can hear, and 130 dB is the threshold of painfully loud sounds. A private office or home generally has noise levels at about 30 dB—the maximum level at which most individuals can concentrate on work.

Residential and commercial spaces are generally zoned so that noisy and quiet activities are separated. For instance, closets and bookshelves may buffer noisy areas (see Chapter 7). Walls may be constructed with additional layers of gypsumboard, dense insulation, alternating studs, or a combination of all three to prevent sound transmission.

Sound may also be controlled by using materials that absorb its energy. Hard surfaces such as concrete floors and tile are dense and although they are good at preventing the transmission of sound, their hardness causes sound waves to reflect back into the room. Carpeting, soft window treatments, upholstered furniture, and acoustical ceiling tiles absorb sound waves and thereby help to quiet a room.

Table 4.1 *Building Codes*

Type	Purpose	Common Codes
Model building codes	Define construction requirements and limit use of hazardous materials.	• National Building Code (NBC), published by Buildings Official Code Administration International (BOCA) • Standard Building Code (SBC), published by Southern Building Code Congress International (SBCCI) • Uniform Building Code (UBC), published by International Conference of Building Officials (ICBO) • International Building Code (IBC), published by International Code Council, a joint commission of BOCA, SBCCI, and ICBO*
Plumbing, electrical, and mechanical codes	Define construction requirements for these specialties. Particularly helpful in determining the number of fixtures in a building.	• Plumbing and mechanical codes published by organizations that publish model building codes • National Electrical Code (NEC), published by National Fire Protection Association (NFPA)
Life safety or fire codes	Establish minimum requirements for fire safety.	• Life Safety Code (LSC, or NFPA 101®), published by NFPA
Residential codes	Define construction requirements in one- and two-family dwellings.	• One and Two Family Dwelling Code (OTFDC), published by Council of American Building Officials (CABO) • International Residential Code (IRC), published by International Code Council*

*The IBC and IRC are planned to be released in 2000. They will consolidate the existing model and residential codes. Universal plumbing, mechanical, and electrical codes will also be released by the International Code Council.

Variations in wall angles direct sounds to different areas. Avoiding the use of right angles and parallel surfaces will improve sound attenuation. Acoustical engineers consult on theatre, concert hall, and large auditorium designs to enhance and distribute reverberating sounds.

Other Concealed Systems

In residential interiors, *central vacuum systems* may be routed through walls. These units are particularly helpful in multistory residences so vacuum cleaners do not have to be moved up and down stairs.

Security systems are another component concealed in the walls of residential and nonresidential structures. Sensing devices activate alarms, turn on lights, or may even dial the local authorities or security company. Alarm systems are the least costly when installed prior to finished construction.

Fire alarms are required by codes in commercial buildings and are integrated into the building structure. These smoke- and heat-sensing devices emit audible as well as visual alarms. Additionally, *sprinkler systems* are located in commercial buildings to help stop or suppress the spread of fire. The systems are usually concealed in the ceiling with only the head of the sprinkler exposed on or below the ceiling's surface. Most sprinkler systems spray water; however, a few emit fire-retarding foam.

In residential environments, homes are equipped with smoke detectors that alert occupants to potential fires. Smoke detectors should be placed in kitchen, family, and bedroom areas.

Codes and Federal Regulations

Interior designers are legally responsible for being aware of and implementing applicable local, state, or federal codes. Because the majority of building codes are updated every three years, designers must check with local code officials to determine which codes are used and from which year. Federal regulations are mandated by law and required regardless of local codes. Codes can be divided into the following general categories: model building codes; plumbing, electrical, and mechanical codes; life safety (or fire) codes; and residential codes. See Table 4.1 for more detailed descriptions.

Federal Requirements

The federal government has passed several laws that relate to the design of interiors. The most common include the Americans with Disabilities Act (ADA), the Fair Housing Act (FHA), and the Occupational Safety and Health Act (OSHA).

The ADA, a civil rights act, was passed in 1990 and has greatly affected building design. Among other things, the ADA requires government buildings, contract design facilities (including all the specialty areas discussed in Table 1.2), public accommodations (residential or otherwise), and public transportation systems to provide equal accessibility to all people regardless of disability. Many of the ADA's physical regulations are based on the 1986 American National Standards Institute (ANSI) codes (which have since been updated). Designers frequently reference the

Figure 4.20 *Minimum clear width for wheelchairs, from the ADA guidelines. http://www.access-board.gov/bfdg.html*

ADA. (A complete copy of the "Accessibility Guidelines for Buildings and Facilities" is available from the U.S. Architectural and Transportation Barriers Compliance Board at 1-800-USA-ABLE.) A sample of these regulations is shown in Figure 4.20. It is important to emphasize that these regulations are laws, not codes or standards. The monitoring of these laws varies from state to state.

The FHA is similar to the ADA, but relates only to residential structures. The OSHA regulations mainly affect contractor and subcontractor work practices.

Summary

This chapter has emphasized the designer's responsibility to understand construction processes, building systems, and related codes. The symbols and terminology relating to the mechanical, plumbing, acoustic, and other concealed systems must be understood in order to communicate with allied professionals and to share accurate information with the client.

Designers have an ethical responsibility to inform clients of alternative design solutions that may conserve energy or lower utility costs. Additionally, designers must take into account the effects furnishings and finishes may have on indoor air quality. The application of low-emission products helps to ensure a safer interior environment. Finally, it cannot be emphasized strongly enough that interior designers are legally responsible for complying with local and state codes and federal regulations.

5

Lighting, Electrical, and Communications

Figure 5.1 *In this vibrant French-styled brasserie, Voila!, the designers used perimeter lighting to visually widen the space and highlight the unique whimsical border. Other decorative pendant fixtures add to the carefree effect. (Architect/Designer: Knauer Inc. Photograph by Steinkamp/Ballogg.)*

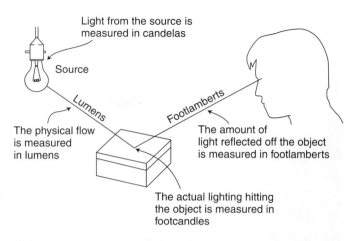

Light from the source is measured in candelas

Source

Lumens

The physical flow is measured in lumens

Footlamberts

The amount of light reflected off the object is measured in footlamberts

The actual lighting hitting the object is measured in footcandles

Figure 5.2 *The four measurements of the quantity of light are candelas (source), lumens (flow of light), footcandle (light falling on an object), and footlambert (reflected light).*

ighting, as discussed in relation to color in Chapter 3, is an essential element in all interiors. Lighting can be one of the most creative avenues in the field of interior design. Light, like color, can alter psychological and physiological reactions. Additionally, the fixtures that house the actual light source can be designed to serve as decorative art or sculpture, adding character and sometimes whimsy to the interior (Figure 5.1).

The quantity and quality of light affect the apparent size, shape, and character of an object. Interior designers can alter the perception of space in a room, focus attention, set moods, define texture, or create a specific atmosphere through the appropriate use of light. Understanding the scientific basis of light, applying this to an interior to create the desired effect, and communicating the plan to engineers and contractors are essential skills of interior designers. To begin to understand how to use light, designers must be familiar with the basic terminology and basic principles of the *quantity* and *quality* of the light source.

The professional terminology for light fixtures and lamps differs from everyday language. The light bulb itself is called the **lamp**. It is the source of light. The physical structure that holds the lamp and other necessary and decorative accoutrements (such as the shade, reflector, or lens) is called the **fixture**. The lamp and the fixture form the **luminaire**.

The Quantity of Light

Light is measured in different ways (Figure 5.2), depending on where the measurement is taken:

- **Candela:** The unit of measure for the intensity of light in a given direction.
- **Lumen:** A measure of flow of light produced by one lamp. Lumens also determine the efficiency, called the **efficacy**, of a lamp. To determine the efficacy of a lamp, divide the lumens by the watts (the amount of energy consumed by the lamp). For example, suppose a new 75-watt incandescent lamp produces 1,180 lumens; 1,180 lumens divided by 75 watts equals an efficacy rating of 15.7. The higher the efficacy rating, the more efficient the lamp. In practice, to select the most energy-efficient lamp, select the lamp with the lowest wattage and the highest lumen.
- **Footcandle:** The unit of measure for the amount of light falling on a surface. One footcandle is equal to the amount of light falling on one square foot of surface, one foot away from a candle. The farther the surface is from the light source, the lower the footcandle measurement. Recommended footcandles for specific tasks are:

Theatre passage	1–2
Passage through a corridor	3–5
Passage though stairwells	5–10
General office work	10–20
Restaurant dining	5–20
Reading	20–30

Intense reading, kitchen preparation, shaving	40–60
Detail work	50–100+
Surgery	500+

- **Footlambert:** The unit of measure for the amount of light reflected from a surface. Generally, this is the amount of light actually seen. For example, a light-colored shiny wall may reflect 80% or more of the footcandles; a dark-colored, rough-textured wall may reflect less than 2% of the footcandles. Reflectance values of common colors are:

White	89%
Ivory	87%
Light gray	65%
Sky blue	65%
Intense yellow	62%
Light green	56%
Forest green	22%
Coconut brown	16%
Black	2%

The Quality of Light

Light is created by wavelengths emitted from a light source (such as the sun or a lamp). Long waves produce warm colors; short waves produce cooler colors.

Natural daylight (the highest quality light) produces a linear color spectrum that evenly distributes the colors we see (Figure 5.3). Artificial light sources do not exactly mimic natural light's color spectrum, although some come close. For instance, a typical incandescent light bulb's color spectrum emphasizes the warmer red wavelengths.

As discussed in Chapter 3, the human eye sees the color of an object when light of mixed wavelengths is reflected into the eye from the object's surface. For instance, if an object is yellow, the surface reflects wavelengths found in the yellow section of the spectrum and absorbs wavelengths of the other colors.

Figure 5.4 *Kelvin temperature lamp comparisons. (Courtesy of GE Lighting.)*

Figure 5.3 *Top: The color spectrum of natural light. Bottom: The color spectrum of incandescent light. (Courtesy of GE Lighting.)*

Color Rendering Index

The closer a lamp's color spectrum is to natural light, the higher the quality of light it produces. The measurement of this quality is called the **Color Rendering Index** (CRI). The CRI is based on a scale of 0–100. A CRI of 80 or better is necessary when color rendering is critical, such as inspecting printing proofs or selecting clothing. A CRI of 60–80 is average; a CRI below 60 may be appropriate for street lighting or other lighting when color selection is not important. Note that a higher CRI requires more energy to support the broader color spectrum.

Kelvin Temperature

Another measurement of light quality is the light's temperature or **Kelvin** rating. This measurement places a candle flame on the lower temperature range around 2000°K. A typical sunny day measures around 6000°K, and a northern night sky is said to be at about 8500°K. This concept seems backwards, but is best related to the heat of a gas fire or burner. Cooler flames burn red, warmer flames are yellow, and the hottest flame is blue. A Kelvin rating between 3000°K (typical of a quality fluorescent lamp) and 6000°K (a sunny day) is considered the natural benchmark (Figure 5.4).

Lighting Location

The quality of light also depends on the physical location of the light source. Designers must carefully locate the light source; otherwise, the resulting glare causes eye fatigue and general irritability (Figure 5.5). To prevent glare when using a portable light fixture, use a soft white bulb, a glass diffuser, and/or a lampshade.

Natural Light Sources

Although light is regarded as a single form of energy, it is commonly divided into two categories: natural and artificial. The main source of natural light is the sun. Its properties, including ultraviolet light, warmth, and radiant energy, are important to people's health and well-being. Sunlight emits all visible wavelengths of radiant energy, as well as invisible infrared wavelengths (long rays felt as heat) and ultraviolet wavelengths (short rays; see Figure 3.2).

Often, the designer's challenge is to control natural light in a living space. Natural light changes from morning to evening. Therefore, a designer may treat a south- and west-facing room with muted, cooler, and darker colors to counter the sun's afternoon warmth and glaring rays. The designer can also determine the most suitable window treatment after considering the position on the site, geographic location, and climate. Natural light can be allowed to enter a space in a manner that enhances the environment and minimizes glare (see Figure 3.27).

The secondary source of natural light is combustion, produced by fire, oil lamps, candles, and gaslights. Until the development of electric lighting, combustion was the only method of producing supplementary light.

Figure 5.5 *Light is reflected off a surface at the same angle as it was received. In these diagrams, this means the angle of A equals the angle of B. Glare occurs when a viewer intercepts the reflected light or looks directly into a lamp.*

Combustion lighting still deserves consideration as a decorative element in residential design and for some commercial projects such as restaurants (Figure 5.6). Candles and a gas or wood fire are frequently used as supplementary lighting or heat. Their main value is in their soft glow that sheds a flattering light and creates an atmosphere of warmth and intimacy.

Artificial Light Sources

Artificial lighting is a manufactured source of illumination derived from electricity. The electrical energy is transformed into visible light and is identified by its wattage. The most familiar artificial light sources are incandescent and electric discharge (which includes fluorescent) lamps.

Incandescent Lamps

Incandescent lighting originated with the familiar light bulb invented by Thomas Edison in the latter half of the 19th century. All **incandescent lamps** provide light by heating an element (usually metal) to a Kelvin temperature of approximately 2500–3000°K, at which point the lamp glows. Incandescent lamps include the typical general

Figure 5.6 *The Canlis Restaurant, a dining landmark in Seattle, was updated from its 1950s origins. The designers used combustion lighting in the Penthouse dining room. (Architect: James Cutler Architects. Designer: Doug Raser. Photograph by Michael Jensen.)*

Figure 5.7 *The incandescent filament lamp. (a) Cross section. (b) Common incandescent lamp styles. A: standard (arbitrary); B: oval or ovoid; C: candelabra; G: globe; P: pear; S: straight side; F: flare; PAR: parabolic reflector; R: reflector; ER: elliptical reflector; T: tubular; TH: tungsten-halogen; LV: low voltage.*

A single-ended 150 watt tubular tungsten halogen lamp

Low-voltage (50 watt) miniature lamp suitable for small task lights.

A standard single ended lamp with a mini base. Available from 50 to 250 watts. Often used for task lighting.

Standard 300 watt linear lamp. Used for small scale flood lighting and other fittings.

Figure 5.8 *Styles of tungsten-halogen lamps.*

service lamp, tungsten-halogen lamps, reflector lamps, and low-voltage lamps (Figure 5.7).

Lamps are designed by a letter identifying their style. The number following the letter indicates the diameter of the lamp in eighths of an inch. (For example, an MR16 is a lamp that is 2″ wide.) Lamps are usually clear or frosted (also called soft white). The frosted lamp emits a more diffused light.

Incandescent lamps:

* are available in a wide variety of sizes, shapes, colors, and types
* are small and adaptable
* produce white light that casts a slight red and yellow hue
* are generally considered complimentary to most skin tones
* effectively highlight textures and forms
* can be easily dimmed
* are relatively inexpensive to purchase, but are costly to run because of their low efficacy
* produce heat, which can burden air conditioning systems
* permit precise optical control for effective accent and task lighting
* can cause glare when exposed
* can neutralize cool colors.

A tungsten-halogen lamp is a type of incandescent lamp, but instead of a filament, the halogen lamp has a piece of hard quartz in a small enclosure. When heated it attains higher temperatures and therefore produces a more intense light and has a better performance output. Tungsten-halogen lamps also come in various styles (Figure 5.8). In addition to the above attributes, the tungsten-halogen lamps also:

Figure 5.9 *Tungsten-halogen lamps dramatically illuminate this contemporary living room. The brightness level is controlled by dimmers that can lower or raise the voltage, allowing the owners to control the mood. (Photograph by Peter Paige.)*

- run warmer (approximately 3000°K), producing a more intense light
- last two to four times longer than a general service incandescent
- are more expensive to purchase
- must not come in contact with the oils on skin; gloves must be worn when changing a lamp
- emit high levels of heat and therefore should not be placed near flammable objects
- must be shielded and therefore cannot be used as a direct light source (Figure 5.9).

Reflector lamps or parabolics have a hard-pressed glass covering and as the name implies, a built-in reflector to enhance light distribution. Reflector lamps are generally $3^1/_2''$ to $6''$ wide. The typical residential exterior flood lamp is an example of a common reflector lamp.

Low-voltage lamps are basically miniature tungsten-halogen lamps commonly used to enhance retail displays. The lamps run on 12 volt or 24 volt electricity and therefore require a separate transformer concealed in the ceiling or walls. (Transformers reduce the standard 120 volt electricity into 12 or 24 volt electricity for use in these lamps.) The transformer must be accessible for maintenance.

Discharge Lamps

Discharge lamps produce light by passing electricity through a gaseous tube. The most common discharge lamps are fluorescent, HID, and neon and cold cathode.

Fluorescent Lighting

Fluorescent lighting, in wide use since World War II, is produced in a glass tube lined with a fluorescent coating,

filled with mercury vapor and argon, and sealed at the ends. When gases are activated by an electric current, ultraviolet rays stimulate the phosphorous lamp coating, which emits visible light. Fluorescent lamps are made in a variety of shapes and sizes (Figure 5.10). The most familiar type is the T12 tubular lamp that is about $1^1/_2''$ in diameter and comes in lengths from two to eight feet.

- Fluorescent lamps emit less heat than incandescent lamps.
- Although the fixtures are expensive, they have a much higher efficacy rate (Figure 5.11). The tubes last up to 15 times longer than incandescent lamps and require about one-third as much energy.
- Small fluorescent lamps may be used in many applications where incandescent lamps were formerly used.
- Fluorescent sources are larger and create broader areas of light than incandescent lights.
- They provide diffused, shadowless light.
- Fluorescent lights are particularly efficient for commercial uses, especially in hospitals, schools, offices, stores, factories, and other large public spaces.
- Fluorescent light can distort colors and details if not color corrected.
- Fluorescent light is not as flexible and as easy to control as incandescent light.

Historically, fluorescent lamps produced a low CRI, but this has improved. Designers need to specify "color corrected" lamps to obtain the best color distribution.

HID Lamp

Another source of discharge lighting is the **HID** (high-intensity discharge) lamp, which incorporates some of the desirable

Figure 5.10 *Fluorescent lamp styles, regular and compact (not to scale). (Courtesy of GE Lighting.)*

qualities of both incandescent and fluorescent lighting. The discharge lamp is similar to the fluorescent in operational design, but in appearance it resembles an incandescent, only slightly larger (Figure 5.12). Three types of HID lamps include mercury (which tends to produce bluish light), high-pressure sodium (which tends to produce orange light and is the most efficient of the three types), and metal halide (which renders colors most accurately).

Characteristically, HID lamps

* last from 16,000 to 24,000 hours
* are highly efficient with about ten times the output of incandescent lighting

* are suitable for commercial and institutional demands for energy-saving lighting
* may show color poorly
* are noisy and therefore have limited use in small commercial and residential spaces
* require up to nine minutes to reach full light capacity from startup.

Because of their intense light, strong glare can occur if HID lamps are not shielded properly. These lamps are commonly used in very high ceilings to distance their intense glare from the occupants.

Neon and Cold Cathode

The well-known neon lamp and the cold cathode are low-pressure discharge lamps. Tubes filled with neon gas produce a reddish glow; tubes filled with argon gas produce a blue-green color. Tubes can be fashioned in many

Figure 5.11 *The SPX41 fluorescent lamp has a good efficacy and a good CRI rating. Its Kelvin temperature is about 4000°K. (Courtesy of GE Lighting.)*

Figure 5.12 *Common HID lamp styles. A: standard (arbitrary); T: tubular; PAR: parabolic aluminized reflector; E: elliptical (conical or dimpled); R: reflector; BT: bulbous tubular.*

cial lighting sources are either architectural (built in) or portable.

Architectural Lighting

Architectural lighting, which includes wall-mounted, ceiling-mounted, and custom-designed fixtures, is closely correlated with the structure of the room. This type of lighting is included in the lighting and electrical plans of the building as an integral part of the complete design. The flexibility of architectural lighting is endless (Figure 5.14).

Wall-Mounted Fixtures

Several types of wall-mounted fixtures are shown in Figure 5.15. A *canopy* overhead provides general illumination. This lighting is used mostly in baths and kitchens.

Cove lighting is placed near the ceiling, directing light upward and giving a feeling of height. When used around a perimeter it can increase the apparent size of the room.

Sconces are decorative lighting fixtures permanently attached to the wall. They may be modern or traditional in style and can be positioned to provide direct or indirect lighting. Commercial sconces must be designed and located to meet ADA requirements.

Valance lighting is positioned over a window. A lamp is placed behind a valance board and the light shines on the drapery. If the valance is open above the lamp, the light produces both indirect (reflected) and direct (downlight) lighting.

Ceiling-Mounted Fixtures

Ceiling-mounted fixtures are attached to the ceiling by one of three methods:

1. Recessed fixtures are hidden in the ceiling. The lamp (or a lens over the lamp) is the only visible component.
2. Surface-mounted fixtures are attached flush to the ceiling, but the fixture itself is exposed below the ceiling.
3. Suspended fixtures hang from the ceiling.

Figure 5.16 illustrates several kinds of ceiling-mounted fixtures.

Can lights (as they are commonly referred to in the industry) house lamps in cylindrical cans. Can lighting may be recessed or surface mounted depending on the design of the fixture. Can lights may be called downlights, wall-washers, or eyeballs. Downlights may focus on a definite object or produce general lighting when used in sufficient numbers. Figure 5.13 shows can lights combined with neon lighting. A **wall-washer** is an adjustable unit that can be directed at any angle to "wash" the wall with light. An **eyeball** is similar to a wall-washer but can swivel, allowing light to be focused where desired.

A *cornice* is usually built on the ceiling to direct the light downward. Cornices are fairly similar to valances. The

Figure 5.13 *Neon lighting adds a playful quality to this pediatric surgery center. Curved ceiling forms and stars enhance its lighthearted atmosphere. (Designer: Kathy Helm & Associates Inc. Photograph by Quandrant.)*

decorative forms, including curves (Figure 5.13). This lighting source lasts for many years but requires a costly, bulky transformer.

Cold cathode lamps are similar to neon lamps but have a higher efficacy and can produce shades of white as well as colored light. They are useful where long stretches of low levels of continuous light are required.

Lighting Fixtures

Fixtures house the light source. All fixtures cast the light either *down* (onto an object or into a room) or *up* (onto the ceiling). **Downlighting** also may be called **direct** lighting; **uplighting** also may be referred to as **indirect** or reflective lighting. The fixtures or luminaires for artifi-

Figure 5.14 *In this Japanese restaurant located in New York City, a variety of lighting techniques have been incorporated. Track lighting is concealed in the wood slat ceiling. Decorative sconces, chandeliers, cove lighting, downlighting, and uplighting define this elaborate use of the stylized yin-yang symbol. Frosted panels diffuse the downlighting over the bar. (Custom lighting by Adam D. Tihany. Architect/Designer: Adam D. Tihany International, Ltd. Photographs by Peter Paige.)*

Valance   Bracket   Cove   Sconce

Canopy

A.

B.

Figure 5.15 *A: Common types of wall-mounted fixtures. B: This decorative sconce was custom designed to meet the needs of the space. Etched glass and metal are combined in this Starfire Select™ fixture. (Courtesy of Starfire Lighting.)*

difference is the physical location of the mounted lamp. When used over a window it can aid in eliminating the black mirror or glare effect produced at night.

Fluorescent panels may be recessed, surface mounted, or suspended. Fluorescent panels are frequently used in 2′ × 2′ squares or 2′ × 4′ rectangles because they are eco-

nomical. Lenses are available in a variety of options to diffuse the light and soften the glare. This is especially important in environments where computer screens or VDTs are used.

Pendants and *chandeliers* (pendants with arms) are hung from the ceiling. Styles and lamp options are limitless (and sometimes custom designed). Pendants and chandeliers, when used over dining surfaces, should be suspended approximately 30 inches above the table in an eight-foot-high room, and raised three inches for each additional foot of ceiling height.

A *soffit* consists of an enclosed light attached to the ceiling and is designed to provide a high level of light directly below. This light is effective in bathrooms, niches, and over built-in desks.

Track lighting consists of a track surface mounted to or suspended from the ceiling. It comes in a broad array of sizes, shapes, and finishes. Fixtures clip or slide along the track or wire frame to create a precisely designed optical system with a vast range of lighting effects. Layout configurations are practically infinite (Figure 5.17).

Custom Fixtures

Custom-designed architectural lighting may be created to highlight steps or handrails, or for other design effects. Recessed floor lighting may be used in airplanes, theatres, or at the base of steps as a safety device.

Fiber-optic fixtures are a type of decorative lighting that often meets custom needs (Figure 5.18). Fiber optics are not in themselves a light source, but rather a style of distributing light. A fiber-optic light fixture is composed of a bundle of thin cylindrical fibers. A ray of light passed through the fibers produces an intense pinpoint of light at the opposite end. Fiber optics can be concealed in handrails and retail display cabinets, or used for spot or downlighting.

Systems Furniture Lighting

Furniture systems (as discussed in Chapter 8) can be purchased with attached lighting systems. The electrical and lighting systems are concealed within the panels of the furniture system. Light may be directed below the upper cabinets onto the desk surface, similar to canopy or soffit lighting. Pendant fixtures may be suspended from the furniture system's walls to provide direct lighting. Lighting may also be directed upward. The area on top of the upper cabinets may conceal a light source that directs light onto the ceiling, similar to the lighting concept of a torchère.

Portable Lighting

A portable luminaire is a fixture that may be transported from one location to another. Portable fixtures (both table and floor models) are the oldest forms of electrical interior lighting. They provide flexible lighting in residential or public

Recessed

Wall washer

Eyeball

Surface mounted downlight

Track lighting

Recessed fluorescent panel

Dropped fluorescent panel

Soffit

Modern pendant or hanging lamp

Traditional hanging chandelier

Cornice

Figure 5.16 *A: Common types of ceiling-mounted fixtures. B: This custom hanging pendant was designed and scaled for a retail mall. Colored neon accentuates the contemporary columns. (Architect/Designer: Anthony Bellucchi Architects Ltd. Lighting design by Roeder Design, a subsidiary of Pacific Lightworks. Photograph by Robt. Ames Cook.) C: This suspended fixture of cone-shaped glass is available with one, three, eight, or twelve pendants to fit the scale of the space. ("Fucsia" courtesy of Flos USA.)*

A.

B.

C.

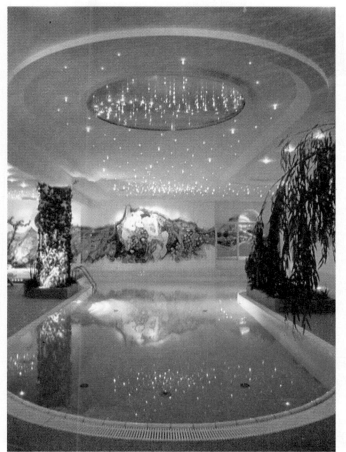

Figure 5.17 *In this gallery space, track lighting suspended from fine cables illuminates the sculpture and framed art. Incandescent halogen lamps pinpoint the selections. (Designer: Ambiance Interiors. Photograph by ©Robert Thien. As seen in* Atlanta Homes & Lifestyles.*)*

Figure 5.18 *Fiber-optic decorative lighting was used in this interior to create a starry sky effect. Strass® Crystal fiber optics from Swaro® Lite Crystal Architecture defines the delicate appearance. (Courtesy of Starfire Lighting.)*

environments and may be purely functional, decorative, or both (Figure 5.19).

Fixture Selection and Placement

All light fixtures in an interior must be selected based on their intended function and the human factor; their aesthetic qualities, and their economic and ecological factors. These same goals were introduced in Part II, "Design Fundamentals."

The Functions of Light

Light sources can serve three functions to meet human needs (Figure 5.20):

1. General or **ambient lighting** is background or fill light that spreads an even, overall luminosity and reduces harsh contrasts between pools of concentrated light.
2. **Task lighting** is functional and localized for a particular activity such as office work, reading, writing, preparing food, or grooming. Task lighting is placed near the activity but is aimed to avoid glare and minimize shadows (Figure 5.21).
3. **Accent lighting** employs a concentrated beam of light focusing on a particular object or area.

Interiors should include a combination of these lighting types in each room.

The size and shape of the lamp, along with the fixture style, produce a typical light distribution pattern. To help determine the correct fixture for a particular function, light distribution charts (or photometric charts) are usually included in manufacturers' catalogs (Figure 5.22). These charts also indicate the approximate quantity of footcandles, depending on the height of the light. By reading the charts, designers can determine the appropriate fixture and lamp.

Figure 5.19 *A: Typical portable lamp fixtures. B: "New Twist" table lamp. (Courtesy of HRS Design, Inc.) C:"Derby" table lamp. (Courtesy of HRS Design, Inc.)*

Ambient or general lighting   Task or local lighting   Accent lighting

Figure 5.20 *Three major functions of artificial lighting.*

Figure 5.21 *Luminaires for task lighting should be placed to minimize glare and shadows.*

Because vision tends to diminish with age, older people and those with visual impairments may require higher levels of light. Designers should provide higher light levels or portable task lighting for individuals with special needs.

Lighting also affects people's emotions. Successful lighting provides a sense of well-being. With respect to human psychological needs, light has the following attributes:

Figure 5.22 *Typical photometric guides. Many manufacturers, including GE, offer these guides on computer disc. (Courtesy of GE Lighting.)*

- Light is associated with the exuberance of life itself and with human well-being.
- It can convey a sense of security, warmth, and comfort.
- It can evoke a mood. For example, low-level lighting can be intimate, cozy, and relaxing; bright light can be stimulating and active.
- Lack of light or insufficient light may provoke feelings of depression, gloom, or even fear. Seasonal affective disorder (SAD) is a medical condition that occurs in some people when they are deprived of natural sunlight.
- Too much light or glaring light can be agitating, uncomfortable, and annoying, even resulting in physical ailments and an inability to function adequately.

It is essential, therefore, when planning light requirements for either residential or commercial interiors to take into account the physical as well as the psychological impact of light on human needs.

Additionally, lighting must be durable. For example, fragile neon fixtures would be inappropriate in a childcare center. Lighting also figures in safety. Emergency light fixtures, operated by batteries, are particularly important during power outages or fires, and are required in contract design.

Aesthetics

Aesthetically, lighting should reflect and enhance the style of the interior. The scale and proportion of a fixture should

Figure 5.23 *The combination of decorative iron screens and back-lit ceiling panels defines the entry into this hotel lobby. (Iron products manufactured by Design Lighting Products Co., Mesa, Arizona.)*

be considered in relation to other furnishings and to the size of the room. Decorative fixtures generally work best when their design is simple, unobtrusive, and suitable to the room's design. Some lighting fixtures serve as a focal point (Figure 5.23).

Designers can create many decorative effects when lighting is properly selected and placed:

- *Spotlighting* accentuates a particular object or point.
- A *pool of light* also focuses attention on a particular area, but a much larger one than that produced by spotlighting.
- A *wash of light*, in between a spotlight and a pool of light, generally covers a particular piece of art or other objects on a wall. An entire wall could be washed with light.
- *Grazing* is similar to a wash of light but the light barely skims the wall. This is usually applied to bring out a wall texture or pattern.
- *Perimeter lighting* is frequently used to expand a space, as seen in Figure 5.1.
- *Silhouette lighting* creates a decorative outline of an object. Sometimes plants or decorative ironwork are silhouetted to produce an interesting shadow effect on a nearby surface.

Economics

The designer's selection of lighting fixtures must not exceed the client's budget. In addition to the initial cost of purchasing and installing the fixtures, light also has continuous costs due to the use of electricity and the maintenance of lamps. Knowledgeable planning and purchasing can give a space sufficient lighting and still save watts and dollars. The following guidelines can help conserve energy in lighting.

- Lighting should fit specific needs. Task areas such as kitchen counters or desks require more light than nonworking areas such as circulation space.
- Dimmers are useful in adjusting light levels, increasing lamp life, and saving energy.
- Installing multiple switches and switches at every exit makes it convenient to use only the amount of light required in a specific area. Three-way incandescent lamps also allow selectivity in the amount of light used.
- Fixtures that can be adjusted and placed where light is needed are a wise choice. For instance, track lighting has great flexibility and permits the light to be directed where it is desired.
- A reflector lamp is good for accent or task lighting. Low-voltage spotlights are especially effective where a tightly controlled beam is required.
- Light sources should be efficient. Light output varies in efficiency according to wattage and color. For example, fluorescent lamps use as much as 80 percent less energy, produce 5 to 30 times as much light, and last 20 times longer than incandescent lamps. For this reason they are often used in commercial spaces, as seen in Figure 5.24.

1. CALL AREA
2. BREAK ROOM
3. RECEPTION
4. TRAINING ROOM
5. LIBRARY
6. EMPLOYEE SERVICE
7. CONFERENCE ROOM

Figure 5.24 *A combination of uplighting and downlighting not only meets the needs of this reservations environment, but also adds visual interest to the 2′ × 2′ lay-in ceiling. The lighting designer selected pendants, fluorescent troffers with high-performance parabolic louvers, and can lights. (Architect/Designer: Hnedak Bobo Group, Inc. Lighting Designer: Benya Lighting Design. Photographs © 1997 Jeffrey Jacobs/Architectural Photography Inc.)*

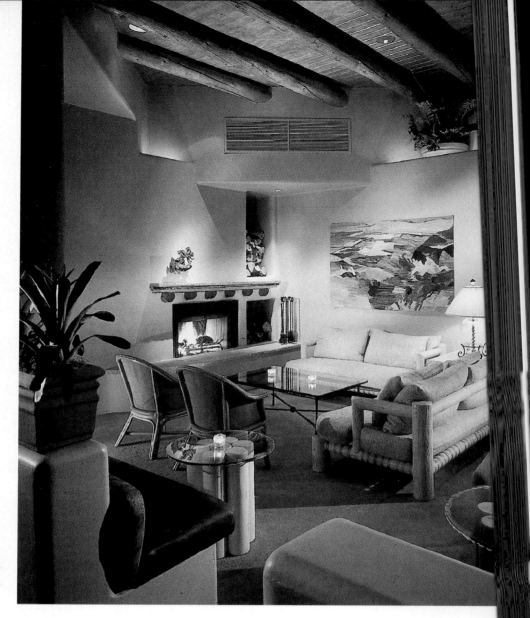

Figure 5.25 *Recessed ceiling lights, cove lighting placed high in wall niches, portable lamps, and firelight contribute to the cozy, warm atmosphere of this Santa Fe–style living room. (Photograph by Mark Boisclair.)*

- Where appearance is not a consideration, as in garages and some basements, industrial reflectors are an economical option.
- Ceilings, walls, floors, and furniture that have light-colored finishes reflect more light. Rooms designed in dark colors absorb light and require more lighting.
- Keeping reflectors, diffusers, and lamps clean helps to maintain lighting equipment.

Lighting for Areas and Activities

The selection and placement of the appropriate fixture is a complex process. This section is a general guide to lighting goals for particular areas or uses.

In the lobby or entrance area, which is the keynote of an interior, lighting plays an important role. During the day the entry or lobby should be bright enough to allow a reasonable transition from the bright outdoors to the darker interior. Illumination needs to be at a lower level at night to aid eyes in focusing, but strong enough to enable visitors to see and be seen. The entrance is an ideal place to try a dramatic lighting effect such as an accented art object. Often the reception desk is more brightly lit to draw visitors.

Waiting rooms and living rooms need soft general background lighting supplemented by special area lighting, as shown in Figure 5.25. Both direct and indirect lighting sources are desirable, although an excess of indirect lighting may result in a washed-out appearance. Well-chosen portable fixtures at necessary locations add a feeling of comfort and accent a room's focal point.

Conference rooms and dining areas deserve versatile lighting around the table area that can be adjusted for a variety of functions. General lighting can provide a low-level background. Dimmer controls allow for a change of mood, or for an audiovisual presentation. In residential or restaurant settings, candles give a flattering glow to skin tones. Creative use of accent light helps to avoid flat downlight and adds interest (Figure 5.26).

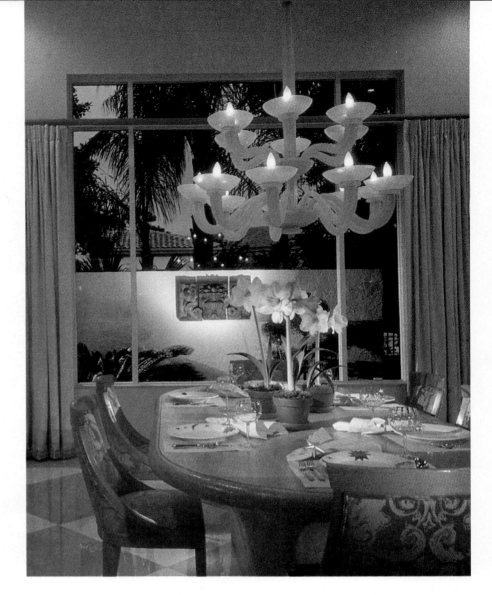

Figure 5.26 *In this elegant dining room of a private residence in Florida, the gently curving shapes of the chandelier and furniture are an effective contrast to the straight-line geometry of the setting. The outdoor area becomes part of the indoor space by the artful lighting of a hanging architectural fragment on the existing privacy wall. (Courtesy of Michael de Santis, ASID, Michael de Santis, Inc. Photograph by Phillip Ennis.)*

Offices, libraries, and studies require general lighting. Where computers are used, overhead lighting should be well diffused to prevent glare. Parabolic louvers that cover fluorescent fixtures function particularly well. Task lighting is also essential for reading and studying. Refer to Figure 5.21 for a review.

Family and recreation rooms accommodate a variety of activities and thus require particularly flexible lighting. General lighting is essential, with task lighting supplied for specific activities. Television viewing is most comfortable when general lighting is at a low level with no strong contrasts or glare. The television or computer screen itself reflects light and contributes to the total lighting effect.

Workrooms, kitchens, classrooms, and utility rooms function best when generous overall lighting for safety and efficiency is planned. Ceiling- or surface-mounted fixtures such as recessed downlights or track lighting can give adequate general light and eliminate shadows. It is also important to provide recessed or shielded lights over work areas and mounted under wall cabinets to illuminate counters (Figure

5.27). Classrooms, like conference areas, also require a low light level option, suitable for slide or video presentation.

Bedrooms need comfortable general lighting with appropriate task lights for reading, grooming, deskwork, and other activities. Direct lighting is also helpful when placed over chests of drawers, in closets, close to seating, and over beds. Dim circulation lighting for safety at night is a basic requirement. Accent lighting can be effectively used to focus on a painting or wall unit.

Bathrooms require shadowless lighting for shaving and grooming, which can be supplied by light from overhead and from both sides of a mirror, and by light reflected upward from a light-colored basin or countertop. Mirror lighting is usually sufficient to illuminate an average-sized powder room; however, general lighting is necessary with the addition of a tub or shower stall. Lighting in the shower needs to be enclosed and certified for use in a wet environment.

Stairways require overall illumination for safe passage. Stairways should be well lit with treads and risers clearly

Figure 5.27 *In this contemporary kitchen, lighting has been designed to create interest while serving the importance of function. The 3"-thick glass shelves, lined with low-voltage incandescent lamps, provide task lighting. (Designer: Steven J. Livingston, owner, Studio Snaidero San Francisco. Photograph by Ellen Perlson.)*

Figure 5.28 *This unique light fixture draws visitors to the front entry. Formed from colored bottles, this fixture is lit by a fluorescent lamp with energy supplied by the sun (see "Green Design: Earthships" in Chapter 13). (Architect: Michael Reynolds. Photograph by Philip A. Jones.)*

defined. Well-shielded light fixtures that avoid blinding glare at the top and bottom of stairs are another safety factor.

Corridors require minimum lighting for passage. Art and other objects can be accented to create dramatic effects.

Outdoor lighting at night enhances exterior architecture, gardens, decks, patios, walkways, and other outdoor living areas and provides visual pleasure. This is true in residential, commercial, and institutional settings. Additionally, outdoor lighting helps alleviate the black glass look seen from inside by balancing and extending the lighting to the outside (see Figure 5.26). Weatherproof luminaires for outside use can be attached under the eaves and on exterior walls. Custom lighting often includes exposed and concealed fixtures placed at various important areas of the garden that throw light upward, downward, or in both directions on trees, plantings, a garden sculpture or fountain, a gazebo, and other garden features to create a visually exciting experience. Front entries commonly serve as focal points (Figure 5.28).

Codes and Regulations

As with other building systems, lighting systems are to some extent regulated by codes. The codes generally relate to lighting for emergencies. Battery- or generator-operated fixtures must route people safely through corridors, stairways, and fire exits.

Some codes set minimum light levels for interiors. Other codes, working to conserve energy, actually limit the consumption of watts per square foot in a building.

Switches and Outlets

Closely related to the selection and placement of the light fixtures is the selection and placement of light switches and electrical and communication (telephone) outlets.

All rooms require at least one light switch to operate an overhead light or to provide electricity to a portable luminaire.

Switches are most commonly placed on the latch side of the door approximately 44″ above the finished floor (**A.F.F.**). Switches are also necessary at both ends of hallways and at the top and bottom of stairways. Lights may be switched at one, two, or three locations to meet the needs of the space. Where task lighting is necessary, switches should be placed within easy reach of the task and not at the entry to the room. Dimmers on switches are effective for incandescent lights but do affect the color of the light as they are dimmed. (Fluorescent dimmers are limited.) Dimmers allow great flexibility for various levels of lighting; they are ideal for creating a mood and also for conserving energy and the life of the lamp.

Typical electrical outlets are technically referred to as duplex outlets (because they have two receptors). Duplex outlets are used for 120 volt appliances. Some high-powered equipment, such as copy machines, require dedicated outlets or must have their own circuit.

Indoor outlets located near water sources (such as the bathroom or the kitchen sink) and all exterior outlets are required to be protected with a ground fault interrupt or GFI. Waterproof outlet covers are also required on exterior outlets. Electric ranges, clothes dryers, and other 220 volt equipment require a 220 volt outlet.

Throughout interior spaces, outlets should be plentiful and located for specific tasks. Outlets should be easily accessible for computer and desk accessories and for appliances in kitchens, utility areas, and bathrooms. When a room's function is determined, outlets can be conveniently located in accordance with local building codes. Outlets placed at regular intervals (approximately 6 ft. apart between doorways and floor-length windows) decrease the need for hazardous extension cords. Outlets are usually mounted 15 in. A.F.F. in barrier-free environments, but can be placed at other heights as needed.

Telephone outlets should be located wherever a telephone may be placed. Because Internet access presently requires connection to a telephone line, two lines should be placed close together in offices, studies, and libraries, or wherever a computer may be located. Like electrical outlets, telephone outlets are placed approximately 15 in. A.F.F. in barrier-free environments, but may be placed at other heights to meet the client's needs.

Other communication lines, such as television, stereo, or computer networking cables, should be located wherever they may be needed. Additionally, telephone and other communication lines should be located away from electrical lines to avoid interference with communication service. In general, it is more cost effective to install additional outlets and communication lines during construction or renovation. Adding one when a space is complete can be very costly.

Visual Communications

Lighting, electrical, and communication systems are documented in construction drawings in the following ways:

1. Lighting location plans indicate where and what kinds of fixtures are used and switch locations.

Figure 5.29 *A floor plan, called an electrical, lighting, and telephone plan or ELT, indicates the wiring and location of electrical outlets and switches as well as light fixtures. This information aids the designer in determining a functional furniture arrangement.*

2. Power and communication location plans indicate where telephone, electrical, and computer outlets are located.
3. Reflected ceiling plans, which are similar to lighting plans, are used mainly in commercial design. They also indicate HVAC and emergency lighting locations, and ceiling materials and heights.

Some projects are small enough or simple enough to combine items 1 and 2 above (Figure 5.29). Figure 5.30 indicates common symbols for lighting, electrical, and communication plans.

No matter how lighting, power, and communication information is communicated, designers must understand three important points:

1. Engineers determine the number of circuits required for the fixtures and outlets. The designer specifies only the style, location, and quantity of fixtures and outlets.
2. Designers need to be vigilant that the HVAC and plumbing systems do not interfere with critical lighting and outlet locations; sometimes a compromise may be required for practical or economic purposes.
3. Lighting design is a collaborative effort among allied professionals. Small residential projects may only require minor assistance from an electrical engineer; larger commercial projects frequently employ a lighting

Figure 5.30 *Lighting, electrical, and communication symbols.*

designer or consultant to assist with the proper quantity and quality lighting decisions.

Creative solutions to lighting problems add depth and distinguish one space from another. Some designers specialize in lighting design and may join the professional chapter of the Illuminating Engineers Society of North America. In the accompanying Design Scenario, a conceptual design for a conference room is produced in a series of drawings. Designers are required to produce drawings such as these to communicate custom detailing and lighting requirements to engineers and builders.

Summary

Interior designers must be familiar with many aspects of light, including the quantity of light, the quality of light, the

proper selection of the lamp, and the proper selection of the fixture. All of these aspects must work together to meet the function of the space in an aesthetically pleasing and economically efficient manner. To accomplish this, designers have many resources including recommendations for foot-candles, reflectance values for various surfaces, CRI ratings, Kelvin temperatures, spectrum patterns, distribution charts, and so on.

Absorbing all this information and correctly applying it can seem overwhelming at first. Many designers may be tempted to delegate lighting design to a consultant. On larger projects, this may be appropriate; however, remember that the consultant is an assistant to the project and still needs direction as to the character and atmosphere desired in the space. Designers should be confident in completing the selection and placement of lighting, power, and communication needs on smaller projects, and visually communicating these needs to engineers and builders.

Project Description

In this commercial office, the client requested an expansion of the existing conference room into a 32'-0" long × 16'-0" wide × 16'-0" high space (Figure DS5.1). The conference space will be located off the reception area, which adjoins an exterior window wall. The conference room itself does not have access to an outside wall.

Programming: The 16'-0" high space must accommodate the HVAC and lighting fixtures. Special effort is required to bring some natural light into the room while maintaining the room's confidentiality. Specific requirements include:

- Minimum of two entry doors
- Seating for a minimum of 16
- Flexible lighting to accommodate slide, video, and presentation formats
- Grid pattern continued from existing office space
- Minimum 10'-0" shelving storage for audiovisual equipment
- Drawer storage for table service and brochures
- Minimum 5' × 5' projection screen
- Accent wall for corporate art collection.

FURNITURE PLAN
¼" = 1'-0"
DINAH WAYNE DESIGNS
FLOWERY BRANCH, GA.

Figure DS5.1 *This schematic furniture plan illustrates the location of furniture and built-in cabinetry. (Design by Dinah Wayne Design, Flowery Branch, Georgia.)*

Conceptual/Schematic Design Solution: The conceptual design solution incorporated these requirements. Figure DS5.2 illustrates an elevation/section of the long wall. Because the room is on the interior of the building, frosted glass panels in and above the door bring light into the space. The panels also form the grid pattern reflecting other design motifs in the office. The textured plaster walls (although costly) also tie into the existing office design. The off-white color forms an appropriate backdrop for the client's artwork.

Figures DS5.3 and DS5.4 illustrate the elevations/sections of the two short walls. Figure DS5.3, which is particularly interesting, defines the projection wall. Note how the designer aligned the chair rail and height of the lower cabinet unit. The paneled wall at the opposite end of the room is designed to accommodate presentation drawings.

Figure DS5.2 *This elevation/section defines the style and finish materials for the long wall in the conference room. (Design by Dinah Wayne Design, Flowery Branch, Georgia.)*

Figures DS5.3 and DS5.4 *These elevations/sections define the style and finish materials for the end wall of the conference room. (Design by Dinah Wayne Design, Flowery Branch, Georgia.)*

Figure DS5.5 illustrates the lighting plan. The cove ceiling is raised above the conference table. Pendants (not yet selected) will be suspended over the conference table and are on dimmers. Fluorescent strip fixtures concealed in the cove are lit separately and provide general ambient lighting for the room. Wall washers, also on dimmers, are separately switched so either short wall or the long walls may be independently illuminated.

Figures DS5.6 and DS5.7 define the details necessary to create the coved ceiling.

After reviewing these conceptual drawings with the client, the designer would proceed with a design development presentation and, on approval, contract documents. (Designer: Dinah Wayne Designs, Flowery Branch, Georgia.)

Figure DS5.5 *This lighting plan illustrates a raised ceiling over the conference table. Switching is located at both entries. (Design by Dinah Wayne Design, Flowery Branch, Georgia.)*

Figure DS5.6 *The drawing details the cove lighting design that surrounds the conference table. (Design by Dinah Wayne Design, Flowery Branch, Georgia.)*

PENDANT

TRIM BOLTS
RECESSED WITH
WOODEN PEGS

VERTICAL TRIM
IN COVE

3 ⅝ METAL STUD

3 PLANES

① ② ③

METAL
BOLTS WILL
KEEP
METAL
STUD IN
PLACE

⑥ COVE CEILING/LIGHTING DETAIL
3" = 1'-0"
DINAH WAYNE DESIGNS
FLOWERY BRANCH, GA.

⅝ " WALLBOARD
3⅝ X 1¼ " METAL STUD

FLUORESCENT

BASE CAP WCM 174

4" ROUTED

BASE CAP (WCM 174)

1" ROUTED

Figure DS5.7 *An exploded (enlarged) view of the actual cove and lighting. (Design by Dinah Wayne Design, Flowery Branch, Georgia.)*

PART IV

Space

Figure IV.1 *This opulent bedroom balances the use of vertical space by placing a tall narrow armoire opposite the larger, yet lower bed. Art over the bed also adds height to the room. Figure IV.2 shows the design progression. (Designer: Marc Michaels Interior Design. Photograph © Kim Sargent Architectural Photography. Residence: Private home, Phipps Estates, Palm Beach. Developer: Addison Development. Courtesy of* On Design.*)*

As discussed in Chapter 2, space is one of the most important elements of design; its appropriate use determines the success of an interior. Well-planned space should be given top priority to ensure an interior where human activity can be carried on with a minimum of frustration. An interior may have exquisite fabrics, brilliant colors, and comfortable seating, but if a person does not have enough space to function (to work behind a desk, for example), the beauty of the furnishings is wasted.

Space is not limited to the area arranged on a floor plan. The designer must also arrange the space in elevation. Upper cabinets that protrude in front of windows, chair arms that will not fit under tables, or counter tops that are too low or high complicate the client's life. The creation of an en-

Figure IV.2 *These drawings show the progression of design from plan view and elevations into the drawing of volume. The photo in Figure IV.1 illustrates the finished room. (Interpretive design drawings by Carol Platt.)*

Perspective: Volume, three dimensions

Plan: Horizontal, two dimensions

Elevations: Vertical, two dimensions

vironment that promotes comfort and convenience requires the designer to analyze the use of all the planes. The horizontal, vertical, and in-between space is known as **volume.** Understanding and visualizing space in three dimensions is the key to using space appropriately (Figures IV.1, IV.2, and IV.3).

In the field of design, the placement of furniture and the arrangement of rooms are part of space planning. As discussed in Chapter 1, in the commercial environment, space planning is a career track. Commercial interior designers may spend days, weeks, or even months working with a client to determine space needs and requirements. In the residential environment, a designer may work with the architect and builder to ensure that rooms are the correct shape and size to meet the client's needs. If the residence is already built, the designer must cleverly select and place furniture to utilize the space most efficiently; if necessary, some walls may need to be relocated. As always, the sooner the designer is involved with the design team on a project, the more successful the design solution.

Form and Space

As discussed in Chapter 2, spaces that designers create form positive areas (the space occupied by the actual furniture pieces) and negative areas (the empty space between pieces). The negative spaces form the pathways or *traffic lanes* that allow people to move throughout a space (Figure IV.4). Hotel lobbies require an immense amount of negative space in order to accommodate the variety of activities and quantity of people moving about the space. Residential dining rooms require less negative space based on the decreased level of activity in the room.

Underfurnishing a room is often more attractive than overcrowding. Studies reveal that overcrowding a space can actually have a negative psychological effect on the occupants. Some empty spaces between groupings help give an uncluttered effect. An occasional open space or empty corner enhances a room and gives the occupants breathing space. On the other hand, a severely underfurnished room may be stark and uninviting. Avoid either extreme.

Space Planning

In many situations, particularly in residential design, the clients may purchase a home and then call upon the services of an interior designer to make the existing space fit their needs. This approach, which may be described as designing from the *outside in,* is taken when the clients fall in love with the look of a home without having truly assessed its practical layout. They may have utilized their entire budget for the purchase, and may resort to substandard interior selections. Although the exterior of the home or building has aesthetic appeal, the interior, the space where people spend 90% of their lives,

Figure IV.3 *Drawings show a progression from plan view and elevations to a drawing of volume. The photo illustrates the finished room. This custom design for a president's office included a flood of exterior window light balanced by a series of bookshelves. (Architect/Designer: Flad & Associates. Photographer: © Norman McGrath. Interpretive design drawings by Carol Platt.)*

**Perspective:
Volume,
three dimensions**

**Plan: Horizontal,
two dimensions**

**Elevations: Vertical,
two dimensions**

Positive space = Furnishings

Negative space = Traffic flow

Figure IV.4 *In these drawings the negative space has been left open to allow for traffic flow. A, use of a bubble diagram. B, furnishings have been placed in the positive space.*

is left to awkward furniture arranging and mediocre design. The designer is required to alter apparent room sizes via clever furniture placement, finish and fabric selection, or portable lighting. In commercial situations, particularly in large spaces, the client often recognizes the need for professional help prior to the selection of the building and therefore avoids this mistake.

The alternative school of thought is to design the home or office from the *inside out*. For many clients this requires a paradigm shift in thought. The designer is contacted before a home or building has been selected, then works with the client to analyze spatial needs. The designer can assist the client in locating an appropriate building or home, or designing a new one that meets the client's needs *and* budget. The following two chapters explore space planning from this inside-out method. Furnishings are planned as part of activity areas. Activity areas are grouped into rooms. Rooms are grouped by interior zones, which then establish the perimeter of the interior environment. Throughout this process, attention is given to the vertical nature of space. Remember that interiors are planned in volumes.

6

Space Planning: Furnishings to Rooms

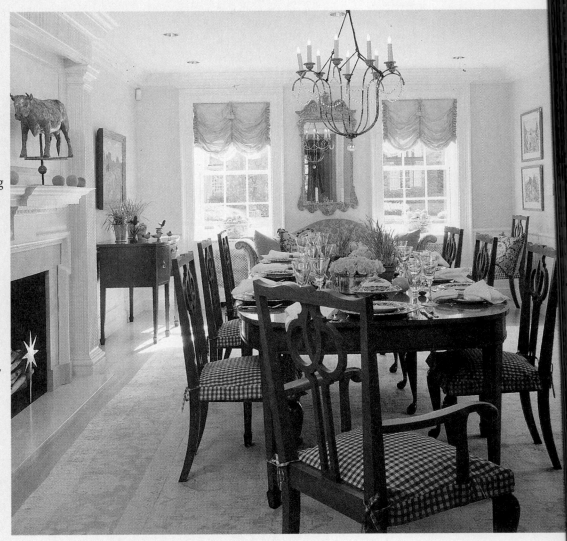

Figure 6.1 *This inviting dining room is based on function. The table allows ample room for each place setting. The sideboard functions as a serving and storage unit. Chairs were selected to promote upright body posture. (Designer: Drysdale Design Associates. Photograph by Antoine Bootz. Courtesy of* Southern Accents.*)*

To be livable, an interior must meet the needs of its occupants. A space must serve its function before fabrics, furnishings, and finishes are specified (Figure 6.1).

Programming Information for Space Planning

Function

During the initial client contact and programming phase, the designer asks numerous questions to determine the function of an interior and the client's design preferences and space needs. The designer working with a residential client may complete a *personal profile* of each occupant and ask questions regarding the client's lifestyle. Nonresidential projects may require interviews with executives of the company and some individual staff members. (Appendix A is an example of a typical initial programming questionnaire.) In essence, the designer must understand the intricacies of the household or the firm in order to carefully plan for spatial needs.

Economic Concerns

Whether clients are searching for a new office space or a new home, the building and its furnishings are probably the most expensive investments they will make. They want the best value possible for every dollar spent. The designer should study costs and look carefully at such criteria as available budget, client needs, materials and components required, time limits, building requirements, and codes.

The cost of a structure varies depending on many factors: its size, structure, geographic location, materials specified, cubic footage or volume (the three-dimensional measurement of the height, depth, and width of the space), special construction features (such as raised ceilings, angled or curved spaces, custom windows and doors), and the cost of local labor. Average building costs per square foot, exclusive of the price of the land, depend on the region where the structure will be built. An excellent source for determining construction costs is the *Means Cost Estimation Index* by Robert S. Means.

Costs also relate to the selection of furnishings. A good-quality low-budget sofa could cost $900, whereas the price of an elaborate custom-upholstered sofa could reach into the thousands of dollars. Designers must determine what level of furnishings will work within the client's budget. The deciding factor is the quality of the product, not necessarily its price. If a client cannot afford a quality product, it is better to wait until the product can be purchased. Placing inexpensive, low-quality furnishings in a space almost always results in an unhappy client and a poor design solution. It is better to have a few well-spaced quality pieces of furniture than a room full of cheap substitutes.

Human Factors

The physical and psychological comfort of the occupants is an important aspect of the space planning process. People

Adult Male and Female Miscellaneous Structural Body Dimensions in Inches and Centimeters by Age and Selected Percentiles														
		A		B		C		D		E		F		G	
		in	cm	in	cm	in	cm	in	cm	in	cm	in	cm	in	cm
95	MEN	36.2	91.9	47.3	120.1	68.6	174.2	20.7	52.6	27.3	69.3	37.0	94.0	33.9	86.1
	WOMEN	32.0	81.3	43.6	110.7	64.1	162.8	17.0	43.2	24.6	62.5	37.0	94.0	31.7	80.5
5	MEN	30.8	78.2	41.3	104.9	60.8	154.4	17.4	44.2	23.7	60.2	32.0	81.3	30.0	76.2
	WOMEN	26.8	68.1	38.6	98.0	56.3	143.0	14.9	37.8	21.2	53.8	27.0	68.6	28.1	71.4

Figure 6.2 *Anthropometric table of structural body dimensions. (From* Human Dimension and Interior Space *by Panero and Zelnick, © 1979, Whitney Library of Design.)*

should be comfortable in relation to the scale and proportion of the architecture. The three-dimensional aspects of a space must be considered, because if the space is too vast or too small, people may feel out of place.

Furniture should be suitably scaled for comfort and arranged for purpose and efficiency. It should also be easy to use and operate. For example, a desk and desk chair should be the appropriate height, and a storage cabinet should have shelves the user can reach. *User-friendly* furniture also should be easy to move or rearrange and clean. Some terms related to design and human comfort are anthropometrics, ergonomics, and proxemics.

Anthropometrics studies the size and proportions of the human body. Research in this area identifies typical human heights, widths, and sizes in various postures and this information can be used to determine optimum space needs and the level of mobility and physical strength required of the end user (Figure 6.2).

Ergonomics is the study of human beings and their responses to various working conditions and environments. Ergonomic data provide designers with information on such subjects as comfortable seating as well as visual and acoustical issues. For example, a computer chair that provides maximum back, arm, and leg support may be said to be "ergonomically" designed (Figure 6.3).

Proxemics studies the use of space by human beings in a particular culture. Everyone has an invisible comfort zone or area of surrounding space called a "space bubble" (Figure 6.4).

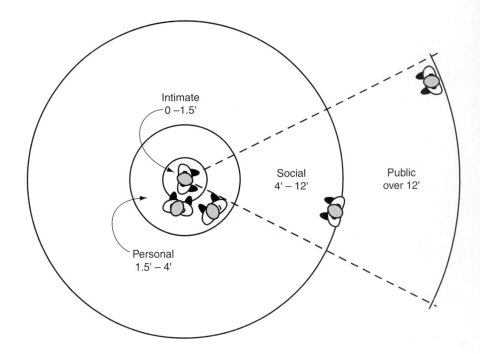

Figure 6.3 *Anthropometric studies combined to form ergonomic knowledge of (A) a work or secretarial chair and (B) a corner seating arrangement. (From* Human Dimension and Interior Space *by Panero and Zelnick, © 1979, Whitney Library of Design.)*

Discomfort may result when a person with a smaller space bubble gets too close to a person with a larger space bubble. Our individual comfort zones vary in relation to our culture and background experiences. The designer can use this information to create environments with furniture that will meet particular needs for comfort and space, especially in a nonresidential setting.

In all environments, most people want a space that belongs to them—like a bedroom, or a certain chair in the family room or breakroom. Observing children who share a bedroom often reveals this need for private space. For example, children may make it clear what side of the room is theirs, or what part of the closet is for their belongings only. This need for a personal space usually carries over

Figure 6.4 *Edward T. Hall, in his book* The Hidden Dimension, *discusses four distance zones: the intimate, the personal, the social, and the public.*

NOTE: x = 12in (305mm) if door has both a closer and latch.

Figure 6.5 *The minimum clear requirements for an accessible swinging door. (Federal Register, Vol. 56, No. 144, Figure 25, Maneuvering Clearances at Doors, July 26, 1991.)*

into adult life and a sensitive designer plans furnishings accordingly.

Universal Design

The elderly, infants, and the physically challenged have special needs that designers must consider. In planning for both residential and nonresidential spaces, designers must adequately satisfy these special users' needs for safety, convenience, and comfort. In universal design, as discussed in Part I, environments are created to meet the needs of individuals regardless of age and ability. One aspect of universal design includes barrier-free environments. **Barrier-free designs** present no physical obstacles or barriers, allowing free movement for individuals with disabilities. Barrier-free access in a public space for users who are physically challenged is required by law. Designers need to be aware of these regulations and implement design solutions that conform to them (see Chapter 4). At a minimum, accessible planning should include the following:

- Parking spaces for individuals with disabilities must be conveniently placed, adequate in number, clearly marked, and not on a slope.
- The environment, both interior and exterior, should be free of architectural barriers so those who may be using a wheelchair, crutches, or a walker can easily circulate throughout various areas. In a commercial environment, doors must be a minimum of 36″ wide and must have lever handles. The pull side of the door should be free of any obstructions for a minimum of 18″ (preferably 24″). Though not required by law, this approach also works best in residential environments for people who are physically challenged (Figure 6.5).
- Traffic lanes or corridors must be kept free of clutter and be wide enough for easy movement in a wheelchair or walker (see Figure 4.20).
- Floor coverings that are hard, smooth, and slip-resistant work most efficiently for safe and easy movement. If carpet is used, a dense, short pile is best. Generally, area and throw rugs should be avoided. Thresholds should be flat, or not more than 1/2″ high.
- In the kitchen, where people are especially susceptible to accidents, heights, clearances, and other measurements should be planned for convenience and safety.

Figure 6.6 *A typical layout for an accessible commercial toilet area. (From U.S. Department of Housing and Urban Development.)*

Working surfaces that pull out and storage areas with open and revolving shelves are an asset. A front-loading dishwasher and washer/dryer, an upright refrigerator, and an oven with front controls are convenient. For those using wheelchairs, oven and dishwasher doors hinged at the side are better; however, controls on the front of the appliances may not be the best solution for households with young children.

- Bathrooms and fixtures must be conveniently and safely located with ample room for manipulating a wheelchair. Grab bars conveniently positioned by the tub and toilet provide added safety (Figure 6.6).
- Signage, water fountains, sconces, telephones, and emergency alarms must also be easily used by people who have physical impairments.

Guidelines for Furnishing Dimensions

Once the functions have been determined and the human needs of each occupant evaluated, the designer determines how much space is required to meet the client's needs. This is a component of programming. In order to accomplish this, designers must have a working knowledge of the actual sizes of furniture pieces and the clearances necessary to move about the space. Study Tables 6.1 and 6.2; refer to them often. In the design industry, furniture size is noted in inches; architectural features are noted in feet and inches.

Traffic Patterns

Once the furniture (positive space) has been determined, the designer analyzes the clearances (negative space) required for major and minor traffic lanes. Study Table 6.3 on clearance requirements, and Figure 6.7.

Table 6.1 *Typical Furnishing Sizes Drawn in Plan View*

Seating

Sofa — 30"–34" × 72"–96"

Love seat — 60"–72"

Lounge chair — 30"–42"

Wing chair — 26"–33" × 33"–38"

Chaise longue — 30"–38" × 42"–76"

Dining chair no arms — 14"–20" × 16"–20"

Dining chair with arms — 18"–24"

Guest chair — 20"–28" × 20"–28"

Desk chair, executive — 26"–33" × 26"–36"

Desk chair, task — 14"–18" × 16"–18"

Ottoman — 18"–22" × 22"–30"

Sectional sofa

Tables

End table/nightstand (wood) — 24"–30" × 18"–30"

Coffee table (glass) — 12"–18" × 26"–48"

Sofa table (wood) — 12"–18" × 38"–60"

Nest of tables

Storage

Shelves attached to wall

Shelves free standing

Lateral file cabinet — 14"–18" × 30"•36"•42"

Vertical file cabinet — 14"–18" × 24"–33"

Executive desk (wood) — 36" × 72"

Standard desk — 30" × 60"

Credenza — 18"–24" × 60"–72"

Returns — 18"–20" × 28"–42"

Dresser or armoire or chest or buffet — 18"–24" × 24"–80"

Corner cabinet — 22"–33" × 22"–33"

Hutch — 30"–48" × 18"–26"

Table 6.1 *Typical Furnishing Sizes Drawn in Plan View*

Table 6.2 *Critical Heights and Depths*

Heights

Chair seat:	18″
End table:	Matches arm of sofa
Sofa arm:	Varies with style
Desk:	29″–30″
Keyboard:	26″–27″ (Should be at user's elbow height when seated with arm bent)
Table:	29″–30″

Depths (and Heights If Critical)

Kitchen base cabinet/counter:	24″D × 36″H
Kitchen wall cabinet:	12″D × 24″–36″H
Space between counter and cabinet:	15″–18″
Bathroom counter:	22″D × 28″–36″H
Bookshelf:	8″–18″

Table 6.3 *Clearance Requirements*

Traffic Paths

Major commercial	60" or more
Major residential	48"–60"
Minor commercial	36"–60"
Minor residential *—Space between furniture*	18"–48"
Physically challenged	32" minimum allowed, but only for a length of 24"
One-way passage	36" minimum
Two-way passage	60" minimum
Corner turn	42" minimum
Wheelchair turnaround	5'-0" diameter

Conversation Areas

Foot room between sofa or chair and edge of coffee table top	12"–15"
Floor space in front of chair for feet and legs	1'-6" to 2'-6"
Chair or bench space in front of desk or piano	3'

Dining or Conferencing

Space for occupied chair	1'-6" to 1'-10"
Space to get into chairs	1'-10" to 3'
Space for person to assist in seating	4'-6"
Traffic path around table and occupied chairs	1'-6" to 2'

Workspaces

Space between desk and credenza	42" to 48"
Space in front of files	30" to 36"
Space for guest chairs in front of desk	42" to 48"

Sleeping Areas

Space for making bed	1'-6" to 2'
Space between twin beds	1'-6" to 2'-4"
Space in front of chest of drawers	3'
Space in front of dresser	3' to 4'

Food Preparation

Workspace in front of cabinets	3' to 6'
Counter space between equipment	3' to 5'
Ventilation for attachments in back of some appliances	3" to 5"

Bathing Areas

Space between front of tub and opposite wall	2'-6" to 3'-6"
Space in front of toilet	18" to 24"
Space at sides of toilet	12" to 18"
Space between fronts of fixtures	2'-6" to 3'

Poor arrangement.

Better arrangement.

Figure 6.7 *Appropriate furniture layout to redirect traffic.*

Space Planning for Specific Activities

There are basically eight activity or functional areas required in interior settings. Table 6.4 illustrates their use in commercial and residential environments. Understanding the specific space requirements for each of these areas allows a designer to space plan an entire room.

Ideally, the designer works with the architect and builder to determine room sizes. Specific functions and space requirements are similar for commercial and residential environments; however, commercial environments typically require wider traffic lanes. The following groupings should be considered when determining square footages. The information in the accompanying box, "Figuring Square Footage," also may be helpful.

Figuring Square Footage

An important aspect of space planning is the ability to figure square footage. Square footage is determined by multiplying the length of a room by the width. Therefore, $L \times W$ = square footage or □. For example, if a room were 10'-0" × 12'-0", it would contain 120 □.

The following charts may be helpful in figuring these problems.

Inches to Decimal Foot Conversion Chart

1" = .08'	7" = .58'
2" = .16'	8" = .67'
3" = .25'	9" = .75'
4" = .33'	10" = .83'
5" = .42'	11" = .92'
6" = .50'	12" = 1.0'

Conversion Chart

1 inch = 2.54 centimeters (multiply the number of inches by 2.54 to determine the number of centimeters)

1 centimeter = .3937 inches (multiply the number of centimeters by .3937 to determine the number of inches)

1 foot = 12 inches = .3048 meters (multiply the number of feet by .3048 to determine the number of meters)

1 meter = 3.2808 feet (multiply the number of meters by 3.2808 to determine the number of feet)

1 □ = 144 square inches = .0929 square meters (multiply the number of square feet by .0929 to determine the number of square meters)

1 square meter = 10.764 □ (multiply the number of square meters by 10.764 to determine the number of square feet)

1 square yard = 9 □ = .8361 square meters (multiply the number of square yards by .8361 to determine the number of square meters)

1 square meter = 1.196 square yards (multiply the number of square meters by 1.196 to determine the number of square yards)

Determining Square Footage in Feet and Inches (Does Not Apply to the Metric System)

If a room is 10'-3" × 12'-9", the process requires the following steps. (A calculator is useful here.) To figure the square footage:

- Using the inches to decimal conversion chart, change the inches to a decimal:
  10'-3" becomes 10.25' and
  12'-9" becomes 12.75'
- Multiply the length by the width:
  10.25' × 12.75' = 130.6875 □
- Square footages or areas are usually figured in whole numbers. Simply round up or down to the nearest whole number, in this case, 131 □.

Determining Square Footage in Odd-Shaped Rooms

It is more complicated to figure square footage when the room has an odd shape. The room below is L-shaped. To figure the square footage complete the following steps:

- Divide the room into two separate rectangles.
- Figure the square footage of each space:
  The square footage of A = 10'-0" × 20'-0" = 200 □
  The square footage of B = 10'-0" × 8'-0" = 80 □
- Add the totals. The total square footage is 200 □ + 80 □ = 280 □.

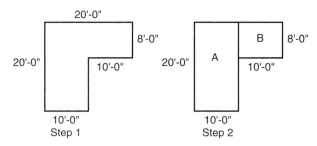

To figure the square footage of a room with an angle, such as in the following figure, more geometry must be used.

- Divide the room into as few rectangles and triangles as possible.
- Figure the square footage of the rectangular spaces:
  A = 16'-0" × 14'-0" = 224 □
  B = 6'-0" × 8'-0" = 48 □
  Hint: 20'-0" − 14'-0" = 6'-0"
- To figure the square footage of C, it is important to know that a triangle is simply a rectangle divided in half. Therefore, multiply the length by the width and divide the answer by 2:
  6'-0" × 8'-0" = 48 □ ÷ 2 = 24 □
- Add the totals of the spaces together to arrive at the total square footage:
  224 □ + 48 □ + 24 □ = 296 □

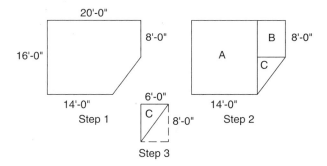

In all cases, convert the inches to a decimal before multiplying. Remember to round off the decimal to the nearest whole number when finished.

Table 6.4 *Specific Activity Areas in Commercial and Residential Design*

Specific Activity	Commercial Use	Residential Use
Conversation area	Hotel and healthcare lobby Waiting room Breakroom Reception room	Living room Family room Bedroom
Dining/conferencing/lecturing	Restaurant Hotel ballroom Corporate office Presentation room Cafeteria Classroom	Dining room Breakfast room
Video/television viewing and presentation	Hotel and healthcare lobby Executive or typical office Classroom Waiting room Breakroom Hotel guest room Conference room Hospital room	Living room Family room Bedroom Media room
Clerical, studying, and computing	All areas of contract design	Home office Library Study Child's room
Sleeping	Hotel room Healthcare patient room Executive suite	Bedroom Guest room
Storage	All areas of contract design	All areas in a residence
Food preparation	Restaurant Hotel Hospital Cafeteria	Kitchen
Bathroom	All areas of contract design	Bathroom

Conversation Area

In both residential and commercial environments, conversation groupings provide the critical backdrop for communication. Conversation groups should be designed out of the line of traffic and planned so that people can hear and be heard. There must be adequate space to access (or walk into) the grouping. The maximum conversation distance is 10'-0", whereas six to eight feet is ideal. Figure 6.8 illustrates the six basic conversation groupings.

1. The *straight-line grouping,* although not conducive to intimate conversation, may work well for public places such as waiting rooms.
2. The *L-shaped grouping* is good for conversation and lends itself to both large and small areas.
3. The *U-shaped grouping* is comfortable and attractive but requires considerable space. Both the L- and U-shapes may be repeated several times in a large hotel, hospital, or office lobby.
4. The *box-shaped grouping* is popular where space is ample. Allow space for a sufficient opening to present an inviting entry.

5. The *parallel grouping* emphasizes an existing focal point such as a fireplace or a special wall feature and provides a pleasant arrangement for conversation.
6. The *circular grouping* may encompass an entire room or an area of a large room. This arrangement can be inviting because it provides an enveloping seating element.

Once the furniture grouping is established, the designer can determine the size of the room (Figure 6.9). If other functions are required in the room, or if special architectural or artistic features are requested, these will be added to the square footage requirements.

Dining/Conferencing/Lecturing

Designers must know how many individuals are to be accommodated in a dining, conference, or lecture area. An area planned for two to six guests is substantially different from an area planned for two to six couples; an area planned for 200 people requires an even greater sensitivity to the human scale. The goal is to plan a space that accommodates all the guests, but does not feel austere when used by a lesser number.

Figure 6.8 *Six basic conversation groupings.*

Figure 6.9 *If a U-shaped grouping to seat seven people is selected, the designer totals the perimeter dimensions to determine the size of the room. This space requires a minimum area of 12'-0" × 13'-0" or 156 ▢.*

Conference and dining tables may be round, square, rectangular, oval, or boat shaped, and in very large conference rooms may form a U-shape. Many conference tables are custom designed to fit a client's needs.

Each occupant requires approximately 2'-0" to 2'-6" of space on the table in front of the chair as a work surface or for dinnerware. Approximately 3'-6" to 4'-0" is required between the table and the wall. Typical arrangements are shown in Figure 6.10.

The process to determine the size of a conference or dining room is the same as for the conversation area (Figure 6.11). When tables are grouped together, such as in a restaurant or cafeteria, a minimum of 44" is needed between them. Additional space is required for serving areas and storage, and in conference rooms and classrooms for presentation areas.

Video/Television Viewing and Presentation

Multimedia viewing has become an important aspect of daily work and home environments. Multimedia centers are custom designed to accommodate stereo equipment, VCRs, computers, and televisions, including HDTV.

Depending on the size of the screen, televisions are best viewed from a distance of 6'-0" to 12'-0". The viewer should be able to look directly at the screen. Straight line, L-, and U-shaped groupings allow for this arrangement. If a parallel grouping is selected and the media center is not the focal point, the media screen may have to be concealed (Figure 6.12).

In offices the systems may also be concealed. Classrooms may require custom mounting systems or portable carts. When televisions are used in lobbies, breakrooms, or waiting rooms, the video/television areas should be separated from conversation areas.

In a conference room, a projection screen should be placed on the narrow wall of the room. A projector for slide

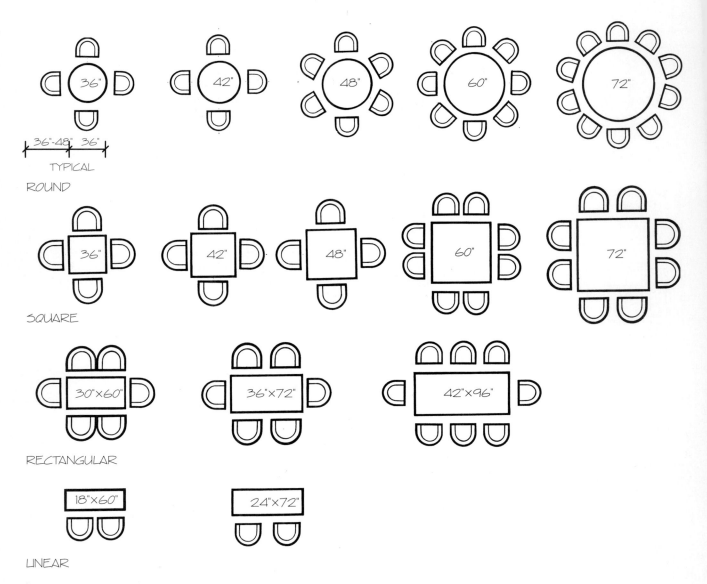

TYPICAL
ROUND

SQUARE

RECTANGULAR

LINEAR

Figure 6.10 *Typical table arrangements. Oval, boat-shaped, and U-shaped tables follow similar requirements.*

viewing or satellite receiving may be concealed in the ceiling or located in another room providing rear screen projection capabilities. Chairs should be on casters to allow ease of movement during presentations.

Clerical, Studying, and Computing

All areas of commercial design from healthcare to hospitality require workspaces to complete daily tasks. The home office is also becoming a standard. More than one-half of American households have a computer. Using the Internet is becoming as commonplace as making a telephone call. Hotels are also catering to these needs. Thus, both residential and commercial designers must have a working knowledge of office design.

The most efficient workspace is the combination of the desk, return, and credenza as shown in Figure 6.13. This allows a clear space on the desk for work. A monitor and keyboard can sit on the return or on the credenza. A printer and

Figure 6.11 *If the room must seat 12, the designer first establishes the minimum table size: 2'-0" to 2'-6" is allowed for each person (depending on the chair size desired), plus an additional 12" to 18" on each end. Then distance is added for chairs and traffic lanes. The smallest room possible would be 12'-0" × 20'-0" or 240 □.*

Figure 6.12 *In this informal breakfast room the television is neatly hidden in the cabinetry. (Designer: Lovick Design. Photograph by Martin Fine.)*

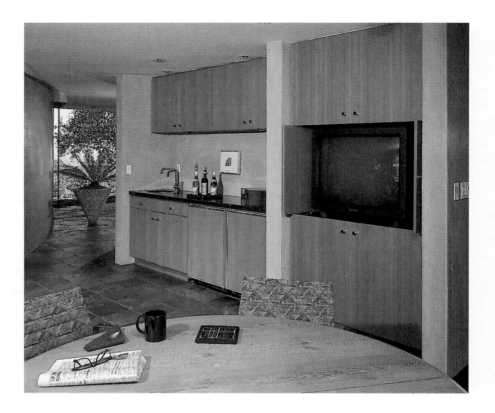

hard drive can sit on or in the credenza. Some clients prefer a pullout keyboard tray in the credenza, or may not want the return. In either case, the space requirements are the same. The office space may also need shelving, guest chairs, filing, storage, or a conferencing area. The designer adds square footage as necessary to meet these needs.

Sleeping

Whether designing a master bedroom suite or a hotel room, designers must be knowledgeable about the space requirements for sleeping areas. Remember that although beds come in standard sizes, ample space must be allowed to move around the bed (Figure 6.14).

Allowances need to be made for storage and seating areas, and television viewing if requested by the client. In hospital design, space should also be allocated to accommodate medical equipment, patient personal care, visitors, and ample traffic areas for mobile equipment.

Storage

Dressers, armoires, chests, filing cabinets, and shelving units come in various sizes as noted in Table 6.1. In planning areas for these spaces, always allow ample room in front of the unit to open the drawers and doors. (A space 2'-6" wide is usually adequate.) Closets need to be at least 2'-1" deep to accommodate hangers.

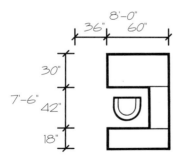

Figure 6.13 *To figure the space required for a typical office arrangement, draw the furniture, allow for a traffic lane, and total the dimensions. The overall minimum space required is 8'-0" × 7'-6" or 60 ☐.*

Figure 6.14 *In this plan for a queen bed, the minimum space needed would be 9'-0" × 9'-7" or 86.22 ☐, or approximately 86 ☐.*

Food Preparation

In residential design, food preparation areas encompass many subactivity zones relating to the refrigerator, sink, and stove or cooktop. Because most of the kitchen layout is based on built-in features, kitchen design is discussed in Chapter 7. Commercial kitchen design is a specialty area of design and requires advanced study.

Bathrooms

Chapter 4 showed typical symbols for bathroom fixtures. Table 6.3 reviews minimum clearances and layouts. Appropriate bathroom layouts, like kitchen layouts, are based on built-in features and are discussed in Chapter 7.

The Floor Plan

The floor plan is a communication tool that illustrates the space planning of furnishings and their relationships to the architectural features of walls, windows, doors, fireplaces, etc. To develop the floor plan, designers must synthesize an immense amount of detailed information, including the following:

- principles and elements of design
- functions of the space
- needs and desires of the client
- furnishing sizes
- three-dimensional aspects of the space and furnishings
- traffic lanes and clearance requirements
- basic furniture groupings and space requirements

The floor plan allows the designer to synthesize all of this information into one drawing. A presentation floor plan, as discussed in Chapter 7, is shared with the client to explain the design. The presentation plan must relate to the elevations and perspectives developed for the client. The next section shows several preliminary floor plans and perspective studies for various rooms.

Space Planning for Specific Rooms

Each room of a home or commercial space presents unique challenges. Because the activities in rooms vary greatly, each room is studied separately; however, throughout the home or office, a sense of harmony must prevail.

Entry Hall or Foyer, Reception, and Lobby

The design of the home or building should be reflected in the details and furnishings of the entry. In a residential setting the entry serves as a passageway, and like all good design should not be cluttered. An *easy flow of traffic* is essential. Ample storage areas need to be designed to accommodate coats, shoes, packages, etc. Furnishings that may be appropriate in an entry include a console or narrow table, a mirror, a coat rack, and accessories. Many clients require a bench or small chair for sitting while changing shoes.

Where the front door opens directly into the living room, a desirable plan is to create an unobstructed entrance to redi-

Figure 6.15 *Before, the front door opened directly into the living room. After, a wall was added, giving a more private entry. A closet provides necessary storage. A mirror and shelf were added for convenience. The furniture was slightly rearranged to pull the conversation group together. The rug works better in this plan because the chair legs all sit on the rug.*

rect traffic and provide some privacy. One successful way to set off an entrance is with a built-in or freestanding storage wall. If space is available, a deeper storage wall may provide closet space for outer garments on one side, and open shelves for books or display on all or part of the opposite side. The storage divider may be a decorative as well as functional element (Figure 6.15).

Where space does not permit a heavy divider, a screen (either freestanding or attached) may serve as a partial divider. In a small room where any type of divider would cut needed space, the furniture may be arranged to redirect traffic by turning a sofa, desk, or chairs toward the room and at right angles to the door, leaving a passageway for traffic (Figure 6.16). Such devices provide limited privacy and create the feeling of an entranceway.

In a reception area, the client will usually request workspace for a receptionist and a waiting area, which may need to accommodate only three or four guests. A waiting room for a doctor's office, however, may require seating for ten or more.

The receptionist may serve more than one function. He or she may operate the switchboard and serve as the office

Figure 6.16 *The designer placed the furniture perpendicular to the front door and added a mirror and console to create the effect of a foyer in this ranch-style home. (Designer: Stephens Designs, Kurt Stephens. Photograph by Simon Watson.)*

manager and secretary. In a doctor's office, the receptionist may double as a nurse or a business accounting employee. It is critical that accurate information be obtained before designing this important workspace. Many times a receptionist works behind a desk that has a *transaction top*. This allows the receptionist a sense of privacy, keeps the paperwork on the desk from looking cluttered to the waiting guests, and serves as a shelf where guests can rest

items while speaking with the receptionist. The ledge is usually placed 12″ above the desk, or at 42″ above the floor.

A guest who enters a reception area should immediately be able to make eye contact with the receptionist. The waiting area should adjoin or be part of the reception area, yet should be out of sight of the workings of the office. Figure 6.17 represents an acceptable reception area solution.

Figure 6.17 *Programming needs: reception work space for telephone, computer, keyboard, and printer; waiting room seating for four; access to conference room; privacy from offices.*

This plan offers many advantages: Guests are immediately greeted by the receptionist. The waiting area easily accommodates four guests. There is a telephone for guest use. The company's name and logo are displayed behind the desk, balanced on the opposite wall by a piece of art over the loveseat. The custom receptionist's desk has an ample work surface and file storage. A tall plant, door and sidelight, console table, and mirror help to balance the window wall opposite.

The conversation area requires approximately 90 ▱; the work area, approximately 60 ▱. The total area for the room is approximately 240 ▱. A room that is approximately 16′-0″ × 15′-0″ satisfies the needs of this client. The hard surface flooring area delineates the entry, provides durable flooring, and gives a pleasing proportion. The carpeted area is 10′-0″ × 16′-0″, meeting the approximate proportions for the golden rectangle.

A.

B.

C.

Figure 6.18 *In this 19th-century New Orleans cottage, furniture has been placed away from the walls to allow for optimum conversation groupings. (Designer: Chrestia & Staub, Inc. Photographs by Tria Giovan. Courtesy of* Southern Accents.*)*

Lobby areas may serve many different functions. For instance, a hotel lobby needs adequate room for seating, luggage, bellhops, a reception desk, a concierge, and a directory; the hotel lobby also requires a focal point for ambience, such as a fountain or sculpture. On the other hand, an office lobby may require only a conversation area. The intricacies of these layouts are beyond the scope of this book, but the basics of space needs remain the same.

Living Room

Living rooms may encompass many of the basic activity areas; conversation areas and video and television viewing are the most common. Other functions may include, but are not limited to, reading, listening to music, writing, and possibly casual dining. The conversation area, however, is usually the most important group. It is designed to enhance or combine with the focal point of the room.

Once the number of people who will regularly use the room is determined, seating can be arranged or selected. *Built-in seating* is usually not as comfortable or flexible as movable sofas and chairs, which may be regrouped for more intimate occasions or opened out to invite more participants. Rigidly placed chairs can make the guests believe that moving them would be a major calamity, so the best choice is to provide comfortable living room chairs of various types and sizes for flexibility.

Bringing furniture away from the walls in a room is more conducive to intimate conversation than placing it directly against the walls (Figure 6.18). An angled or slightly curved sofa is more conducive to conversation than a long, straight sofa. The curve in a sectional sofa is invariably oc-

cupied first, just as the corner table in a restaurant is the most popular.

Another solution to providing a flexible seating arrangement is *modular furniture*. Two or three separate pieces that fit together may be purchased at once; others can be added later (although fabric matching may present problems). Modular furniture can be arranged in a variety of ways depending on space and the number of pieces.

Soft, low-level lighting adds a feeling of intimacy to a conversation area; however, the area should not be in semi-darkness. People need to see the features of those with whom they are talking. A low-hanging light can pull a grouping together and allow light for reading.

Finding the right wall space for a piano is often a challenge. Direct sunlight and changes in climate can have a damaging effect on a piano, limiting possible placement within the room. An upright piano can be placed against an inside wall. A grand piano may be more difficult to place in the average room because of its size. The curved side should be toward the listeners, not facing a wall or corner, so that when the lid is raised the sound will be projected toward the audience. In addition, the pianist and the listeners should be able to see one another, as shown in Figure 6.19. A bay window furnishes a beautiful setting for a grand piano if temperature and light conditions permit. In a large room a grand piano may be placed to serve as a room divider.

In the living room, most tables are placed where a functional need exists. Every seat in a room should have access to a side table. The scale, shape, and height of each table should be right for the purpose and size of the chair or sofa it accompanies. A good height for a coffee table is generally 16 inches. Tables placed next to sofa and chair arms should

Figure 6.19 *Designer Laurence Lake placed the grand piano on a diagonal with the room's architecture and in relation to the other furnishings in this living room, so the occupants can better hear the music and watch the pianist. (Photograph by Pam Singleton.)*

Figure 6.20 *Programming needs: conversation seating for six; grand piano; fireplace. This plan has these advantages: The conversation grouping complements the focal point of the fireplace. The piano faces into the room, balances the doors on the opposite wall, and is away from the windows. Ample tables are placed for beverages and lighting. A console table and large piece of artwork balance the fireplace. A plant softens the corner of the room and provides height on the far left wall. Furniture floats in the room, not aligned against the walls. There is a variety of furniture shapes and heights.*

The conversation area requires approximately 160 ☐ ; the room is approximately 280 ☐ . A room that is approximately 14′-0″ × 20′-0″ works well for this client's needs. This size also meets the proportions of a golden rectangle.

be the same height as the arm to help people avoid knocking items off the table. *Console tables* can be decorative as well as functional, and when combined with a mirror or picture are assets to almost any room. *Writing tables* may be placed flush or with their short end against the wall.

Large case or wall pieces are usually located to lend a feeling of balance. If the area is small, careful planning is necessary to place the large piece where it will be most functional and will complement the wall space. A combination of furniture heights in a room provides interest and helps balance architectural features such as columns, windows, doors, and fireplaces.

Pairs can enhance a living room in many ways. Identical items can be a unifying factor; they give balance and pull together unrelated furniture. A pair of chairs can create a conversation grouping in a number of ways: placed side by side to balance a sofa on the opposite side (see Figure 6.18 A and C), placed on either side of a fireplace, or angled about a table to give an intimate corner feeling (see Figure 6.18 B). Where space is adequate, a pair of love seats or sofas may be used in place of single chairs. A pair of tables may be placed in front of a sofa, creating a flexible substitute for a standard coffee table. Two similar chests placed on either side of a doorway or a fireplace enhance almost any room. Pairs of lamps, candelabras, or wall accessories can be pleasing. When carried to an extreme, however, the use of pairs can be boring. Figure 6.20 indicates a good solution for a living room.

Family Room

The family room is probably the most used room of the house. Here, family members congregate around an entertainment center, read, converse, play games, and often entertain. More than in any other area of the house, the arrangement of furniture is of utmost importance to accommodate easy adjustment for various activities. Use, convenience, and practicality are guiding principles in arranging furnishings, as shown in Figure 6.21.

- *Seating* for conversation incorporates similar solutions discussed for the living room. When television viewing is an important activity, plan seating for easy viewing. Include additional flexible seating for various activities where space permits.
- A number of *tables* can add to the occupants' comfort, including a large coffee table to accommodate beverages and food and side tables for lighting and other necessary items.
- Convenient and adequate *lighting* is essential in a family room and must be comfortable and flexible enough to accommodate all activities (see Chapter 5).
- An *audiovisual entertainment system* is an important part of the family room. Special planning is necessary to place a television set, movie screen, stereo, or complete entertainment center to take best advantage of the space.

Figure 6.21 *The warm reds and rich blues of the area rug are picked up in the painting over the fireplace, the chair upholstery, and the accent pillows. A clear Plexiglas table allows the rug to be seen from all angles. A fascinating mix of African tribal pieces and objects from the American Southwest testifies to the personal interests of the owners. (Photograph by Mark Boisclair.)*

- Family rooms may also serve as an area for quiet games. A *game table* can be incorporated into the space.

Family rooms are extremely difficult to design because of their multiple uses. Figure 6.22 illustrates an example of a well-designed family room.

Dining and Conference Room

Except for the selection of the actual furniture pieces, the space requirements for dining and conference rooms are very similar. Dining chairs need to be relatively small in width in order to fit around a table. Conference room chairs may be larger, but a larger table will also be required. Conference chairs should be on casters for ease in mobility. A practical pedestal-base table gives maximum knee room, and round and oval tables make it easier to squeeze in an extra person.

A serving area is required in conference and dining rooms. A *buffet* may be placed against a wall to be used for food service or the display of a client's product. Storage pieces also may be needed. A high piece of furniture, such as a *breakfront* or *china cabinet,* can provide space for displays and adds dignity and vertical interest to the room. Cor-

Figure 6.22 *Programming needs: comfortable seating for four to view the television; game area for four; storage and shelving; entertainment area; comfortable reading chair. The advantages of this plan include: The adjoining breakfast room is used as the game area to conserve space in the family room. The television is opposite the windows to balance their height. The sofa placed beneath the window balances the archway leading into the breakfast room. There are four oversized seating areas for watching television. One of the seats is canted and has appropriate lighting to serve as a reading chair. Extra large pillows can serve as additional floor seating. Shelving and cabinets flank the entertainment system for storage.*

The conversation area requires approximately 100 ☐. The room has approximately 150 ☐. Therefore, a room that is approximately 10'-0" × 15'-0" is a good design solution, as long as the breakfast room doubles as the game area. The rectangular room also meets the dimensions required by the golden rectangle.

ner cupboards are appropriate storage and display items for a residence. Figure 6.23 indicates a design solution for a dining room.

Lighting is a key element in dining and conference rooms. Dimmed lights may be required for presentation purposes in the conference room, and are usually desirable for setting a mood in the dining room. Refer to Chapter 5 for further discussions on lighting options.

Video conferencing, slide viewing, and presentation display areas may be needed in conference rooms (Figure 6.24), which may then require blackout draperies or shades.

Figure 6.23 *Programming needs: seating for four to eight; storage and display for china and linens; surface for serving. The advantages of this layout include: The buffet is located near the kitchen door. A china cabinet for storage also balances the large windows and adds height and interest to the room. A large painting balances the buffet. There is comfortable seating for eight.*

The table area requires approximately 176 ▢. The area of the entire room is approximately 234 ▢. A room that measures 13'-0" × 18'-0" could accommodate this design solution.

Figure 6.24 *At Balis & Co., Inc., in Philadelphia, this traditional conference room seats 18. The audiovisual equipment is concealed. Lighting is flexible to allow for a variety of presentation needs and the sideboard functions well for additional service needs. (Designer: Daroff Design, Inc. Photograph by Elliott Kaufman.)*

(Window treatments will be discussed further in Chapter 12.) Some conference rooms may include a conversation area for informal discussions.

Office

Home and commercial office spaces require much of the same equipment. Aside from the desk, credenza, and desk chair there needs to be ample shelving and filing storage. Commercial spaces require guest seating, usually for two. The designer needs to know if the client desires to sit across the desk from the guests, or to have guests sit next to the desk. Executive offices may include a conferencing area or a conversation grouping (see Figure IV.3). It is not uncommon in a commercial space for furniture to be placed against a glass window wall.

When designing an office it is best to place the computer at a 90° angle to the window to avoid glare. If the computer is placed against the window the bright contrast between the sun and low-lit screen causes eye fatigue. When the screen faces the window an immense amount of glare is created. Also, the person sitting at the desk should be able to easily see who is entering the office. It is disconcerting to be seated facing away from the door.

Finally, consider the placement of electrical and telephone outlets. Cords should not be strung across the room or hidden by the base molding. In a residence, a reading chair or two may be requested, as well as substantial shelving for the client's personal library. There should be a comfortable, ergonomically designed desk chair to fit the occupant. In a residence, the chair may be used by different family members and therefore should be easily adjusted. Figure 6.25 presents a scheme for a commercial office.

Bedroom

Whether in the home, hospital, or hotel, bedrooms are a place of retreat. Because of the size of the bed, it usually becomes the focal point of the room. Traffic lanes are established around the bed with careful attention to nighttime walking. Built-in units or nightstands placed beside the bed are essential to accommodate necessary items. Like tables next to sofa arms, nightstands should be the same height as the top of the mattress.

In residential settings chests, dressers, storage chests, or other case pieces are essential for storage. Built-in under-

Figure 6.25 *Programming needs: desk and credenza; two guest chairs; filing and shelf storage. This layout provides these advantages: ample storage and shelving space; view to the door by employee; seating for two guests; ease in accessing file cabinets and shelving. These items, with the door, balance the long window wall. The computer can be placed on the credenza at a 90° angle to the windows. An accent furniture piece adds interest.*

The work area requires 68 ☐. The entire room requires 120 ☐. A room that is approximately 10'-0" × 12'-0" will accommodate this typical office.

the-bed drawers can convert unused space into storage. A cedar chest can serve as storage and also works well as a bench for sitting. It is practical to have at least one chair or seat in the room.

Hotel rooms require minimal storage facilities, but do require a writing surface and seating area (Figure 6.26). Careful consideration is given to the location of the television and a place to set luggage. Hospital rooms require an immense amount of attention to the location of medical equipment. Although hospitality and healthcare design solutions are beyond the scope of this text, space requirements are determined in a similar manner.

In a residential setting, a master bedroom may incorporate an intimate seating group for two, or possibly a *chaise longue* (an elongated chair that supports the feet and legs).

If a television is requested, the designer must know whether it is to be viewed from the bed, seating area, or both.

Children's and teenagers' bedrooms require special attention. Work areas, play areas, and toy storage areas need to be accommodated.

All bedrooms require a mirror. It can be freestanding, mounted on the wall, or attached to a piece of furniture or a closet door. Also, all bedrooms should have lighting conveniently located next to the bed. Figure 6.27 shows an acceptable layout for a small master bedroom suite.

Making the Most of Space with Furniture

In many instances designers are required to work with an existing space and do not have the option of increasing or decreasing the actual room size. Therefore, through the clever use of the principles and elements of design, a small room can be made to appear much larger than it is, or a large room smaller than it is. The designer should first examine the room carefully and define the traffic lanes, then apply space planning principles to expand or contract the apparent size of the room.

Lightly scaled furniture can be accommodated more readily in a small space than heavily scaled pieces (Figure 6.28). Lightweight furniture is usually supported on legs rather than flush to the floor. It may have rounded corners and clear glass or plastic tops. Lightly scaled seating lacks arms and has backs and sides that are see-through or made of caning.

Upholstered pieces covered in a plain or small all-over patterned fabric blended to the room's background provide visual space. Repeating the same fabric on other pieces helps unify furniture and has a space-making effect. Upholstery that is neatly tailored and without skirts also gives an uncluttered look. Furniture aligned with walls leaves the center of the room free.

Floor-to-ceiling shelves and high shallow storage units add visual height, and if terminated approximately one foot from the floor and two feet from the ceiling allow the perimeter of the room to be seen, adding to the sense of space. Smaller storage units such as serving tables, consoles, buffets, and desks can be wall hung, eliminating the need for space-using legs (Figure 6.29).

It may be possible to add a projecting window or a skylight. Space could also be arranged so the eye can easily travel through a room to outside areas like a garden, terrace, or view. Finally, rooms should be free of clutter, with an occasional empty corner.

The challenge of making a big room livable is not a common one, but it does occur. The most important consideration is *scale*. Massive furniture, overscaled patterns, and large pictures can be chosen; all furnishings, however, need not be big. After large pieces have defined the grouping of the room, lighter pieces can be used to complement the spaces.

Too little furniture in a big room can result in a cold, uninviting interior. More important than quantity, however, is arrangement. The best technique is to plan separate areas

Figure 6.26 *Located on St. John, Virgin Islands, Caneel Bay Hotel boasts simple, elegant, and sophisticated rooms in the tropical style. (Designer: Vision Design Dallas. Photograph by Mike Wilson.)*

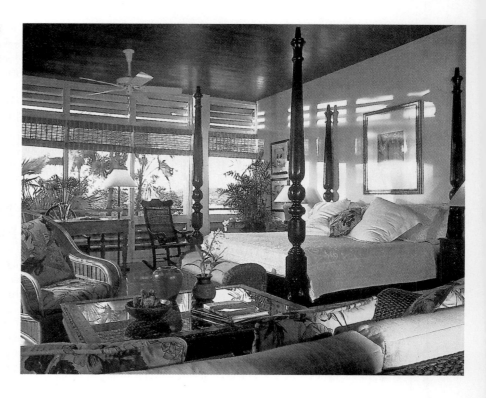

Figure 6.27 *Programming needs: queen-sized bed; triple dresser; seating area for two; television in armoire (viewed from bed). Advantages of this layout include: clothing storage near the closets and bath; the tall armoire, door, and cased opening into the closet and bath balance the bed and window wall; the triple dresser with mirror provides storage and balances the seating group on the opposite wall; ample walking space for making the bed and accessing drawers and storage units; lighting at the sitting area and on both sides of the bed.*

The sleeping area requires approximately 86 ☐; the sitting area, 60 ☐. The room requires 204 ☐. A space approximately 12'-0″ × 17'-0″ would accommodate this master bedroom suite. This is close to the ideal size of the golden rectangle.

To closet and bath

Heavy

Light

Light

Heavy

Heavy

Lighter

Light

Light

Heavy

Heavy

Lighter

Figure 6.28 *These line drawings indicate heavily and lightly scaled furniture. Lightly scaled furniture creates the feeling of a more spacious room.*

Figure 6.29 *A wall-hung shelf with rounded corners takes little space.*

of different sizes. Utilize the architectural elements, such as flooring and ceiling changes, to create human-scaled spaces within the big area. Some may be small and intimate; others, more open (Figure 6.30). Occasional chairs may be moved from one group to another, forming a link between groupings.

Summary

When space planning furnishings for clients, successful designers remember the following key philosophies:

- Design to meet the function(s) of the space.
- Design for the client's needs and within the client's budget.
- Allow for ample traffic lanes and clearances.
- Follow the principles and elements of design as they relate to space and space planning.
- Scale the furniture to match the scale of the room or the desired feel of the room.

Whenever possible, design from the *inside out*. In new construction, work with the architect or builder to establish the appropriate room sizes and shapes prior to construction. In existing construction, move walls (where possible) to meet the needs for the function of the space, but be prepared to use space planning and design principles to make the most of an existing space. And above all, *space plan furniture in the third dimension*.

Figure 6.30 *In this large living area designed by architect Charles Gwathmey, the space is visually divided by marble tiles inset into the wood floor and the sweep of a dropped section of the ceiling. Separate furniture groupings encourage conversation. (Photograph © Paul Warchol. Courtesy of Charles Gwathmey.)*

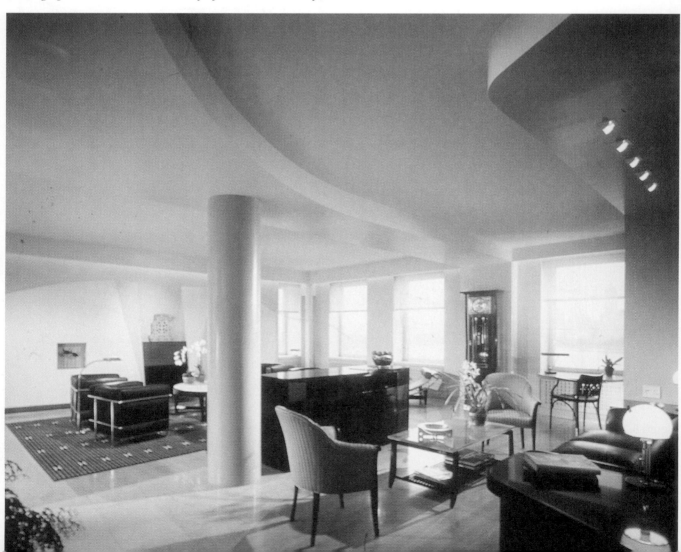

7

Space Planning: Rooms to Buildings

Figure 7.1 *In this formal traditional foyer, a limestone floor with oak inlays sets an elegant tone. (Designer: Ewing-Noble Interiors. Photograph by Tria Giovan. Courtesy of* Southern Accents.*)*

In the last chapter, furnishings were the smallest elements of the interior space planning puzzle that were grouped together to define activity areas. Activity areas were then grouped together based on the functional needs of specific rooms. This chapter explains how these rooms are grouped together into *interior zones* that are combined to form residences and commercial working environments.

When space planning rooms into buildings, a designer frequently serves in a support role to the architect, collaborating with the design team to establish appropriate zoning and massing of spaces. However, professional and/or legal guidelines may restrict the designer from developing the footprint of the building. Certainly a designer is not qualified to design the structural, electrical, or mechanical components of the building, jobs that are performed by the architects and appropriate engineers.

Defining basic areas in residential and nonresidential projects is helpful to the designer during the space planning process. Zoning interior spaces for a project depends on their intended functions. (Note that the term "interior zoning" is used in this chapter as it relates to spatial assessment; this should not be confused with zoning established by building codes and regulations.) Broad categories of zoning include divisions between public and private places. For instance, in a restaurant, the "back of house" is referred to as the kitchen and storage areas; the "front of house" is where the guests eat. In commercial office design, the public spaces include the reception area and conference rooms. Executive offices, accounting areas, copy rooms, and the like are considered the private spaces. In residential design, a similar division exists in private and public zones.

Residential Zones

The zones in residential design combine related activities. Public or social zones include formal areas such as the entry, living room, and dining room. Informal public areas include the kitchen, breakfast room, and family or recreation room. Private zones include bedrooms, dressing areas, bathrooms, studies, and laundry rooms. Offices may be considered part of the public zone if open to visitors; otherwise, they are part of the private zone. Zones should be viewed as a whole and should have compatible spatial organization. Analyzing and designing for individual differences, lifestyles, and activities that take place within the spaces contributes to the smooth functioning of the residence.

Public Zones

The public zone is where people meet for various activities. In years past, many of these areas, such as kitchens, may have been "off limits" to guests. However, kitchens and recreation rooms have now become common gathering places.

The Entry

The entry is usually placed to allow for access into the formal and informal areas of a residence. The entry may be open to the formal social zones, but it is best when it provides a visual block to informal rooms. Entries may include a large closet for occupants' and guests' coats, a mirror, and seat. A bathroom or powder room should be near (see Figures 7.1–7.3).

Figure 7.2 *The warm yellow hues in this foyer add casualness and give a fresh, informal look to a typical traditional setting. The dining room glimpsed above is shown in detail in Figure 6.1. (Designer: Drysdale Design Associates. Photograph by Antoine Bootz. Courtesy of* Southern Accents.*)*

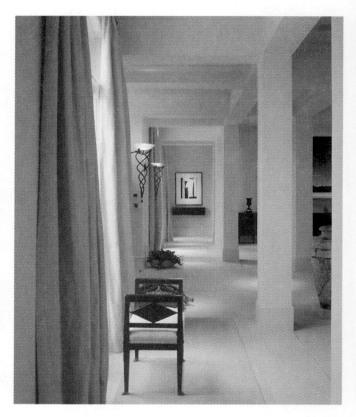

Figure 7.3 *In this warm contemporary environment, the foyer sets the tone. The simple elegant lines and refined finishes are restful. (Designer: Gandy/Peace, Inc. Photograph by Chris A. Little. Courtesy of* Southern Accents.*)*

Figure 7.4 *This space shows a successful transition from the foyer to the dining area and the conversation area. Emphasis is on the conversation grouping; the fireplace serves as a backdrop. A soaring ceiling, warm lighting, and plants add to the comfortable yet sophisticated character of the space. (Interiors: Fine Decorators, Hallandale, FL/Ted Fine with Robert Perlberg. Photography by Brantley, Ocean Ridge, FL. Courtesy of On Design.)*

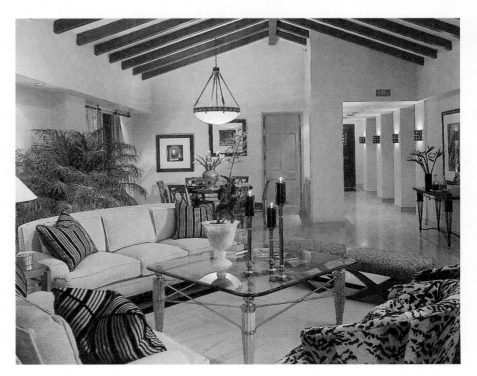

Living Room

The transition from the entry to the living room is important. The entrance area should flow easily into the living room with a smooth transition of design elements.

The formal living room works well when placed away from major traffic lanes. It may be planned for privacy as well as various functions such as conversation, listening to music, reading, relaxing, and other activities (Figure 7.4).

A fireplace in the living room is often a natural focal point. It can be emphasized through such elements as texture, color, lighting, and the arrangement of other furnishings.

If the living room lives up to its name, it will provide for all household members and guests as well. The space may be relatively large or a cloistered parlor area, depending on requirements, preferences, and budget restrictions. In many homes, the formal living room or dining room may

Figure 7.5 *In this renovated space, the dining area is distinguished by the use of an Oriental rug. Traditional French chairs are accented by the sleek lines of the glass-topped table. (Designer: Dana Maye. Photograph by Erica George Dines.)*

be converted into a library, study, or music room. The room then functions as a quiet sanctuary where owners can relax.

Dining Room

An inviting formal dining area requires privacy from informal areas. It should be close to the food preparation area but shut off from the clutter of the kitchen. Keeping the dining room in the same basic theme and mood as the living room makes a pleasing transition (as seen in Figure 7.4).

If the dining room is an alcove or part of a living room, any number of treatments can set it apart. Walls may be papered or painted a different but coordinated color. Free-standing screens, a plant grouping, or an area rug can help define the space (Figure 7.5).

Kitchen

In many residences, the kitchen has become the hub of the home—an area where food preparation, serving, eating, and other socializing take place. The kitchen needs to be adjacent to the formal dining room, but also screened from its view. The kitchen also should be adjacent to the breakfast room, family room, and pantry. Additionally, the kitchen

should be near the garage or the door where groceries are brought into the home; however, it is very important that the kitchen not be part of a major traffic lane. The location of the kitchen is obviously central to the residence.

The layout of the kitchen should be based on household needs, the physical limitations of the client, and the number of cooks working at the same time. The basic kitchen shapes are U-shape, L-shape, island, parallel, and one-wall, as illustrated in Figure 7.6.

The kitchen is generally planned around three work centers, which may also include subcenters.

* The *refrigerator/storage area* is generally the first area used as items are removed for preparation. An 18″ wide counter adjacent to the handle side of the refrigerator is needed for holding items.
* The *sink area* (preparation and cleanup) is truly multipurpose and therefore is usually positioned between the other two centers. The sink center may include a dishwasher, a garbage disposal or trash bin, cabinet space, and a minimum of 18″ of counter space on both sides of the sink. Lighting is particularly important over this area.
* The *cooking area* (stovetop or range, oven, convection oven and/or microwave) receives particularly heavy use just before a meal. In a kitchen designed for two cooks, the microwave or oven may be separated from the stovetop. Eighteen to 24″ of space should be included on either side of the cooktop. Ventilation should be provided for the range and oven. When the oven door is open, it should never obstruct a main walkway.

Subactivity zones include the *mixing area* (which is often located between the refrigerator and sink and includes an uninterrupted counter space of 36″) and a *serving center* (usually located near the eating space out of the general work triangle). The serving center is particularly convenient when it is near the dishwasher and away from the cooking area, because the table is frequently set while the final cooking is completed. Cabinets and counter space of at least 24″ are important features.

Efficient and adequate cabinet storage is necessary for a successful kitchen plan. There must be storage for food (dry food, perishables, staples, and canned food), tableware (flatware, dishes, tablecloths, napkins, etc.), cleaning supplies (floor cleaners, soaps, paper products, towels, etc.), and cooking utensils. Portable appliances such as blenders, food processors, mixers, juicers, coffee grinders, and other task-related appliances may be placed in lower cabinets, hung from upper cabinets, or concealed in appliance garages. Portable appliances should have a convenient and concealed home and not be left to clutter countertops that are needed for food preparation.

Breakfast Room

Informal eating areas for quick snacks and everyday family meals are most conveniently located in or near the kitchen. The eating area close to the kitchen can vary depending on the space and shape allocated. Some kitchens have eating areas at a bar or counter, often with bar stools or attached seats

U-SHAPE KITCHEN
U-shape kitchens are generally considered the most comfortable and efficient. Work centers are out of the way of traffic and more conveniently located. Accommodates 1 person best.

L-SHAPE KITCHEN
L-shape kitchens are a little more efficient than the parallel since traffic lanes do not intrude into the space. Work centers are conveniently located. Can accommodate 2 people.

ISLAND KITCHEN
The island kitchen has similar qualities as the U-shape, but with the unwelcome addition of possible traffic through the space. Can accommodate 2 people.

PARALLEL KITCHEN
Parallel kitchens provide undesirable traffic, especially when doors are located at each end. Work centers are more convenient than one-wall kitchens. Best with 1 person.

ONE-WALL KITCHEN
One-wall kitchens economically use one plumbing wall, can be concealed with folding doors, and do not take up much space. They are usually most suitable for apartments and small living spaces. They have very little counterspace and work space pattern is long. Best with 1 person.

Figure 7.6 *Basic kitchen arrangements.*

(Figure 7.7). Other kitchens may have the eating area in a bay window or alcove close by, as shown in Figure 7.8.

Family or Recreation Room

Family rooms should be located near the kitchen and away from quiet areas of the home, such as bedrooms, living rooms, and studies. Family rooms also should have immediate access to the outside. Of all the rooms in a house, the family room probably needs the most well-planned storage to take care of such items as a card table, folding chairs, games, CDs, videotapes, books, or even a screen and projector. Freestanding walls, built-ins, or wall systems may be set up to provide floor-to-ceiling banks of drawers, cabinets, and shelves.

The television and VCR are generally standard equipment in a family room. Locating the television in a central section of a wall of built-ins is an excellent way to incorporate this

piece with other furnishings (Figure 7.9). Another good solution is to place the fireplace and television in an L-shape (Figure 7.10). With this arrangement, the television and fireplace are not in competition as the focal point. The television should always be placed so that several people can view it comfortably.

As discussed in Chapter 6, family rooms may have different activity areas for dining and game playing, television viewing, and conversation. The designer's goal is to allow for ample free-flowing and flexible space that can accommodate a variety of activities.

Bathroom

A half-bath or powder room (one that includes a toilet and sink) should be located in the public zone, so guests do not have to enter the private zone to use the restroom. Typical bathroom layouts are discussed later in this chapter.

Figure 7.7 *This transitionally styled kitchen includes a breakfast bar for quick meals and snacks. Particular attention was given to the clean lines and contemporary finishes. (Designer: Burns Century Interiors. Photograph by Billy Howard. Courtesy of Brenau University.)*

Figure 7.8 *This kitchen work zone is designed in a parallel arrangement with a traditional casual dining area at one end. The Mediterranean style of the residence was carried into the kitchen area. (Interiors: Perla Lichi, Perla Lichi Design, ID 1727, Tamarac, FL. Photograph by Barry Grossman. Courtesy: On Design. Residence: Condominium, private residence, Essex model at L'Hermitage, Ft. Lauderdale, FL.)*

Figure 7.9 *Audiovisual equipment is tastefully displayed in a custom cabinet. The television and fireplace function together in this angled arrangement. (Interiors: Marc-Michaels Interior Design. Photograph ©Kim Sargent Architectural Photography. Residence: Private home, Phipps Estates, Palm Beach. Developer: Addison Development.)*

Figure 7.10 *This floor plan illustrates a quality solution in a family room that has both a fireplace and a television.*

Laundry Rooms and Utility Rooms

Function and convenience are major considerations when locating laundry and utility areas. Laundry rooms are best placed near the dressing and bathing area. Unfortunately, laundry rooms are frequently relegated to a space close to the kitchen or garage, requiring occupants to haul clothes up and down stairs or across the social areas of the home. Some clients prefer to have the laundry area near the kitchen to facilitate daily activities. Designers should check with clients to determine their preference. Placing the washer with easy access to water lines is also important. A laundry tub or sink, adequate counter surfaces, space for the dryer and ironing board, sufficient storage, hanging space, and good lighting are also desirable.

Sewing, workshop, office, garden, and other work areas should be conveniently located with well-arranged space for required storage, furnishings, equipment, and lighting.

Libraries, Studies, and Offices

These areas, when used by visitors, may be part of the public zone. As more people operate businesses from their homes, clients may be invited there. If this is the case, the office should be located near an entry that is easily accessible from the front of the house, away from noisy rooms, and screened from the formal social areas. If only the occupants use the office, library, or study, the room should be located in an area away from noisy areas such as family rooms, kitchens, and utility rooms (see Figure 13.3).

More and more households have computers, which are becoming central to daily household operations. In many families children have their own computers and study spaces. Furthermore, the laptop computer has allowed virtually any surface to become an office. Although the study may be located in the private zone, additional computer stations may be located near the kitchen or family room and also in children's rooms.

Private Zones

For maximum quiet and privacy, sleeping, dressing, and hygiene areas function best when located away from the social zone of the residence. Guests, except for those in the guestroom, rarely visit this zone of the home.

Master Bedroom

The master bedroom has become a refuge from the pressures and stress of everyday living—a place for relaxation and sleeping. Often the master bedroom is a luxurious part of the home (Figure 7.11). There may be space for a fireplace, a bar, a television set, a study, a conversation arrangement, an office, and even a physical fitness area. The master bedroom is best located at a distance from all other rooms. It does not have to be adjacent to any other room except the master bath and, if appropriate, a nursery.

Bedrooms for Children and Young Adults

These rooms, like the master bedroom, should be located in quiet areas of the house. Children's rooms require ample storage, access to a bathroom, and perhaps a study or computer area. Designers should also be sensitive to the needs of children in blended families. When possible, the designer should talk directly with the children to determine their needs and desires in this specialty area of design.

Dressing and Clothes Storage

The dressing area may be in a separate space, in a closet, in the bedroom itself, or adjacent to or in the bathroom. Storage for clothing should be close to the dressing area and bathroom and planned for convenience. Closets should not protrude into the bedroom (Figure 7.12). A space for soiled clothing should be conveniently located. Storage for clothing, jewelry, and other dressing items is generally limited, so using space to advantage is a challenge.

Guestrooms

Rooms set aside for guests are many times considered a luxury; however, where space permits, a warm and inviting guestroom is a welcomed retreat for visitors. As in other bedrooms, traffic lanes should be allocated around the bed. A side chair for reading and a television are also appreciated. Minimal storage is needed for clothing and other personal items.

Guestrooms should be located away from noisy activity areas and private zones and need to have access to a bathroom. Guests may desire access to public areas, such as the kitchen or family room.

Bathrooms

Since the beginning of the 20th century, the bathroom has undergone many changes. Originally, it was one shared room at the end of the hall; then it became a personal adjunct to the

Figure 7.11 *In this seaside model home, the master bedroom faces the ocean. A writing area and a relaxed conversation area are included. (Interiors: Fine Decorators, Hallandale, FL/Ted Fine with Robert Perlberg. Photograph by Brantley, Ocean Ridge, FL. Courtesy of* On Design.*)*

Figure 7.12 *Poor and proper placement for closets.*

Poor closet placement

Proper closet placement

bedroom, and became smaller and more utilitarian. Today, utility and luxury are combined, and the bathroom—once hidden behind closed doors—is frequently exposed to sky, garden, terrace, and sometimes to other rooms of the house. What was once a small, sterile room with three basic plumbing fixtures (lavatory or sink, toilet, and tub or shower) has become a powder room, dressing room, and even sitting room, often with additional luxury features such as whirlpool, sauna, spa, hot tub, television, or fireplace (see Figures 4.19 and 7.13).

Most homes have more than one bathroom. Some may have half or three-quarter baths (with a sink, toilet, and shower stall) as well. The designer must determine the space available, the needs of the users, and the most efficient arrangement of plumbing fixtures and supportive furnishings, storage, and lighting for each hygiene area in the residence.

Bathroom design is still centered on the three basic fixtures—the tub, toilet, and sink. Ample storage for towels, medicines, and grooming and cleaning aids is essential. A place for soiled clothing is also desirable. Master bathrooms commonly contain two sinks, a separate area for the toilet, and a shower stall in addition to the tub. Tubs may be located almost anyplace, including the center of the room. They are available in all shapes, designs, colors, and sizes. Sometimes tubs are placed beside large windows to take advantage of a view. It is safest for the user if the tub is sunken, because steps up to the tub can be treacherous when wet. Figure 7.14 illustrates some common bathroom layouts.

Figure 7.13 *In this contemporary remodeling project, the designer created a tree house effect for the master bath. (Designer: T. Duffy & Associates, Inc. Photograph ©Robert Thien. As seen in:* Atlanta Homes & Lifestyles.*)*

Figure 7.14 *Typical bathroom layouts. A and B are appropriate for half-bath layouts. A is extremely tight, but acceptable when a closet is converted to a bath; B is a better solution. C is the most compact three-fixture layout. D is a common inexpensive solution for a larger master bath. E illustrates one of an endless variety of solutions for an upgraded master bath.*

General Zoning Guidelines

Allowing enough space for each member of the household is an essential requirement in planning interiors. Space requirements vary for each individual, and in some cases may reflect clients' preferences rather than their needs. Generally, 1,000 square feet of space meets the needs of one person; and additional 500 square feet per person provides sufficient space. Designers must be able to guide clients and meet their essential needs while staying within financial boundaries.

Commercial Zones

Like residential zones, commercial zones also are divided into broad categories of private and public spaces. The myriad options for the specialty areas of design, such as hospitality, healthcare, or institutional design, require separate study well beyond the scope of this text. It is, however, feasible to consider the space planning needs of a typical commercial office. As was discussed in Chapter 6, commercial buildings must also consider accessibility standards, from the entry to the snack bar at the rear of the office complex. Space planning can be greatly affected by these requirements. Figures 7.15 through 7.19 illustrate a successful corporate office design and are used throughout this section as examples.

Public Zones

The public zone consists of the area where clients, or guests, arrive. Clients should feel welcome but should not be aware of activities in progress in the private spaces.

Reception Room

As illustrated in Chapter 6, the reception room includes two activity areas—the conversation/waiting area and the office workspace for the receptionist. The reception room needs to be adjacent to the front door and therefore also serves as the entry or foyer. The reception room should be near the public conference room and be easily accessible to other private office areas (see Figures 2.23, 7.15, and 7.16). The reception room needs access to a breakroom or coffee area so guests may be served refreshments while waiting. A storage area for coats and umbrellas and a small private telephone room also may be required.

Conference or Presentation Room

This room also should welcome clients. Access should be directly off the reception area (see Figure 7.16). In some conference rooms, an adjacent audiovisual area conceals equipment and doubles as a storage area for presentation materials.

Figure 7.15 *Figures 7.15-7.19 illustrate an excellent solution to a commercial office space. The radial lobby (see Figure 2.23) defines the interior and sets the tone for the entire office. (Architect/Designer: VOA Associates, Inc. Photographs by Steve Hall/Hedrich Blessing.)*

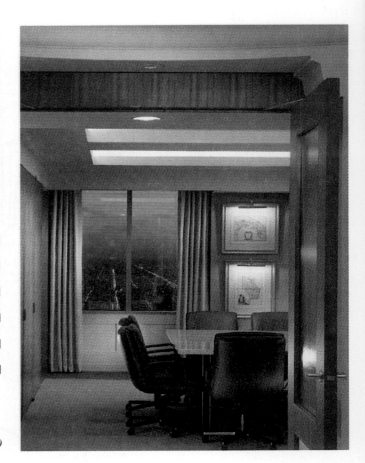

Figure 7.16 *Two conference rooms are located directly off the reception area.*

Private Zones

In commercial spaces, private zones could more accurately be called semiprivate zones, because clients and guests may frequent almost all areas of a commercial office.

Offices

Offices are grouped together based on the company's division of departments. In large commercial establishments, entire floors may be dedicated to a particular division. Offices may also require flexible spaces; for example, individuals may share an office space, at other times working at home or on the road. Offices should be in quiet zones of a building away from breakrooms and near the support staff.

Executive offices may comprise a suite of rooms that includes a private administrative assistant's office, private conference room, office, bathroom, and storage closet. Executive suites are generally located in private areas of a building, frequently on the top floor (Figure 7.17).

Open Offices

In many commercial establishments, employees work in open offices or systems furniture environments (see Chapter 8). Open office areas should be grouped by department away from noise and adjacent to support staff (Figure 7.18).

Support Staff

In many firms, the support staff, secretaries, or administrative assistants serve more than one individual. Locating support staff to meet the needs of those they serve can be difficult. Support staff also must be near copy, file, and storage areas. In very small firms, the receptionist may be the support staff for the entire firm. In larger corporations, support staff may be in an area of their own, sometimes referred to as a "secretarial bay."

Ancillary Areas

Ancillary areas include copy, mail, file, and other related rooms necessary for processing various tasks. These areas are generally used only by the employees, but need to be centrally located to expedite the flow of work. Noisy copiers and printers should not interfere with the need for a quiet office.

Breakrooms

Although the size of this room varies greatly depending on the client's needs, the space planning remains the same. Breakrooms are potentially noisy areas that need proper sound attenuation. They also should be separated from the public zone. Because most breakrooms require a sink, they must be located near plumbing lines (Figure 7.19).

Bathrooms

In commercial design, the location of the bathroom depends on the location of plumbing lines. In high-rise buildings, bathrooms are located in a central core that serves the entire floor. In smaller offices, the bathroom should be located between the public and private zones to accommodate both employees and guests. Commercial bathrooms must meet universal design requirements (see Chapter 6).

Figure 7.17 *Private offices are located out of sight from the main public areas.*

Figure 7.18 *Open office spaces and support staff areas maintain the formal design characteristics. Employees are provided ample lighting.*

Figure 7.19 *Ancillary areas are centrally located and out of public view, yet even the lunchroom maintains the character and classical design details found throughout the office.*

General Zoning Requirements

Whether designing for a residential or commercial client, the designer should consider the principles of design, as well as various space and traffic flow guidelines.

The Principles of Design in Relation to Space

Space, like all the elements of design, affects the principles of design. When arranging furniture or space planning rooms, designers should consider the following points.

- The *proportions* of a room can be altered through appropriate space planning. For instance, long, tall pieces can divide a room into smaller areas. Dropped ceilings and area rugs can delineate an area needing a more intimate space (Figure 7.20). Furniture placed perpendicular to a wall can define a smaller area.
- The *scale* of a room is greatly affected by the room's furnishings. As discussed in Chapter 3, the scale of the furniture must be in line with the scale of the room. If the furniture is too large the room will appear cramped; too small, and the room will appear stark and uninviting (see Figure 2.16).
- Furnishings should be arranged to give the room a sense of *balance*. Large architectural features, such as picture windows and fireplaces, require heavier furniture opposite them. In rooms with slanted ceilings, heavier furniture should be placed against the taller wall.
- Balance also can be achieved through a mixture of high and low pieces of furniture and furnishings. Exclusive use of tall pieces makes a room appear heavy and

Figure 7.20 *In this square room, a rectangular rug was added to define the seating area and to control the proportions of the room.*

Figure 7.21 *In this casual café in a shopping mall, patrons are led to the maître d' stand through the use of an architectural axis, accentuated ceiling, and lighting. (Architect/Designer: Engstrom Design Group and To Design. Photograph ©Greg Murphey.)*

overbearing, whereas a consistent use of low pieces makes a room look squatty, as if designed for children.

- Achieving *rhythm* in an interior allows the eye to move easily about the room. The repetition of a side chair or end tables adds continuity. A person may be drawn from the living room to the dining room through a progression of steps. An architectural detail, combined with furniture and carpet placement, may form an axis drawing the person to an appointed location (Figure 7.21). In large office buildings, hotels, and airports, corridors should be placed in systematic locations to aid visitors' directional sense. In retail design, this repetition is intentionally altered to encourage shoppers to wander through the store.
- All rooms or groups of rooms must have a *focal point*. The center of interest may be an information desk, painting, sculpture, coffee table, or panoramic view. In a group of rooms, the main conference room, reception area, living room, or great room may serve this purpose. Once the focal point of a room is decided, it should be supported by the arrangement of furnishings and corridors (see Figure 2.26).

- *Harmony* can be achieved only when space planning utilizes unity and variety. Offices need desks and chairs; living rooms require sofas and end tables. Bathrooms should be located near bedrooms and reception rooms near the front door. It is this typical placement of furnishings and rooms that allows the client to feel comfortable in a space; however, it is the unusual juxtapostition of a wall, chair, accessory, or architectural element that enhances a room and keeps the client's interest elevated (Figure 7.22).

Space and Traffic Flow Guidelines

Arranging space to meet clients' needs requires general guidelines that should be applied in all situations.

- The style of the home or office may guide the layout of the rooms. Some clients prefer a formal design balanced in all dimensions with distinctly defined interior zones. Other clients may prefer open planning and an informal approach to interior zoning.
- Floor and wall space must be adequate to support large pieces of furniture, shelving, files, and art. Doorways, although convenient, cannot encompass every wall.

Figure 7.22 *This presidential suite located in the Westin Grand Hotel illustrates harmonious use of the principles and elements of design. Warm tones, soft lighting, and contemporary furnishings provide unity. Black accents and a sweeping window treatment create drama and variety. (Architect/Designer: NBBJ. Photograph by Assassi Productions.)*

- Traffic patterns should not cross conversation groupings, television viewing, workspaces, or the kitchen preparation area.
- A view to the outside should be accessible from every major room or workspace. Only storage rooms, closets, baths, file rooms, movie theatres, and similar spaces should be without natural daylight.
- Windows should be located to preserve the function of the wall space. Properly placed windows allow for ease in operation and for placement of window treatment (Figure 7.23).
- Doorways should not be located at the end of corridors. A corridor should end with a wall or other focal point.
- Bathrooms, bedrooms, kitchens, breakrooms, copy rooms, and offices, along with any other private or back of house function, should not be visible from an entry.
- Sufficient storage should be located throughout a house or office building.
- Rooms that require plumbing save costs when grouped near or on top of each other.
- Rooms should have the most pleasing proportions possible. Ancillary areas such as closets, stairwells, or bathrooms should not protrude into a room (see Figure 7.12).
- Designers must adhere to federal, state, and local building codes (see Chapter 4). Understanding these codes prior to initial space planning may prevent having to make changes later in the design process.
- Designers should consider the need for future space. A good plan can effectively accommodate projected expansions.

Site Orientation and Selection

The selection of the site must work in conjunction with the selection of a floor plan. Although the physical placement of a building is not the responsibility of the designer, on certain projects the designer may have input into selecting the site. Before making a selection, the architect and designer should have

Poor placement   Good placement

Figure 7.23 *Window placement.*

the general plan of the structure in mind. Not until the site has been analyzed should the plan be finalized. For example, when selecting a site for a residence, many factors should be considered including such criteria as location of schools, transportation, availability of police and fire protection, quality of the neighborhood, availability of utilities (water, sewer, power, garbage collection), taxes, and building codes and restrictions. Depending on the building's intended function, criteria when selecting a site for a nonresidential structure might include public convenience, efficiency, accessibility, and aesthetic appeal.

A gently sloping lot that provides good natural drainage and allows sewer lines to be connected easily is desirable. A steep lot may cost less initially but may require expensive retaining walls and have other hidden costs; however, a view or a wooded site may be what the client wants. Effective positioning of the structure on the site and orienting it to take advantage of solar properties are also important. "Green Design: The Economy of Space Planning" addresses additional space planning and site selection criteria.

GREEN DESIGN

The Economy of Space Planning

One of the most important aspects of a green environment is the physical layout of the building. Several design criteria assist in the conservative use of materials and energy.

- The more square the shape of the exterior walls, the less the cost per square foot. Cost does not increase in direct proportion to a structure's square footage—jogs and angles drive construction costs higher, as illustrated in Figure GD7.1. Two stories cost proportionally less than a low, rambling plan, because the roof and foundation can serve twice the space, and the second story provides extra insulation against summer heat and winter cold.

Square 40'

40'

= 160 ft perimeter
= 1600 sq ft floor space

Rectangle 20'

60'

= 160 ft perimeter
= 1200 sq ft floor space

(A loss of 400 sq ft of floor space
with the same wall perimeter)

40'

8'

20' Rectangle with jog 20'

12'

60'

= 160 ft perimeter
= 1040 sq ft of floor space

(A loss of 160 sq ft of floor space
plus the extra expense of the jog)

Figure GD7.1 *Price and square footage. The three enclosures, each requiring the same number of linear feet of exterior wall, illustrate how the price per square foot increases as the space deviates from the square.*

- Adequate insulation reduces heating costs, as do wood- or coal-burning stoves that meet strict EPA requirements.
- Locating the structure to take the best advantage of the climate saves on heating and air conditioning bills. The winter sun should strike long walls and large windows, but in the summer large areas of glass should be screened from the afternoon sun (see Figure GD7.2). Positioning the house wisely also reduces the cost of connecting other utilities from the road to the house.

Winter

Summer

Figure GD7.2 *A well-designed roof can permit the warm winter sun to flood the interior spaces in December and block out the hot summer sun in July.*

The Economy of Space Planning—cont'd

- Centralized plumbing saves energy. Bathrooms can be placed back to back as seen in Figure GD7.3, or one above the other. Kitchen and utility room plumbing can be located to take advantage of the same major drains.
- Fireplaces can be planned to take advantage of a common chimney (Figure GD7.4).

Figure GD7.3 *Back-to-back plumbing.*

Figure GD7.4 *Two fireplaces can be combined to share the same chimney.*

- Materials found on-site in the construction area, called **indigenous materials,** offer great savings. Flawed materials may cost less and character can be gained by making a feature out of a fault.
- Consider the cost of upkeep of building materials over a long period of time. This is called life-cycle costing. Some items that are more costly initially are the most economical in the long run. For example, brick may cost more than frame facades, but it never needs painting and the building's resale value is usually higher than for one made of wood. Hardwood balusters are more expensive than pine, but pine balusters are easily broken and replacement may soon add up to more than the cost of the hardwood.

G R E E N D E S I G N

The Economy of Space Planning—cont'd

Figure GD7.5 illustrates a very efficient three-bedroom floor plan of only 1464☐.

Figure GD7.5 *In this efficient home the laundry room is conveniently located adjacent to the bedrooms. The kitchen is out of the circulation zone yet near the garage and out of view from the main entry. (Designer: Alan Mascord Design Associates, Inc.)*

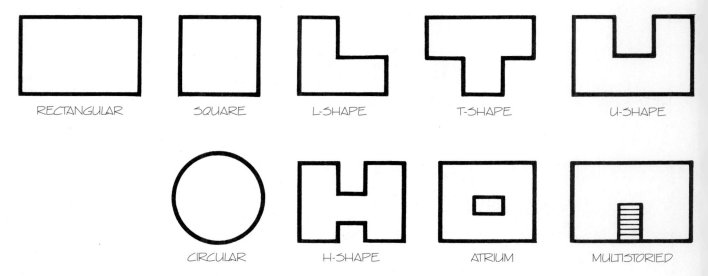

RECTANGULAR   SQUARE   L-SHAPE   T-SHAPE   U-SHAPE

CIRCULAR   H-SHAPE   ATRIUM   MULTISTORIED

Figure 7.24 *Basic floor plan shapes.*

Analyzing Residential Floor Plans

Floor plans for residential design come in a variety of shapes or styles, some of which are illustrated in Figure 7.24. These floor plans often have a few jogs, angles, or window extensions that do not change the basic shape of the structure. To serve the client better, the designer should keep these points in mind:

- The house should be positioned on the site to enhance the landscape. For example, square and rectangle shapes can be more difficult to position and landscape attractively than shapes with more interesting angles.
- Each angle and jog of a floor plan shape adds to the expense of the structure.
- The shape of the residence may affect the interior arrangement of activities. For instance, it is more difficult to arrange various functions in a square because of the limited flexibility of the shape.
- Traffic patterns are usually more efficient in shapes with more angles than the square or rectangle offer.
- Heating and cooling costs are higher with added wings.
- Shapes with more wings or extensions allow additional light and ventilation in the residence.
- Some shapes offer more interesting ways to arrange furnishings, the T, U, H, and atrium shapes, for example.
- Private outdoor living space is possible with shapes like the T, U, H, and atrium, but very difficult with the square.
- Aesthetically, garage doors should open from the side of a home instead of the front; however, such an arrangement may require a larger lot and therefore is more expensive.

Square Plan

The square plan is a simple and inexpensive arrangement of space with distinct advantages and disadvantages, similar to the rectangular plan. Most designers try to minimize or even change the boxy shape—both for interiors and exteriors—through creative manipulation of the elements of design (Figure 7.25). Some considerations when employing the square plan include the following:

- The square plan is one of the least expensive to build because corners are limited to four. It requires only a simple roof and foundation—generally the most costly elements in house construction.
- Rooms should be arranged so traffic can flow freely. The placement of an entrance and hallways can be a challenge in the square plan.
- Good planning should provide adequate light and air circulation—often a problem with the square plan. The center may be poorly lit. A centrally located skylight is one method of eliminating this condition.
- The square plan generally does not provide interesting and inviting outdoor living spaces; however, through skillful landscaping this problem can be eliminated. Sometimes the square plan is turned on an angle to the lot, providing a diagonal or diamond shape.
- Good separation of interior living spaces, such as the sleeping and activity areas, is more difficult to arrange in the square plan.

The basically square plan seen in Figure 7.26 incorporates many open planning concepts in its interior, including the following:

- The house was designed to fit its beachfront site. Upper floor windows provide an ocean view.
- The garage is enclosed and attached.
- Public and social zones are well defined.
- Closets and storage areas are incorporated into the plan.
- First and second floor bathrooms are stacked.
- Rear steps provide a secondary entry/exit to the second and third floors.

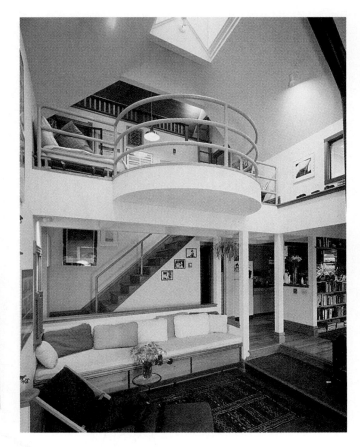

Figure 7.25 *This relatively small house plan, based on the square, efficiently utilizes less than 1300 square feet. The soaring living room ceiling adds the feeling of a grander space. (Designer: Wolff-Lyon Architects.)*

STOR
CLOS
BATH
BEDROOM
12 X 10
ENTRY
UP
KITCHEN
12 X 10
UP
LIVING
14 X 17
DINING
9 X 10
Main Level
32' wide
36' deep

UPPER LOFT ABOVE
BATH
DRESS
MASTER BEDROOM
12 X 13
DN
LOFT
14 X 6
DECK
OPEN TO LIVING
Upper Level

THIRD FLOOR
14 BALCONY
15 LIVING AREA
16 DINING AREA
17 STAIR
18 KITCHEN
19 SITTING AREA

0   8

SECOND FLOOR
5 MASTER BEDROOM
7 MASTER BATH
8 SHOWER
9 BEDROOM
10 HALL
11 BATH
12 ENTRY / STAIR
13 STUDY

0   8

FIRST FLOOR
1 DEN
2 PATIO
3 BATH
4 LAUNDRY
5 GARAGE

0   8

Figure 7.26 *This unique plan was developed to fit the site. Public areas are on upper floors for the best view of the ocean. An open stairway unites the floors. Closets, storage areas, and bathrooms do not infringe upon the space. (Architect/Designer: Rockefeller/Hricak Architects. Photograph by David Glomb.)*

Figure 7.27 *This plan, basically rectangular in shape, has a few jogs and window extensions to provide additional interest. (Courtesy of Knight and West Construction.)*

FAMILY ROOM 18'X23'6"

LIVING ROOM 17'X13"

MASTER SUITE 3 21'8"X13'

BREAKFAST AREA

DINING ROOM 11'X12'

BEDROOM 2 12'4"X 14'6"

KITCHEN 13'6"X12'3"

LAUNDRY ROOM

GARAGE 22'X21'5"

MUD ROOM

BEDROOM 4 12'6"X 12'6"

BEDROOM 3 12'4"X 14'6"

1340 sq. ft.

1560 sq. ft.

Rectangular Plan

The simplest floor plan is the rectangle. The more the plan departs from this shape, the more complicated and costly it becomes. Each jog and additional roof angle mean added expense, and thus more dollars per square foot of floor space. The rectangular plan is readily adapted to both traditional and contemporary exteriors. Figure 7.27 illustrates a rectangular plan with the following features:

- An entrance hall routes traffic to all areas of the house.
- Basic private and social zones are well defined and conveniently located.
- Plumbing is back to back in the private zone.
- Windows and openings are somewhat limited but allow adequate ventilation and light.
- The family room has easy access to the outside and is convenient to the kitchen. Although the fireplace is awkwardly placed off-center, there is room for an entertainment center on the same wall.
- Access from the kitchen and utility rooms to the outdoors and to the garage is convenient.
- An average amount of storage is provided.
- The garage door could be relocated to the side of the home. An access door to the garage could be added from the porch.

Multistoried Plan

Multistoried plans provide living space on two or more levels, which allows versatile living. Features of the plan in Figure 7.28 include the following:

- The basically rectangular plan and the addition over the garage eliminate most unnecessary jogs.
- All zones are well defined on two levels.
- An entry hall channels traffic through the house.
- Doors and windows are well placed.

- Traffic lanes permit easy access. The rear stairway is particularly important for a large family home.
- Closets and storage areas generally do not infringe on basic room shapes.
- The laundry room is well placed upstairs.
- As with the rectangular plan, the garage doors could be relocated to the side of the home if the lot permits.

L-Shaped Plan

The L-shaped plan (Figure 7.29) allows variety in space planning through an extension from the rectangular shape. Features of this simple L-shaped plan are the following:

- The plan incorporates the basic requirements for functional space allocation.
- A central entrance hall welcomes visitors.
- The great (or family) room is combined with the kitchen for informal activities.
- The garage has a convenient access door to the kitchen. The garage door is located on the side of the home.
- The second bath is well situated between public and private zones. The third half-bath is well placed when access is needed from outside.
- The bedroom wing is away from the social areas. This split bedroom plan allows for a more private master suite.
- Closets are well placed.
- The bar in the great room is handy for quick snacks. The separate dining room invites more formal meals.
- The bonus room serves the needs of larger families, or may double as an office.

T, U, and H Plans

The T, U, and H plans allow additional space extensions, with advantages including more variety in room arrangement, easy

PLAYROOM
14 X 12

PORCH

BRKFST
9 X 9

PORCH

UP   MUDRM

FAMILY
21 X 15

KITCHEN
14 X 11

MECH

UP

GARAGE
21 X 26

LIVING
14 X 15

ENTRY

DINING
14 X 16

PORCH

MAIN LEVEL

MASTER
BEDROOM
16 X 21

DRESSING

BATH

CLOS CLOS

DN

HALL

DN

BEDROOM
12 X 12

BATH

LDRY
W D

BEDROOM
14 X 13

BATH

BEDROOM
14 X 13

BEDROOM
12 X 12

UPPER LEVEL

Figure 7.28 *A well-designed multistory home with five bedrooms. (Architect/Designer: Cooper Johnson Smith Architects.)*

Figure 7.29 *A well-designed L-shaped plan gains character from a columned foyer. (Plan #/367 ©1994, Donald A. Gardner Architects, Inc.)*

master
bath

skylights

MASTER
BED RM.
14-0 x 17-4

walk-in
closet

PORCH

w d

UTIL.

pd.
rm.

stor.

BRKFST.
11-4 x 8-8

up

64-2

attic storage

BONUS RM.
23-2 x 19-0

down

BED RM.
11-4 x 11-0

GREAT RM.
15-4 x 18-6
(cathedral ceiling)

fireplace

KIT.
11-4 x
12-10

GARAGE
23-2 x 22-8

cl

lin.

bath

BED RM.
13-8 x 11-8

cl

FOYER
7-4 x
11-8

cl

DINING
14-8 x 11-8

PORCH

FLOOR PLAN

64-7

©1994 Donald A. Gardner Architects, Inc.

PLAN NO. 367

192

Figure 7.30 *A well-designed U-shaped plan with a split bedroom arrangement is similar to Figure 7.29, but has a more varied floor plan. (Plan #/339 ©1994, Donald A. Gardner Architects, Inc.)*

separation of noisy and quiet areas, effective traffic lanes, opportunity for more efficient natural lighting and cross-ventilation, and more interesting landscaping possibilities. Disadvantages may include additional costs for heating and cooling; added expenses for foundation, roof, and jogs; and the need for a larger lot to accommodate these shapes. Figure 7.30 illustrates a U-shaped plan with the split bedroom design.

Atrium Plan

The atrium plan (Figure 7.31), with its inner courtyard, was used by the ancient Romans and is common in locations with a pleasant climate. This courtyard can be completely enclosed as the central focus of the entire house or built within

Figure 7.31 *Atrium plan.*

a U shape or to one side. The atrium can be open to the sky or topped with a skylight.

Circular Plan

The circular plan is often considered the least preferable shape because of problems involved with designing in a circle. Its unusual design, however, can provide a unique living dimension when well planned. Figure 7.32 illustrates a well-designed plan based on a portion of a circle.

Attached and Multifamily Plans

Architects are currently designing high-density housing units accommodating a variety of lifestyles and tastes. Main concerns include efficient use of space, noise control, privacy, easy upkeep, security, and energy conservation. Apartment houses, duplexes, garden apartments, clustered condominiums, and townhouses are planned inside much like single detached houses. Floor plans for attached and multifamily housing may vary from large, two-level multiroom units to compact one-room arrangements.

The one-bedroom unit in Figure 7.33 illustrates a well-arranged space that is convenient for a couple or for a single person. In a *tandem arrangement* the individual units can be placed side by side or one behind the other.

A Poorly Arranged Floor Plan

Figure 7.34 illustrates a poorly arranged plan that includes the following undesirable features:

- Lack of an entranceway makes the living room a major traffic lane
- Poorly located front door causes traffic-pattern problems and prevents a private conversation area around the fireplace

Figure 7.32 *The sweeping arrangement of these interior spaces gives fluidity and movement to the interior. Curvilinear design features are repeated in chair backs, bathroom cabinets, and ceiling details. (Architect: The Steinberg Group. Designer: Brukoff Design Associates. Photograph by Richard Barnes.)*

0 5 10 15 20 25

Figure 7.32 *Continued*

Figure 7.33 *One-bedroom unit.*

- No privacy in eating areas
- Inconvenient placement of garage makes transporting groceries a chore
- Necessity of crossing through a bedroom to reach three-quarter bath from kitchen
- Uneconomical placement of plumbing
- Inconvenient location of washer and dryer in kitchen
- Window size and placement undesirable; window in small corner bedroom abutting the wall; windows in living room too small, providing inadequate light
- Noisy and quiet areas not adequately separated
- Private informal living space ignored; for example, television set would have to be placed in living room

A Well-Arranged Floor Plan

The well-arranged plan in Figure 7.35, although expensive because of numerous shapes, angles, and jogs, meets many requirements for a successful and livable residential space. Some positive advantages of this plan include the following:

- Well-defined and spacious public (both formal and informal) zones and private zones
- Creative and unusual arrangement of space to meet individual needs of occupants with the use of both open and closed planning
- Well-placed and convenient wall space and openings; adequate space for required furnishings
- Well-arranged traffic patterns; easy access to outdoors from social zones; spacious hallways throughout; large entry area
- Garage conveniently located to the kitchen; garage doors face away from the street side

Analyzing Commercial Floor Plans

Like residential floor plans, different styles of commercial office buildings meet clients' needs in varying ways. Although a detailed analysis of building styles is beyond the scope of this text, the beginning designer should be familiar with the following basic building options.

Figure 7.34 *A poorly arranged floor plan.*

Stand-Alone Building

- Provides client with opportunity to design and own the building to meet a specific need.

Strip Shopping Center

- Spaces are leased from an owner who usually takes care of maintenance and utilities.
- Allows drop-by customers easy access.

Mall Location

- Benefits are the same as above, but encourages even more drop-by customers.
- Owner may find that the design and operating hours are restrictive.

Multistoried Building

- Clients may occupy a partial floor, an entire floor, or several floors within the building.
- Restroom facilities are centrally located and maintained by others.
- Cleaning services may be provided by the owner of the building.
- Exterior building design may add prestige to the firm. Buildings may have multifaceted walls that allow for many corner offices. Curved and angled walls add interest and style to the interior.

In the accompanying design scenario, the client is considering relocating to a multistory, historic building. The client's floor plan will be developed from programming information. As part of the design process, the information will be gathered, the facts analyzed, and several ideas and plans will be generated from this information. Once a solution has been selected, a final plan will be developed.

Figure 7.35 *A spacious and well-arranged two-story plan. (Courtesy: L & T Design, Orem, Utah. Architect: Gordon Jacobsen.)*

Summary

Analyzing furnishing options, grouping them into areas, and synthesizing those areas into zones begins the space planning process. Sketching and resketching various options is the essence of analyzing space usage that eventually leads to the design of the *volume* of space. Figure 7.36 graphically illustrates this process.

Designers are fluent in the use of space and understand the relationship of space to volume. Space planning is similar to putting together a puzzle; however, there is no predetermined solution. Designers create the solution to fit the design parameters unique to each client.

Figure 7.36 *In the space planning process furnishings are analyzed based on the client's needs. The furnishings are grouped together in specific activity areas, allowing for ample passageways. Activity areas are then analyzed and grouped together in rooms. Through the use of the design process and the elements and principles of design the volume of space is composed.*

DESIGN SCENARIO COMMERCIAL REAL ESTATE OFFICE

A commercial real estate firm is relocating. The firm, specializing in historic properties, has found tenant space in a 1915 structure (Figure DS7.1). The designer was hired to analyze whether the space would meet the firm's needs. After meeting with the client and visiting the site, the designer gathered the following programming requirements:

Reception Area

- Needs secretary/reception desk with room for computer/printer, typewriter, and 200 linear inches for filing/telephone and typewriter
- Needs room for four guest chairs
- Receptionist must be able to receive guests and guests should not see the workings of the office when seated
- Receptionist must work closely with president

President/Marketing Representative

- Needs desk, credenza, and two other chairs for seating
- Needs some bookshelves and wants a window

Three Assistant Marketing Representatives

- Need office space for desk, credenza, and two other chairs for seating
- Need some bookshelves and window exposure

Conference Room

- Needs comfortable seating for six
- Needs display area to show presentation boards and facility to show slides and videos of real estate

Supply Room/Breakroom

- Needs access to deliveries, copy machine, small refrigerator, counter for postage machine

Figure DS7.1 *Proposed tenant space.*

Figure DS7.2 *Spatial needs assessment.*

- Needs cabinets for storage of paper and stationery supplies, coffee, etc.
- Needs to be close to receptionist

To analyze the information, the designer produced the spatial needs assessment as noted in Figure DS7.2. The designer informed the client that the space would be very tight.

Because the firm was new and had only three employees (but planned to add two more assistant marketing representatives), the owner requested further analysis of space planning options. In order to understand spatial relationships further, the designer developed a compatibility matrix and also studied the relationships between individual areas through the use of a bubble diagram (Figures DS7.3 and DS7.4).

Based on the synthesis of these facts, the designer then created blocking options A and B (Figures DS7.5 and DS7.6). From these blocking diagrams, rough floor plans were developed defining potential walls for options A and B (Figures DS7.7–DS7.12).

The best solution was selected. The final presentation plan, Figure DS7.13, utilized the development of option B.

Figure DS7.3 *Compatibility matrix.*

Figure DS7.4 *Bubble diagram.*

Figure DS7.5
Blocking diagram option A.

Figure DS7.6
Blocking diagram option B.

Figure DS7.7 *Option B: Step 1.*

Figure DS7.8
Option A: Step 1

Figure DS7.9
Option A: Step 2

Figure DS7.10   *Option A: Step 3*

Figure DS7.11
Option A: Step 4

Figure DS7.12   *Option B: Step 2.*

Figure DS7.13   *Final presentation drawing.*

PART V

Furnishings, Fabrics, and Background Elements

Figure V.1 *Designers created an "18th-century, membership only" atmosphere in the Sheraton Russell Hotel, Manhattan. The exquisite wood paneling, fringed pillows, and fine rugs contribute to the living room's exclusive ambiance. (Interior by Brennan Beer Gorman Monk/Interiors. Photograph by Jim Raycroft and Anthony P. Albarello.)*

Part V encompasses five chapters that review the options available in furniture, accessory, and textile selection as well as the material and finish options available for floors, ceilings, and walls. The final chapter elaborates on door, window, and fireplace options. In all interiors, these varied components must work together to create a harmonious, unified environment and to set the mood for the room (Figure V.1).

As was discussed in Part II, "Design Fundamentals," the goals of design include *function and the human factor, aesthetics,* and *economics and ecology.* Designers have the same goals when selecting furnishings, fabrics, and background elements.

Function

The interior materials and components in an environment must meet the functional needs of the space. The functional needs of the space are intermingled with the *human factor, durability, safety,* and *acoustics.*

The Human Factor

In the selection of all interior materials, designers must be aware of the client's needs in order to meet the goal of the human factor. Different individuals require different furnishings to complete the same task. Meeting the needs of the specific individual is particularly important when selecting

Figure V.2 *Quality Steelcase products were used to furnish this open office. Special attention was given to employees' ergonomic needs. (Designer: Steelcase, Inc. Courtesy of Steelcase, Inc.)*

furniture. Like clothing, what fits one client does not necessarily work with the next. In furniture, one size does not fit all. Designers must pay special attention to the ergonomic needs of the client (see Part IV, "Space").

For example, elderly clients may require chairs with high armrests and firm cushions to make it easy to get up. Younger clients may desire overstuffed sofas for lounging. Commercial office clients may require chairs that can be adjusted to suit various employees (Figure V.2). Suitable furniture may be required to meet the functional needs of users who are physically challenged.

Durability

Products selected must be durable; this is particularly important for flooring. White carpet may look great in a master bedroom suite, but would be a disaster in a reception area, for example.

Equally important is the durability of wall finishes and fabrics. Washable wallcoverings, for instance, are critically important in public corridors, but may not be as important in a library. Fabrics must also meet cleaning and durability requirements.

Furniture must withstand expected wear and tear. Residential dining room chairs may look good in a commercial conference room, but without proper bracing, they will quickly begin to fall apart. File cabinets that may be appropriate for occasional residential office filing will not withstand the rigors of an accounting office.

Safety

Products must also meet safety and fire regulations. Designers must consider regulations relating to flame resistance, slip resistance, and accessibility in order to meet functional requirements.

Acoustics

Textiles, wallcoverings, and floor coverings greatly affect the acoustics of an interior environment. These materials serve as a transition, softening the edges (both physically and visually) from the hard architectural elements. Proper selection is particularly relevant in restaurant design, where the noise from clattering dishes in the kitchen is not desirable in the dining room (Figure V.3). Other areas of concern include private offices, studies, libraries, classrooms, and conference areas.

Theatres and recital halls require a collaborative effort with acoustical engineers.

Aesthetics

The selection of the furnishings, fabrics, and background materials must be in line with the basic principles and elements of design; however, the client's personal preferences also must be considered. Just as the function of the room conformed to the human factor, so must the aesthetics. Client preferences are particularly important in residential design. The designer must not only listen to the client's requests but also observe the client, ideally in his or her personal surroundings (Figure V.4).

The color, texture, and feel of the finishes and materials help to define the character of the space. Each component of the design needs to support the overall theme and architectural background of the space. As discussed in Chapter 1, designers develop a discerning eye through careful observation and experience.

Economics

The value of a particular furnishing, fabric, or background element must

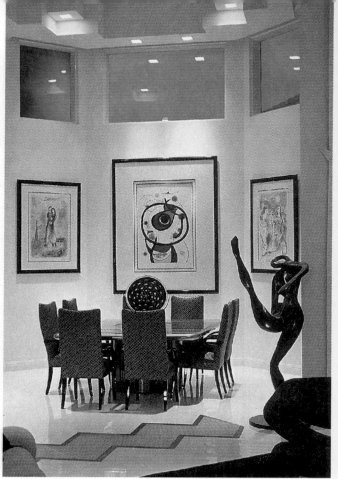

Figure V.3 *Unique torchères and custom ironwork add warmth and vibrant character in this restaurant. Suspended accent lighting focuses on a series of botanicals. Control of unwanted noise is critical in this upscale environment. (Architects/Designers: Engstrom Design Group and To Design. Photograph by Andrew Kramer AIA.)*

Figure V.4 *The designers worked very closely with the clients to create a dining space encircled by art. The custom glass inset flooring makes a visual delineation between the dining room and the living room (Figure 8.1 shows the adjoining living room). (Designer: Stevenson Design Group. Photograph by Robert Brantley.)*

be considered in respect to the *quality, cost,* and *ecological nature* of the product.

Quality

How a piece of furniture (or any other architectural component) is made and the quality of the materials used are of vital concern to both the designer and the end user. The quality of construction, materials, and finishes varies, and designers often depend on the integrity of the manufacturer and the word of a salesperson. A good manufacturer takes great pride in the skilled workmanship

that goes into the product because the company's reputation depends on it.

Cost

The client's budget is a necessary consideration when planning and furnishing a space. The cost of the furnishings must be in line with the budget allocation. Almost all design projects have a certain spending limit that must be respected.

In addition to the initial cost, the costs over the life of the product (lifecycle costing) must be considered: the cost of maintenance, repairs, and re-

placement parts. Fine quality and good design are always wise investments and, if carefully selected, can be obtained at reasonable cost.

Ecology

The designer is also responsible for encouraging the use of products and materials that do not harm the environment or create health hazards through the emission of toxic fumes. See the special sections on green design in the following chapters on furniture and accessories, textiles, and backgrounds.

8

Furniture and Accessories

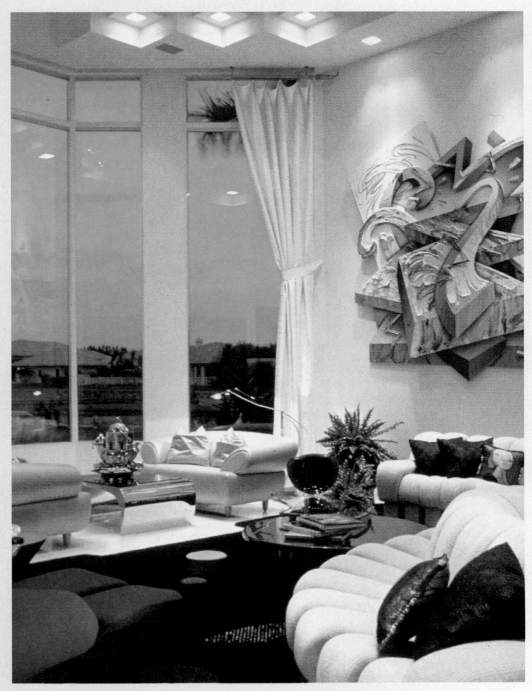

Figure 8.1 *In this vibrant contemporary living room, the designers carefully placed the art to visually pull the room together. Note the accent pillows and custom rug design. (Designer: Stevenson Design Group. Photograph by Robert Brantley.)*

FURNITURE

Selecting furniture for residential and commercial projects is a major responsibility of the designer. Furniture is used to meet a range of human needs in a variety of spaces. Furniture can function as a simple utilitarian item (such as a barstool or bench) or it can serve as an artistic focal point in a room. Accessories and art placed on or around furniture can enhance and complement the furniture selection (Figure 8.1).

Furnishing a space can be a rewarding experience, and furniture can last a lifetime. Careful study and planning enable the designer and client to make wise purchases. This approach requires time and effort but pays long-term dividends. The ability to discriminate between long-lasting and faddish designs is a necessity. Different styles of furniture can be used together providing there is similarity of line, shape, proportion, and so on. Knowledge of the principles and elements of design and understanding of how a fine piece of furniture is made aid in the selection process. A well-designed piece of furniture will always be a quality piece.

Figure 8.2 *This design is inspired by the French rococo and neoclassic styles. The original ceiling was removed to expose a circular attic window. Note the variety of patterns and textures working together. (Designer: Holly Hock Design, Suzanne Rheinstein. Photograph by Tria Giovan. Courtesy of* Southern Accents.*)*

Types of Furniture

Furniture has evolved from pure function to an important art form. By the time of the ancient civilizations of Egypt, Greece, and Rome, furniture was elegantly formed and decorated, satisfying the need for both function and beauty. In later periods, various styles have had lasting influence on following generations. English and French designs are particularly influential in North America (Figure 8.2). Systems furniture, built-ins, and modular units emerged on a grand scale during the 20th century. Figure 8.3 illustrates many furniture types.

Chairs

People use chairs every day for a variety of functions; they are essential pieces of furniture. Materials generally include wood, metal, plastic, leather, and textiles. Sizes range from simple and lightly scaled side chairs to oversized upholstered lounge chairs, with styles from all periods available to suit any taste. Generally, a variety of chair sizes and designs are required within an interior environment. Figures 8.4 through 8.10 show examples of different types of chairs.

Figure 8.3 *Furniture types: Seating pieces and beds; tables, case furniture, desks, and pianos.*

Nested tables

Harvest table

Pedestal table

Tilt-top pedestal

Tier table

Butterfly table

Console

Pembroke

Gateleg

Lamp table

Hutch

Secretary

Breakfront

Armoire

China cabinet

Buffet

Double chest

Chest on chest

Chest of drawers

Four-poster bed

Canopy bed

Ottoman

Grand piano

Console piano

Figure 8.3 *continued*

Figure 8.4 *This Queen Anne "wing chair," so named for the curved half-sides that rise to the height of the high back, originally offered protection from the drafts and chills of poorly heated rooms. The arms are made up of two scrolls, one vertical and one horizontal, which meet to outline a graceful flat C-shaped scroll. (Courtesy of Kindel.)*

Figure 8.5 *This reproduction of a Philadelphia Chippendale side chair, originally made between 1760 and 1780, features heavily carved acanthus leaf clusters with cabriole front legs that terminate in claw-and-ball feet. (Courtesy of Kindel.)*

Figure 8.6 *Charles and Ray Eames experimented with various wood forms. The Eames® DCW chair (1943–1953) is an early example of a molded plywood chair design. (Courtesy; Herman Miller, Inc. archives.)*

Figure 8.7 *This lounge chair by Loewenstein, called the "Royale," is upholstered in fine, tight-fitting leather. The chair is appropriate in commercial office lobbies, lounges, and contemporary residences. (Courtesy of Loewenstein.)*

Figure 8.8 *The Seconda armchair (1982), designed by Swiss architect Mario Botta, is constructed of perforated sheet metal with a backrest of polyurethane. (Courtesy of ICF.)*

Figure 8.9 *This ergonomic desk chair, called Aeron, is designed to support the lower lumbar region or the user's back. Adjustable arms, seat, and back, along with a variety of sizes, provide personalized comfort for the user. (Photograph by Nick Merrick/Hedrich Blessing. Courtesy of Herman Miller, Inc.)*

When selecting chairs, consider the following:

- The height, depth, and width should comfortably accommodate the human form.
- An adjustable chair gives flexible service to a variety of users.
- Ergonomic designs, based on extensive anthropometric studies, provide maximum comfort.

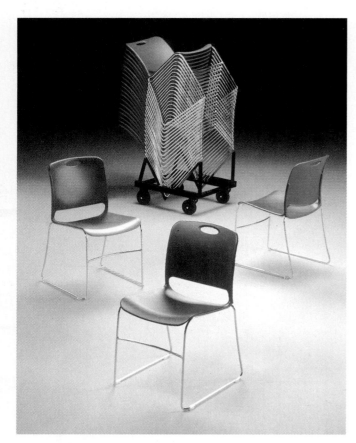

Figure 8.10 *The Maestro by KI is one of many styles of stacking chairs for corporate training areas, auditoriums, and offices. The chairs have polypropylene seats and chrome legs. The stackers allow for ease in storage and mobility. (Courtesy of KI.)*

Figure 8.11 *When Le Corbusier designed the Grand Confort Collection in 1928, he eliminated the traditional construction of an upholstered piece and used a light support of tubular steel with loose cushions. (Courtesy of Cassina USA Inc.)*

Sofas

Sofas are upholstered seating units usually accommodating two or more persons (Figure 8.11). Through the ages particular terms have been associated with certain designs, although many times the terms are used interchangeably.

- The *Lawson* is a type with flat armrests lower than the back support (Figure 8.12).
- The *chaise lounge* accommodates one person and is a cross between a sofa and a chair plus ottoman.
- The *tuxedo* is a completely upholstered piece with armrests the same height as the back (Figure 8.13).
- The *chesterfield* is a large, tufted, upholstered sofa with upholstered ends and no exposed wood.
- The *divan,* a low sofa without arms or back, is derived from stacked rugs used in Turkey for seating. It is commonly placed against the wall and piled with cushions.
- The *love seat* is a smaller sofa for seating two persons.
- The *settee,* also generally for two people, is a lightly scaled piece, often with some upholstered sections (Figure 8.14).
- *Settles,* completely constructed of wood with very high backs, originally were used in early American homes to retain heat from fireplaces.
- *Davenport* is an old term for a sofa that converts into a bed. It originally referred to a small writing desk named after its designer.
- *Modular* and *sectional* sofas consist of several units placed side by side to form one large sofa unit.

Sofas, like chairs, should be selected to comfortably accommodate the user. Care should be taken to ensure the stiffness of the seat is appropriate for the intended use. For example, an elder care center would require firm furniture seats with high arms to assist patients in standing up. An environment for individuals using wheelchairs might include a firm sofa without arms to allow a person to transfer easily from the wheelchair to the sofa.

Figure 8.12 *Lawson arm sofas.*

Figure 8.13 *Tuxedo arm sofas.*

Tables

Tables, like sofas, come in many forms, including dining and kitchen tables, coffee tables, end or occasional tables (Figure 8.15), game tables, and sofa tables. All tables should be sturdy and of appropriate size and height. Dining, kitchen, and game tables are usually 29″–30″H (Figure 8.16). End tables should match the height of the arm of the sofa as closely as possible (Figure 8.17). Sofa tables should match the height of the back of the sofa. Coffee tables are about the same height as the seat cushions on a sofa.

Desks and Credenzas

Desks, credenzas, and associated computer furniture are particularly important because of the surge in home offices and the increased understanding of the importance of ergonomic furniture. A desk is a combination of a storage unit and a table. Typically desks are 29″–30″H. Desks (as discussed in Chapter 6) are available in a variety of sizes; however, the most common is 30″W × 60″L. Some desks are accompanied by left- or right-hand return. Returns are approximately 20″D and 30″–42″L. Like credenzas, they commonly house computer equipment. Credenzas are thinner than desks, but usually the same length, commonly 20″W × 60″L.

Desks and credenzas with articulating keyboard trays are especially beneficial to the user's comfort (Figure 8.18). Ideally the tray is at the same height as the bent elbow when the person is seated at the computer. Keyboard trays, however, should be adjustable.

Desk drawers should vary in size. There should be a drawer to accommodate hanging file folders; at least one shallow drawer for pencils, paper clips, and other office

Figure 8.14 *"Old Hickory" settee, used in historic lodges since the early 1900s. (Courtesy of Old Hickory Furniture Company. As seen in:* Fine Furniture International.*)*

Figure 8.15 *This occasional table, the "Vector" from Carolina Business Furniture, is available in wood or metal. The pinwheel top defines its distinctive character. (Courtesy of Carolina Business Furniture.)*

Figure 8.16 *This comfortable deck furniture is designed to endure harsh weather elements while folding to allow for portability. Tables are available in a variety of sizes. (Courtesy of Smith & Hawken.)*

Figure 8.17 *This custom-designed table cleverly meets the needs of the high-armed sofa and the armless side chair. (Designer: Gandy/Peace Inc. Photograph by Chris A. Little.)*

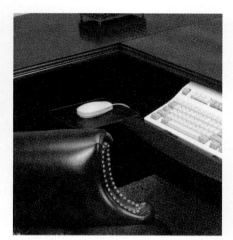

Figure 8.18 *Reception area desk, return, and credenza unit. The unit also has a transaction top. Also shown is the retractable keyboard tray. (Courtesy of Inwood Office Furniture.)*

Figure 8.19 *A modern casepiece, Sideboard 2, designed by Charles Rennie Mackintosh at the beginning of the 20th century, was put in production in 1974. The piece, made of ebonized wood and contrasted with pearlized and stained glass, can be used for a variety of functions. (Courtesy of Cassina USA Inc.)*

supplies; and a medium-depth drawer appropriate for storing stationery, computer disks, and CD-ROMs. Desks also may contain grommets that conceal channels for routing computer cables, telephone wires, and electrical cords. Custom desks may be designed to meet a specific user's needs.

Storage

Many innovative pieces designed for functional storage are available. Built-in systems house stereos, televisions, and VCRs. Chests, cupboards, hutches, secretaries, china cabinets, shelves, armoires, and filing systems provide convenient and efficient storage (Figures 8.19 and 8.20).

Beds

A bed may be built-in or freestanding. It may serve dual purposes, such as a day bed or convertible sofa. Different styles include four-poster beds (Figure 8.21), Murphy beds (a type of bed that folds down from the wall), trundle beds (a bed that pulls out from under another bed), bunk beds, and waterbeds.

Built-In Wall Units

Built-in furnishings may function as seating, tables, beds, and storage space and are integrated with wall construction. Built-in units have the advantage of providing architectural unity and a more spacious feeling (Figure 8.22); a disadvantage is the inability to move the components.

Figure 8.20 *Dakota Jackson, New York furniture designer, created these unique storage units called the Nuevo Tango Series. (Courtesy of and design by Dakota Jackson.)*

Figure 8.22 *A built-in work counter was developed for this office suite. The maple and cherry woods are accented by rich black stone. Notice that wires, paper, and files are concealed. (Architect/Designer: Leers, Weinzapfel Associates. Photograph by Chuck Chói.)*

Systems Furniture

Systems furniture are modular pieces used for office design projects. They consist of work surfaces, storage units, and vertical panels that make up a workstation (these may be private, semiprivate, or a combination of the two). These flexible pieces can be set up in a variety of configurations to fit the space available. They serve the needs of executive, management, secretarial, clerical, and word processing workstations (Figures 8.23 and 9.14).

General Classifications of Furniture Styles

Furniture styles typically are referred to as traditional or contemporary; however, designers should be familiar with the following terms:

- **Antique**—A piece of furniture or work of art that, according to United States law, must be at least 100 years old.
- **Reproduction**—A copy of an original period piece. Some reproductions are made so meticulously that

Figure 8.21 *A four-poster bed of brushed metal is the central focus of the eclectic master suite in designer Montie Simmon's home. Sheer Fabrics hung at the corners soften the effect. (Photograph by Pam Singleton.)*

Figure 8.23 *This contemporary office space illustrates the use of open office systems furniture. Wires are concealed in the system's walls. Fabric-covered insulating wall panels are available in a variety of options. Task lighting is concealed below overhead storage bins. (Photograph by Nick Merrick/Hedrich Blessing. Courtesy of Herman Miller, Inc.)*

only the well-trained eye can detect the difference; other modern reproductions are far from exact copies.

- **Adaptation**—A piece in which some elements from the original have been adapted into a new design.
- **Period style**—A term used to designate a single item or a complete interior, including the architectural background, furniture, and decorative arts prevalent in a specific country or a particular time in history. This type is often referred to as traditional.
- **Contemporary style**—A term referring to designs that to some degree have been adapted from historical or modern influences. Usually considered a clean and elegant 20th-century design.
- **Modern style**—Any time in history when a new art form emerges, breaking ties with previous design forms—whether in music, architecture, or furniture—it is referred to as modern.

Quality and Craftsmanship

The quality of construction and craftsmanship of a piece of furniture help to define the value of the item. Designers need to understand the nature of furniture construction in order to purchase wisely for clients. Some construction features to look for:

- Furniture should be well proportioned and comfortable. Sit on a chair or sofa to test its comfort. Check the depth of the seat and height of the back and arms. If a chair is being chosen for a particular person, have that person try it out.
- A fine-quality finish is smooth and evenly applied, with no spotting, sticky areas, running, or buildup of coats. Good wood furniture has the look of a fine **patina** (a mellow, refined appearance) resulting from much rubbing, a practice requiring time and effort and therefore adding to the cost.
- Back panels should be recessed and smoothly finished.

Figure 8.24 *Inner characteristics of furniture determine durability: selected hardwoods; mortise and tenon joints; heavy-duty center drawer guides; drawers dovetailed front and back; durable dust panels between drawers; durable drawer bottoms held in grooves; strong casebacks recessed into ends; well-mounted top and sides; drawer interiors sanded and sealed.*

- Movable parts like drawers and door panels must be durable and easily operated (Figure 8.24). Drawer runners are best when made of metal, plastic, or durable hardwood. Well-made drawers have solid sides, three-ply nonwarp bottoms that are sanded and sealed against snags, and dovetail joints, and are separated by dust barriers. All drawers should have drawer stops to prevent the drawer from being completely pulled out.
- Hardware, such as drawer pulls and handles, should be securely fastened.
- Furniture with flat areas like tables, cabinets, and desktops should be constructed of durable material to maintain function and appearance. Although some materials are practical, each may have a particular hazard; for example, marble may stain, glass may break, plastic may chip, and hardwood may scratch.
- The edges of tables and other pieces are especially susceptible to damage and wear. Rounded edges, reinforced strips, and edges made of solid hardwood are more practical.

In general, all sections of furniture must be securely joined. The following pages discuss some of the specific materials and methods used in furniture construction.

Wood

Wood is the major material used for furniture construction. Furniture is made from both hard and soft woods. Hardwoods come from deciduous trees (those that drop their leaves), such as oak and maple. Hardwoods are more durable and dent-resistant than softwoods, but because they grow slowly they cost more. Hardwoods are generally more attractive than softwoods and often are preferred for fine furniture. Softwoods come from coniferous trees (those with needles that are mostly green year round), such as pine and spruce. Softwoods are used for less expensive furniture and in combination with hardwoods.

The woods most widely used in furniture construction are pine, birch, maple, oak, cherry, walnut, mahogany, beech, pecan, and teak. Labels describing the finish such as "fruit wood finish" or "walnut finish" refer to the color only, not to the species of wood used. Each wood has its own special properties. Wood selected for a particular furniture piece should be properly dried, well suited for its intended construction, purpose, finish, size and style, and resistant to warping, splitting, swelling, and shrinking. Table 8.1 lists the most common woods and their uses.

Solid Wood and Veneers

Solid wood refers to the parts of the piece of furniture made from one piece of wood, such as legs in chairs or tables, the frames, and trim. A **veneer** is a thin layer of finishing wood applied to the body of a less refined wood or a polymer (a material added to wood to strengthen it). Veneers may be cut in different methods that result in characteristic wood grains (Figure 8.25). With advanced methods of cutting and adhering veneers, a piece of veneered furniture can be stronger and more resistant to warping than a solid wood piece. The label *genuine* indicates that all the exposed solid pieces and the veneers are made from the same wood species.

Other Forms of Wood in Furniture

Plywood, commonly used in building construction, is made by laminating together a number of thin layers of wood, with the grain of each layer turned 90°. In furniture design plywood is sometimes used on the inner core of veneers.

Particleboard (also known as fiberboard, chipboard, or composite board) is made by combining chips of wood with resin and compressing the mixture to form a larger piece of wood. Because high-quality particleboard does not warp as easily as plywood, it is commonly used as a base in veneer furniture construction.

Hardboard, also made of compressed wood, is commonly used in the bottoms of drawers, dust panels, and on furniture backs. It is thinner than particleboard and gives the appearance of a thin sheet of solid wood.

Bentwood is made by placing thin strips of wood under pressure and softening them with steam to fit around molds. Michael Thonet's bentwood chairs, developed in the 1800s, remain popular (see page 44).

Construction Methods

The quality and type of wood joining indicate the durability and aesthetic appeal of a piece of furniture. The most common construction methods for joining wood follow (also refer to Figure 8.26):

- **Mortise and tenon:** The mortise (hole) joins with a piece that has a projecting piece (tenon). This forms a strong joint used particularly where arms and legs join the frame.
- **Dowel:** Rounded dowels (pegs) are joined and glued into corresponding holes. The strength of this design relies on the strength of the dowel.
- **Miter:** Edges are cut at a 45° angle and must have a supportive strip straddling the joint to be strong.

Table 8.1 *Most Common Wood Types*

Wood Type	Characteristics	Uses in Home
Acacia	Hardwood. Light brown.	Furniture. Woodwork. Often used for religious decorations.
Alder	A light, weak wood. White to light browns.	Furniture. Framing for construction.
Ash	A blond hardwood. Texture resembles oak. Relatively inexpensive.	Cabinetry and furniture. Furniture framing. Flooring.
Bamboo	A tropical tubular woody plant with a raised joint.	Asian-style furniture. Decorative accessories.
Beech	A blond hardwood. Fine-grain texture. Strong.	Informal furniture. Popular in Scandinavia. Flooring.
Birch	Subtle wavy grain. Hard and durable. Takes stain well, or beautiful in natural finish.	Furniture. Popular in Scandinavia. Flooring, doors, and cabinetry. Furniture framing.
Cedar*	Reddish-brown, often with yellow streaks. Soft. Lightweight. Strong odor. Moth repellent.	Closet lining, chests. Informal furniture. Shingles. Siding. Paneling.
Cherry	Reddish-brown hardwood. Resembles mahogany. Durable. Strong.	Used in small quantities. Inlay and marquetry work. Popular for early American furniture.
Cypress	Color varies from light yellow to darkish-brown. Soft. Warp resistant. Inexpensive. Weathers silver gray.	Particularly used as a finish wood. Outside finish work. Doors, shingles, and siding. Some informal furniture.
Ebony*	Exquisite dark heartwood with brownish-black streaks. Ebony, sometimes red or green. Hard and heavy.	Modern and Asian furniture. Inlay and marquetry designs.
Elm	Light brown with gray overtones. Takes stain well. Slight undulating grain. Hard and heavy.	Particularly used for veneers. Furniture. Interior finish work. Furniture framing.
Fir*	Strong and durable. Wavy grain. Takes stain well. Resembles pine.	Plywood and laminated sheets. Cabinetry. Trim pieces. Inexpensive furniture.
Gum	Reddish-brown. Medium hard. Resembles mahogany. Interesting grains.	Veneers. Doors. Interior trim. Furniture parts.
Mahogany*	Reddish or reddish-golden brown with fine grain. Can be beautifully finished.	Fine expensive furniture. Especially popular for Queen Anne, Chippendale, and other 18th-century furniture. Paneling and cabinetwork.
Maple	White to pale yellowish-brown. Fine grain. Hard and heavy. Resembles birch. Relatively inexpensive.	Informal furniture. Popular for early American style. Flooring. Cabinetwork. Furniture framing.
Oak*	White oak is light to golden brown. Red oak has pinkish tones. Straight to strong wavy grain. Hard and durable.	Most important wood for furniture, trim, and cabinetwork. Quarter-sawn (straight grain) usually preferred for fine furniture and paneling.
Pecan	White to reddish brown. Refined grain, often with darkish streaks. Hard, strong, and heavy.	Fine furniture. Furniture parts. Cabinetwork, paneling, and trim.
Pine	Off-white to pale yellow. Soft. Not strong. Lightweight. Inexpensive. Close grain with occasional wavy grain.	Flooring, doors, and trim. Early American or provincial furniture and paneling. Cabinetwork.
Poplar	Off-white to yellowish brown. Softwood. Lightweight. Subtle straight grain. Inexpensive.	Informal furniture. Works well painted. Trim, cabinetwork, and exterior siding. Furniture framing.
Rattan	A jungle vine from Asia. Pale yellow to light brown. Soft and pliable.	Informal furniture with Asian feeling. Can be nicely painted and stained.
Redwood*	Uniform red color. Grays when exposed to weather. Available in large planks.	Exterior finishes. Beams, paneling, etc. Cabinetwork. Outdoor furniture.
Rosewood*	Fine-textured reddish-brown hardwood with black streaks. Beautiful when highly polished.	Popular for fine 18th-century furniture. Inlay designs. Danish modern furniture.
Satinwood*	Pale blond color with smooth satin finish. Unique grain. Expensive.	Fine furniture and finish work. Inlay and parquetry designs.
Teak*	Yellow to reddish-brown with fine black streaks. Strong and durable. Beautiful with oiled finish.	Popularly used for Asian- and Danish-designed furniture. Decorative and functional accessories.
Walnut	Light to dark golden brown. A variety of beautiful grains. Hard, strong, and durable. Expensive.	Used for fine furniture in many styles. Especially used during 18th-century Queen Anne period, called the "Age of Walnut." Paneling.
Yew*	Dark reddish-brown hardwood particularly found in England. Close grained.	Cabinetwork and some furniture.

*Make sure these woods are obtained from companies with sustainable forest practices before specifying.

Figure 8.25 *Veneer cutting patterns.*

Knife

Rotary

Plain slicing

Quarter slicing

Rift cut

- **Dovetail:** Semi-triangular or fan-shaped protrusions fit into notches of the same size and shape. This type of joint secures drawer fronts and sides.
- **Tongue and groove:** The tongue and groove joint is similar to the mortise and tenon but runs the entire length of the joint.
- **Rabbeted or rebated:** One edge has a groove cut the entire width to accommodate a straight-edged piece.
- **Butt:** This type of joint is not used for fine furniture. The joints are merely glued or screwed together. It is sometimes found on inexpensive furniture, but it must have cross-supports or corner blocks to reinforce it.
- **Blocking:** Corner blocks or hidden blocks of wood help to reinforce joints such as those at table or chair legs.

Types of Finishes

Principle types of finishes applied to wood furniture include stain, paint, oil, varnish, shellac, lacquer, and polyurethane (see "Paints and Finishes" in Chapter 11). Special or unusual finishes include stenciling, faux finishes (simulating other materials such as marble and granite), spattering, stippling, glazes, sponging, and hand-painted designs.

Metal

Metal is a common material in furniture construction and can be shaped in many forms. It can be riveted, bolted, or welded, providing great flexibility of design. The most common metals used for furniture construction are aluminum, chrome, iron, and steel.

Aluminum appears in tubes, cast leg frames, and sections of angles and channels. It requires a unique finishing process called anodizing to prevent corrosion. Aluminum is relatively weak in strength.

Chrome or *chromium* is used as a metal finish on furniture. It is characterized by its highly polished sheen, but is also available in a satin finish. Quality chrome plating is difficult to achieve and should be backed by a reputable manufacturer.

Iron, a black metal, is commonly used in outdoor furniture and on railings or grills. "Wrought" iron simply means "worked" iron.

Steel, a combination of iron and carbon, is the most commonly used metal in furniture construction. When formed into sheets, this metal is used in office furniture, cabinetry, shelving, and other products. The *gauge* or thickness of the steel determines its quality. Thin sheets are flimsy, easily dented,

Figure 8.26 *Types of wood joining.*

1. Mortise and tenon   2. Dowel   3. Miter   4. Dovetail

5. Tongue and groove   6. Rabbeted or rebated   7. Butt joint   8. Blocking

and when struck may produce a drumming noise. Quality metal furniture should be able to withstand normal dents and dings. Tubular steel furniture was perfected in the late 1920s through the works of several Bauhaus designers (Figure 8.27).

Steel rusts, and therefore must be finished with paint or be chrome plated. Stainless steel, a combination of steel and chromium, is used in hardware and trim. Other metals used in furniture, such as *brass, copper,* and *tin,* are primarily decorative elements.

Synthetic Materials

Machine-made products for furniture construction have revolutionized the design field. Synthetic materials such as laminates, molded plastics, and acrylics are used for almost all furniture types. Plastic *laminates* are commonly used on cabinet surfaces and writing surfaces. Available in a wide variety of colors, thicknesses, textures, and patterns, plastic laminates are actually sheets of paper laminated together with resin.

Molded plastics such as nylon, vinyl, and polyethylene are only used in small parts in furniture construction (though they are often used in textile design). Fiberglass, a molded plastic mixed with glass fibers, is commonly made into chairs. These durable pieces of furniture can be molded into almost any shape (Figure 8.28). Other lightweight plastics are widely used in institutional and outdoor furniture design. Plastic chairs should be tested for durability and stability, because there are many grades of plastic on the market.

Acrylics such as Lucite and Plexiglas can be either transparent or translucent. They are commonly used for contemporary furnishings or as a safe substitute for glass.

Synthetics are durable and easy to keep clean; however, some synthetics may dull over time, break, or scratch. Some synthetics are flammable and when damaged can rarely be repaired. Because synthetics are mainly petroleum-based, they use up nonrenewable oil resources. Not all synthetics are biodegradable; however, some can be recycled. Synthetics used as upholstery fillers are discussed in the section on upholstered furniture.

Palms and Grasses

Bamboo, rattan, cane, rush, and the materials used in wicker come from natural sources such as palms and grasses. Because of their nature, rattan, wicker, cane, and rush are compatible with an informal setting; in an eclectic formal room, they can add interest to the decor (see Figure 8.14). These materials can be used effectively in both inside and outside spaces.

Bamboo is a grass characterized by woody, hollow stems and ringed joints. It is used in lightweight furniture.

Rattan poles are cut from the rattan palm and can be bent to form a variety of designs. They are mainly used for chairs, tables, and beds.

Cane is split rattan or bamboo that is woven to form a mesh. Cane was introduced into England about 1660. It was used for chair seats and backs and some outdoor tabletops (Figure 8.29).

Rush is tightly twisted long grass (paper is often used as a substitute) made into a cord. The cord is then woven and mainly used for seats and backs of chairs.

Figure 8.27 *The Barcelona chair, couch, and X table, designed by Mies van der Rohe, combine leather and steel. The Barcelona chair has become a classic statement of contemporary design. (Courtesy of Knoll, Inc.)*

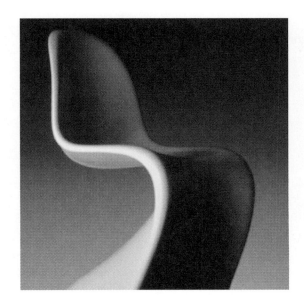

Figure 8.28 *Danish designer Vernor Panton created his classic stacking chair in the 1960s. Now made of polyurethane, this graceful cantilever design is the first example of a single-form molded fiberglass chair (Courtesy of Vitra.)*

Figure 8.29 *Marcel Breuer combined cane with tubular steel for his famous Cesca chair while he was a faculty member at the Bauhaus design school during the 1920s. He was the first designer to use tubular steel for furniture construction. (Courtesy of Thonet Industries, Inc.)*

Wicker (or basketwork) is a *method* of woven chair construction rather than a specific material. Used since ancient times, wicker chairs can be made of rushes, twigs, or reeds.

Upholstered Furniture

People in ancient civilizations first created "upholstered furniture" by stretching textiles, animal skins, or other natural materials over a sturdy frame. Chairs with fabric stretched over seat and back frames are still used for lightweight pieces. During the Renaissance, simple cushions were placed on top of the stretched fabric. Later, fabrics were stretched over those cushions. By the 16th century, padding made of horsehair, feathers, wool, and down made cushions deeper and more comfortable. In the 19th century, springs were introduced and modern upholstered furniture had arrived. After that, little change occurred in upholstery construction until the introduction of synthetics during the 1930s, which had a tremendous impact on the furniture industry. There are two basic types of upholstered furniture: overstuffed (furniture that has padding or stuffing attached over the frame), and partially exposed (furniture that has some exposed frame pieces). The padding or stuffing is covered with a fabric or natural hide, which is referred to as upholstery.

Parts of Upholstered Furniture

Hidden beneath the upholstery are the components that should produce durability, comfort, and quality in upholstered furniture (Figure 8.30). Because these elements are hidden, the designer must rely on the manufacturer's written specifications.

Frame

A frame is constructed of metal, plastic, or kiln-dried hardwood such as maple, poplar, oak, ash, birch, or elm. (Softwoods tend to split.) The wood frame should be firmly assembled and usually joined by double dowels that are spiral grooved and then glued in place. Reinforcement braces of metal or wood should be glued and screwed to the corners. Nails are never used in the frames of good-quality furniture. Frames should be smooth to prevent the fabric sagging.

Figure 8.30 *Upholstery construction.*

Cotton
Burlap
Sinuous wire springs
Fiberfill
Foam
Spring edge construction, single cone coil, prefabricated unit

Figure 8.31 *Single- and double-cone coils.*

Webbing and Felt

Generally made of linen, jute, plastic, or rubber, the webbing is arranged in a basketweave to provide support for the springs and cushions. Good-quality webbing measures 3 to 4 inches in width and is tightly woven with little to no space between the bands. Cotton felt may also be used to protect springs and other materials.

Springs

Springs are constructed of either sinuous wire or coils. The sinuous wire is simpler, and may be more desirable for slim-line modern furniture and lightweight occasional chairs. The cone coil comes in both single and double cone (Figure 8.31). The single-cone coil is a prefabricated all-wire unit. To create a spring cushion, single coils are tied to each other and attached to top and bottom border wires. Double-cone coils are affixed to a resilient base such as strips of webbing or metal and are hand tied at the top to prevent slipping. This construction provides maximum comfort and is used in more expensive deep-seated upholstery. In fine-quality furniture individual coil springs are contained in muslin; however, in most furniture burlap is used to protect and cover springs and prevent the filling from working into the springs.

Filling, Stuffing, and Padding in Cushions

Filling, stuffing, or padding materials of various types and qualities are used for cushioning, either alone or in combination. These materials are listed on the label. The most commonly used fillings include the following:

1. *Polyester* is lightweight, resilient, odorless, and resists mildew and moths. It may be used alone or combined with cores of foam, down, or innersprings. Polyester or fiberfill fillings should be wrapped with fabric (such as muslin) to retain their shape and prevent abrasion on the final covering.
2. *Polyurethane foam* is commonly used and is available in a variety of densities. It is often wrapped with polyester fiberfill to add softness. Polyurethane resists liquids, moths, and mildew and is very resilient.
3. *Down* or *feathers* are used in seat cushions, usually in combination with polyester and a thin foam core for shape. Although historically considered luxurious, 100 percent down is expensive and because it is not resilient, it requires frequent plumping.
4. *Rubberized fibers* (which have less resiliency than the previously mentioned filling materials) are used in moderately priced furniture.
5. *Shredded fibers* from natural sources (such as certain types of leaves) or synthetic felts are generally used in low-priced furniture.
6. *Cotton* is occasionally used for small pieces.

Upholstered cushions may be used on some or all of the construction of the furniture piece. Seat and back cushions and pillows are added to complement the furniture's style, and cushions may be fastened or loose, depending on the style and preferred degree of flexibility. Cushions may also be tufted, a process in which the final covering is securely tied to the inner springs. Tufting is often accented with fabric-covered buttons. Cushioning should be comfortable, resilient, durable, and should stay in place. Three types are shown in Figure 8.32.

Fabrics and Finishing Touches

Upholstery fabric is used to cover the cushions and other parts of the furniture frame as dictated by the style. Guidelines for selecting durable, stylish, and functional upholstery fabrics are discussed in Chapter 9. Finishing touches add character and detail to upholstery pieces. Welts (a cord around the edge of cushions and/or wood trim wrapped

T-shaped cushion   Square cushion   Slip Seat

Figure 8.32 *Types of cushions.*

GREEN DESIGN

Selecting "Green" Furniture

The process of furniture manufacturing, if not carefully undertaken, can harm the environment. When selecting "green" furniture, designers should look for products that utilize lumber from renewable wood resources or select furniture made from recycled materials.

Many furniture companies have strict policies regarding the use of wood from threatened or endangered species of trees, many of which are found in rain forests. In some cases federal and state laws restrict the use of certain woods for furniture construction. Some species, such as maple and oak, are easier to replenish than other rare woods, such as mahogany, teak, and rosewood. Wood species that are endangered but are grown specifically for furniture industries and replenished are often used only as fine thin veneers. These woods may be farmed as plantation-grown lumber or in a sustainable forest. More plentiful wood byproducts, such as particleboard, are used for the veneer backing.

According to *Design Solutions* magazine, the Tropical Forest Foundation is one organization that works to educate consumers and producers about the benefits of conservation and forest management. One of their primary goals is to educate individuals and companies on the benefits of low-impact logging.

Another alternative is to select furniture made from recycled products. For example, HAG, a furniture manufacturing company, has designed the adjustable Scio chair whose seat and back are made of recycled bottle caps (Figure GD8.1). Environmental Furniture Company produces chairs from used automobile tires utilizing fire-retardant padding processed without formaldehyde and dichloro-fluorocarbons.

GD8.1 *The ergonomic Scio chair with seat and back made from recycled plastic bottle caps. (Courtesy of HAG, Inc.)*

Proper selection of green furniture also includes ensuring the items have safe, environmentally friendly finishes. The process of applying paint to furniture can cause the release of toxic volatile organic chemicals, or VOCs, into the air. These solvents are carried into the exhaust stacks and released directly into the atmosphere. VOCs contribute to smog and harm the ozone layer, allowing damaging ultraviolet rays to reach the earth.

The Clean Air Act passed by Congress in 1990 requires companies to reduce these harmful emissions. Some companies have developed alternative painting processes to reduce emissions. At an Interior Design Educators Council conference, Elizabeth Rylan and Gordon Kerby outlined several ways this can be accomplished. For example, paint can be applied to wood as it rides on a conveyor belt, reducing the VOCs emitted into the air; metal furniture can be given an electrical charge and coated with paint of the opposite charge, bonding the two together electrically. Additionally, substituting water-based stains and natural coatings for paint, and using carbon filters can also lessen the release of VOCs.

In order to help protect the environment, designers should ask manufacturers for their policies and statistics on sustainable forestry and about their compliance with the Clean Air Act before specifying their products.

with fabric) can be applied in single or double rows in the same or contrasting fabrics. Cording, a wrapped decorative piece of rope, may also be added in these places. Nail heads (usually brass) give a masculine feel to a piece of furniture. Decorative trims and fringes create interest in a design.

Selecting Quality Upholstered Furniture

In selecting a piece of upholstered furniture, consider the following criteria:

- Precise tailoring is necessary for a well-finished appearance. Seams, welts, and cording should be smooth, straight, and firmly sewn with no loose threads. Hems and pleats should hang evenly.
- Large patterns should be carefully centered and matched on each cushion and skirt.
- All patterns, including those on the sides of the seat cushions, should run in the same direction.
- When fabrics are quilted, smaller stitches prevent snagging.
- Cushions should fit snugly.
- If zippers are used, they must be sewn straight with no puckering, and they must operate easily.
- If a nap is present, it should run in only one direction.
- Fabric should be smoothly stretched over the frame with no buckling.
- Back panels should be firmly and neatly tacked or stitched.
- Exposed wood parts should be of well-finished hardwood.

Labeling

As mentioned previously, federal and state laws require labels providing specific information about the piece to be attached to furnishings. Reputable manufacturers warranty the materials used, and guarantee that the furniture's performance will meet the specifications outlined on the label.

ACCESSORIES

Furniture and accessories work together in defining the style and feeling of a space. Because accessories can do so much to enhance a space, the process of selecting and arranging accessories for both residential and commercial settings deserves thoughtful consideration. Accessories add the finishing touches to a room, reflecting the personal taste and individuality of the user more than any other element. Accessories may have sentimental value to the client and may incorporate personal collections. Accessories can also be a powerful tool in establishing the design theme or expressing a cultural background. Interiors are enriched by the addition of both functional and decorative accessories.

Functional Accessories

Functional accessories serve a utilitarian purpose but may become an interesting display item as well. Some items, such as towel racks, drapery rods, door handles, or accent plumbing fixtures (Figure 8.33), may be attached to the architectural background. Other practical accessories such as a mir-

Figure 8.33 *In this bathroom with a 15' ceiling and a view of the Hawaiian mountains, the designers chose lighting and accessories to complement the clean, contemporary lines of the building. (Architect/Designer: Gensler. Photograph by Marco Lorenzetti/Hedrich Blessing.)*

ror, lamp, clock, or tray may be moved from one place to another within the space.

The purpose or use of the room should be the prime consideration when selecting functional accessories. For example, if lighting is required beside a lounge chair in a living room, choose an appropriate lamp that will meet the needs of the user. Making a list of accessories necessary in each room will help with the successful selection and placement of each item.

Lamps

Lamps, known in the industry as *portable luminaires,* are attractive accessories serving the purpose of providing light when and where needed. Common types of lamps include table lamps, floor lamps, sconces, torchères, and pendants (chandeliers). Lamps are available in a wide range of styles—traditional or modern, decorative or structural. A lighting fixture that is carefully chosen for a specific room, style, mood, location, or purpose can be an important contributing element, as shown in Figure 8.34. (Refer to Chapter 5 for further information on lamps and lighting considerations.)

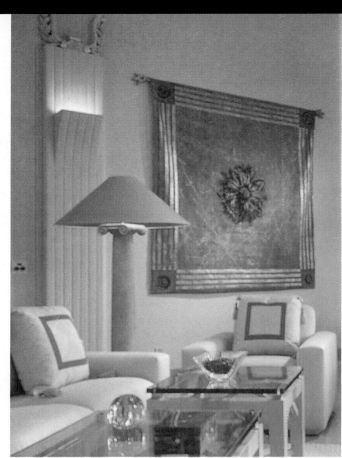

Figure 8.34 *Floor lamps with Ionic scrolls and opaque shades flank the seating areas in this large living space designed by Michael de Santis. Uplighting comes from an unexpected source—tall, fluted pilasters that appear to be peeled open to release the light within. Seating groups angled out from the walls encourage conversation and circulation. (Courtesy of Michael de Santis, ASID, Michael de Santis, Inc. Photograph by Phillip Ennis.)*

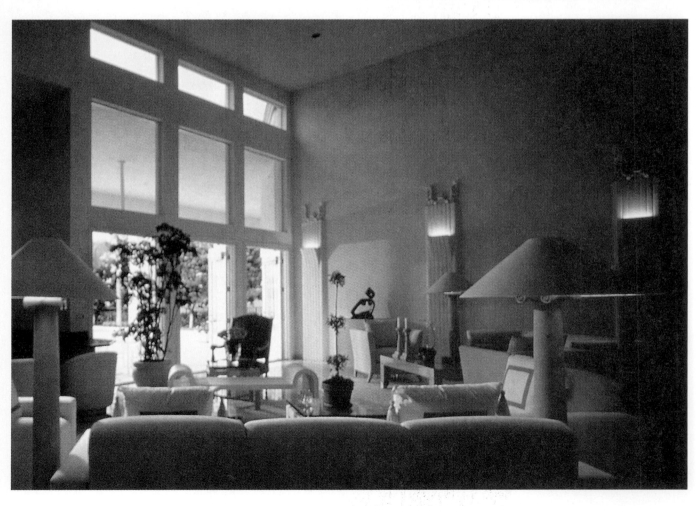

Books

Cicero said, "A room without books is a body without a soul." Books add friendliness to a home. Usually no room has a mood that precludes their use, or a color scheme so complete it could not benefit from their warm tones and textures. Bookshelves can go in almost any room, require little space, and create a warm, friendly atmosphere, as illustrated in Figure V.1. Children need bookshelves in their rooms at a height they can easily reach. Other bedrooms can accommodate shelves where space permits—usually close to the bed for nighttime reading. Kitchens need handy shelves for reference books and cookbooks. Conference rooms benefit from shelves used to display company memorabilia, awards, and reference books. Bookshelves often can be fitted into unused spaces and odd corners. They can also work around or over doors and windows, or as a space divider.

Additionally, books can add a decorative quality to a room with their textures, colors, and shapes. They also mix well with other accessories; for example, a few books flanked with interesting bookends, next to a plant and a small sculpture, or placed on a coffee table with other items add interest to a room (Figure 8.1).

Mirrors

Since the 14th century mirrors have been used as functional and decorative objects in homes and public places. Mirrors are available in almost any size and in frames to fit any decor. Mirrors are a helpful tool for the interior designer; they can add beauty, multiply space, conceal unattractive structural features, distribute and double light, brighten dark areas, and bring life into an otherwise drab room. Because of their myriad uses, mirrors have steadily increased in popularity and now play an indispensable role in all styles of interiors (Figure 8.35).

Clocks

Clocks have long been important accessories in the home and office. From the handsome antique grandfather clock encased in an elegantly carved case to the high-tech clocks of the late 20th century, timepieces not only serve a necessary function but can also add a calming background "tick-tock" sound to any room. Naturally a clock must be placed where it can be seen easily. Outdoors, clocks frequently serve as landmarks in metropolitan settings. In smaller communities the chime of a clock tower helps to define the "sense of place".

Screens

In addition to its decorative value, a screen may serve many functional purposes. Screens can set off an entrance where the front door opens directly into the living area, act as a divider between living and dining areas, close off a kitchen, or set off a private area by making a room within a room. They also can redirect traffic when strategically placed, extend the apparent size of a room by replacing a door, control the flow of air and the direction of light, camouflage an old-fashioned radiator or air conditioning unit, or conceal storage. A decorative screen

Figure 8.35 *This custom-designed table is accentuated by the use of a mirror and floral accessories. The table, designed by Jeffrey Jurasky, ASID, is fabricated from steel and slate. (Designer: Jurasky & Associates. Photograph by Kaminsky Production.)*

can give an architectural quality to a room, enhance the room's decor, provide a backdrop for a furniture grouping, substitute for side drapery, or serve as the room's focal point.

Hardware

A contemporary room can be made strikingly modern and a traditional room can take on an authentic feeling through the discriminating use of small accessories such as doorknockers, doorknobs, switch plates, curtain rods, and tiebacks. Drawer pulls, **escutcheons** (the plate behind the pull), and hinges can give a piece of furniture the feeling of a particular period (see Figure 8.36 and Chapter 12).

Doorknobs   Drawer pulls

Door knockers   Tiebacks

Figure 8.36 *Finishing touches.*

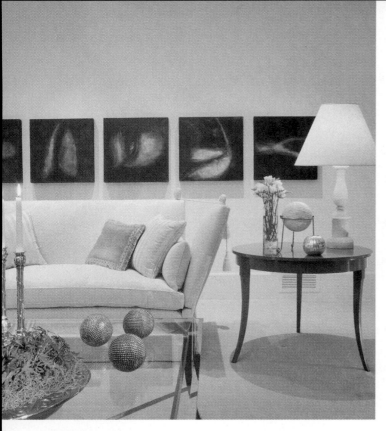

Figure 8.37 *The series of paintings by artist Alice Nesbitts complements the fine fabric on the racket-arm sofa. Accessories add texture and sparkle to the room. (Designer: Gandy/Peace, Inc. Photograph by Chris A. Little. Courtesy of* Southern Accents.*)*

Decorative Accessories

Decorative accessories generally provide no other value than the pleasure derived from looking at them. Decorative items abound in furniture and antique stores, galleries, design studios, art and craft exhibitions or shows, and numerous other sources. Accessories are available in traditional or contemporary styles and may be handcrafted or machine-made, old or new.

Following is an outline of the basic accessories that complete a room and give it an attractive, desirable, lived-in feeling.

Art

In residential design paintings, drawings, original prints, photographs, sculpture, and other types of art are usually selected personally by the client. Corporate art collections are usually selected by a professional curator. Designers should be aware of the following types of art and related terms in order to assist clients with their personal selection or to work effectively with a curator.

Paintings, Drawings, Prints, and Photographs

Original *paintings* in oil, acrylic, watercolor, or tempera are usually the most expensive type of art. They range from the works of famous painters to those of local artists, as shown in Figure 8.37.

Original *drawings* are usually executed in ink, charcoal, pencil, pastels, or crayon.

Original *prints* such as etchings, lithographs, woodcuts, steel engravings, and drypoints are *not* photographic copies. They are designed by an artist and usually produced by her or under her supervision. Limited edition prints are numbered and signed by the artist. A piece numbered 27/100 for example, is the twenty-seventh of a total of 100 prints made. The fewer prints produced, the rarer the piece. Limited prints are usually less expensive than one-of-a-kind paintings and drawings.

Posters, originally called "poor man's art," are available at minimal cost. They are usually considered a low-budget accessory but are often seen framed in fine contemporary settings. Photographic reproductions of original paintings, drawings, or prints are also inexpensive and widely available. Some early posters are now collector's items.

Family or artistic *photographs* personalize a space.

Frames and Mats

Frames and mats are most effective when they do not detract from the work but complement the medium, colors, and subject. The frame and mat should work with the style and architectural background elements. The size, line, and form of the frame should not overpower the art but enhance the overall composition. *Slip molds,* small gold inserts, are frequently used when a little sparkle is required between the frame and mat, or between mats.

A mat usually complements drawings, etchings, watercolors, and prints of all types. Oil paintings are seldom matted, but may have a liner made from linen, velvet, or leather. Mats protect original art from direct contact with the glass, where condensation can occur when the temperature changes. Quality mats are acid-free, protecting the displayed work from discoloration and serious damage.

Glass is usually used over prints, watercolors, and etchings but is almost never used over an oil painting. Regular glass, nonglare glass, and acrylic are available. Nonglare glass tends to give a clouded appearance but does cut down on reflections. Acrylic works well in environments where broken glass could be highly dangerous. Glass may also be purchased with built-in ultraviolet light protection to preserve colors in original and poster art.

Sculpture

Three-dimensional works of art can be treasured accessories in residential or commercial settings (Figure V.4). Sculpture is fashioned in many media, including metals, marble and other stone, wood, glass, and ceramics. Placement often depends on the size of the piece. If small, the piece may be best displayed on a shelf, mantel, or tabletop. If the sculpture is large, it can dominate an area or provide a focal point. A pedestal may be used for either a small or large sculpture to give it greater prominence. Lighting that spotlights the art but does not wash it away adds visual interest.

Other Types of Art and Crafts

Ceramics are accessories made of clay and include sculpture, dishes, bowls, platters, pots, and tiles. Clay ranges from

Figure 8.38 *This ceramic sculptural vase,* Perianth, *was created using the process called raku. Originally used in Japan in the 16th century for ritualistic tea ceremonies, today raku refers to clay pieces fired rapidly and cooled quickly, often by immersion in cold water. The vessel stands 30" high and would serve as an excellent focal point or accent piece in an interior. (Artist: Mary Jane Taylor. Photograph by Light Sources, Inc.)*

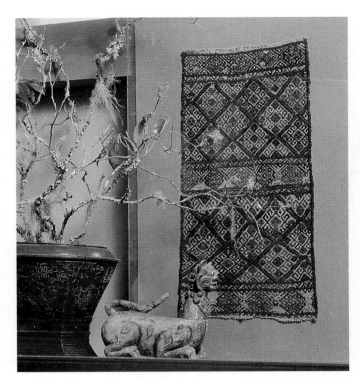

Figure 8.39 *This exquisite weaving protected by Plexiglas complements an antique dragon on a rustic glass cabinet. The textures and form enhance a Thai-influenced interior. (Designer: Jerry Pair. Photograph by Peter Vitale. Courtesy of Veranda.)*

coarse to fine and comes in a wide variety of colors. The artisan may create a unique ceramic piece by applying different types of ornamentation, colors, textures, and shapes (Figure 8.38). Ceramics fall into four basic categories—porcelain, china, earthenware, and stoneware.

A *mosaic* is made up of small, usually square pieces (called tesserae) of ceramic, stone, or glass arranged in an artistic design and set in cement. Used for floors and murals in ancient times, mosaics currently are used for a variety of small decorative objects including trays, boxes, and small tables.

Glass art accessories include vases, dishes, bowls, and sculpture. Glass can be etched, colored, enameled, pressed, gilded, cut, and engraved. Hand-blown glass has been a popular art for centuries, and exquisite pieces from many countries, each with their own design approach, have been widely appreciated in America. Modern designs have been pioneered most notably by Italian and Scandinavian artists, who fashion beautiful and unique pieces.

Stained glass, an artistic composition of small pieces of colored glass held together by lead, has also been known through the ages, particularly during the medieval period when stained glass was used to create extraordinary windows in Gothic cathedrals. Stained glass can be made into window and door panels, hung at a window, or designed as a freestanding piece of art.

Weaving and *textile art* has been known for centuries in almost every country of the world, and each has developed distinctive cultural designs (Figure 8.39). Historically, most weavers have employed a simple handloom, wool yarns,

and natural dyes. Tapestry is an intricate, usually pictorial, multicolored hand-woven textile design with a ribbed surface. Presently, most tapestries used as accessories are machine-made. Some copy patterns used in previous times, and some are more modern in design. Tapestries can be used as accessories in a similar manner as paintings.

Handcrafted and custom-designed rugs and blankets are often used as a focal point in a room or as the basis for a room's color scheme, as seen in Figure 10.14. Blankets such as those produced by the Navajo Indians and the Finnish add a pleasant decorative touch in a room. The traditional process of quilting involves arranging small pieces of colored plain or patterned fabrics into an overall design. Quilts are frequently employed in provincial design.

Animal hides may be hung as paintings, draped over furniture, or used as rugs in low-traffic areas. Before selecting a hide for use, the interior designer must be able to verify that the hide was legally obtained. Designers should be sensitive to ethical treatment and conservative use of all animal products. Endangered species should never be used.

Painted brain-tanned animal hides such as deer, elk, or bison are a popular art form in Western design. The art form, developed by Native Americans, requires the hide to be tanned using the animal's brain instead of harsh commercial chemicals. The designs painted onto the skin may be inspired by authentic pictographs, geometric designs, or original concepts of the artist (Figure 8.40).

Figure 8.40 *These painted brain-tanned hides work well in a contemporary or rustic setting. Hung from custom-designed poles or draped over furnishings, they create an intriguing focal point. (Artist: Lee Secrest. Photograph by Laurie Lane.)*

Baskets and the art of basket weaving have changed little since ancient times. Artists have further developed this art by introducing new colors, forms, patterns, and styles. Traditional baskets created by particular cultures display distinctive characteristics and styles that are highly valued.

Handcrafted *candles,* originally used for purely functional purposes, are a highly intricate art form. Candles are created in many colors and in a wide range of textures and forms suitable for both traditional and modern settings. Candles are often used for decorative accents in the interior; when lit, they provide a warm, inviting element in the private or public environment.

Flowers, Foliage, and Plants

Of all accessories making up the final touches of a residence or commercial space, almost nothing can duplicate the effect of fresh flowers. Three popular flower arranging styles are Oriental (ikebana), traditional, and contemporary freestyle. The container contributes to the total success of the arrangement and generally works best when the texture, pattern, and size complement the surroundings. Glass, metal, porcelain, pottery, and baskets are often used because they can be effectively combined with traditional or modern furnishings.

Living plants placed around interior environments contribute to the total design scheme and help to bring something of the outdoors into the interior (Figure 8.17 shows the use of both living plants and fresh-cut flowers). Personal preference for texture, form, color, and size is a consideration in selecting plants, as well as special care requirements for light, water, and temperature.

Dried flowers, branches, pods, and other foliage are often used as alternatives to fresh plants and flower arrangements. They have the advantage of being permanent, and require no upkeep other than dusting. Well-made artificial flowers, foliage, and plants look amazingly natural. They may be manufactured from silk, polyethylene, or polypropylene. (The latter two materials can be cleaned more easily than silk.) Like dried arrangements, they are permanent and require only occasional dusting. Many commercial and institutional organizations use artificial flowers and plants instead of fresh ones because of the easy upkeep and one-time investment.

Selecting Accessories

When determining what accessories are suitable for a particular space, consider a wide range of possibilities. Reviewing an outline of numerous items often sparks an idea of the accessory or accessories that tie an entire grouping together. Table 8.2 lists commonly selected accessories for both residential and commercial settings.

The accessories may be utilitarian or displayed for aesthetic pleasure. The items may be incorporated into the scheme to enhance the background or they may function primarily as a point of interest (Figure 8.41). The principles and elements of design must always be used. For example, the item must be suitable in texture, color, and form to the style, background, and other accessories and furnishings in the room. The item should be in scale with the other furnishings and the space allocated. The accessory should help to bring balance and harmony to the room.

Accessories can either be authentic to a certain historic style or mixed to support a variety of styles. The latter approach is often considered more creative. Accessories can also support the architectural background. For example, an informal arrangement of flowers in a basket enhances a rustic wood wall, and an elegant porcelain vase enhances a formal French paneled wall.

Designers often play an important role in selecting accessories for commercial and institutional spaces. The previous guidelines should be followed, but the art and accessories should be placed so as not to interfere with the function of the facility. Usually, commercial spaces do not incorporate personal items except in private offices; however, accessories in public areas do reflect the corporation's image and character.

Adding art and accessories to a commercial setting can give an inviting, warm character to an otherwise institutional setting. Often the designer is limited in purchasing fine-quality items for the commercial setting because of budget restrictions and the possibility of theft. Obtaining accessories that project an aesthetic appeal and that will last through the years are additional challenges. Such items as plants and artwork—usually large in scale—are often chosen for schools, offices, hospitals, libraries, hotels, retail stores, restaurants, and other public settings. Also, accessories that relate to the function of the facility itself can add character to the space; for example, prints in a restaurant might pertain to the history or theme of the establishment. All accessories selected for the commercial setting should enhance the environment and humanize the space.

Table 8.2 *Accessory Idea List*

Animal hides	Ceramics	Kitchen and cooking utensils	Serving carts
Aquariums and fish	Clocks	Kites	Shells and rocks
Arms and armor	Coat racks	Lamps	Shelves (a small, decorative,
Art (two-dimensional)	Collections (coins, guns,	Maps, charts, and documents	carved wood shelf, for
Artificial flowers and foliage	stamps, antique items, etc.)	Mirrors	example)
arrangements	Cushions	Models (airplanes, ships, etc.)	Silverware
Ashtrays	Desk accessories (pen and	Mosaics	Stools
Baskets	pencil holders, letter holders,	Musical items (instruments,	Tablecloths, mats, and napkins
Bath accessories (soap dish,	desk pad, address book,	music stands, sheet	Tapestries
toothbrush container, towel	small clock, etc.)	music, etc.)	Telephones
racks, towels, washcloths,	Dishes	Music boxes	Tools (antique spinning wheel,
scales, toilet-paper holder)	Dolls	Needlework	for example)
Birdcages	Doll houses	Pedestals (for displays)	Toys
Blankets	Figurines	Photo albums	Toy furniture
Bookends	Fireplace tools and firescreen	Pillows	Trays
Books and magazines	Flowers	Pitchers	Trophies
Bottles	Flower and plant containers	Plants	Umbrella stands
Bowls	Foliage	Plates and platters (decorative)	Vases
Boxes	Frames (for art, photos, etc.)	Pottery	Wastebaskets
Brassware	Games	Puzzles	Weavings
Calendars	Glassware	Quilts	Wreaths
Candles	Hardware (door knobs, hinges,	Rugs	
Candlesticks	racks, pulls, tiebacks, hooks,	Screens	
Canisters	escutcheons, rods, etc.)	Sculpture	

Figure 8.41 *This creative art piece establishes the whimsical feeling in the Galaxy Café. The restaurant, which can seat more than 500, draws 2,500 visitors a day from Boston's Museum of Science. (Architect/Designer: Prellwitz/Chilinski Assoc. Photograph by Steve Rosenthal. Artist: David Tonneson.)*

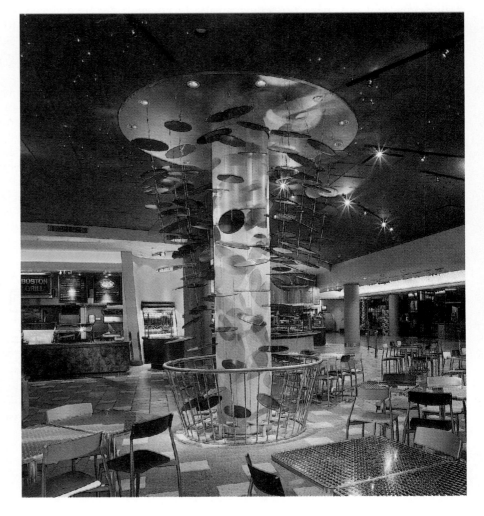

Grouping and Placing Accessories

The desire to display prized possessions is universal; the challenge for a designer is to arrange these treasured objects into an appealing composition. If the collected items are worth acquiring, they are worth displaying. Successful placement of accessories lies in training the eye to see beauty in color, texture, form, and spatial relationships. Applying the principles and elements of design is helpful when choosing the best location for each item.

Grouping items in an artistic arrangement can be an effective means of creating an interesting display in the room. By themselves, small things may be insignificant, but through skillful arrangement even the simplest items can take on special meaning. When grouping small objects, keep in mind that they are seen against a background of walls and furniture, which can be considered part of the arrangement. Be aware of the relationships of the items to each other. Perhaps a grouping of round objects of varying sizes is pleasing, but adding a rectangle can provide an interesting contrast. In an arrangement with three elements—a horizontal piece, a higher intermediate piece, and a tall vertical piece—the eye moves from the low horizontal to the high vertical, providing a sense of transition. This rhythm is seen in nature when the eye observes the earth, flowering plants, and towering trees. A common color subtly running through each element can add unity to an arrangement; varying colors and textures can create a sense of interest and variety.

Two-Dimensional Art in Wall Composition

Pictures can be hung individually or in groupings, but they should always relate to the sofa, desks, chairs, tables, or other furnishings constituting the wall composition. Usually a picture relates best to the composition when not "floating" alone on the wall. A table, console, or other piece of furniture beneath the picture can stabilize the artwork. Following are considerations for selecting and arranging two-dimensional art for a wall composition.

- Positive spaces are the areas filled with the two dimensional artwork; negative spaces are the areas in between these pieces. Regardless of shape and size, each picture should have a pleasing space surrounding it (Figure 8.42).
- A single picture on a wall may work best when hung at eye level.
- A picture hung above a chair or sofa should be placed high enough so the head of the seated person does not touch the frame; if hung much higher, the picture lacks continuity with the furniture arrangement. Approximately 6 to 8 inches above a sofa or chair back provides sufficient clearance. Additionally, pictures are best seen and appreciated when not obstructed by lamps, flower arrangements, or other accessories.
- To assemble an arrangement, lay a large sheet of brown paper the size of the area to be covered on the floor. Arrange pictures and other objects on the paper until the final composition is created. Trace each object around the perimeter, and mark a point where it will be hung on the wall. Then hold the paper up against the wall with marks made where nails or hooks will be placed. The pictures can then be hung easily in the planned arrangement.

Arranging Art in Storage Units

The arrangement of accessories on wall units, bookcases, secretaries, breakfronts, or even baker's racks requires a sensitive eye. The elements and principles of design are the key to a successful design solution. The following ideas are helpful.

- Taller, heavier pieces look best on lower shelves.
- Books may fill an entire shelf, or be combined with accent plates, figurines, photographs, or small plants. Books also may be laid flat and stacked to serve as a bookend. Brass accessories or accent pieces may be placed on top of the books. It is common to group books in relationship to their height in ascending or descending order. Antique books with leather covers may be purchased if a client's collection requires additional character.

Asymmetrical

Symmetrical

Figure 8.42 *Symmetrical and asymmetrical arrangements of art are hung with careful attention to the relationship of positive spaces (the art itself) and negative spaces (the spaces between the art pieces).*

- Bookends can add a special character or accent to a row of books.
- Two-dimensional art may be placed on shelves at a slight angle.
- Accents from nature, such a geodes, shells, or driftwood, can add warmth and texture.
- Photographs and unusual frames can add interest.
- Clear, simple glass objects look best when grouped together and placed at or near eye level.

It is important to remember that the composition of accessories is not a static element in the room. Collections of books and accessories will grow. (Landscape architects continually deal with this dimension of growth.) Designers must allow empty space for new prized objects. Conversely, some objects will be moved to other rooms where the client finds them more useful or appropriate.

Summary

Knowledge of the various furniture types and their proper construction will aid the designer in the development of a successful interior. Furnishings that withstand years of use will be remembered by the client and produce positive referrals; conversely, furniture that falls apart will also be remembered by the client, most likely in the form of negative referrals. Because of the financial investment, longevity is the expected outcome and designers must be able to specify and recognize quality construction.

Accessories work directly with the room's furniture and should complement the selections. Accessories should include items of personal value to the client or company. Items for functional or decorative use in all areas of the interior add visual pleasure, whether displayed alone or in groups (Figure 8.43).

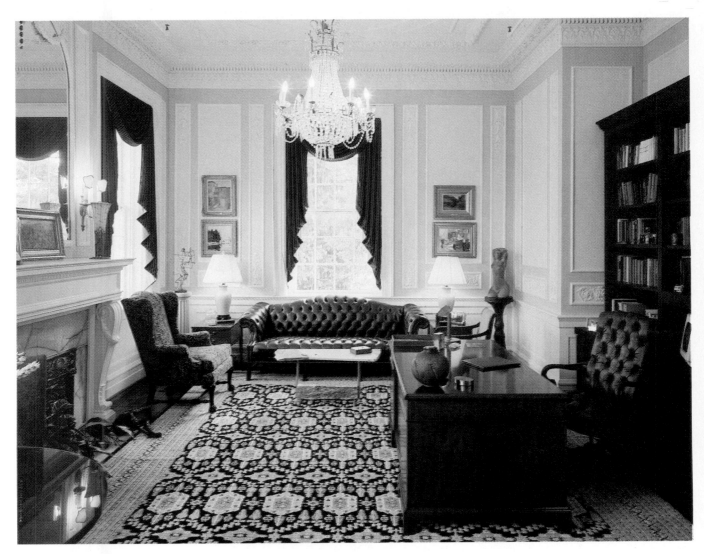

Figure 8.43 *In this award-winning university president's office, art and accessories from the university's collection add warmth and variety to the traditional setting. (Designer: Lynn M. Jones. Photograph by J. J. Williams.)*

9

Textiles

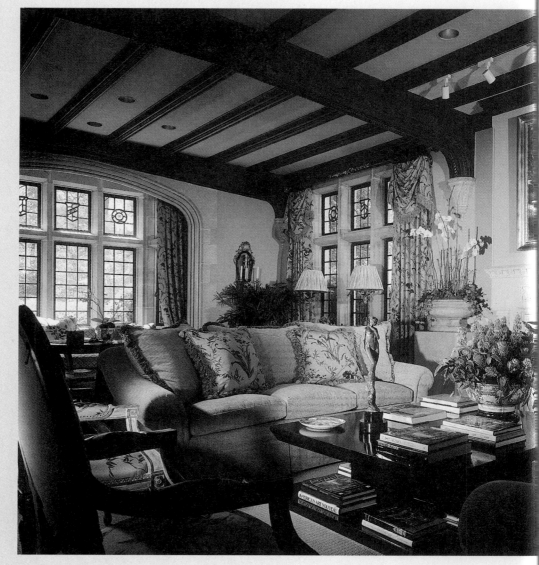

Figure 9.1 *In this masculine Tudor home, warm tones were selected by the designer to humanize the interior. Note the addition of trims and fringes on draperies and pillows. (Designer: James Essary & Associates. Photograph © Robert Thien. As seen in:* Atlanta Homes & Lifestyles.*)*

Textiles enhance both residential and commercial interiors; they are probably more versatile than any other element used for interior design. Textiles are pliable; they can be sewn, draped, bent, folded, wrapped, pleated, gathered, and stretched. Textiles are used in every room for upholstery, window treatments, slipcovers, pillows and cushions, bedspreads, blankets and throws, towels, table linens, wall coverings, ceiling coverings, lamp shades, and trim.

As discussed in the introduction to Part V, there are several basic considerations in the selection of interior materials: function, aesthetics, and economics. One of the primary purposes of textiles, however, is to humanize living spaces. Textiles provide a transition between architecture and furniture, and bring comfort, warmth, and softness to homes and public places (see Figures 9.1 and 9.2).

Textile is an overall term used to describe a fiber, yarn, or fabric. The terms *fibers, yarns, fabrics,* and *textiles* are often used interchangeably in the profession, and are defined as follows:

- **Fibers** are the raw materials, either natural or synthetic, that produce yarns and fabrics.
- **Yarns** are fibers that are twisted or assembled together to form the strands that produce fabrics.
- **Fabrics** are the results of the weaving, knitting, twisting, felting, or lacing of fibers and yarns. Fabrics also may be formed from plastics.

Fibers

Fibers, such as raw cotton, silk, or polyester, are the most basic element of a fabric. A perfect fiber that will adequately serve every general design purpose does not exist. Each fiber has its own advantages and disadvantages. Manufacturers have found that by blending certain fibers, the most desirable qualities of each can be incorporated into a single fabric.

Yarns are made by spinning various lengths of fibers into strands used for fabric construction. A fabric's performance and appearance are affected by the method and the amount of twisting of the fibers. A high twist produces more strength and durability but takes away some of the luster. Long filaments with little twist generally maintain a high luster but lose much of their stability. *Ply* is the result of twisting two or more single yarns together before weaving to give added strength or create a surface effect.

Natural Fibers

Fibers that come from nature fall into four classifications: protein, cellulose, metallic, and mineral.

Protein Fibers

Wool and silk are the most important protein, or animal, fibers.

Figure 9.2 *For a commercial lounge and dining area, the designer selected upholstery and drapery fabrics to add warmth and visual appeal. The colors and patterns complement the plush floral-patterned wall-to-wall carpet. (Designer: Carolyn Henry. Photograph by Pam Singleton.)*

Figure 9.3 *In this child's room, a berber wool carpet adds warmth and durability. The short looped pile provides a soft flooring, as well as a masculine appeal appropriate in a boy's room. (Courtesy of Wools of New Zealand.)*

Wool is the fleece of sheep, Angora goats (known as mohair), camels, and other animals. It has been used since the 7th or 8th century B.C. In early Egypt, Greece, Asia, and the Middle East, it was used for clothing and some household articles. Wool has several advantages. It is resilient, flame retardant, resists abrasion, is a good insulator, and can be woven in a variety of textures. It can be dyed from the palest to the deepest colors, cleans well, resists dirt, and can absorb up to 20 percent of its weight in moisture without feeling damp. Its disadvantages include a tendency to yellow with age (particularly when exposed to sunlight), shrink, and be damaged by moths and other insects. Additionally, wool can be expensive and it requires professional cleaning. It may also cause allergies. Wool is used for both residential and commercial applications including upholstery, carpeting, draperies, and wall coverings (Figure 9.3).

Silk is an ancient fiber that, according to legend, was discovered in China about 2540 B.C. The process of producing it from the larvae of silkworms, known as sericulture, was kept secret for many years but gradually became known in countries around the world. The advantages of silk are that it is a beautiful, long fiber that is soft and luxurious, and surpassed in strength only by nylon (Figure 9.4). It takes and holds dye well and drapes beautifully. One disadvantage is that the sun's rays break down the fiber, requiring it to be protected from direct sunlight. Silk also is susceptible to deterioration by soil, beetles, and moisture. It is expensive as well.

Raw silk, or uncultivated silk, is a shorter and coarser fiber with less luster. Both types of silk fibers are used for draperies, some upholstery applications (when backed), wall coverings, trim, and fabric art.

Cellulose Fibers

Cellulose (or vegetable) fibers include stems, leaves, and seed hairs found in plants. The two most common cellulose fibers are cotton and linen (or flax).

Figure 9.4 *Donghia's* Sleight of Hand *collection of four silk fabrics includes* Abracadabra *(a silk shantung),* Hocus Pocus *(a stripe),* Shazam! *(a zigzag design), and* Presto! *(a quilted matelassé). (Courtesy of Donghia Textiles. As seen in:* Fine Furniture International.*)*

Cotton is believed to have been grown in India during the 4th century B.C. and used in early Rome; it is the most plentiful of the natural fibers. Its advantages are that it takes and holds color well, washes easily, and can be woven to produce sheer or heavyweight fabrics. Its flexibility allows it to be adapted for such functions as upholstery, floor coverings, and window treatments (Figure 9.5). Its disadvantages are that it is not as durable as other fibers, and it wrinkles. It can mildew and fade. The cost of cotton varies according to the quality of the fiber, weave, and finish.

Figure 9.5 *Constructed of mercerized cotton, this fabric assures heavy-duty wear for contract use. (Courtesy of ICF Group/Unika Vaev.)*

Figure 9.6 *Touches of metallic gold add opulence to this patterned fabric from Girmes, a German manufacturer.* (*Courtesy:* Fine Furniture International.)

Linen, made from flax fibers, is the most ancient of all fibers. It was used for weaving in Egypt as early as 4000 B.C. Its advantages are that it is strong, pliable, lustrous, and washable, and it takes and holds color. It is absorbent. The disadvantages of linen are that it wrinkles readily unless chemically treated, which then reduces its wear potential; it fades; it is stiff; and it is difficult to clean. Linen is used for upholstery, drapery, table linens, and slipcovers.

Mineral and Metallic Fibers

Mineral and metallic fibers are created from naturally occurring minerals, including metals. *Metallic fibers* include strips of gold, silver, or copper that are used chiefly as accents in decorative fabrics (Figure 9.6). Metallic fibers glitter without tarnishing and are washable.

Manufactured Fibers

Manufactured fibers are derived either from synthetic chemicals or natural solutions chemically treated. Manufactured fibers are designed to improve upon the quality, durability, and ease of care of natural fibers, as well as their resistance to soil, mildew, and insects. Although costs vary, manufactured fabrics tend to be less expensive than those made from natural fibers. Manufactured fibers are made by creating a liquid or viscose out of the original substance, then forcing the liquid through holes in a showerhead-like device called a **spinneret.** Varying the size and shape of the holes in the spinneret changes the characteristics of the fiber. Manufactured fibers fall into two categories: regenerated cellulose and synthetic fibers.

Regenerated cellulose fibers are produced by changing the physical and chemical properties of cellulose (plant and

Figure 9.7 *This high-tech tapestry, called Lancelot, is woven of Trevira polyester. It is inherently flame-retardant, durable, and classic in design. (Courtesy of Anzea Textiles.)*

wood fibers). Some examples are rayon, acetate, and triacetate. *Synthetic fibers* are produced from chemicals and carbon compounds. Some examples are nylon, acrylic, modacrylic polyester, olefin, and glass (Figure 9.7).

During the past five decades, the production and consumption of manufactured fibers has steadily increased. In 1940, manufactured fibers accounted for only 10 percent of the fibers used. Today, over 80 percent of fibers used are manufactured fibers. Table 9.1 lists the most common manufactured fibers, their qualities, their most important decorative uses, and recommendations for care to maintain appearance.

Table 9.1 *Properties of Manufactured Fibers*

Generic Name	Appearance	Abrasion	Resilience	Heat Tolerance
Acetate (regenerated cellulose)	Smooth; silky; drapes well; holds shape well	Fair	Poor	Poor
Triacetate (a subdivision of the acetate group)	Crisp; smooth; silky; drapes well; strong colors	Fair	Good; resists wrinkling; retains pleats	Less sensitive than acetate
Acrylic	Wool-like; soft; bulky; warm; may squeak; rich colors; pilling depends on quality	Good; needs treatment for static	Good; holds heat-set pleats	Sticks at 450°F
Modacrylic (modified acrylic)	Similar to acrylic; good color retention	Good	Fair to good	Does not melt
Aramid	Stiff and smooth	High; exceptional strength	Excellent; low stretchability	Not affected
Fiberglass	Soapy; lustrous; silky; color range fair; Beta Fiberglas has remarkable sheerness	Strongest of all fibers	Excellent	Fireproof
Nylon (polyamide)	Squeaky; silky; cold; natural luster; good color range; drapes well	Excellent	Very good; resists wrinkling; can be heat set to hold shape	High resistance
Olefin (propylene and ethylene)	Waxy; wool-like; color range fair	Good to excellent	Good; resists wrinkling	Poor; heat sensitive
Polyester	Silky, cotton, or wool-like; drapes well; color range fair	Good to excellent	Excellent; resists wrinkles	Sticks at 400°F
Rayon (regenerated cellulose)	Soft; drapes well; excellent color range; bright	Fair to good	Low to medium; crease retention poor	Excellent; does not melt
Saran	Soft; drapes well	Tough	Crease retentive	Shrinks in intense heat
Vinyl (thermoplastic resins)	Smooth; variety of weights; expanded vinyl closely resembles leather	Good	Low	Shrinks at 212–230°F in dry heat, less in moist heat

Notes: All manufactured fibers are resistant to moths and mildew. Insulation depends on construction and is primarily a function of thickness. Hollow polyester fibers provide particularly good insulation. Costs are variable, depending on construction.

Fabric Construction

The history of textile arts is almost as old as the history of humanity. The exact origin of the loom is not certain, but evidence suggests that it was used in Mesopotamia before 5000 B.C. Although modern mechanization has brought great changes in textile production, weave structures are much the same as they were at the beginning of the Renaissance; these simple weaves are still standards in the industry. More intricate weaves that originated in Asia, such as damasks and brocades, are now produced on special **Jacquard** looms. Invented in France in 1801 by Joseph-Marie Jacquard (1752–1834), a Jacquard loom can create multicolored fabrics with intricate patterns.

Woven Textiles

This section discusses the most common weaves (illustrated in Figure 9.8), as well as some more intricate ones used in decorative fabrics.

Flammability	Light Tolerance	Decorative Uses	Care
Slow	Long exposure weakens fiber; colors fade unless protected by special finish	Curtains, drapery, upholstery, rugs; for shower curtains in blends with other fibers	Soil resistance fair; wash in lukewarm water or dry-clean, depending on dyes, finishes, decorative designs; quick drying; iron at moderate heat
Slowly combustible	More resistant than acetate	Same as acetate	Same as acetate
Resists fire; burns with yellow flame	Good	Rugs, carpets, blankets, curtains, drapery, upholstery	Keeps buoyancy when washed with warm water; machine dry; does not shrink, sag, or stretch; steam pressing reduces loft
Self-extinguishing	Excellent	Curtains, drapery, in carpet blends, furry rugs, blankets	Similar to acrylic; resists chemical stains; washable; use warm iron; shrinks unless stabilized; does not dry-clean well
Low flammability	Weakens with long exposure	Carpets	Not affected by moisture
Nonflammable	No loss	Curtains, drapery, bedspreads; Beta Fiberglas used for bedspreads	Impervious to moisture; hand wash; drip-dry; needs no ironing
Melts slowly	Poor	Upholstery, bedspreads, carpets	Washable; quick drying; use warm iron; resists soil; easy spot removal; static electricity unless treated
Slow to burn	Good	Rugs, blankets, upholstery, webbing, seat covers	Wash or dry-clean; iron at very low heat; good soil resistance
Burns slowly	Loses strength in prolonged exposure	Curtains, drapery, upholstery, carpets and rugs, pillows, blankets	Soils easily; machine wash in warm water; dries quickly; use warm iron; resists stretching and shrinking
Burns quickly	Fades when not solution dyed	Curtains, upholstery, drapery, table linen, rugs; probably most versatile fiber	Same as acetate; fair soil resistance
Nonflammable	Excellent	Outdoor furniture, upholstery, and screening; curtains, drapery, wall coverings	Excellent ease of care; resists wrinkling and stains; water-repellent
Burns with difficulty	Weakens with long exposure	Shower curtains, wall coverings, upholstery when backed with fabric	Stain resistant; waterproof; wash and wipe clean

Plain Weave

A plain weave is made by the simple interlocking of **warp** (vertical or lengthwise) threads and **weft** or filling (horizontal or crosswise) threads, and may be single or double, regular or irregular. In the *plain single weave,* one weft thread passes over one warp thread and under the next. When the warp and weft differ because of different weights or textures of yarn, the weave is called irregular or unbalanced. In the *basket weave,* two weft threads are interlaced with two warp threads. This weave may also be irregular from variations of weight or texture.

Twill Weaves

Twill weaves are those in which two or more threads pass over or under another set of threads, skipping at regular intervals to produce a diagonal effect. Twill weaves may be regular or irregular. Irregular twills are used for many decorative fabrics such as denim, gabardine, and herringbone.

Satin Weave

The satin weave floats one warp yarn over four or more weft yarns. This combination produces a fabric with luster, softness,

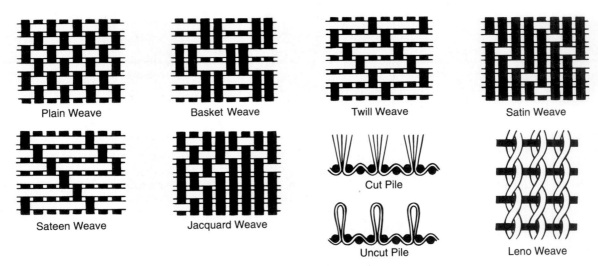

Plain Weave

Basket Weave

Twill Weave

Satin Weave

Sateen Weave

Jacquard Weave

Cut Pile

Uncut Pile

Leno Weave

Figure 9.8 *Common types of weaves.*

and drapability, especially when the fiber is smooth, as with satin and sateen.

Jacquard Weaves

The Jacquard weave requires an intricate series of hole-punched cards that tell the machine which threads to raise and which threads to drop. Some of the most common fabrics created on the loom include damask, tapestries, and brocades (Figure 9.9).

Pile Weave

Pile weaves are produced by additional threads in the weft or warp that form loops or tufts of yarn that stand out from the surface of the fabric. These loops may be cut, uncut, or a combination. Pile weaves are used in a wide variety of fabrics. The basic weave of the carpet industry is the raised-warp pile. Numerous fabrics are produced using pile weaves, including terry cloth, corduroy, and friezé. Velvets, originally woven by this method, are generally made today in a double cloth that is cut apart to produce the pile.

Double-Cloth Weave

Double-cloth weaves are woven in two attached layers, often resulting in a quilted appearance. These fabrics, known to the ancient Peruvians, are both durable and beautiful. The Jacquard loom is used to weave these fabrics for commercial applications.

Leno Weave

The leno weave is a loose, lacelike weave in which the warp threads are wound in half twists around each other, alternating positions on each row. Sheers, semisheers, and casements (coarsely woven sheers) use these weaves.

Figure 9.9 *This fabric selection includes a Jacquard drapery fabric of 74/24 viscose/acrylic, a cotton/silk bed cover, and pure silk decorative pillows from Zimmer & Rohde, Germany.* (*Courtesy:* Fine Furniture International.)

Nonwoven Textiles

Knitting

Knitting is a process of interlocking a series of yarn loops by means of blunt needles. Through a variation of stitches, patterns are formed. Knitted fabrics, either hand- or machine-made, range from loose, open construction to a close, fine mesh. Finely knit fabrics are used for many home furnishing needs because of their wrinkle resistance, tight fit, and ease of care. The tendency of knitted fabrics to stretch is being overcome by new methods of production.

Twisting

Twisting, interlocking, and knotting of yarns account for various types of mesh construction, such as nets, laces, and macramé. The intricacies of twisting are unlimited.

Felting

Felting is a process of subjecting a mass of fibers to moisture, heat, and pressure, which produces a compact sheet that does not fray, absorbs sound, and provides good insulation against heat and cold. Felt was formerly made from wool and hair fibers. Through modern technology, new fibers and fusing methods are employed to produce a variety of nonwoven materials.

Bonding

A bonded fabric results when two fabrics are adhered (or bonded or laminated) together chemically or with heat. By bonding a layer of fabric to the underside, the face fabric can be stabilized. If care is not taken, however, cleaning may cause separation of the layers. Bonded fabrics may be used as interfacing in upholstery to add stability.

Textile Coloring/Dyeing

Fibers are dyed or colored throughout the various stages of textile fabrication. In general, the most colorfast products are dyed early in the manufacturing process; however, greater color variety (and therefore design options) occurs when dyes are added later in the process. The various methods of dyeing fibers, yarns, and fabrics include:

- **solution dyeing**—the coloring agent is added to the viscous liquid of the synthetic before it is forced through the spinneret to be formed into a fiber
- **stock dyeing**—the dye is applied to the fibers before they are processed into yarns
- **yarn dyeing**—the skeins or hanks of yarns are dyed before they are woven into fabrics
- **piece dyeing**—fabrics are dyed after they are woven

Each time a new dye solution or dye bath is mixed, it may vary slightly in color from the previous one. Each solution is called a *dye lot*. When using a fabric from more than one bolt for a certain project, it is important to make sure the bolts are from the same dye lot or that the colors still match. A unique alternative to dyeing is to select fibers in the desired colors to produce the fabrics (see "Green Design: Colored Fibers").

Finishing

The finish is a treatment that may be applied to the fabric before or after construction to change its appearance and performance. When the unfinished fabric comes from the loom it is referred to as **greige** or **gray goods.** Before the cloth is ready for the market it goes through a series of finishes: the preparation or *prefinish*, the *functional finish*, and the *decorative finish*.

Prefinishes

Prefinishes and preparation of the gray goods consist of a variety of treatments including:

- beetling or pounding to give luster
- bleaching to whiten
- boiling to rid the fabric of grease or other unwanted substances
- calendering to provide a smooth finish and tighten the weave
- durable finishing to strengthen the textile
- gigging or napping to produce a flannel-like texture
- heat setting to add stability, especially for permanent pleating
- preshrinking to shrink the textile and make it ready for finishing, and prevent fiber contraction when exposed to moisture
- singeing to remove surface fuzz or lint

Following the prefinishing, the cloth is ready for the functional and decorative finishes.

Functional Finishes

Functional finishes are applied to improve performance. These standard textile finishes include

- antibacterial finishes to help prevent mold and mildew
- antistatic finishes to help guard against static
- carefree finishes to help resist creasing or wrinkling
- flame-retardant finishes to help retard burning
- insulating finishes to improve insulation qualities; a coating of foam or other material is bonded to the fabric
- mothproofing finishes to help prevent damage by insects
- soil-repellent finishes to help resist soiling
- water-repellent finishes to resist stains and moisture

Soil-resistant finishes are particularly important. Water-repellent, soil-resistant or soil-repellent, and soil-release

GREEN DESIGN

Colored Fibers

One of the purest means of ensuring environmentally safe interiors is to use natural, untreated, nondyed organic fibers. Designers developing green interiors need to consider the source of the fibers and their hidden environmental costs. For instance, according to Natural Cotton Colours, Inc., the process of dying fibers can be five times more expensive in the United States than in other countries. This is because government agencies in the U.S. require the residue from the dying process to be purified. Obviously, this should be required worldwide, but other countries do not apply these restrictions and thereby pollute the environment. Natural Cotton Colours found an answer to this problem—they grow cotton in different colors; dyes are not applied to the fibers. FoxFibre® has developed several lines of fabric from these fibers (Figure GD9.1).

In all textile specifications, designers should look for products made from natural, regenerated, recycled, or reproduced fibers. Remember, however, that the fabric must fulfill its intended function.

Figure GD9.1 *FoxFibre® color chart shows that after repeated washings the color of the natural fiber actually darkens. (Courtesy of Natural Cotton Colours, Inc. Photograph by Cary S. Wolinsky.)*

---

finishes are all chemical finishes that increase a fabric's resistance to dirt and stains and help make cleaning easier. For example, Scotchgard™ is a trade name for a finish that makes the surface of the fabric stain resistant. It is best when this finish is applied to the fabric at the mill; however, it is possible to purchase the soil-resistant or water-repellent finish separately and apply it manually. Manufacturers' labels or instructions accompanying the fabric inform the consumer about what to look for, how often to clean, and how effective the finish is.

Decorative Finishes

Decorative finishes include printing by hand or machine, custom finishes, and needlework.

Printing (Hand Processes)

In general printing is completed after the fabric is woven. Obviously, hand processes require human labor. Some popular hand processes are:

- *Batik printing:* Sections of the cloth that are not to be colored are blocked out with wax; then the cloth is immersed in a dye solution. The wax is then removed, revealing the pattern.
- *Hand block printing:* A carved wooden or linoleum block is inked and stamped onto a piece of fabric to create the design.
- *Tie-dye:* A resist process that employs strings or knots tied on the fabric. The fabric is then immersed in dye, creating abstract patterns.

- *Silk-screen:* A specially prepared fabric screen resists the color penetration except in desired areas. Dye in paste form is forced through the screen onto the fabric below. A separate screen is prepared for each color used in the design. Only the silk-screen process produces hand-printed textiles on a commercial scale.

Printing (Mechanical Processes)

Many prints are produced mechanically by the transfer of color from an engraved copper roller onto the fabric. This process is called *roller printing.* A separate copper roller must be engraved for each color of the design, but once prepared, the rollers can be used in a variety of color schemes on thousands of yards of fabric. Other types of roller printing include:

- *Embossing:* engraved rollers produce a pressed high-low design into the fabric
- *Moiré:* a type of embossing in which rollers press a watermark design into the fabric
- *Warp printing:* printing is completed on the warp yarns of a fabric before it is woven

Printed fabrics come in designs of unlimited styles, including documentary prints (designs copied from patterns of a particular historical period). These designs help establish an authentic feeling in a room.

Custom Finishes

Some examples of custom finishes include:

- *Etching:* acid burns out one fiber, resulting in a design on a sheerer fabric
- *Flocking:* small fibers are bonded to the fabric in a patterned design
- *Softening finishes:* chemicals are added to a fabric to soften the feel
- *Texturing:* chemicals applied to the fabric create a puckered surface

Needlework

Needlework, embellishing fabrics with intricate stitchery, is an ancient art form. A wide variety of needlework, such as embroidery, needlepoint, candlewicking, appliqué, and quilting, is utilized, usually in residential applications.

Fabric Testing and Safety Codes

Fabrics, particularly those for commercial uses, must meet standard tests for *durability, colorfastness,* and *flammability.*

Durability

Durability generally refers to the fabric's resistance to abrasion. The Wyzenbeek test is commonly used to indicate the number of double rubs, or revolutions, required before a fabric is damaged. A typical commercial-grade fabric may sustain 15,000 or more double rubs. Another way to test durability is to measure the fabric's stability, its resistance to sagging or elongation, its flexibility, and its resistance to tearing (its *tenacity*). Fabrics also should be *resilient,* which means they return to their original shape after stretching or crushing.

Colorfastness

As previously discussed, the colorfastness of the fabric is partially a function of the dyeing method. Colorfastness measures a fabric's resistance to fading from the sun's rays and from various cleaning methods. Fabrics also may be tested for crocking (the color rubbing off onto another fabric or the skin).

Flammability

The speed at which a fabric will ignite and spread flames, its ability to extinguish itself, and the quality of the fumes emitted are all measurements of flammability. Fabrics used in most commercial applications are subjected to two tests of flammability: the Tunnel Test (ASTM 84) and the Vertical Flame Test. Interior finishes are rated from Class A (the most flame resistant) to Class C (the least flame resistant).

Labeling

To help consumers differentiate among the huge array of manufactured fibers, the Federal Trade Commission (FTC) established the Textile Products Identification Act. Under these regulations, each manufactured fiber is defined in specific terms and given a *generic name,* which along with the company's trade name must appear on the label attached to the fabric. The generic name is the term assigned to a chemical family of which all members exhibit certain traits. For example, all members of the nylon family are characterized by unusual strength and resistance to abrasion, but they will not hold up well under direct sunlight. The polyester family is known for its drip-dry quality and resistance to sun deterioration. The *trade name* identifies the manufacturer. Because manufacturers need to give specific names to their products, there are hundreds of trade names for manufactured fibers, making it virtually impossible for the consumer to recognize them all. Familiarity with the general properties of each fiber family, however, and checking the label to make sure of the fabric content help when selecting the fabric that best serves specific needs. The label alone, however, does not ensure good performance if the construction, dyes, and finishes are not properly handled.

Textiles used for most commercial applications should be labeled to indicate their flammability and their fiber content (with percentages of natural and manufactured fibers when applicable), and whether they have been treated with protective finishes such as Scotchguard™.

The Association for Contract Textiles (A.C.T.), founded in 1985, has established performance guidelines to make fabric specification easier. Figure 9.10 defines these specifications and accompanying symbols.

Flame Resistance

Flame resistance refers to a fabric's ability to resist burning.
The appropriate flammability test is dictated by the intended end use for the fabric.

The two testing methods most commonly used to measure flame resistance are the Tunnel Test (ASTM E-84) and the Vertical Flame Test (used by California Bulletin 117 and NFPA 701).

In the Tunnel Test, the fabric to be evaluated is clamped (unadhered method) or glued (adhered method) to a substrate. The substrate is placed on the ceiling of the test chamber and ignited by a flame from below. The fabric sample is then evaluated for the density of the smoke formed, the amount of fuel contributed and the extent of the flame spread. Based on these factors, a rating is established.

In the Vertical Flame Test, the fabric to be evaluated is mounted in a vertical holder and exposed to an open flame for a specified amount of time. Once the flame is removed, the after flame and char length of the test sample are measured against various code standards to establish a classification.

The NFPA 701 utilizes the Vertical Test but unlike California Bulletin 117, the test is conducted in "oven dry" conditions, meaning the fabric to be tested is heated and thoroughly dried out prior to testing. The test then proceeds under the standards described above and a classification is established.

APPLICATION	PASSES
Upholstery	California Bulletin 117 Section E
Direct Glue Wallcoverings	ASTM E 84 (adhered method)
Panels and Upholstered Walls	ASTM E 84 (unadhered method)
Drapery	NFPA 701 Small Scale

Colorfastness to Wet and Dry Crocking

Colorfastness is a fabric's ability to retain color in various conditions. Crocking refers to the rubbing off of color from a fabric when subjected to abrasion.

To measure for colorfastness to crocking, the fabric to be tested is rubbed with squares of white cotton fabric (both wet and dry) under controlled pressure for a specified number of times. The amount of color transferred to the white test squares is matched to a control chart and a rating is established.

Class 5 = no color transfer

Class 1 = high degree of color transfer

APPLICATION	PASSES
Upholstery	AATCC 8 Dry Crocking, Class 4 minimum Wet Crocking, Class 3 minimum
Direct Glue Wallcoverings	AATCC 8, Class 3 minimum
Panels and Upholstered Walls	AATCC 8, Class 3 minimum
Drapery	AATCC 8 (solids) AATCC 116 (prints) Class 3 minimum

Colorfastness to Light

Colorfastness to light refers to a fabric's ability to resist fading when exposed to light.

To measure for colorfastness to light, the fabric to be tested is exposed under specific conditions to a controlled light source which simulates the sun's rays. At timed intervals, the test swatch is compared to a gray scale and the degree of fading is rated.

Class 5 = no fading

Class 1 = high degree of fading

APPLICATION	PASSES
Upholstery	AATCC 16A or AATCC 16 E Class 4 minimum at 40 hours
Direct Glue Wallcoverings	AATCC 16A or AATCC 16E Class 4 minimum at 40 hours
Panels and Upholstered Walls	AATCC 16A or AATCC 16E Class 4 minimum at 40 hours
Drapery	AATCC 16A or AATCC 16E Class 4 minimum at 60 hours

Figure 9.10 *A.C.T.'s textile performance guidelines. (Courtesy of Association for Contract Textiles.)*

Physical Properties

APPLICATION	PASSES
Upholstery	Brush pill ASTM D3511, 3 minimum Breaking strength ASTM D3597-D1682-64 50 lbs. minimum in warp & weft Seam slippage ASTM D3597-D434 25 lbs. minimum in warp & weft
Panels and Upholstered Walls	Breaking strength D5034 Grab Method 35 lbs. minimum in warp & weft Seam slippage ASTM D3597-434 25 lbs. minimum in warp & weft
Drapery	Seam slippage ASTM D3597-434 for fabrics over 6 oz./sq. yard 25 lbs. minimum in warp & weft Seam slippage ASTM D3597-434 for fabrics under 6 oz./sq. yard 15 lbs. minimum in warp & weft

Abrasion

APPLICATION	PASSES
General Contract Upholstery	ASTM 3597 modified (#10 cotton duck) 15,000 double rubs Wyzenbeek method ASTM D4966 (21 oz. weight) 20,000 rubs Martindale method
Heavy Duty Upholstery	ASTM 3597 modified (#10 cotton duck) 30,000 double rubs Wyzenbeek method ASTM D4966 (21 oz. weight) 40,000 rubs Martindale method

Pilling is the formation of fuzzy balls on the surface of a fabric. Pilling occurs when loose fibers in the fabric are worked to the surface after the fabric is subjected to abrasion.

The Brush Pill Test uses nylon bristles to rub the surface of the fabric to be tested for a specific amount of time. The number of balls or pills that form on the surface of the fabric are counted and the fabric is evaluated in a 1 to 5 rating system.

Class 5 = no pilling
Class 1 = severe pilling

Breaking strength measures a fabric's ability to resist tearing or breaking when subjected to tension.

To evaluate breaking strength, the fabric to be tested is gripped by clamps at one end while weight is applied to pull it from the other end. This test is performed in both the warp and the filling directions. The number of pounds required to cause the fabric to break or tear determines the rating.

50 pounds minimum = upholstery
35 pounds minimum = panel and vertical surface fabrics
15 pounds minimum = drapery

Seam slippage refers to the condition when fabrics pull apart at a sewn seam.

To measure a fabric's ability to resist seam slippage, a seam is sewn in the fabric to be tested. These sewn fabrics are then clamped at one end and pulled by weights at the other end. This test is performed in both the warp and filling directions. The weight is increased until the seam separates a specified distance. The number of pounds required to cause this separation determines the fabric's rating.

25 pounds minimum = upholstery
25 pounds minimum = panel and vertical surface fabrics
15 pounds minimum = drapery

Abrasion resistance is the ability of a fabric to withstand surface wear from rubbing.

Two of the test methods used for measuring abrasion resistance are the *Wyzenbeek* and the *Martindale*.

Wyzenbeek Test Method (modified)

The fabric to be tested is pulled taut and rubbed in both the warp and filling directions, using a piece of cotton duck fabric as the abradant. The number of cycles, or double rubs endured before the fabric shows "noticeable wear" is counted. This number determines the fabric's abrasion rating.

15,000 = general contract upholstery
30,000 = heavy duty upholstery

Martindale Test Method

The fabric to be tested is mounted flat and rubbed in a figure eight-like motion using a piece of worsted wool cloth as the abradant. The number of cycles endured before the fabric shows an objectionable change in appearance is counted. This number determines the fabric's abrasion rating.

20,000 = general contract upholstery
40,000 = heavy duty upholstery

Figure 9.10 *Continued*

Textile Care and Maintenance

Although not required, after a design project is complete, interior designers can offer the client a valuable service by providing manufacturers' manuals, booklets, and other care instructions. Knowledge of the cleaning properties of particular fabrics is essential for upkeep. For instance, water-repellent and soil-repellent finishes must be reapplied periodically, especially after a fabric has been cleaned.

The designer also may recommend added protection from the sun for certain fabrics. Many fabrics are susceptible to sun damage, and glass can multiply the destructive element in the sun's rays. Even the winter sun and its reflection from snow can be harmful. Lined and interlined draperies help protect fabrics from sunlight, especially when fragile materials are used. Blinds drawn during the day and exterior awnings are practical. Trees or shrubbery that shade windows can help prevent interiors from becoming damaged by the sun. Protective coatings can be applied to glass to prevent harmful UV rays from entering the interior.

Textile Uses in Interior Design

Interior designers have a wide choice of textiles with new fabrics always in production. The market abounds with fabrics suitable for every taste, style, and decorative purpose in every price range. Adding to the appeal of improved fibers is the seemingly unending variety of designs, ranging from folk patterns from around the world to traditional and contemporary designs. Following is a discussion of the principal decorative uses of fabrics.

Window Treatments

Styles of window treatments are discussed in Chapter 12. Typical fabrics used for these styles are covered here.

Drapery

Fabrics for drapery should have a light to medium weight, like silk, antique satin, chintz, and damask. Fabric should drape gracefully, clean without shrinkage, and meet the decorative needs of the room in which it is used (see Figure 9.1).

Sheers or Semisheers

Sheers filter the light, giving softness to the room and providing daytime privacy. The fabric should be sunproof but sheer enough to permit light, and should wash or clean well without shrinkage. Batiste, voile, ninon, and chiffon are four popular fabrics.

Casements

Casements are usually made of a coarser weave than a sheer, and are available in a variety of patterns. The fabric should be drapable, sun resistant, and should wash or clean well without shrinkage. Leno weaves especially help control sagging and are commonly used in commercial environments.

Figure 9.11 *Inspired from famous 19th- and 20th-century archeological discoveries, these intricate woven patterns achieve luxurious lines by use of bouclé and chenille yarns and a unique weave structure from Pallas. (Courtesy of Pallas Textiles.)*

Linings

Drapery linings are necessary to protect the drapery from sunlight and provide a uniform exterior appearance. Acrylic and modacrylic fibers are particularly resistant to sunlight.

Curtains

Lightweight and decorative curtains are frequently made from cottons and cotton-polyester blends. Curtains used in kitchens and restaurants should be constructed of washable material. Curtains are a relatively inexpensive window treatment solution and will have a shorter useful life than a drapery treatment.

Upholstery

Upholstery is a fabric, animal skin, or other material that covers furniture permanently, adds beauty and comfort, conceals or emphasizes the furniture design, and adds to or sets the theme or mood of the room.

Upholstery Fabric

Fabric used for upholstery should have a tight weave, be durable, comfortable, and easy to clean. Common upholstery fabrics include heavyweight fabrics such as matelassé, tweed, tapestry, velvet, bouclé (Figure 9.11), and friezé; mediumweight fabrics such as damask, brocatelle, and canvas; and lightweight fabrics such as chintz, linen, homespun, and moiré.

When purchasing upholstered furniture, fabric is a primary consideration because it is an expression of personality and individual taste. In selecting the fabric, use is generally the determining factor. Selecting suitable upholstery fabric involves answering questions such as the following:

1. What type of fiber and weave are employed? An upholstered fabric, for example, will last longer if the warp and fill are the same weight and tightly woven.
2. Is the fabric attractive and comfortable to the touch?
3. Is a patterned or plain fabric preferred? Fabrics with small overall patterns tend to show soil less than solid colors. If a pattern is chosen, is it in scale with the furniture and the room, and does it support the style?
4. Is the fabric suitable for its intended function? For example, will the upholstery be used by active children in a family room, or by a single professional in a seldom-visited area?
5. Is the fabric the best quality the budget will allow, considering long-term wear and maintenance? It is usually inadvisable to buy expensive fabric for cheap furniture and fabric of lesser quality for fine furniture.
6. What maintenance process is necessary? Does the particular upholstery fabric require a water- and soil-repellent finish like Scotchguard™ or Zepel?
7. Does the upholstery fabric fit the style, mood, and character of the room? Is the fabric formal or informal? Does it conform to the lifestyle of the occupants and complement its environment?

Upholstery Leather

Leather (tanned animal skin) is a product that has long been used for aesthetic and utilitarian purposes (particularly the hides of cattle and swine). Its advantages are that it is pliable and durable, may be dyed or used in its natural color, and may be embossed or made into suede (Figure 9.12). Genuine leather can be expensive; simulated leather (vinyl) is available, but needs to be carefully selected to ensure proper aesthetic qualities. The disadvantage of leather is that it is susceptible to marks, holes, and tears. Leather is also used for wall coverings and floor tiles.

Slipcovers

Slipcovers may cover worn upholstered furniture, protect more expensive fabrics, and brighten or change a room's atmosphere. Usually, slipcovers are used only in residential settings.

Slipcovers are made of light- to mediumweight fabrics that should be tightly woven. Some manufacturers offer furniture upholstered in muslin or other plain fabrics that can be purchased with several changes of slipcovers to help dress the furniture for seasonal changes. Sailcloth, ticking, chintz, whipcord, and corduroy are all good choices for slipcovers.

Walls

Fabrics can be used on walls to add beauty (as illustrated in Figure 9.13) or to solve a decorative problem. (See Chapter 11 for uses of fabric wallcoverings.) The fabric should have a tight weave with firm body. Canvas, burlap, moiré, ticking, heavy cotton or linen, velveteen, and damask are often used for wall coverings. In commercial environments, flammability codes for wallcoverings must be followed.

Figure 9.12 *A variety of finishes have been developed for these leathers. Some are treated to produce a weathered look; others are given a high-sheen appearance or made to look antique. The velvet-napped leather is shrink-retardant and wear-resistant. The leather second from the right is part of a group of leathers laced into patterns. (Courtesy of Cortina Leathers.)*

Figure 9.13 *Framed fabric on a wall can add interest and style.*

System Furniture Panel Fabrics

In commercial interiors, and particularly in commercial offices, panel systems create office spaces. As discussed in Chapter 8, panel systems are an effective solution in offices where employees communicate frequently. One of the design challenges of the open office panel system is the redirection of noise. Covering the panel with fabric assists with noise reduction.

Fabrics on the panels must meet several criteria. First, they must be durable. Employees and visitors will lean their hands and bodies against the panel. Second, the fabric must be able to accommodate pushpins. Although tackboards are incorporated in panel systems, the experienced designer knows that, over time, notes, calendars, pictures, etc. are pinned up everywhere. Finally, the fabric must be cleanable; food and drink stains and marks from fingerprints will occur.

The fabric may be used as a subtle background color or it may be patterned to add interest to a space (Figure 9.14). Sometimes vinyl wallcovering is used below desktop level and fabric is used above. Fabrics may vary on different sides of the system or from panel to panel. Panel manufacturers

Figure 9.14 *The open office system designed for MTV employees incorporates a variety of textile choices. Upholstery fabrics add interest to the walls. Colored lampshades create a warm, friendly glow and contrast well with the crisp metals and geometric edges. (Designers: Felderman & Keatinge Design Associates.)*

Figure 9.15 *Trims are available for drapery tiebacks, skirts on upholstery pieces, edges, and borders. (Photograph ©F. Schumacher & Co. Permission has been granted by F. Schumacher & Co. to use copyrighted work.)*

supply many optional fabrics that have been tested for panel use. If a designer selects a custom fabric, the fabric may require testing to insure its appropriateness for use on the panel systems.

Accents

Textiles also may be used as accents in a room. Trims, fringes, and braids add character and distinction to an interior (see Figures 9.1 and 9.15). (Chapter 10 discusses the use of textiles as accent floor coverings and Chapter 8 discusses fabrics as a form of art for wall accessories.) Textiles can be used for accent throw pillows, adding interest as well as comfort and continuity to a room. For instance, a particular silk fabric may not be suitable to cover an entire sofa, but may function well on accent pillows.

Selecting Textiles for Interiors

Perhaps the most common question clients ask professional interior designers is, "What fabric goes with what?" This question has no absolute answer. Combining fabrics is a matter of training and skill. Some people seem to have an aptitude for this; others require much patient study and practice.

Combining Fabrics

Although an unexpected combination of materials may create a feeling of great interest and charm, some general principles will be helpful to the inexperienced designer when combining patterns, textures, and colors.

- The selection of any combination of textiles must coincide with the desired feeling or mood in the room. For example, a formal contemporary studio apartment would have crisp shiny fabrics, possibly with leather accents; a woven flamestitch upholstery would appear out of place.
- Many designers coordinate textiles based on a patterned fabric or rug, called the *color source* (Figure 9.16). This method is fairly safe because the basic colors of the scheme are already coordinated; however, without careful consideration this approach can become static or uninteresting.
- Select a textile scheme appropriate for the chosen style. For example, a Victorian-style room would include deep purples, mauves, greens, and reds in rich brocades, velvets, and heavy tapestries.
- To be certain the colors and fabrics are harmonious, compare textiles under all the natural and artificial lights to be utilized in the interior.
- Often, predictable color and fabric combinations and those that match exactly are not interesting or creative. Trying out fabric combinations trains the eye and helps develop a sense of what fabric selections are complementary and what groupings do not work well together. Some manufacturers develop "mix and match patterns" for wallcovering and fabrics; designers with a discerning eye generally select alternative textures and fabrics to enhance these predetermined schemes.

Pattern

Pattern indicates that the design has motifs sufficiently large in scale, or with enough contrast in color or tone, to be distinguished clearly. The skillful use of pattern can camouflage defects, create beauty and glamour, and perform decorating miracles. As with color, no absolute do's or don'ts govern the successful use of pattern. A few general guidelines, however, may be helpful:

- Patterns used within the same room should be related. Common elements such as color, texture, or motif tie them together and unify the design.
- The principal pattern need not be repeated in the room so long as one or more of the colors in that pattern are carried over into another area (as seen in Figure 9.16). The pattern, however, may be repeated on furnishings or used on windows or walls, depending on the overall effect desired. Odd pieces of furniture can be unified by covering them in the same fabric, and repetition of the fabric brings continuity to a room.
- Using no more than one bold pattern of the same type of design, such as a floral, is usually more effective. Once the dominant motif is established it can be interestingly supplemented with more subdued patterns, stripes, checks, or plaids, with complementary plain textures added.
- When combining patterned fabrics, consider the scale or size of the pattern. For example, if a bold floral print with a large scale is combined with a plaid, a stripe, or both, a smaller scale pattern in these complementary

Figure 9.16 *Contemporary fabrics are mixed with traditional fabrics and furniture styles in this refreshing interior. The color source is found in the antique rug. Simple yellow walls with crisp white trim and floral fabrics contribute to the eclectic blend of old and new. (Designer: Spectrum-Interior Design. Photograph ©Kim Sargent.)*

fabrics will be most effective (Figure 9.17). If an unobtrusive floral pattern is used, accompanying fabrics with bolder characteristics may blend well.
- Success in combining patterns can be achieved with practice, experience, and consideration of basic guidelines. It is helpful to observe pattern combinations assembled by experienced professional designers in design periodicals, design studios, showrooms, and at home shows.

Texture

The surface quality of a textile is also an important element to consider when combining fabrics in a specific project. Knowledge of what makes a fabric formal or informal is essential for successfully combining textiles.

Formal fabrics are primarily those with smooth and often shiny textures, displaying elegant stylized and geometric patterns. Some examples of formal fabrics include velvet, damask, brocade, brocatelle, satin, shantung, and taffeta. Formal fabrics are often creatively used in both traditional and modern interiors in a wide range of colors and patterns.

Informal fabrics are generally those with a rougher texture and matte finish, such as burlap, canvas, hopsacking, muslin, tweed, and bouclé (Figure 9.18). Fabrics with a handcrafted

Figure 9.17 *In this room the designer combined several patterns for an interesting interior. A pale paisley pattern on side chairs and the tablecloth contrasts with the strong plaid chair and formal swag and jabots draperies. Crushed velvet and a sisal rug add three-dimensional textural character. (Designer: Bill McGee. Photograph by Antoine Bootz. Courtesy of* Southern Accents.*)*

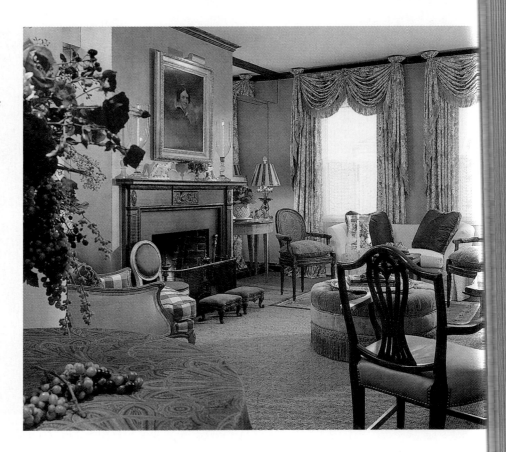

quality often fall into this category. If the informal fabric employs pattern, the design may be bold, naturalistic, abstract, or geometric.

Many fabrics can be used in either category. For instance, cottons and linens may have textures, colors, and patterns that fit into a formal setting or are at home in an informal room. Leather also may be used in formal and informal settings. When designing a room, keep in mind that a combination of textile finishes is important to add interest. Some fabrics should be glossy, where others should have a deeper nap or pile. For example, a room of furnishings covered only in cotton chintz lacks depth.

The unique surface quality or *hand* (rough, smooth, hard, soft, shiny, or dull) of each fabric should be considered when coordinating them. The relationship should be appropriate for the room's style and mood. For example, informal monk's cloth is not at home in an elegant 18th-century English room with smooth and shiny damasks and satins, but is compatible with a wicker chair in a country style.

The character of the texture should be appropriate for its intended use. For example, for a comfortable chair in a family room, a smooth, soft leather would be preferred over a rough burlap.

Color

When coordinating fabrics, another goal is to select colors that are compatible and harmonious. When selecting colors for fabrics, remember from Chapter 3 that color has three dimensions: hue, value, and chroma.

Hues fall into warm or cool color classifications. One of these can be selected to dominate the scheme. The best hues will fit the needs and preferences of the occupants. Such criteria as climate, positioning of the space in relationship to the sun, and lifestyle should be considered.

Fabrics are either light, medium, or dark in value. Most fabric coordination is enhanced by including fabrics in all three levels of luminosity. For example, if the major fabrics in the room are light in value, the fabrics for smaller furnishings or accessories might be medium and dark in value. Many designers use darker values below, medium values in the middle areas, and lighter values on the upper portions of the space; of course, this method can be reversed for a more unusual effect. Using only dark and light values in a space creates drama, as in a color scheme using black and white.

Fabrics are either muted or bright in chroma. A color scheme is usually successful when varying levels of chroma are selected (Figure 9.19). For example, if the major fabrics for the room are muted in chroma, some accents of bright fabrics are visually interesting. A room with all muted colors can be dull and boring; a room with all intense colors can be tiring or even agitating.

Textiles for Period Rooms

Design in textiles was used in ancient times as a symbolic medium for religious purposes. With the passage of time, fabric became a significant medium for aesthetic expression. The design motifs used in the early rugs of East Turkistan are much the same as the designs used in the early rugs of the

Figure 9.18 *Nubby wool textures and dull matte finishes on the upholstered furnishings, pillows, and throw enhance the effect of informality in this living space. The leaf-textured rug further supports the informal and artistic mood of the contemporary style. (Courtesy of Steve Chase and Associates. Photograph by Mary E. Nichols.)*

Figure 9.19 *In this sophisticated boardroom the predominant muted tones are accentuated with small amounts of black on chair seats and in furniture details. The bold artwork adds interest to the space. (Designer: Spector Group. Photograph by Peter Paige.)*

Inca and Navajo peoples halfway around the world. This similarity occurred because people represented natural phenomena in their early art forms. For example, the sun and stars were represented in identifiable form. The difference in early textile weaves is minimal because all were completed on simple looms, using natural fibers and dyes. Although each country developed different characteristic styles, a common quality in their early crafts blends them together harmoniously.

A close relationship often existed among the designs of European, Near Eastern, and Asian countries during the Middle Ages and the Renaissance. The conquerors brought artisans of all kinds to their newly acquired lands, where the

artisans continued to carry on their trades. In time they were influenced by the designs of their new environment, eventually blending different methods and motifs. During the Renaissance and the 17th and 18th centuries fabrics from Asian countries, with their unique motifs and colors, were in great demand in Europe and America.

Historic designs can establish an authentic feeling of a specific period or style. Documentary fabrics bearing designs from a wide range of historic periods are produced by manufacturers. Seldom, however, does a client wish to create an entirely authentic period room; this is usually reserved for restoration projects and museums.

Figure 9.21 *In this Seattle medical facility, the children's play area utilizes bold colors and durable fabrics. Upholstered and built-in furniture is sized to meet the children's needs. (Designer: NBBJ. Photograph by Steve Keating.)*

Figure 9.20 *In this restaurant, named "Stars," the theme is carried through the clever design on the rug, in the fabric (repeated on chairs and booths), the lighting, and even in the poster art. (Architect/Designer: DES Architects+ Engineers. Photograph by Paul Bardagjy.)*

Textiles for Commercial Interiors

Although the previous discussions on fabric testing and safety codes and on combining patterns, textures, and colors apply to commercial interiors, additional design criteria are important for commercial use as well.

In general, commercial interiors will not have as much variety in fabrics as residential interiors. Fabrics for restaurants, offices, and hospital or hotel rooms will be repeated to obtain unity and flow throughout the interior (Figure 9.20). Corridors or hallways must unite the spaces while allowing for high traffic flow, requiring durable textiles.

Commercial interiors in general contain more understated classic materials and colors. Bold colors are reserved for accent walls, children's areas (Figure 9.21), and for use in theme restaurants and hotels. Occasionally, however, a client will request a strong, bold look.

All fabrics must be durable. Designers should select fabrics from reputable commercial manufacturers who have tested their products to meet flammability and abrasion tests.

Fabrics used in commercial interiors should be treated to resist stains. A lovely peach chair will not look so lovely after coffee has sunk into its fibers. At home, the spill may be cleaned within minutes; in a hotel lobby or office environment, it may remain for hours until housekeeping can clean it. Additionally, medical facilities such as hospitals and nurs-

ing homes require fabrics that are easily washable as well as highly resistant to blood and urine stains. To help clients, designers should supply maintenance procedures for cleaning all textile products. Some solution-dyed products can be bleached; piece-dyed fabrics are more sensitive.

Finally, remember that in most commercial situations, the design selections are not for the client, but for the client's client (the customer at the restaurant, for example). Sometimes designers must select items in the end user's best interest and gently explain this to the client.

Solving Design Problems with Textiles

Design problems often can be solved through the skillful use of fabric. A well-chosen fabric can:

- Lighten or darken a room. Fabrics in high values can work wonders to visually lighten the room. If the room has too much light, fabrics in low values help darken the room.
- Emphasize walls, windows, or furnishings to attract desired attention.
- Conceal walls, windows, or furnishings. A designer may want to draw attention away from or cover up a particular wall, window, or piece of furniture.
- Bring harmony and unity to a room by repeated use of the same or complementary fabrics.
- Provide balance to a room. For example, a bold-patterned fabric at a window or on a small piece of furniture balances a larger piece of plain furniture at the other side of the room. A spot of bright color balances a larger area of muted color.

Large or conspicuous pattern tends to
make furniture appear larger.

Small pattern diminishes size.

Figure 9.22 *The effect of pattern and size.*

- Change the apparent size and proportion of a piece of furniture or an entire room. For example, a sofa covered in a large pattern or bold-colored fabric appears larger than the same sofa covered in a light, plain color, or a small unobtrusive pattern, as illustrated in Figure 9.22. A chair or love seat upholstered in a vertical stripe looks higher than the same piece covered in a plain fabric.
- Establish the room's color scheme. A successful method by which to color scheme a room is to choose a favorite patterned fabric as a starting point.
- Establish the historic or modern style of a room. If the room is based on a certain period, the fabric, more than any other item or furnishing, can set the desired feeling. Documentary fabrics can provide historically authentic styles.
- Change the look of a room for different seasons. For example, a sofa and chairs in deep warm colors may be slipcovered in light-colored ticking for summer. Heavy winter drapery may be changed to light sheers in summer to create a cool atmosphere.

Figure 9.23 *This living area provides a secluded and comfortable retreat. The warm browns and rich textured fabrics create a relaxing environment. (Designer: BRITO Design Studio. Photograph ©Robert Thien. As seen in:* Atlanta Homes & Lifestyles.*)*

Summary

All fabrics supply softness and comfort to an interior. Fabrics also add character, absorb sound, and provide for textural enrichment in a space (Figure 9.23). Selecting the appropriate fabric requires knowledge of fibers, fabric construction, coloring or dyeing procedures, finish selections, and product testing and safety codes. Combining fabrics demands careful discernment and an appreciation for the human factor and the elements and principles of design. Careful fabric placement can solve unusual architectural or interior construction dilemmas.

According to Jack Lenor Larsen, "Fabric is one of the principal devices for introducing color, texture, and pattern into interiors and certainly the most easily manipulated one." The beginning designer will find great satisfaction in selecting fabrics that fit the unique needs of each client in each situation.

Textile Terminology

The information in this section can assist the designer in getting maximum service from fabrics. The following are common fabrics, their qualities and uses, as well as terms relating to the textile industry. Fabrics are listed under their common decorative name. Pronunciations of difficult terms follow in parentheses.

Antique satin A satin weave fabric with textured horizontal striations that imitate antique silk. Antique satin is lightweight, usually a solid color. Draperies.

Bastiste A fine, soft, sheer fabric of plain weave made of various fibers. Sheers.

Bouclé French word meaning "curly." It indicates yarns are curled or looped in a flat or pile fabric. Heavyweight. Upholstery.

Broadcloth A lightweight fabric in a plain or twill weave. Cotton, wool, or synthetic fibers popularly used. Draperies, bedspreads.

Brocade A mediumweight fabric woven on a Jacquard loom. An embroidered multicolored pattern stands out in relief against a satin or ribbed background. Drapery and upholstery.

Brocatelle A mediumweight Jacquard fabric with an extra set of wefts for backing, unevenly twisted, which results in a high-relief embossed appearance on the surface. Upholstery and draperies.

Buckram Stiffened material sized with glue. Reinforcement for draperies and valances.

Burlap A mediumweight coarse fabric woven of jute in a plain, loose weave. Drapery and lamp shades.

Calico A lightweight plain cotton weave with a small all-over print. Curtains.

Cambric Plain weave cotton or linen. Called "handkerchief linen." Originally made in Cambrai, France. Very sheer to coarse. Linings.

Canvas A mediumweight, closely woven cotton. A plain, diagonal weave in solids or prints. Upholstery, drapery, walls.

Casement A broad term covering a relatively coarse fabric used like a sheer. Usually light neutral colors in leno or open weaves. Commonly used in commercial settings.

Challis A lightweight wool, cotton, or synthetic soft fabric in a plain tight weave. Printed designs or plain. Drapery, upholstery.

Chenille A heavyweight fabric woven with chenille yarns. When woven in a fabric, can create a pile similar to velvet; if woven on a Jacquard loom can look similar to cut velvet. Upholstery.

Chiffon A translucent fabric. Tight weave, lightweight. Sheers.

Chintz A plain, tightly woven, lightweight cotton fabric with fine yarns. Sometimes processed with a glazed finish. Can be either a solid color or printed. Draperies, slipcovers, bedspreads.

Color flag The series of clippings attached to a purchased fabric sample to show the colorline.

Colorline The complete color range of a given fabric series.

Colorway The color of an individual fabric.

Corduroy A heavyweight cotton or synthetic pile fabric, ribbed or corded lengthwise. Drapery, slipcovers, upholstery, bedspreads, and other uses.

Crepe Crinkled or puckered fabrics of many types. Usually produced by twisting the yarn when weaving or by a chemical process. Cotton, silk, wool are typical. Plain weave.

Cretonne First made in Creton, France. Similar to chintz but heavier. A cotton fabric with a printed design. Plain or rep weave.

Crewel embroidery A heavyweight plain-woven fabric of cotton, linen, or wool embroidered with fine, loosely twisted, two-ply worsted yarns. Usually worked by hand in the Kashmir province of India. Drapery and upholstery.

Crocking The rubbing off of color from dyed or printed fabrics.

Customer's own material or **COM** The "COM" designation is used when designers supply material to the furniture manufacturer. The fabric is purchased separately and shipped to the upholstery company to be used on a particular piece of furniture.

Cutting A sample of a fabric for presentation or design purposes.

Damask A Jacquard-woven mediumweight fabric with patterns providing unique weave effects. Can be woven self-tone, one-color warp, different-color filling, or multicolor in design. Distinguished from brocades because face of fabric is flatter. The color is reversed on the wrong side. Drapery and upholstery.

Denim A mediumweight, tightly woven cotton twill made of coarse yarns. Usually in a solid color, but can be patterned. Drapery, upholstery, bedspreads, walls, and numerous other uses.

Dotted swiss Sheer fabric woven with extra yarns forming dots when clipped. The effect may be produced by flocking. Curtains.

Duck Similar to canvas. Tightly woven and durable cotton textile. Often striped and used for awnings.

Embroidery Needle and thread art. Originally handwork designs. Can also be machine produced.

Faille (fīl) A lightweight, flat-ribbed fabric woven with fine yarns in the warp and heavier yarns in the filling using a plain weave. The ribbed effect is flatter than grosgrain and smaller than rep. Faille can be the base cloth for moiré. Drapery, upholstery.

Felt Wool or mixed fibers pressed into a compact sheet. A heavyweight fabric used for walls, table covers, and other uses.

Fiberglass Fibers and yarns produced from glass and woven into flexible lightweight fabrics. Noted for its fireproof qualities. Beta Fiberglas is a trademarked glass fiber. Curtains.

Film A lightweight thin or thick plastic sheet used for upholstery, shower curtains, or table coverings. Can be textured, patterned, or plain.

Flannel Twilled fabric made of wool or cotton. Soft yarns are brushed to produce a napped texture. Used for interlinings.

Friezé (frē-zā′) A strong heavyweight fabric with a fine, cut or uncut, low-loop surface woven on a wire loom to maintain loops of an even size. Upholstery.

Gabardine Twill fabric with a distinct diagonal design. Durable, lightweight or mediumweight, made with natural or manufactured fibers.

Gauze Sheer, thin textile constructed of leno or plain weave or both. Originally silk, now also cotton, wool, linen, and synthetic fibers. Used for sheers.

Gimp Ornamental braid used to cover upholstery tacks.

Gingham Medium- or lightweight cotton or cottonlike fabric for informal use. Made of colored yarns forming checks, plaids, or stripes.

Grenadine A leno weave textile similar to marquisette, but thinner. Often woven with dots or patterns. Sheers.

Gros (grō) point Heavyweight needlepoint embroidery. Upholstery.

Homespun Loosely woven lightweight fabric made to resemble handwoven material. Curtains or drapery.

Hopsacking A rough-surfaced mediumweight fabric loosely woven of various fibers in a plain basket weave. Mainly for drapery and slipcovers.

Insulating Fabrics processed with reflective metallic or foam plastic on one side to provide insulating qualities.

Jacquard Damasks, brocades, tapestries, and all fabrics requiring the Jacquard loom.

Khaki A coarse lightweight to mediumweight cotton twill weave dyed an earthy green color.

Lace Open needlework fabric. Originally handmade, now produced by machine. Often has net background with floral and geometric designs. Curtains and tablecloths.

Lampas Fabric having narrow ribs with satinlike figures formed of warp threads and contrasting figures formed of weft thread. Drapery and upholstery.

Leather Animal skin, usually from cows. Upholstery.

Lining A term applied to plain cotton or sateen fabrics that line or back support draperies or other decorative textiles.

Marquisette (mär′-kĭ-zĕt) A sheer lightweight leno woven textile used for sheers. Made of natural or manufactured fibers. Looks like gauze.

Matelassé (măt-lä-sā′) A double-woven heavyweight fabric with a quilted appearance. From the French *matelasser,* meaning "to cushion" or "to pad." Upholstery.

Memo sample A sample of a fabric that must be returned to the fabric showroom.

Moiré (mwä-rā′) A wavy, watery effect pressed into a ribbed surface such as taffeta or faille. A lightweight fabric suitable for drapery, upholstery, or bedspreads.

Monk's cloth A coarse mediumweight fabric in a loose weave of flax, jute, or hemp mixed with cotton, generally in neutral colors. May have sagging problems.

Muslin Bleached or unbleached plain, lightweight cotton weave. Has many uses in decorating, especially in Early American and modern rooms. Walls, draperies, slipcovers. Solid colors or printed patterns.

Needlepoint A heavyweight handmade or Jacquard fabric. Fine and delicate effect is known as petit point; larger needlepoint is known as gros point.

Net A sheer lacelike fabric with a consistent mesh texture available in a variety of fibers. Suitable for sheers.

Ninon (nē′-nŏn) A plain tight weave. Has a smooth, crisp, gossamer appearance. Sheers.

Organdy A sheer crisp cotton fabric with good pleating qualities. Available plain, embroidered, or printed. Sheers.

Osnaburg A light- to mediumweight fabric similar to homespun. A loose, uneven, coarse cotton with solid color or printed motifs.

Oxford A plain-weave fabric. Large filling yarn goes over two warp yarns. An informal fabric with many uses.

Paisley A printed design inspired by original motifs from India and shawl motifs from Paisley, Scotland. Exaggerated curved raindrop or pear shape most typical design. Lightweight to mediumweight. Usually cotton.

Percale A tightly woven and durable lightweight textile. Can be plain or printed. Most often used for bed sheets.

Pilling Formation of fiber fuzz balls on fabric surface caused by wear or friction; encountered in spun nylon, polyester, acrylic, cashmere, or soft woolen yarns.

Piqué (pĭ-kā′ or pē-kā′) A mediumweight to heavyweight cotton textile with raised cords or geometric designs running lengthwise. Often used for bedspreads and curtains. Many variations of this textile type.

Plissé (plĭ-sā′) A lightweight fabric with a crinkled or puckered effect created by chemical treatment. Curtains.

Plush A heavyweight pile fabric with greater depth than velvet. Usually has a high sheen. Upholstery.

Polished cotton A plain- or satin-weave cotton cloth characterized by a sheen ranging from dull to bright. Polish can be achieved either through the weave or by the addition of a resin finish.

Pongee (pŏn-jē′) Term derived from Chinese words for "natural color." Made from wild silk and left in its natural tan color. Lightweight and durable. Used for curtains.

Poplin Lightweight. Similar to rep. Has a lightly corded surface running through the fabric. Made of natural or manufactured fibers. Often used for draperies.

Quilted fabrics A pattern stitched through a printed or plain fabric and through a layer of batting. Outline quilting traces around the pattern of a printed fabric. Loom quilting is a small repetitive design made by the quilting alone. Ultrasonic quilting produces thermally bonded welds in place of stitching threads.

Rep Plain weave, lightweight fabric with narrow rounded ribs running the width or length of the fabric. Usually a fine warp with heavier filling yarns. Drapery, upholstery, slipcovers, bedspreads, and other informal uses.

Sailcloth A mediumweight fabric in a plain weave similar to canvas. Popular for informal indoor or outdoor upholstery.

Sateen A highly lustrous fabric usually made of mercerized cotton with a satin weave. Drapery lining.

Satin *Plain:* Fine yarns woven to give a more lustrous surface. May be lightweight or heavy enough for upholstery. Has many decorative uses when a formal style of decor is desired. *Antique:* A smooth satin face highlighted by slub (or twisted) yarn in a random pattern. An important fabric for drapery.

Serge Twill weave with a hard clear finish. Made from rayon, silk, cotton, or wool.

Shantung A heavy pongee. Usually made of wild silk and has a textured, striated surface. Antique satin simulates shantung.

Sheer General term for thin, lightweight textiles.

Suede Leather with a napped surface. Polyester suede washes and wears well. Upholstery.

Swiss A fine, thin cotton textile originally made in Switzerland and often used for sheers. May be plain, but usually is embroidered or designed with dots (dotted swiss) or figures that have been chemically applied. Manufactured fibers also used.

Taffeta *Plain:* Tight, crisp smooth weave with slight horizontal ribbed effect. When woven of silk, it is a luxury fabric for drapery, bedspreads, and lampshades. *Antique or shantung:* A smooth, soft weave with random slub yarn creating a texture effect. A lustrous fabric with many decorative uses, especially drapery and lamp shades.

Tapestry A figured multicolored fabric woven on a Jacquard loom made up of two sets of warp and weft. The design is formed by varying weave effects brought to the surface in combination with colored yarns. The surface has a rough texture. A heavyweight upholstery fabric.

Terry cloth A mediumweight cotton or linen pile fabric. May be cut or uncut. Loops may be on one side or both. Bedspreads, upholstery, and towels.

Ticking A mediumweight, tightly woven cotton or linen fabric. A strong, usually striped fabric in a satin or twill weave. Mattresses, pillows, wall coverings, slipcovers, and drapery.

Toile de Jouy (twäl də zhwē′) A floral or scenic design usually printed on a plain cotton or linen ground. Originally printed in Jouy, France.

Trapunto (trə-pün′-tō) Quilting that raises an area design in one color on the surface of upholstery fabric.

Tweed Plain-weave, heavyweight upholstery fabric with a tweed texture because of flake (or knotted) yarn, in multicolors. Upholstery.

Union cloth Half linen and half cotton fabric that is plain or patterned. Coarse weave. A variety of uses.

Velour A French term loosely applied to all types of fabrics with a nap or cut pile on one side. Specifically, it is a cut-pile fabric similar to regular velvet but with a higher pile. Heavyweight upholstery fabric.

Velvet A heavyweight fabric having a short, thick warp pile. May be of any fiber. *Crushed:* Most often the fabric is pulled through a narrow cylinder to create the crushed effect. *Cut:* Jacquard design, usually cut and uncut pile on a plain ground. *Antique:* Velvet that has an old look. Upholstery.

Velveteen A heavyweight weft-pile fabric with short pile, usually of cotton. Drapery, upholstery, bedspreads, and innumerable other uses.

Vinyl A heavy nonwoven plastic fabric capable of being printed or embossed to produce any desired finish such as a leather, wood, floral, or textured design. Cloth backing prevents tearing. Walls and upholstery.

Voile (vȯyl) A fine, soft, translucent fabric in a variety of textures, used for sheers.

Webbing Heavyweight jute, cotton, or synthetic strips, generally 1 to 4 in. wide. Interwoven and plain or printed. Particularly used for sofas and chairs. Can also be used to support springs for an upholstered piece.

10

Backgrounds: Floors

Figure 10.1 *In this carpet showroom the variety of flooring materials serve to showcase the flooring industry. The design center includes options for compatible wallcoverings and fabrics, along with an abundance of layout space. (Architect: White Associates. Designer: Chute Gerdeman. Photograph by Michael Houghton Studio. Courtesy of Stanley Steemer International.)*

The general scheme of any room is established by the architectural background: floors, ceilings, walls, and other items such as trim, doors, windows, and fireplaces. The decorative treatments added to these backgrounds (as well as to the movable objects in the room) should be in keeping with the overall feeling to give the room harmony and unity (Figure 10.1). This chapter focuses on the material and finish options for floors.

Floors are designed primarily to be walked on and to provide a foundation for furnishings; therefore, floors must be made from or covered with durable, stain-resistant materials. Due to improved technology, developments in old and new materials, and methods of production, today's flooring materials are both beautiful and practical. The decision to select a specific type of flooring is based on the same criteria discussed in the introduction to Part V: *function and the human factor, aesthetics,* and *economics.*

HARD FLOORING

Recent decades have witnessed a renaissance in hard-surface floor coverings, both nonresilient and resilient. The term *resilient* refers to a material's ability to spring back when pressed. In contrast, *nonresilient* materials lack flexibility.

Nonresilient Flooring

Masonry

The initial cost of nonresilient flooring is generally high; however, hard-surface **masonry** flooring such as brick, stone, and tile remain popular because of their extreme durability, versatility, low maintenance requirements, and timeless character. Masonry floors are installed in either thin or thick mortar.

Figure 10.2 *Chinese slate and bleached pine flooring are combined in this retail store. Note how traffic is directed by the changes in flooring material. (Architect/Designer: Area Design, Inc. Photograph by Jon Miller/Hedrich Blessing.)*

Figure 10.3 *Ceramic tile offers a broad range of finishes from aged and weathered stone to polished marble. The square on the left is Cerdomus Ceramiche, the rectangle is Graniti Fiandre, the bottom two squares are Emilceramic and Vives Azulejos y Gres. (Calmenson, Diane Wintroub. 20/20 Foresight.* Interiors & Sources, *April 1998.)*

Figure 10.4 *Natural stone borders are available in intricate designs. Shown from left are waterjet-cut marble borders from the Corolla and Victoria collections by Stoneworks, and the Wrought Iron border in carved St. Croix travertine by StoneArt. (Calmenson, Diane Wintroub. 20/20 Foresight.* Interiors & Sources, *April 1998.)*

Figure 10.5 *A travertine floor and rusticated columns provide an interesting contrast to the fringed tablecloth, glass top, and faux animal print. (Design and Architecture: Wells Design. Photograph by Hickey-Robertson. As seen in:* Southern Accents.*)*

The durable qualities of tile, stone, and other masonry floors allow these materials to be used throughout the home and commercial environment. In the home, masonry floors may flow from the entrance hall to the porch or patio, thus providing unity and beauty and minimizing upkeep. Designers of restaurants, hotel lobbies, and shopping malls find masonry flooring an extremely durable and creative solution (Figures 10.2 through 10.7).

Table 10.1 contains information on the most commonly used nonresilient hard floor coverings, their characteristics and uses, and suggestions for treatment and care.

Concrete

Concrete floors or slabs are common base floors in commercial office structures. Left plain the floors can give a harsh or institutional feel to the interior; however, concrete floors can be etched or scored into a variety of patterns. Concrete floors also can be faux painted and imprinted to resemble marble, brick, or other decorative motifs (see Figure I.1). Bits of stone or gravel can be added to the cement mixture to create a rough surface; however, these surfaces can be difficult to negotiate.

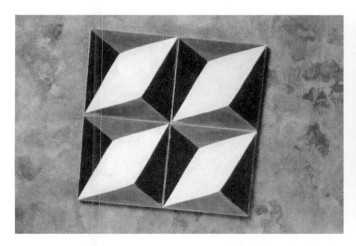

Figure 10.6 *This tile creates a* **trompe l'oeil** *(three-dimensional) effect: Astra from Wholesale Tile & Accessories. (Calmenson, Diane Wintroub.* 20/20 Foresight. Interiors & Sources, *April 1998.)*

Figure 10.7 *This rich, vibrant color palette of ceramic tile is offered by Briare Tile. (Calmenson, Diane Wintroub.* 20/20 Foresight. Interiors & Sources, *April 1998.)*

Table 10.1 *Hard-Surface Flooring: Nonresilient*

Material	Characteristics	Uses	Treatment and Care
Brick	Durable, little upkeep needed Comes in many textures, sizes, and colors Transmits moisture and cold readily, and absorbs grease unless treated Absorbs and stores solar energy, but not sound Rough to touch	Walks, patios, foyers, greenhouses Adds a country look or historical appearance	Careful waxing softens rugged effect and produces soft patina Coating of vinyl protects from grease penetration Dust with dry mop, wash occasionally For stubborn stains, use trisodium phosphate
Ceramic tile (see Figures 10.3, 10.6, 10.7)	Has unique aesthetic quality One of the hardest and most durable floor and wall coverings Versatile Common type using small squares is called mosaic May be glazed or unglazed; comes in many colors, patterns, and textures Glossy surface squares usually 4 1/2 in. New developments producing handsome tiles 12 in. square with variety of designs, textures, and colors Pregrouted tile sheets up to 2 by 14 ft. now available Absorbs and stores solar energy, but not sound Expensive	Especially attractive for bathrooms, and may be suitable for any commercial interior	Unglazed: may be waxed to give soft sheen Glazed: dust with dry mop, wash when needed with soap and warm water
Concrete	May be solid or in squares, smooth or textured, polished or unpolished Color may be added before pouring or after Absorbs and stores solar energy, but not sound Easy upkeep Inexpensive Tends to give cold, industrial feeling when brought inside	Particularly desirable for some hard use areas and for support of heavy equipment Usually used commercially	Heavy waxed surface necessary for maintenance Do not use lacquer, varnish, or shellac Special finishes available Wet before cleaning and use detergent Easy to maintain
Exposed aggregate	Stones are laid in concrete and polished to smoothness, but surface remains uneven Absorbs and stores solar energy Can be too uneven and difficult to walk on	Especially appropriate for exterior walks	Dust, wash occasionally
Flagstone	Any flat stone; varies in size, thickness, quality, and color Versatile, durable, handsome Easy upkeep Colors range from soft grays through beiges and reddish browns May be cut geometrically or laid in natural shapes Surface slightly uneven Absorbs solar energy, but not sound Expensive Difficult to repair if damaged Cold when not heated	Walks, patios, foyers, greenhouses, any heavy traffic area May be dressed up or down, making it appropriate for wide range of uses	Treatment and care same as for brick
Granite	An igneous hard stone of cooled molten rock Has a fine- or coarse-grain (crystal or grain) texture Main colors are variations of gray, brown, black, pink, green, yellow, or combinations of these Has a coarse finish or can be polished until it shines Easy to cut for various uses Harder than marble Expensive Cold to touch Difficult to repair if damaged Does not absorb sound	Floors, walls, tabletops, countertops, and steps Highly durable and excellent for heavy traffic areas Especially popular for commercial use	Easy maintenance: sweep clean, wipe with water when necessary

Table 10.1 *Continued*

Material	Characteristics	Uses	Treatment and Care
Marble (see Figure 10.4)	Extremely hard Available in many varieties, colors, and veining Gives feeling of elegance, luxury, and formality More expensive than most other flooring materials, but is permanent New stone-cutting techniques make it lighter and less expensive Tiles are reinforced by epoxy-fiberglass coating Cold to touch Difficult to repair if damaged Does not absorb sound Slippery when wet	Wherever elegant durability is needed Especially appropriate with classic styles of furnishings Not appropriate in settings where water may be prevalent	Wash with soap and warm water Easy maintenance
Mexican tile or terra-cotta	Crude base made of unrefined clay Hand shaped and sun dried Allows little control of color and shape Durable, informal, inexpensive Absorbs solar energy, but not sound Easy upkeep Difficult to repair if damaged Cold when not heated	Wherever a hard, cementlike surface is desired or wherever solar energy storage is desired	Dust with dry mop, wash occasionally with detergent Surface seldom waxed
Quarry tile	Type of ceramic tile One of the hardest and most durable tiles May be glazed or unglazed Heat and frost resistant, easy upkeep, durable Both ceramic and quarry tiles are practically impervious to grease and chemicals Absorbs and stores solar energy, but not sound Variety of shapes to select Inexpensive Difficult to repair if damaged Cold when not heated	Suitable for many period rooms, especially Italian, early English, and rooms with Mediterranean feeling Can be used wherever hard surface is appropriate Coolness makes it desirable in hot climates	Care same as for ceramic tile
Slate (specific type of stone)	More formal than flagstone Qualities similar to flagstone except for color, which runs from gray to blue-green to black Absorbs solar energy Easy upkeep if sealed Expensive Difficult to repair if damaged Cold when not heated Shows dust easily when polished	May be used in traffic areas in formal rooms Appropriate for some period rooms Particularly appropriate for sunrooms, foyers, and greenhouses	May be polished or unpolished, but more often waxed and highly polished
Terrazzo	Consists of cement mortar (matrix) into which marble chips (aggregate) are mixed Custom or precast; comes in large or small marble chips Larger chips give more formal appearance Available in limited range of colors Sanitary, durable, and easy to clean Cold to touch Difficult to repair if damaged Does not absorb sound Slippery when wet	Patios, foyers, halls, recreation rooms, bathrooms, or wherever traffic is heavy	Care same as for Mexican tile Some varieties need occasional waxing
Travertine (see Figures 10.4 and 10.5)	Porous limestone characterized by irregular cavities that should be filled with either clear or opaque epoxy resin Clear resin has three-dimensional appearance Cold to touch Difficult to repair if damaged Does not absorb sound Slippery when wet	Formal settings where durability is required	Wash with soap or detergent and warm water

Figure 10.8 *The flooring in this entry foyer is bleached oak. The opulent, dramatic design complements the owner's collection of black and white photographs. (Designer: Dilger-Gibson. Photograph by Cheryl Dalton. As seen in Southern Accents.)*

Wood Flooring

Wood has both resilient and nonresilient properties; it is considered the most versatile of all flooring materials. Wood combines beauty, warmth, resistance to indentation, durability, and availability. It also has resistance to cold, which gives wood flooring the additional advantage of comfort over masonry floors. Wood floors can provide an attractive background for any style of furnishings, as seen in Figures 10.2 and 10.8. New methods of treatment have made wood a practical flooring choice for many environments.

Methods of Laying Wood Floors

The three basic methods of laying wood floors are in strips, planks, and parquetry. In the *strip* method, pieces of wood, usually about 2 in. wide with tongue and groove edges, are nailed in place. In the *plank* method, the planks may be uniform or random, varying in width from 3 in. to 7 in. Some have square edges; others are tongue and groove. The *parquetry* method makes use of short lengths of boards, arranging them in various designs such as checkerboard and herringbone

(Figure 10.9). For economy and ease of installation, 9″ to 12″ squares are assembled at the factory.

Stained and Stenciled Wood Floors

Wood flooring is available in a variety of colors in addition to the familiar tones of natural wood. Stain may be applied without obliterating the natural grain of the wood. (Some stain tones even emphasize the pattern in the wood.) A colored wood finish can be achieved by a *stain and sealer method,* in which the surface is stained and then sealed with polyurethane, or the *stain wax method,* in which the stain penetrates into the wood, leaving a wax residue on the surface. When the latter process is repeated and the wood is thoroughly rubbed, the surface has a soft, protective patina.

Stained and sealed wood floors require vacuuming and occasional damp mopping with a vinegar and water solution. Waxed floors must be protected from water and do require occasional rewaxing.

Stenciling, a process of applying paint through a stencil, was used historically as a substitute for expensive carpets. Today, stenciled floors are still an attractive alternative for residential environments.

Figure 10.9 *Patterns of wood flooring.*

Random plank

Checkerboard parquet

Herringbone parquet

Figure 10.10 *A variety of design characteristics are now available in laminate floors. (Courtesy of Perstorp Flooring, Inc.)*

Alternative Wood Flooring

Laminate flooring was introduced to the American market from Sweden. The flooring consists of a moisture-resistant particleboard core and a melamine top layer with a matte or glossy finish. Beneath the finish is a photographic layer that reproduces the pattern and color of wood (Figure 10.10). Laminate floors have many of the same warm characteristics of wood, but have a greater resistance to water. Additionally, they may capture the appearance of rare woods, some of which may no longer be available.

Resilient Flooring

As previously mentioned, resilient hard-surface flooring has the ability to "spring back." The majority of resilient floors are made of vinyl and rubber; however, cork and leather are also used. Table 10.2 lists characteristics, uses, and methods of care for resilient hard-surface floors.

Vinyl

Sheet vinyl is one of the most common forms of vinyl flooring. The sheets are available in rolls 6′, 9′, and 12′ wide for installation with as few seams as possible. Sheet vinyl is available in various grades and qualities. Some high-grade varieties have antimicrobial finishes and resistance to urine and bloodstains, which makes them a good choice for medical facilities.

Vinyl composition tiles, or *VCTs,* are a type of resilient flooring commonly used in commercial environments. The tiles are available in a variety of colors and textures. Laying the patterns on the tiles in the same direction gives a uniform appearance; a checkerboard effect appears when the pattern tiles are alternately turned. Different colors and textures of tiles can create a pattern, define an area, or lead to a destination.

Because tile floors have seams where bacteria can collect, they are not recommended for healthcare areas. VCTs resist water, but should not be used in pool areas where extensive water damage could cause loose tiles. A type of vinyl tile called *conductive tile* is made especially for hospitals and chemical and electronics laboratories to protect against static electricity.

Rubber

Rubber tiles, with a raised dot or other dimensional surface, are designed for high traffic areas or areas around water. The raised areas allow dirt and water to settle below the walking

Table 10.2 *Hard-Surface Flooring: Resilient*

Material	Characteristics	Uses	Treatment and Care
Cork tile	Provides maximum quiet and cushiony comfort underfoot Cork with vinyl or urethane surface highly resistant to moisture and stains, but natural cork not suited for abuse of kitchen traffic, water damage, etc. Colors range from light to dark brown Dented by furniture Rich color and texture Good insulation properties Shows dust easily Fairly expensive	Especially appropriate for studies and other rooms with little traffic Good green design alternative	Maintenance not easy Dirt hard to dislodge from porous surface Wash with soap and water, coat with wax Vinyl coating protects surface
Laminate	Available in a variety of patterns and finishes Offers the beauty of wood with greater durability Easy to install Very durable One of the newest concepts in flooring; as much as 25 times tougher than laminate countertops	Appropriate in any environment except in areas with a lot of water, such as bathroom or poolside	Vacuum and damp mop
Leather tile	Resilient but expensive Natural or dyed colors Quiet Luxurious look and feel Cleans well Rich colors, can be embossed	Studies and other limited areas with little traffic	Warm water and mild soap
Linoleum	Natural linoleum made from linseed oil, tree resin, cork, wood flour, ground limestone, and pigments Jute backing provides good resiliency Available in a variety of patterns and colors First resilient flooring material (manufactured since the mid 19th century)	Can stain if liquids are allowed to soak in Good green design alternative	Warm water and mild soap
Rubber tile	Tiles available 9 in. × 12 in., thickness 3/16 in. and 1/2 in. Usually marble or dot pattern Sound absorbing, durable, nonskidding Safe when wet Raised surface knocks off dirt Relatively expensive	Kitchens, bathrooms, utility rooms Any commercial environment with heavy traffic	Easy to clean Wash with soap and water Avoid varnish or shellac
Sheet rubber	Available in 36 in. × 3/4 in. untrimmed widths Plain or marbleized Durable, nonskidding Safe when wet Raised surface knocks off dirt Relatively expensive	Hard traffic areas Safe covering for stair treads	Same as for rubber tile
Vinyl composition tile or sheets	Excellent all-around, low-cost flooring Resists stains and wears well Hard and noisy Tiles may have self-adhesive backing	May be used in any interior environment	Exceptionally easy to maintain Wash with soap and water
Vinyl, cushion backed	Vinyl chips embedded in translucent vinyl base Has pebbly surface Shows no seams Has cushion backing, making it resilient May tear or dent	Wherever desired in residential setting	Same as for other vinyl
Vinyl, sheet	Lies flat with adhesive only on edges	Wherever vinyl flooring is desired in residential setting	Same as for other vinyl
Vinyl tile	Tough, nonporous, resistant to stains, durable Comes in clear colors or special effects, including translucent and three-dimensional effects The more vinyl content, the higher the price Comes in great variety of patterns and colors	Extremely versatile, may be used in any room depending on grade of vinyl	Easy care Some varieties have built-in luster and require no waxing

Figure 10.11 *In this interior, raised rubber flooring was used for its durability and resistance to water. (Courtesy of Roppe Corporation.)*

surface. This surface is commonly used in airports and near pools (Figure 10.11).

SOFT FLOOR COVERINGS

Soft floor coverings are valued for their practicality, relatively low cost, and design characteristics. They insulate the floor, muffle noise, and create a feeling of comfort. A well-anchored soft floor covering gives sure footing and helps prevent accidents; it is also easy to maintain with regular vacuuming.

Essentially, there are two types of soft floor coverings: carpets and rugs. *Carpets* are sold by the yard from a roll (generally 12 ft. wide) and are called **broadloom.** (Some broadlooms are available between 27 in. and 18 ft. wide.) Pieces of broadloom are taped or seamed together where necessary and attached to the floor to form wall-to-wall carpet. Carpets may also be sold in tiles 12 in. to 24 in. square.

Rugs come in standard sizes or can be custom sized. They have edges finished with a binding thread, fringes, or other materials and are generally not attached to the floor.

A room's décor may be based on the soft floor covering, as seen in Figure 10.12. It can bring furnishings into harmony, create personality and a feeling of luxury, and alter the apparent size and proportion of a room (Figure 10.13). The same carpet carried throughout an interior can serve as a transition from room to room, providing a feeling of unity, whereas an art rug may be a room's focal point (Figure 10.14).

History of Rugs and Carpets

Carpets were used in Egypt as early as 3000 B.C. Writers of the Bible and poets of early Greece and Rome allude to rugs, although walking on such floor coverings was usually the privilege of royalty. Colorful Oriental rugs have been produced in Persia (Iran), Turkey, China, and other Asiatic countries for centuries, where they were the principal item of home furnishing. In the Middle Ages, the later Crusaders came into contact with Constantinople, Antioch, and other

Figure 10.12 *The rug, a Tabriz from Iran (Persia) c. 1850, forms the color source for this room. (Designer: Francis □ Russell. Photograph by Peter Vitale. As seen in Veranda.)*

Wider   Larger

Longer   Smaller

Figure 10.13 *Carpet can change the apparent size and proportion of a room.*

Eastern cities. They carried back many fine rugs, which created a great demand in the West. These floor coverings soon became a symbol of status in Europe and America. Since the time when the first rug looms were established in Aubusson, France, weaving fine floor coverings has been a continuously growing industry. In the 20th century, the introduction of machine-made carpets revolutionized the floor covering industry.

Design Characteristics

The selection of carpet and rugs is based on an understanding of carpet terminology and several design characteristics. Carpet quality is determined by the combination of several components including the *fiber, yarn, construction, backing,* and *surface characteristics.*

When evaluating the quality of carpet, designers should look for products that are resilient, resistant to abrasion, soil, and moisture, easily cleaned, and that do not produce static electricity. Soft floor coverings (particularly carpets and their padding) should also be environmentally friendly (see "Green Design: Flooring Materials"). Overall, carpets and rugs should be durable and maintain their appearance.

Figure 10.14 *This art rug, influenced by the Art Deco style, forms the focal point for this Philadelphia penthouse living room. (Designer: Daroff Design, Inc. Photograph by Mary E. Nichols. Project: Philadelphia penthouse.)*

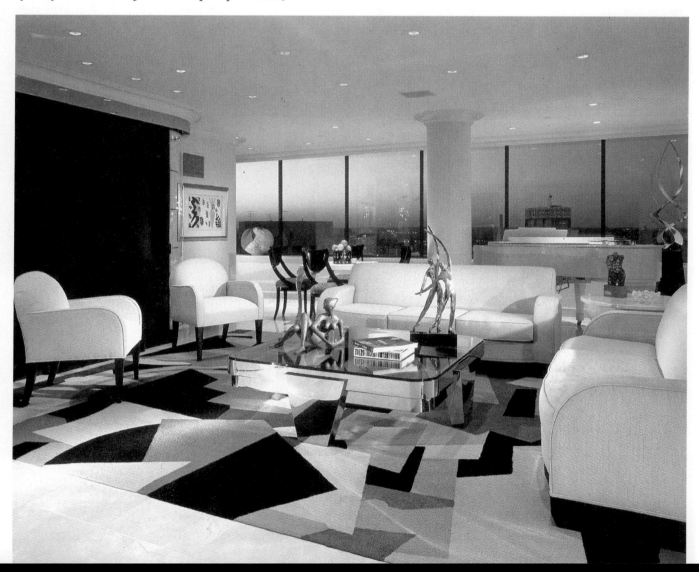

GREEN DESIGN

Flooring Materials

A variety of options are available when specifying flooring materials that help protect the environment. Carpet can be one of the most costly finishes in an interior and creates a disposal problem when it must be replaced. The Partnership for Carpet Reclamation, created by DuPont, a manufacturer of carpet fiber, is one of the many solutions to this problem. The program reclaims used carpets and recycles them into new carpet fibers. Another interesting recycling program uses recycled polyethylene terephthalate (PET), also known as #1 plastic. Consumer products made of PET such as ketchup bottles and soda bottles are cleaned, ground up, melted down, and then extruded to form new fibers (Figure GD10.1).

From ketchup bottle to carpet

Plastic is the latest entry into household recycling programs, joining glass, aluminum and paper. Here's how one system turns bottles made of the light plastic polyethylene terephthalate (PET) into carpet fibers.

Plastic bottles are collected at recycling centers and shipped in compacted bales about 3 x 4 x 5 feet and weighing about 1,200 pounds to a processing plant.

At the processing plant

1 Bottles are washed and heavy plastic bottoms and caps are removed. The heavy plastic is recycled in a separate process.

2 Grinder cuts plastic bottles into one-inch strips

3 Second grinder reduces strips to a mixture of quarter-inch chips containing:
PET
Other plastics
Aluminum chips from leftover bottle caps
Paper from labels
Glue from bottle and label

4 Paper is blown out of the mixture by air jets

5 Chemical solution strips off glue

6 Two-step water/electrostatic process isolates PET chips from other impurities. The chips are shipped to carpet plant

7 At carpet plant, PET chips are melted to the consistency of honey and forced through molds that create fibers about the thickness of a human hair.

About 35% of all carpet fibers made in the USA contain recycled plastic.

Other uses of PET include new food and beverage containers, paint brush bristles, fiberfill material for items such as sleeping bags or ski jackets and strapping material for packagers.

Pounds of PET recycled

175 million — 1988
190 million — 1989
215 million[1] — 1990   1 – Estimate

Source: National Association for Plastic Container Recovery

By Julie Stacey, USA TODAY

Figure GD10.1 *This diagram illustrates the recycling process of used PET plastic into new carpet. (Copyright, USA TODAY. Reprinted with permission.)*

GREEN DESIGN

Flooring Materials—cont'd

As discussed in Chapter 4, another common problem with carpet and carpet pads is that they may emit volatile organic compounds, or VOCs, some of which are harmful to breathe. The Carpet and Rug Institute (CRI) has developed an Indoor Air Quality Testing Program, which evaluates carpet, carpet cushions, and floor covering adhesives, and labels products that have been tested and that meet stringent indoor air quality (IAQ) requirements. Carpet pads made of felt or a natural fiber such as jute are the best choice because they are low-emission products. Specifying low-emitting adhesives or selecting the strip method of installation also may limit the emission of VOCs (see "Green Design: Indoor Air Quality" in Chapter 4).

Vinyl tiles and sheet vinyls can produce high levels of VOCs. Natural linoleum is a better choice. Cork flooring from renewable sources is also an appropriate environmental choice. Cork is taken from the bark of live trees that continue to grow after the cork is harvested. Although not appropriate for all situations, a cork floor is warm and resilient.

One of the best solutions to improve indoor air quality and to diffuse VOCs is to install the flooring materials three to four weeks before an interior is occupied. Recognizing that in many situations this is next to impossible, it is wise to consider installing flooring materials late in the week and then opening the building or home to the fresh air over the weekend. Many businesses are closed on weekends and residential clients possibly could relocate for a weekend. In general, designers should look for labels that mark the product as "low emission" and remember that natural products are generally a more renewable resource.

Fiber

Over the years, virtually every type of fiber has been used in carpets. Today, however, almost all carpeting sold in the United States is made of synthetic fibers, principally *nylon, acrylic, polyester,* and *olefin. Wool* is the most-used natural fiber. Fibers are often blended to bring out the best characteristics of each type.

Wool

Wool is the luxury fiber and has long been regarded as the top carpet fiber. Other fibers express their aesthetic qualities in relation to how nearly they resemble wool. Great resilience accounts for the vital quality of wool in retaining its appearance. Wool has warmth, a dull matte look, durability, and soil resistance. It takes colors beautifully, cleans well, and when cared for, keeps its new look for years. Although more expensive than synthetic fibers, natural wool is the fiber of choice for many designers.

Nylon

Nylon is the single most important synthetic fiber, accounting for about 90 percent of carpeting sold today. Nylon has excellent abrasion resistance, resists crushing and matting, and reduces static electricity, pilling, and fuzzing. When regularly vacuumed it maintains its soil repellency. It is nonallergenic and is mold-, mildew-, and mothproof.

Acrylic

Acrylic's outstanding characteristic is its wool-like appearance. Resistance to abrasion and soiling is good. It is also fairly resilient.

Polyester

Polyester is an exceptionally soft fiber offering good abrasion resistance, but lacks resiliency. Stain and soil resistance are good, and it is easily cleaned.

Olefin

Olefin (or polypropylene) is predominant in needle-punch carpets, which are especially popular for indoor-outdoor use. Ease of care and a nonabsorbent nature are its outstanding characteristics. Most stains lie on the surface, making it the easiest fiber to clean. However, olefin melts easily and when poorly constructed, lacks resilience.

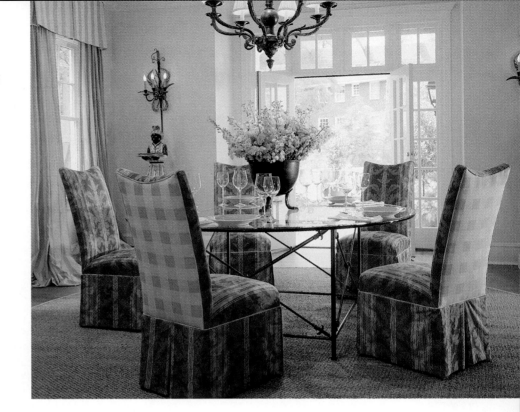

Figure 10.15 *A rug made from seagrass delineates the circular dining area. (Designer: Oetgen Designs. Photograph by Antoine Bootz.)*

Cotton

Although not as durable or resilient as wool and synthetic fibers, cotton is soft, takes dye well, and is less expensive. It is used most often for flat woven area rugs like dhurries from India. Cotton fabric strips are braided into rugs and used in informal settings.

Sisal, Jute, and Hemp

Sisal, jute, hemp, and other grasses are inexpensive floor coverings generally limited to area or room-size rugs (Figure 10.15). These fibers can be woven into simple or intricate designs, and are often made in sections and assembled. Although they provide a natural look, they are not as comfortable underfoot. Japanese tatami mats are made from grasses; however, they are flammable and not particularly durable.

Yarn

The performance of a carpet also depends on the quality, height, density, and quantity of the yarn. Yarns are produced by twisting fibers together into tufts. A tight twist helps the yarn spring back, creating a resilient carpet. Proper heat setting of the yarn holds the twist in place.

The pile height is the length of the yarns; the pile density is the number of tufts per square inch. Taller carpets with greater density contain a greater quantity of yarn. The combination produces a face weight measured in ounces per square yard. Face weights are commonly between 24 and 48 ounces.

A simple test to determine the quality of a piece of carpet is to fold the carpet back on itself. If there are wide spaces or gaps between rows and large amounts of backing show (called the "grin"), the carpet probably will not wear well. A short pile carpet will require a denser pile (more tufts per inch) than a taller pile carpet to pass this test.

In theory a tightly twisted yarn, properly heat set, with the appropriate combination of pile height and pile density produces the best carpet. In addition to fiber and yarn composition, other factors such as construction, backing, and surface characteristics also affect the outcome of these combinations.

Construction

Because of technological developments, the old carpet construction methods (weaving, needle-punching, flocking, and handmade construction) are not often used. Most carpets on the market today are tufted.

Tufting

Tufting accounts for approximately 90 percent of all carpet construction. Based on the principle of the sewing machine, this method involves inserting thousands of threaded needles into a backing material. Heavy latex coating is applied to the backing to permanently anchor the tufts. Some tufted carpets have a double backing for greater strength.

Weaving

The three types of woven carpets are Wilton, Axminster, and velvet, illustrated in Figure 10.16. The *Wilton* carpet takes its name from the town in England where it was first made in 1740. It is woven on a loom with a special Jacquard attachment. The yarns are carried along the background of the carpet until they are drawn to the surface to form loops.

Axminster carpet. Top diagram shows different colored yarns. Bottom diagram shows use of curled down yarns for multilevel effect in face of carpet. (Courtesy of James Lees and Sons Company.)

Wilton carpet (loop pile). Pile is woven over strips of metal, which are removed during weaving process.

Velvet carpet (cut pile). Backing of jute and cotton holds pile yarn in place.

Figure 10.16 *Three types of woven carpets.*

Figure 10.17 *This inviting feminine room, designed by Mario Buatta, features a custom-woven rug. (Room design by Mario Buatta. Carpets and fabrics courtesy of Stark Carpets.)*

After more than 200 years, the Wilton carpet is still regarded as a standard of high quality.

The *Axminster* carpet also derives its name from the town in England where it was first manufactured in 1755. Originally a hand-knotted carpet, it is now made on a specialized American loom in which yarns are set in a crosswise row, permitting each tuft to be controlled individually. This process makes possible an almost unlimited combination of colors and patterns. High-end residential clients and many hotels may require or request the Axminster technique to achieve the desired appearances and quality.

Velvet, the simplest form of carpet weaving, is traditionally a smooth-surface pile, cut or uncut, in a solid color. The pile loops of velvet carpet are woven over long wires extending the full length of the carpet.

Needle-Punching

In the needle-punching process, an assembly of corded fiber webs is compacted and held together by felting needles that mechanically interlock the fibers. The back of the carpet is coated with latex or other weather-resistant materials. This method can produce a wide variety of textures and the carpet sells at a low cost.

Flocking

Flocked carpets have short clipped fibers providing the appearance of velour. They may be produced by three basic methods: *beater bars, spraying,* or an *electrostatic method* (the latter accounts for most flocked carpets). In the electrostatic method, chopped fibers are introduced into an electrostatic field where they become charged. The charged fibers are then projected toward a backing fabric coated with adhesive, where they become vertically embedded. Flocked carpets have a low level of abrasion resistance.

Handmade Construction

Various types and styles of rugs are made by hand. These methods are discussed later in this chapter.

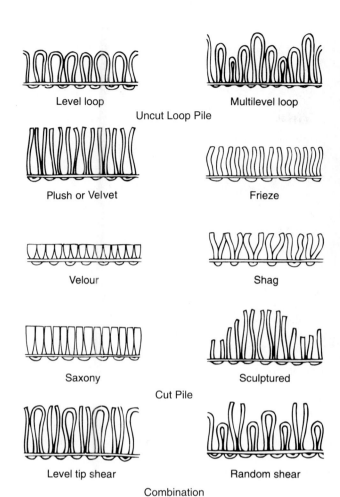

Uncut Loop Pile

Level loop   Multilevel loop

Plush or Velvet   Frieze

Velour   Shag

Cut Pile

Saxony   Sculptured

Level tip shear   Random shear

Combination

Figure 10.18 *Surface characteristics of carpet:* Level loops: *Level loop; multilevel loop.* Cut piles: *Cut or plush; velour; shag; Saxony; friezé.* Combinations: *Sculptured; random shear; level tip shear.*

Backing

The unseen parts of a carpet—the backing and the glue that hold the backing—are important. Together they secure yarns to the foundation and prevent stretching, buckling, and shrinking. Polypropylene and jute are the most common backing materials. Jute is strong but may mildew and therefore is not suitable where floors may be damp. Polypropylene resists mildew and is also strong. Tufted carpets may have a secondary backing applied for extra strength. It may be jute, polypropylene, rubber latex, or vinyl.

Surface Characteristics

Carpets are described by their surface characteristics as either an uncut *level loop* or a *cut pile* (Figure 10.18). The length of the yarn and the texture or design created by the uncut or cut yarns produce these characteristics.

Figure 10.19 *In this high-tech interior a sculptured level loop carpet adds warmth and tactile interest to the sleek wood and metal finishes. (Photograph courtesy of Holey Associates and Cesar Rubio Photography.)*

Level Loop

Level loop carpets are tufted or woven with looped tufts. Because the yarns are not cut, level loops wear extremely well when produced from durable fibers. Level loop carpets are available in solids, heathered solids, and a variety of geometric, stylized, and abstract patterns. Level loops are used in many commercial environments (Figure 10.19). When the heights of the loops are varied the carpet is called a multilevel loop.

Berber carpets, a type of level loop carpet, utilize thick, relatively untwisted yarns. Strong fibers must be used to compensate for the lack of twist. Berbers are found in neutral tones and occasionally soft pastels.

Cut Pile

Cut pile carpets are formed when the loops of yarn are cut or sheered. Various designs have the following characteristics:

- *Plush* or *velvet carpets,* the original style of cut piles, have a dense upright and evenly cut pile under 1″ in height. The carpet is enhanced by highlights and shadings, which provide an extra dimension. Plush carpets are generally more appropriate for formal areas with little traffic. Plush carpets are more resilient and appropriate in short pile heights, under 3/8″, for commercial wear. A short, fine, dense plush is called a velour.
- A *friezé* carpet has a tightly twisted yarn, giving a rough, nubby appearance. Friezés are resilient and resist abrasion.
- *Shag carpets* have pile yarns that are more than 1 in. in height and low in density. The tufts are designed to lie flat giving a shaggy, informal appearance.

- A *Saxony carpet* is similar to a plush, but has more yarns twisted together. The surface of the Saxony appears rougher than that of the plush.

Combination Loops and Piles

Sculptured carpets combine various heights of cut pile and/or level loops to create a design. Sculptured carpets, such as the *random shear,* are most effective when the design is subtle. Too much variety in the heights of the yarns can cause poor resiliency. Yarns that are left all the same height and then selectively cut produce subtle patterns and are called *tip shear* carpets.

Custom-designed *hand-sculptured carpet* is one in which part of the surface has been cut away to form a pattern, or the pattern itself has been cut away from the background. This carpet style is often custom-made and expensive.

Flat Woven

Flat-woven cellulose fiber rugs are machine-made of coarse flax fiber, paper pulp or "kraft" fiber, sisal, hemp, and other grasses and rushes. They come in full-sized rugs or in one-foot squares to be sewn together. Fiber rugs are usually in natural colors but are sometimes dyed. Popular in warm climates, they also provide inexpensive year-round floor coverings in many contemporary settings. Other flat-woven styles include *dhurries* from India, *Navajo rugs* from America, and *Rollikans* from Scandinavia.

Special Features

Additional design features may be necessary when selecting carpets for specialty commercial uses. To control static electricity, synthetic fibers can be altered during the viscose stage or covered with a special coating after they are manufactured. A low static electricity rating, usually less than 3.5 kilovolts, is required in all areas where computers or electronic equipment will be used. An antimicrobial treatment is necessary in healthcare environments. Advanced soil-resistant treatments may prove beneficial in areas with extremely high traffic.

Handmade Rugs

Oriental Rugs

The making of Oriental rugs is a great art, and these rugs have been coveted possessions for hundreds of years. During the 18th and 19th centuries, rugs from China and the Middle East were in great demand among wealthy Americans who wanted to adorn their Georgian- and Federal-period mansions.

With the advent of wall-to-wall carpeting, Oriental rugs were in less demand in America, but during the past few decades they have been rediscovered and are again desirable for contemporary use, regardless of style. To meet the current demand, American manufacturers are duplicating authentic Oriental designs in loom-woven rugs retailing at a

Ghiordes or Turkish knot, used in Turkey and elsewhere

Sehna or Perrsian knot, used in many parts of Iran

Figure 10.20 *Principal knots used in making Oriental rugs.*

fraction of the cost of the handmade ones. These rugs are called "Oriental design rugs" to distinguish them from the hand-loomed rugs made in the Orient called "Oriental rugs."

Oriental Rugs from Persia and Turkey

The great majority of Oriental rugs imported into America have come from Persia (Iran) and Turkey. These rugs are made by hand-tying a knot in each weft thread as it crosses the warp. The knot is either the *Ghiordes* (Turkish) or the *Sehna* (Persian) type, depending on the area in which it is made (Figure 10.20). Rugs are frequently made by members of a family who use the same pattern generation after generation. The name of the particular rug is usually that of the family or is taken from the name of the village or area in which the rug was made.

Given the myriad types with distinct design origins from different areas, towns, tribes, and families, the study of Oriental rugs can be a lifelong pursuit. A logical beginning is to become familiar with the three Oriental rugs from the Near East that are particularly pleasing to American tastes: the Kirman, Sarouk, and Tekke, commonly called Bokhara.

A top-grade *Kirman* is among the most costly of Oriental rugs. The most familiar type has a central medallion surrounded by a plain ground with a wide border of intricate design (Figure 10.21). Sometimes the entire ground is filled with delicate blooms. This rug is one of the few Oriental rugs that are available with an ivory background.

The predominant colors in the *Sarouk* are exotic jewel tones of red, rose, and deep blue, with black and ivory as accent colors. Although the pattern is predominantly floral, it does feature some geometric devices. The Sarouk may also have a vibrant medallion outlined in dark colors. The pile is usually heavy (Figure 10.22).

Figure 10.21 *The most familiar of the Kirman designs: an open ground, a wide, uneven border, and a medallion center. (Courtesy of Karastan Rug Mills.)*

Figure 10.23 *A Bengali rug from India, made in the Chinese Peking design. (Courtesy of Stark Carpet Corporation.)*

Figure 10.22 *The all-over floral with rose or red ground is typical of Sarouk rugs. (Courtesy of Karastan Rug Mills.)*

The *Bokhara,* originally from Turkistan, is made in many Middle Eastern countries. The background of the Bokhara may be red, cream, or blue, but the predominant color is always red. The easily recognizable design is made up of octagons or polygons called *guls* (roses), which are repeated uniformly about the field. When the guls are quartered by narrow lines running the length and width of the field, the design is popularly called *Royal Bokhara.*

Oriental Rugs from China

The art of rug making has been practiced in China for more than 12 centuries. The oldest known rugs were from the T'ang dynasty (618–906). The oldest existing rug dates from the Ming dynasty (1368–1644). Early designs were taken from ancient Chinese silk weaving and are symbolic of ancestor worship. Ancient symbols, of which there are over 100, fall into a number of categories. Chinese rugs can be recognized by the following characteristics:

- Colors of Chinese rugs are typically blue and white (often used for the field), with yellow-orange, red-orange, gold, and cream also used in various combinations.
- Geometric designs are used primarily as border ornamentation. The Chinese "T," key, or fret designs are the most familiar. The circle with a square in the center and two curved cells within a circle, symbolizing male and female, are common motifs.
- Religious symbols are commonly used, including the dragon, which symbolizes God and emperor, and waves and closed bands (eternity). Among the mythological symbols are the lion (authority), horse (strength), fish (abundance), and stag and crane (longevity).
- Flowers most commonly used are the lotus (purity), peony (prosperity), and chrysanthemum (fidelity).

Chinese rugs are made from complete paper models, and the design is outlined on a cotton warp. The pile is higher than on rugs made in the Middle East, and designs are sculptured by clipping the yarns along the contour of the pattern.

Rugs made in eastern China usually have allover patterns reflecting the Middle Eastern influence. The two most familiar Chinese rugs are the *Mandarin,* which has no border, an open ground, and a different asymmetrical floral spray in each corner, and the *Peking,* which has a wide border, similar corner motifs, and a round central medallion. Peking design rugs made in India are called *Bengali* (Figure 10.23).

Oriental Rugs from India

Today many rugs of excellent quality are handmade in India for export to Europe and America. Rugs employing old and authentic designs from China, Iran, Turkey, and France are made from top-quality wool (mostly from New Zealand) and sell at moderate prices.

Numdah rugs, used in India for centuries, have been imported into the United States for many years and recently

Figure 10.24 *This Numdah rug is made of rough felt with wool embroidery in the "tree of life" design. (Photograph by Mark K. Allen.)*

Figure 10.26 *The French Savonnerie is a velvety pile carpet, typically with intricate French designs. (Courtesy of Designer Rugs Limited.)*

have revived in popularity (Figure 10.24). This rug is an informal type made of felt. The wool surface is traditionally enriched with bird and floral motifs worked with a long, open stitch.

Dhurries are flat-weave rugs hand-woven in India (Figure 10.25). They are tightly woven in wool or cotton and incorporate both stylized and geometric designs. Colors are frequently pastels and medium tones on a natural field.

French Rugs

Two French-style rugs have been produced with little interruption since the 17th century: the Savonnerie and the Aubusson.

The *Savonnerie* is a pile carpet made by hand with knotted stitches in the manner of Orientals but with French pat-

Figure 10.25 *The dhurries were used originally as sleeping bags for travelers. The thin wool or cotton rug could be rolled up and easily carried.*

terns (Figure 10.26). The Savonnerie factory, established in France in 1663 by Louis XIV, was an outgrowth of a workshop founded earlier in the Louvre. Although it was the first factory to produce tapestrylike rugs, it is best known for its velvety pile rugs, usually made in strong colors on a dark ground with elaborate designs sometimes take from formal French gardens.

Aubusson rugs are distinctive. During the late 17th century when the upper classes of France became interested in beautifying their homes, long-established, privately owned workshops at Aubusson strove to imitate the weaving completed at Savonnerie. Some of the oldest Aubusson rugs have an Oriental flavor, but later ones follow the French textile designs employing small-scaled, stylized floral themes. Colors are usually soft, muted pastels, giving a faded effect (Figure 10.27).

Other Types of Rugs

Moroccan Rugs

The Moroccan is a type of Oriental rug made primarily in northwest Africa. The character of the rug has changed little in 1,000 years. Its distinctive informality has made it a favorite in contemporary decor. The most common Moroccan rug is the Berber.

Berber rugs (the inspiration for American berber carpets) are traditional types made primarily by Berber tribes in the Atlas Mountains. The designs are abstract and geometric. Some are primitive, often of natural wool color with simple black or brown designs; others are vividly colored.

The Spanish Matrimonia

The Spanish matrimonia, the traditional bridal gift in Spain, is the fringed, bold-figured Manta rug. Woven on the Jacquard loom, these rugs have subtle shadings, a handcrafted-like texture, and a three-dimensional quality. Patterns are brightly colored and inspired by medieval motifs, classic Aubussons,

Figure 10.27 *Aubusson rugs are made of tapestry weave, usually with French designs in pastel colors. (Courtesy of Stark Carpet Corporation.)*

Figure 10.28 *The elaborately woven matrimonia rugs are created based on the bride's status. Handed down through generations, the fine rug is used in the marriage ceremony and may be made of linen, cotton, wool, silk, or gold and silver threads. (Courtesy of Designer Rugs Limited.)*

Far East Orientals, mythical figures, and the tree of life (Figure 10.28).

Navajo Rugs

The Navajo rug is a hand-woven rug or blanket made by the Navajo Indians in the American Southwest. Those of finest quality are made of wool and colored with vegetable dyes. Designs are usually geometric with frequent zigzag, chevron, and diamond motifs combined with stripes (Figure 10.29). Stylized representations of birds, animals, and human figures are sometimes used.

Rya Rugs

Rya is a name derived from an old Norse word meaning "rough." This hand-hooked rug is a traditional import from Scandinavia, where it has been used for centuries. The rya is a high-pile shag rug combining a blend of multicolored yarns forced into a wool backing with a rug hook. The yarns are cut at an angle and at various heights, creating the "shaggy" appearance. Geometric designs of all types are often combined with stylized nature themes. Rya rugs are ideally suited for use as area or art rugs in contemporary settings.

Rag Rugs

Rag rugs were one of the first floor coverings made by American colonists. Scraps of cotton, linen, or wool fabric were cut in narrow strips and then sewn together to form long strands, then woven in a plain weave on a cotton or linen warp. The craft of making rag rugs is still practiced.

Braided Rugs

Braided rugs were originally made in the home from scraps of clothing and blankets. They are still a favorite for rooms with a provincial atmosphere, especially in colonial Ameri-

can and country French rooms. Strips of rags are stitched together (on the bias), then braided into long ropes, which are either sewn or woven together in rounded or oval shapes (Figure 10.30). Rugs of this type are also produced commercially at reasonable cost.

Hooked Rugs

Hooked rugs are made by hooking colored rags or yarns through a tightly stretched piece of burlap, canvas, or wool to form a design. The foundation fabric and the type of material used for filling determine the degree of durability.

Figure 10.29 *This Navajo rug is characteristic of much of the art of the North American Indians and is similar to Peruvian rugs. (Photograph by Mark K. Allen.)*

Figure 10.30 *A braided rug can be used in any setting where a country look is desired.*

Needlepoint Rugs

Needlepoint rugs were originally made by embroidering wool yarn on a heavy mesh canvas. Designs range from simple to highly complex floral motifs in a wide array of colors.

Padding

Most carpets and rugs require a quality pad or cushion, which provides tremendous value for the initial cost. Cushioning improves and helps to maintain the appearance of the carpet and enhances its resiliency. Carpet pads absorb noise, help to control the room's temperature, and create a feeling of luxury. Padding is particularly beneficial in areas where the subfloor is uneven, because the pad assists in smoothing out the floor. There are three general categories of padding: fiber, rubber, and urethane foam.

- *Fiber cushions* can be made from natural products (such as animal hair or jute), synthetics (such as nylon or polyester), or recycled textile fibers. A fiber cushion creates a "firm" feel.
- *Rubber cushions* can be either flat or ribbed. The flat gives a firm feel and the ribbed a stiffer feel.
- *Urethane foam cushions* come in a variety of types. *Conventional* and *grafted prime urethane* foams are manufactured from a chemical mix and are available in a variety of densities. *Densified polyurethane* has undergone a further process to meet specific guidelines. *Bonded* foam is made by fusing shredded pieces of urethane foam together. *Mechanically frothed urethane* foam was originally developed as a cushion attached to the back of carpet. It typically has a higher density and firmer feel.

When selecting a pad for residential use, keep in mind the following recommendation from the Carpet Cushion Council (CCC): "The heavier the traffic, the thinner the cushion." For commercial use the CCC has developed a labeling system based on volume of traffic. Pads with a Class I rating are acceptable for moderate traffic, those with Class II for heavy traffic, and those with Class III for extra heavy traffic.

In some commercial office environments when level loop carpet is used, no padding is laid beneath the carpet. The carpet is said to be "direct glue," and is literally glued to the plywood or concrete subfloor. Thick padding is inappropriate in commercial environments because it gives the appearance of a luxury residence.

Design Considerations

Aside from the performance characteristics of the carpet and pad, designers must also consider aesthetic factors. These factors include the *size and space, color and pattern,* and *texture.*

Size and Space

The size of the carpet or rug depends on the characteristics and intended use of the particular space. For instance, wall-to-wall carpets have distinct uses, but may also be bordered to give the appearance of an art or area rug.

Wall-to-wall broadloom carpet has some distinct advantages: It creates continuity within a room or from room to room, makes rooms look larger, adds warmth and a feeling of luxury, requires only one cleaning process, and provides maximum safety from accidents. This carpet treatment also has some disadvantages: It must be cleaned in place, and it cannot be turned for even wear.

Carpet tiles have many of the same benefits as wall-to-wall carpet with the additional advantage that a tile can be replaced should it become soiled or damaged. Carpet tiles are glued directly to the floor. They allow for greater flexibility in design and access beneath the floor (see Figure 9.14).

A *room-sized rug* is one that comes within a foot or so of the walls, leaving a marginal strip of floor exposed. The room-sized rug has most of the advantages of wall-to-wall carpeting, plus some extra benefits. It can be turned for even distribution of wear and removed for cleaning. Two processes, however, are necessary for complete cleaning—one for the rug and the other for the exposed flooring material around it.

An *area rug* does not cover the entire floor but is used to define an area of a room according to its function. The area rug should be large enough to accommodate all the furniture used in the area grouping. This type of rug is versatile and may easily be changed for different grouping arrangements.

An *art rug,* which is usually smaller than an area rug, is generally handcrafted and used as an accent or treated as a focal point. This rug is often placed so that furniture does not encroach on it, enabling it to be admired like a piece of art on the floor. Sometimes an art rug functions as an area rug (see Figure 10.14).

Scatter or *throw rugs* are smaller rugs often used as accents or as protection for a spot that receives hard wear.

Color and Pattern

Color is a critical factor in the selection of a carpet. As with textiles, dyeing processes vary and some fibers accept color better than others. As with fabrics, generally the earlier the color is added in the manufacturing process, the longer the color will remain.

Neutral color carpet allows for a variety of changes in other finishes. In apartments, tenant offices, and other places with frequent turnover rates, neutral colors are the best choice. In restaurants or other high traffic areas, patterns and colors in middle values hide dirt the best. A light color will easily show stains, whereas a dark color will show lint and dust.

Lighting also affects the carpet's color. Fibers, style characteristics, and textures of carpet absorb and reflect light differently. A sunny room may call for a carpet in cool colors, whereas a northern exposure or dark room may require warm colors in lighter tones. Carpets should be tested for color in their final environment.

Wall-to-wall carpets in solid colors or overall texture give a feeling of spaciousness. Large patterns tend to fill up space and are usually best reserved for larger areas. If the carpet selected has a pronounced pattern, then walls, drapery, and upholstery tend to be complemented when plain colors or unobtrusive patterns are employed (see Figure 10.12). Carpets with a plain overall effect permit a wider choice of furnishings.

Texture

Each carpet or rug type has a unique texture, such as smooth, shiny, dull, rough, etc. The surface quality of the carpet should be aesthetically compatible with other furnishings. The same considerations discussed in Chapter 9 for selecting textures of textiles also hold true for the selection of carpet textures. A carefully chosen carpet or rug can coordinate all furnishings of the room and provide unity.

Codes and Regulations

Federal, state, and local laws or codes and regulations set particular standards (especially for flame resistance, flame spread, and smoke generation) regarding the performance and quality of a floor covering. There must be a label attached to the floor covering indicating the name of the manufacturer, the Federal Trade Commission number, the fiber content, the weight of the fiber, and flame-resistant qualities. Building codes vary in different areas; therefore, the designer must be knowledgeable about local codes and regulations before specifying a particular floor covering.

Measuring and Installation

Before purchasing the selected floor covering it is necessary to figure the amount of material needed to complete

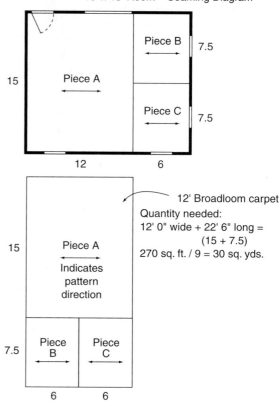

Figure 10.31 *A seaming diagram for a 15′ × 18′ room covered with 12′ wide broadloom carpet.*

the job. To arrive at an estimate, determine the square footage of the space to be covered and divide by 9 (the number of square feet in a yard). This will give the approximate square yardage needed; however, additional yardage is required for piecing the carpet and for matching pattern repeats. Many designers prepare a cut or seaming diagram for figuring the correct yardage (Figure 10.31). Try to avoid specifying carpet seams in major traffic areas. The *nap* of the pile (sometimes called the *pile sweep*) must be laid in a uniform direction to prevent light variation.

When specifying carpet for a residential or commercial project the designer indicates installation methods and techniques. There are two basic installation methods: the stretch or tackless strip and pad method and the glue-down method. In the *stretch and pad method* a 1-inch-wide plywood strip with small projecting metal pins is nailed around the perimeter of the room and the pad is nailed, glued, or stapled inside the strip. The carpet is stretched over the pad and then attached over the pins of the strip. TACFAST™, by Karastan Bigelow, also offers a hook and loop technology that secures carpet to the floor through a system similar to Velcro™. In the *glue-down method* glue or adhesive is applied to attach the carpet to the floor.

Figure 10.32 *This foyer sets a formal, masculine tone for the residence. The stone flooring unifies the interior and is an excellent selection for the high traffic area. (Courtesy of Renaissance Reclamation.)*

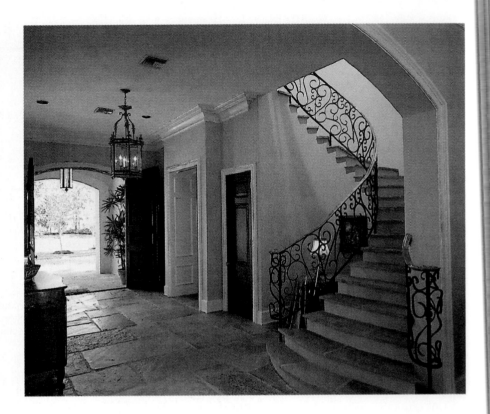

Summary

The decision to select a particular floor covering forms an important piece of the interior environment puzzle. Broad design decisions must first address the need for a hard or soft flooring material. The floor covering can create the interest or focal point, or serve as the neutral element unifying a room or series of rooms (Figure 10.32). Carpet selection requires close attention to design characteristics and construction methods to ensure durability. Considerable time should be devoted to selecting the proper floor covering that not only looks great, but also maintains its appearance through years of foot traffic.

11

Backgrounds: Ceilings and Walls

Figure 11.1 *This extravagant, opulent drawing room in the Kip's Bay Showhouse was designed by Juan Pablo Molyneux. The elegant backgrounds, including walls, ceiling, floors, windows, and fireplace, clearly establish a formal, eclectic French style and support the 18th- and 19th-century furnishings. (Antique Aubusson courtesy of F. J. Hakimian, Inc., NY, and Juan Pablo Molyneux. Photograph by Peter Vitale).*

CEILINGS

The ceiling—the largest unused area of a room—has been given special attention for hundreds of years. The ceilings of Renaissance palaces were magnificently sculpted and adorned with decorative plaster. (A contemporary version of this treatment is seen in Figure 11.1.) Ceilings during the settlement period in America were usually low and plain with visible support beams. During the Georgian, Federal, Greek Revival, and Victorian periods ceilings were generally not as ornately designed as in earlier periods in Europe, but did include some decorative treatment.

The functions of the ceiling include providing (1) protection from the elements, (2) insulation for heating and cooling, (3) a source for artificial lighting (and natural lighting, when skylights are used), (4) an acoustic barrier for absorbing or reflecting sound, (5) a flame-resistant barrier that meets standard fire codes, and (6) an important element of the character and atmosphere of a room (Figure 11.2).

In many current interiors, the ceiling's potential to add character and atmosphere to a room has been neglected. It has been covered with gypsumboard (a type of wallboard) and painted white. The following section discusses some of the various types of ceilings that designers can use.

Types of Ceilings

Ceiling designs can be distinguished according to various structural forms and their placement or direction.

- The *flat ceiling* is usually plastered, painted, or covered with wood strips. The flat-beamed ceiling is one in which the structural beams are exposed or lightweight beams have been applied.
- The **shed** or *lean-to ceiling* rises diagonally to one side in a single slope. The furnishings in a room with this ceiling must be arranged carefully to achieve a comfortable balance.
- The *gabled, double-pitched,* or **cathedral** *ceiling* expands vertical space, especially when beams extend upward (Figure 11.3). Placing beams horizontally emphasizes the room's length.
- A ceiling whose middle portion extends vertically up about 6 in. to 18 in. is called a **tray** ceiling. Trays may be formed in many shapes and may conceal lighting around the perimeter.
- The *sculptured, custom-designed ceiling* may call attention to itself as the room's focal point. Sometimes designed in highly dramatic ways, sculptured ceilings follow no set pattern and usually require ample space for construction and effect (Figure 11.2).

Figure 11.2 *The sculptured ceiling in this retail center not only adds interest and entertainment but also opens to skylights in the roof. Architect/Designer: Anthony Belluschi Architects Ltd. Lighting Designer/Roeder Design, a subsidiary of Pacific Lightworks. Photograph by Robt. Ames Cook.)*

Figure 11.3 *In this library, located at Culver Academy in Culver, Indiana, the designers used a gabled and beamed ceiling to contrast with the refined traditional columns. (Architect/Designer: Hellmuth, Obata & Kassabaum. Photograph by Balthazar Korab Ltd.)*

- The **coved** *ceiling* meets the wall with a curve instead of a right angle, so the ceiling and wall flow into each other. Sometimes the perimeter is made to accommodate recessed lighting, allowing light to shine upward on the ceiling surface.
- **Vaulted** and *domed ceilings* are arched structures as opposed to flat planes and can be considered a complete extension of the coved ceiling.
- **Coffered** *ceilings,* popular in past centuries, are constructed of wooden members in a grid manner, often with moldings and sunken decorative panels.
- A *dropped ceiling* has a portion or its entire area lowered below the main structure (Figure 11.4). This type of ceiling can define an area of a room (a dining area in a dual-purpose living room or a reception area in a lobby, for example), provide indirect lighting, and add interest to a living space.
- In many commercial settings, the ceiling is actually nonexistent and is formed by the exposed structure above. This type of ceiling allows for extensive flexibility in lighting placement. Furniture showrooms and other retail establishments use this method of ceiling treatment to accommodate the great variety and abundant changes in the merchandise displayed. Restaurants may use this design to create an informal or high-tech feeling. In residential settings, this type of ceiling may be used to add drama (Figure 11.5).
- Designers often create custom-designed ceilings for specific residential or commercial projects (Figure 11.6).

Figure 11.4 *Dropped ceiling.*

Ceiling Construction and Materials

Ceiling materials may be divided into two general categories: those that attach directly to the structure (such as plaster, gypsumboard, glass and plastic panels, stamped metal, fabric, and wood), and those that hang from the structure (such as suspended ceiling tiles).

Plaster and Gypsumboard

Plaster is the most versatile of all ceiling treatments. Plaster is a thick mixture of gypsum, water, lime, and sand. This mixture is applied to a metal lattice, a special hardboard, or any rough masonry surface. The finished surface may be smooth, textured, wallpapered, or painted. Sometimes a plaster ceiling is stenciled or has applied decoration or moldings. Plaster has been used for centuries, but currently the cost is relatively high.

Because of the high cost of plaster, gypsumboard is more commonly used. The 4 ft. × 8 ft. panels have a finished surface like plaster. Gypsumboard provides insulation and is available in many thicknesses. When layered it is highly fire resistant.

Glass and Plastic

Glass or plastic panels, either translucent or transparent, are sometimes used in ceilings to provide overhead light—either natural daylight or recessed artificial light. These panels may provide overall illumination or striking lighting effects from high-up windows. Skylight views add a new dimension to any interior.

Figure 11.5 *To give the illusion of endless space, designer Harry Stein painted the beams and part of the ceiling black and strategically placed numerous lamps. Other sections of the ceiling are mirrored, adding to the effect of depth in this New York penthouse. (Photograph by Norman McGrath.)*

Figure 11.6 *The theme of the Enchanted Lobby at the Walt Disney World Swan Hotel, designed by Michael Graves, is fantasy and entertainment. Large palm-frond sconces and colorful parrot light fixtures reinforce the tropical illusion. The high-pitched ceiling is painted with dramatic stripes resembling fabric. Handsome swan benches provide a warm touch. (Photo ©Disney Enterprises, Inc.)*

Stamped Metal

Stamped metal ceilings were popular during the 19th century and add a historical feel to interior environments. These ceilings are used in the restoration and construction of Victorian buildings and are commonly seen in commercial interiors such as restaurants or retail spaces. This treatment involves stamping or pressing designs onto metal panels, providing a unique embossed effect.

Fabric

Fabric, although not commonly used, can be stretched, shirred, or pasted (like wallpaper) to the ceiling surface. Its softness provides a comfortable, warm feeling, and when used as a repeating fabric in the room can unify the interior. Figure II.4 illustrates an unusual treatment of a fabric ceiling.

Wood

Wood, in strips, panels, beams, or planks, can provide a warm, inviting atmosphere. Because of its visual weight, wood tends to lower the ceiling and may create a feeling of heaviness unless the ceiling is higher than average. Often wood is used in combination with plaster; for example, wood beams can stretch across a plaster ceiling. Wood can be left natural, stained, or painted. Where natural beams are not feasible, ceiling beams of polyurethane (which simulate hand-carved wood to a remarkable degree) can be glued to the ceiling.

Suspended Ceilings and Tiles

Suspended ceilings are common in commercial construction. Metal tracks are suspended from the structure, forming a 2 ft. × 2 ft. or 2 ft. × 4 ft. grid pattern, which is then filled with tiles. The tiles come in a wide variety of materials, colors, and patterns. Many have acoustical properties for absorbing noise. Others have a foil backing, which cuts down on air conditioning and heating costs. Some manufacturers wrap ceiling tiles in fabric to create a warm, plush look. Another type of suspended ceiling system is the 1 ft. × 1 ft. concealed spline. Although this ceiling is more difficult to install, it gives a more uniform appearance than the larger grids.

Suspended ceilings are versatile. Lighting and HVAC are concealed above the grid system in the space called the **plenum.** As interior furnishings are moved, the ceiling lighting may be moved to adjust to the new needs. Additionally, if HVAC or plumbing systems need to be upgraded, repaired, or moved, they are easily accessed.

Ceiling Illusions

If a ceiling is much above or below the average main-floor height of eight to nine feet, it alters the general feeling of the room. A high ceiling emphasizes space and tends to create a feeling of dignity and formality. A low ceiling, which decreases space, can produce a warm, informal atmosphere. Designers should note the ceiling height with respect to the

Figure 11.7 *Wallpaper extended beyond the walls and into coved ceilings gives the appearance of greater height.*

width and length of the room. A low ceiling in a very large room can be confining, whereas a high, tall ceiling in a small room can create the impression of living in a barrel. To accommodate the human factor, ceilings may be made to appear higher to suit an owner's preference for a more spacious feeling, or lower to provide a cozy, intimate atmosphere. To create the illusion of height, observe the following guidelines:

- Run the wall color or covering a short distance onto the ceiling, especially when the corners are coved. This treatment causes the eye to move upward and makes the ceiling appear higher (Figure 11.7). Use a light color on the ceiling.
- Use a predominance of vertical lines in the architecture of the room and in the decorative elements, like patterned wallpaper.
- Add a skylight to open up space.
- Use diagonal beams, which draw the eye upward, to make gabled ceilings appear even higher (see Figure 11.2).

To create a lowered ceiling effect:

- Paint the ceiling a darker color or use a patterned finish.
- Extend the color or covering down onto the wall a short distance and end it with a border or a small molding. As attention moves upward, it stops at the molding and the ceiling seems to begin at that point. In this way the ceiling can be psychologically lowered as much as three feet.
- Use a predominance of horizontal lines in the room's architecture and decorative elements.
- Use wood ceilings and horizontal beams, particularly in natural wood or a bold or dark color.

In recent years changing interior styles have produced exhilarating ceiling designs, which add new dimensions to interior spaces. Through the use of creative materials and finishes, and by incorporating a variety of ceiling

Figure 11.8 *In this refined restaurant Adam D. Tihany utilized a multilevel grid pattern to create a bold yet simple architectural statement. The texture of the materials provides warmth and adds depth to the interior. (Architect/Designer: Adam D. Tihany International, Ltd. Photograph by Peter Paige.)*

heights within a residence or commercial setting, the ceiling can become the focal point or an important backdrop for other interior elements (Figure 11.8).

WALLS

The vertical background elements of a room are important factors in setting and maintaining the decorative scheme. Walls, windows, doors, and fireplaces are all part of the room's enclosure and provide the background elements for furniture and fabrics; however, their most important function is to provide a background for people.

Walls occupy the largest area of a room, define its size and shape, and serve purposes of both function and beauty. Functionally, walls provide protection and privacy from the exterior surroundings and create interior areas of various shapes and sizes for particular activities. Walls also provide space for plumbing pipes, electrical and telephone wires, and HVAC, as well as insulation against heat, cold, and noise. Aesthetically, they contribute significantly not only to the success of a room but also to its general atmosphere and personality.

Wall Construction

Walls are generally defined as load bearing or non-load-bearing. Load-bearing walls support other parts of the

structure such as the roof or upper-level floors. Non-load-bearing walls function as dividers and do not support the structure, but may support shelves, cabinets, or other interior elements. Before moving or cutting an opening in a load-bearing wall, a designer must consult with a builder, engineer, or architect to determine alternative structural requirements.

Some non-load-bearing walls are freestanding and stop at desk or counter height, or just short of the ceiling. These walls provide some degree of privacy, but permit the flow of air, light, and sound from one area to another.

Nonresilient (Rigid) Wallcoverings

There are many materials available for wall treatments. Each type has advantages and disadvantages with regard to appearance, cost, upkeep, noise, insulation, and longevity. Some wall treatments are extremely versatile; others belong to certain period styles or are used to evoke certain moods. When selecting materials for wall backgrounds designers should consider aesthetics, function and the human factor, economics and ecology, as discussed in the introduction to Part V.

Table 11.1 lists the most frequently used nonresilient wallcoverings, plus information on their general characteristics, fire ratings, insulation properties, uses, and care.

Table 11.1 *Nonresilient Wallcoverings*

Material	General Characteristics and Cost	Finishes	Fire Rating	Insulation Properties	Uses and Care
Brick (fired clay)	Solid and durable Variety of sizes, shapes, and colors Old, natural brick has feeling of warmth May be laid in regular or varied patterns Pleasant texture High cost	No finish necessary May be painted or waxed	Fireproof	Reflects noise Conducts heat and cold	Interior and exterior walls Appropriate for large- or small-scaled rooms in a wide range of styles, and for fireplace facings and hearths Little or no upkeep
Concrete blocks (lightweight aggregate)	Substantial, cold, regular shape, large scale, textured Moderate cost	No finish necessary May be painted Waterproofing necessary for exterior	Fireproof	Fair insulator	Interior or exterior walls, fireplace facings Best when used in large-scaled rooms Lacks domestic warmth Little or no maintenance
Ceramic tile (clay)	Comes in variety of shapes, sizes, colors, and patterns, and in pregrouted sheets Durable, resists water and stains, but may crack or break Moderately high cost	No finish necessary	Fireproof	Reflects noise Poor insulator	Bathrooms, kitchens, utility rooms, breakrooms Particularly appropriate for dadoes in Spanish- and Mexican-style rooms Minimum upkeep
Fiberglass (panels)	Translucent panels of reinforced fiberglass Most often ribbed or corrugated Also available in flat sheets and in several thicknesses Comes translucent, white, or colored Moderate cost	No finish necessary	Fireproof	Good insulator	Room dividers, folding screens, tub enclosures, translucent lighting panels for ceilings, built-ins, and sliding doors Easy upkeep
Glass (architectural)	Can be clear, rubbed, corrugated, pebbled, frosted, colored, or curved Metal mesh core will prevent breakage May be tempered Moderately high cost	No finish necessary	Fireproof	Poor insulator	Sliding doors, screens, room dividers, clinical purposes, numerous other uses Mirrors can usually expand space and add dramatic element to rooms One-way glass has many functional uses
Glass (block)	Excellent light transmission High-impact strength Moderately high cost	No finish necessary	Fireproof	Solid glass blocks conduct heat Blocks with hollow air centers are good insulators	Contemporary settings Suitable to lighten most dark areas Easy upkeep
Metal (panels and tiles)	Stainless steel: plain or grained (nonreflective finish) Serviceable, sturdy, not affected by acid, steam, or alkalies Solid copper: attractive May be plain, hammered, or antiqued Sealed to prevent tarnish or corrosion Aluminum glazes: solid aluminum Coated with permanent vitreous glaze of porcelain, enamel, or epoxy enamel Sturdy, easy to maintain Lightweight and strong, but subject to dents that are difficult to repair Tends to have commercial effect Moderate cost	Factory finished with grain, or enameled in variety of colors	Fire resistant	Reflects heat	Kitchens, bathrooms, utility rooms, and wherever sturdy wall is desired Unusual decorative uses residentially and commercially Easy maintenance

Table 11.1 *Continued*

Material	General Characteristics and Cost	Finishes	Fire Rating	Insulation Properties	Uses and Care
Plaster and stucco	Smooth or textured, no seams or joints Tends to chip and crack Moderately low cost	Paint, paper, or fabric	Fireproof	Special types have good insulation against noise	Most versatile of all wall treatments Appropriate for any room and any style Washable
Plastic (sheets)	Durable, resilient Comes in variety of colors, patterns, and textures Moderately high cost	No finish necessary	Poor Some do not burn but emit noxious gas	Poor insulator	Wherever durable, resilient walls are needed Resists stains and cuts Easy maintenance
Stone	Great beauty If covering too large an area, may appear cold, depending on color Natural colors and textures Feeling of strength and durability Improves with age High cost	Waterproofing sometimes required	Fireproof	Poor insulator Reflects sound	Fireplace surround or entire wall No upkeep
Wallboard (gypsum, drywall, or sheetrock)	Surface may be finished in attractive colors and patterns, or imprinted with woodgrain appearance Lowest cost	Same as plaster: paint, paper, or fabric	Fire resistant	Excellent insulator	Any room in which low cost is primary consideration Care depends on finish
Wallboard (hardboard, pressed wood)	Extremely durable, dent resistant, available in many woodgrains and colors Woodgrain applied via high-fidelity photo process Factory coated, virtually indestructible, easily installed Also available in embossed and textured surfaces simulating fabrics Moderate cost	May be stained, painted, or waxed	Surface melts Pressed wood burns	Reflects noise Insulation depends on thickness of pressed wood	Any area in which wood paneling of low cost and durability is required Wash with damp cloth
Wallboard (plastic laminate)	Extremely durable Surface of laminate similar to plastic countertop Photo process can produce textured appearance, woodgrains, colors, or patterns Matte or shiny surface High cost	Finished at factory Needs no additional finish	Smokes and melts	Reflects noise Fairly good insulator, depending on density and thickness	Hard-use areas of house (family rooms, children's rooms, basements) Resists stains and moisture Scratches are irreparable Wash with damp cloth
Wood (plywood)	Thin surface of wood veneer bonded to rugged and inexpensive panel backing Appears much like solid wood, but less expensive Comes in 4-ft by 8-ft sheets for easy installation May or may not have vertical grooves Moderately high cost	Same as solid wood—usually not considered a finished look	Susceptible to burning	Good insulator and noise reducer	Depending on type of wood and method of installation, will go in any room—period or modern Beauty improves with age and care Dust only
Wood (solid)	Natural grain throughout Comes in variety of natural grains from rough barn wood to rich grains for formal rooms Can be installed tongue and groove, plain edged, flush joint, or grooved Natural colors vary, but may be stained any color Subject to denting, but can be refinished indefinitely High cost	Needs protective finish to seal against stains and water	Susceptible to burning	Good insulator and noise reducer	Same as plywood

Figure 11.9 *This warm, inviting interior (18′ W × 24′ L × 20′ H) was originally a cold, vacant room. To give the room a more human scale, the designer created custom furniture scaled to fit the room. A subtle faux rag finish on the walls helps to envelop the occupants. (Designer: Pharr Design Group. Photographs ©Robert Thien. As seen in:* Atlanta Homes & Lifestyles.*)*

Plaster and Wallboard

In addition to its use as a ceiling material, plaster makes a versatile but costly wallcovering. A less expensive alternative is wallboard, which may be made of gypsum, pressed wood, or plastic laminate. Gypsum wallboard—called drywall or by its brand name of *Sheetrock*—is the most common and is used extensively.

Drywall and pressed wood are inexpensive wallboard treatments that come in 4 ft. × 8 ft. panels that are secured to the wall's vertical stud supports. Wallboard provides insulation against heat, cold, and noise, and when painted produces a variety of effects from rough to smooth (Figure 11.9). Rough, plasterlike walls are appropriate for informal rooms and for some period rooms (such as those in the Spanish style). Smooth surfaces can be used in any style room and with any style furniture. Consequently, the plain wall is considered the safest background treatment for rooms whose furnishings may be changed from time to time. Plastic laminate wallboards are available in a wide range of colors and simulate a variety of textures.

Wood

Wood walls have been a favorite background treatment for centuries. Wood may be applied to walls in boards or panels. Boards can be of any wood type, cut in various widths, stained any color, and laid vertically, horizontally, or diagonally. They can be joined with tongue-in-groove, butted, or beveled edges. A wide variety of wood sheet panels (known as *paneling*), some with thin veneers, is also available with numerous finishes, colors, and styles, and is considerably less expensive than boards.

Masonry

Masonry used for walls includes brick, tile, concrete block, and stone. Brick, which has been used since the time of the ancient Babylonians and the pharaohs, has a timeless quality of warmth and adaptability. Its natural look is equally at home in traditional or modern settings and in residential or commercial spaces. Ceramic tile, available in many shapes, sizes, colors, patterns, and finishes, can be used for almost any style and room. It is especially popular for use in kitchens and bathrooms.

Marble, travertine, limestone, slate, fieldstone, flagstone, and quartzite, all types of stone, are available in a variety of textures and colors. Some stones, like marble, can provide a formal and elegant look, and some, like fieldstone, give an informal and casual feeling. Stone is popular for fireplaces, and in contemporary homes is widely used for walls (Figure 11.10). For additional stone characteristics, see Table 11.1.

Other Wallcoverings

Mirrors

Mirrors can expand an area visually—an advantage in smaller living spaces. Mirrors are available in large sheets and precut panels ready to install. They can cover an entire wall or be spaced on a wall for function or aesthetic appeal. Mirrors also have great light-reflecting qualities and can be used to brighten a room.

Metal

Metals such as stainless steel, copper, and aluminum are available in sheets and tiles. Finishes may be smooth and

Figure 11.10 *Sofas, accessories, and other furnishings are placed to achieve a sense of balance and harmony in this living area. The geometry of the asymmetric fireplace wall and the irregular curves of the stone and wood divider add interest and complexity. (Courtesy of Steve Chase and Associates. Photograph by Arthur Coleman.)*

shiny, or brushed. The latter has easier upkeep. Metal interior walls are contemporary in feel and provide a strong textural quality (see the wall design in Figure 11.8).

Plastics

Plastics are available in either sheets or tiles in a wide range of colors and styles. They are easy to clean and are completely waterproof. Although durable, plastics may appear inexpensive if used to simulate marble, wood, or other natural finishes.

Moldings

Moldings are used most often where walls meet ceilings and floors. The molding hides the joinery at the corners and it also provides a transition from one surface to another. Moldings may also be used as a decorative treatment on walls. Figure 11.11 illustrates typical molding terminology.

Wall Moldings

A *chair rail* divides the wall horizontally, usually about three feet above the floor. The area between the chair rail and the base molding is called the **dado.** *Base moldings* usually consist of a *baseboard* (the taller portion) and a piece of quarter-round (usually called *shoe molding*).

Wainscoting, a common practice in medieval interiors, is ornately carved wood paneling that extends partway to the ceiling. A *picture rail* usually runs around the top of the wall, or may extend one to two feet down the wall in a room with a 10- to 14-foot ceiling. The picture rail traditionally was used

to suspend wires for hanging pictures. It also may be used as a decorative element (Figure 11.12).

Panel moldings may be achieved in one of two ways. True panel molding is created by applying wood in various layers on the wall, and applying strips of molding at the intersections. A simpler form of panel molding consists of a flat plaster or sheetrock wall with strips of moldings added to form frames. A series of panel moldings is commonly used in traditional dining rooms and conference rooms. **Boiserie** is a French term describing ornately carved paneling.

Figure 11.11 *Molding terminology.*

Crown Moldings

Ceiling moldings are called **crown moldings.** Crown moldings may have three parts. The uppermost is called the **cornice,** the middle the **frieze,** and the lower the **architrave.** Together they are referred to as the **entablature** (see page 26).

Moldings come in a variety of styles and shapes (see Figures 11.13 and 11.14). By combining these individual pieces, more ornate forms of moldings are developed. Higher ceilings (those above eight or nine feet) may accommodate a series of moldings. Ornate moldings add a feeling of dignity and grandeur, but if a ceiling is already low, a heavy crown molding may cause it to appear even lower. Chair rails and base moldings also may consist of one or more pieces of trim.

Trims are manufactured in wood, fiberglass, and foam. The latter are more versatile in design than wood and are lighter in weight (see Figures 11.15 and 11.16). When properly installed and painted, they are difficult to distinguish from their wood counterparts.

Figure 11.13 *Moldings add warmth to this traditional library. The interior perspective (top) illustrates the room and indicates where the moldings are placed. The line drawing (bottom) indicates the molding shapes used. (Reprinted with permission from Architectural Woodwork Quality Standards, Seventh Edition, published by the Architectural Woodwork Institute, Reston, Virginia. All rights reserved.)*

Figure 11.14 *Stock moldings add architectural interest.*

Figure 11.15 *This traditional sunburst design can add formality to a front door. It is sturdy, lightweight, and easily installed. (Courtesy of Focal Point.)*

Figure 11.16 *This exquisite fretwork cornice, made of tough, lightweight modern material, is molded directly from notable wood or plaster originals. (Courtesy of Focal Point.)*

Paints and Finishes

To change the character of a room quickly with a minimum of expense, nothing works as well as paint. Of all wall treatments, paint is the easiest to apply. It is made to adhere to any surface and is appropriate for any room or any style. Some paints resist rust, fading, and fire. Paints come in numerous colors, producing unlimited shades, tones, and tints. A painted wall surface can be smooth or given the illusion of texture by use of a stiff brush, sponge, or special embossed roller. Paints are made from a vast array of synthetic and natural materials.

Types of Paint

Alkyd Paint

Alkyd paint has virtually replaced oil paint. It is resin enamel that is fast drying, resists yellowing, and cleans better than latex. Depending on the color, one coat is generally sufficient. Alkyd paints must be thinned with solvent. They are recommended for moldings, woodwork, trim, and anywhere moisture, fingerprints, or scuff marks may be a problem. They are probably the best choice for painting metal.

Acrylic Paint

Acrylic paint is a water-based synthetic resin paint. The more acrylic the paint contains, the higher the quality. Acrylic is extremely durable, odorless, easily applied, quick drying, and washable. Some acrylic paints resemble baked-on enamel and are almost impervious to damage. Straight acrylic paints are not commonly used on interior finishes.

Latex Paint

Latex is a type of acrylic and is frequently used on interior finishes. It is a water-based paint, so cleanup is easy. Latex leaves no overlap marks, dries quickly, and the characteristic odor soon fades. Latex, however, does show brush marks. A difference between indoor and outdoor latex is that outdoor latex "breathes," thus allowing moisture to escape, which eliminates blistering. Latex paints are recommended for plaster, gypsumboard, masonry, wood siding, acoustical tile, and occasionally metal.

Enamel Paint

Enamel is a special type of paint similar to oil paint and is made with varnish or lacquer. Its finish is exceptionally hard and durable.

Epoxy Paint

There are two types of epoxy paint. The first type is ready-mixed in a single can. The second type is a two-stage finish, or catalyzed epoxy, which puts a tilelike coating on almost any surface. Once it hardens, this coating can be scratched, struck, or marked with crayon or pencil and still be washed back to a high gloss. Epoxies can be used on such surfaces as basement walls, shower stalls, and swimming pools.

Types of Finishes

Sealers and Fillers

Sealers and fillers are special substances applied to new surfaces as a base coat, ensuring a more professional finish.

Paint Finishes

Most paints are available in various finishes. Different manufacturers use different terms, but essentially there are three variations—*gloss, semigloss* or *eggshell,* and *matte* or *flat.* The higher the gloss, the easier it is to clean; however, higher gloss paint also shows the most imperfections in the wall.

Flat finishes tend to look richer than semigloss finishes; however, a matte or flat finish is easily marred by furniture, fingerprints, and spills. A semigloss or eggshell finish will prevent some scarring, and for an active family room or office space it is the best solution.

Stain

Stain penetrates wood pores and contains various colorants that can enhance natural color or give a different color to wood. Stains should be tested on an inconspicuous area first, because different woods react differently to the same color stain. A varnish is generally required over the stain to seal it.

Varnish

Varnish is a word sometimes used as a generic name for all clear resinous finishes. A resin is a natural or synthetic substance that, when dissolved in a suitable solvent, leaves a hard glossy film. Natural resins are the saps of certain trees or deposits of insects that feed on the sap. Synthetic resins are also available that duplicate natural ones. Varnish is made from natural resins with alcohol or a drying oil, and volatile thinners and dryers. A varnish is usually a transparent coating and is commonly used on wood to protect the surface and allow the natural grain to show through. Some varnishes have a colorant added to darken the wood, but the result is usually less satisfactory than staining before applying clear varnish. Varnish comes in high-gloss or matte finishes.

Shellac

Shellac is a protective coating similar to varnish. It is made of a resinous substance called lac, which is deposited on trees in India and Asia. Its solvent is alcohol. Shellac dries more quickly than varnish but is less durable and is subject to water spots. Clear shellac does not discolor when applied to a light-colored surface.

Lacquer

Lacquer is a superior, quick-drying, varnishlike finish made from resin from an Asiatic sumac (Chinese or Japanese lacquer) or from a synthetic nitro-cellulose resin. The finish ranges from matte to high gloss and comes in white, black, brown, or beige. Commercially made furniture may be finished with lacquer.

Polyurethane

Polyurethane is a varnishlike finish that provides an exceptionally tough plastic surface coating. It comes in matte, medium-, or high-gloss finish. It is an excellent protective surface for hardwood floors in heavy traffic areas and walls where moisture is a problem. Polyurethane is also used to protect furniture surfaces and wood paneling.

Paint Textures

There are several methods of achieving unusual textures with paint. The following techniques involve applying one or more colors of wet (often thinned) paint over a dry base coat of another color:

- *Sponging*—Paint is applied with a sponge over a base coat, giving a mottled or blotchy texture (Figure 11.17).
- *Spattering*—Paint on a brush is flipped onto the base coat, giving a speckled appearance.
- *Stippling*—Similar to sponging, but a more delicate effect is achieved by using a stippling brush to apply a colored paint lightly over the base color.
- *Ragging*—One or more colors are applied over the base coat, then partly removed by blotting or rolling with a rag to achieve a marbleized effect.

Figure 11.17 *A variety of soft neutral tones were sponged on this wall to create a textured background for a contemporary Spanish-style bedroom. (Photograph by Pam Singleton.)*

- *Color washing*—A coat of thinned paint or glaze is lightly applied over a base coat of another color.
- *Glazing*—Layers of one or more transparent colors are applied on top of a base coat. The result gives the illusion of various depths on the wall.

Decorative Finishes

Faux is French for "false." Faux finishes simulate the look of another material, such as stone or wood, by using various techniques to apply paints to a surface. Among the more popular finishes are marble, granite, and woodgrains. More exotic faux finishes include tortoiseshell and malachite. In addition to being used on walls, faux finishes are used on moldings, doors, mantelpieces, and furniture.

Trompe l'oeil is a delightful wall treatment, especially for those who desire an unusual effect or perhaps want to inject a note of humor into their design. The French term literally means "to fool the eye." Trompe l'oeil is a hand-painted wall or wallcovering, in almost any subject matter, giving a three-dimensional look. Very simple or extremely complicated designs can be used (see the ceiling in Figure 11.1).

Painted scenes, patterns, and borders that do not attempt the illusionistic effects of trompe l'oeil can be created either freehand (Figure 11.18) or with stencils. A stencil is a masking sheet with a pattern cut out so that the pattern can be re-

Figure 11.18 *In this residential foyer, a painted faux finish creates a Renaissance courtyard illusion. Wisteria falls over the garden wall; bluebirds and robins gather in the sky. (Designer/Artist: Shannon Pable. Photograph by John Orth.)*

peated. Stenciling is especially popular for rooms with an informal or country look. Stenciling designs can be purchased or personally created.

Resilient (Flexible) Wallcoverings

Wallpaper

Using decorative paper as a wallcovering has been important in enhancing interiors since the late 16th century in Europe and early colonial times in America. Although wallpapers have been more fashionable during some periods than others, they have always been esteemed as a valuable tool in transforming the visual aspect of interior space.

History of Wallpaper

Hand-painted wallpapers were made as early as 200 B.C. in China, where they were used for decorating tombs. The first manufacture of wallpaper on an organized basis was in France toward the close of the 16th century. The first papers were painted in a marbleized effect—a design copied from imported Persian papers—and made for facing book covers and lining boxes. These were called *domino papers.*

The introduction of flocked papers (wallpaper with a three-dimensional fuzzy texture) during the early 17th century made it possible for people to simulate the elegant damasks used in the homes of the wealthy. In the latter half of the 17th century a new printing method developed by Jean Papillon produced wallpaper that could be matched to make the pattern continuous around the room.

During the latter half of the 18th century, pictorial murals became popular through the works of Baptiste Reveillon in France and John Baptiste Jackson in England. During the 18th century in America, hand-painted papers from China were in vogue for the great Georgian mansions built along the Atlantic seacoast.

Copper printing rollers turned by a rotary machine were invented in northern England in the second quarter of the 19th century. Although wallpaper was frequently used during the 19th century, it was not until the Industrial Revolution that the wallpaper industry flourished in America. When the industry developed a new method of silk-screen printing in the mid-20th century that produced papers of high quality at affordable prices, the demand multiplied. *Documentary wallpapers* are used in replicating historic interiors (Figure 11.19).

Methods of Producing Wallpaper

The three most common methods of producing wallcoverings are roller printing, hand blocking, and silk-screen printing. *Roller printing* is the most common process and the least expensive. It is a cylinder process in which each color is applied in rapid succession. In *hand blocking,* each color is applied separately after the preceding one is dry. This method is slower and more costly than the roller method. *Silk-screen printing* is a more complicated process in which a wooden or metal frame tightly stretches a silk, nylon, or metal screen made for each color of the pattern. Portions of the pattern not to be printed are heavily varnished or bleached out. Each repeat is made by applying pigment, which seeps through the screens as it is pushed

Figure 11.19 *A documentary wallpaper establishes an authentic feeling of the period. (From the Winterthur Museum Collection. Courtesy of Van Luit and Company.)*

across by a squeegee. Each color is allowed to dry before the next frame is printed. This method produces a high-quality wallcovering at reasonable cost.

Embossed and flocked wallcoverings have unique surface qualities. *Embossed* paper is made by a machine process producing high and low surfaces. This method is used where texture and three-dimensional effects are desired. *Flocked paper* is produced by a method in which the design motif is outlined and covered with glue or an adhesive material. Fine wool-like fuzz is then blown onto it, producing a surface resembling cut velvet.

Common Wallpaper Terms

Following are the most commonly used wallpaper terms:

- *Washable*—Usually refers to a wallcovering that may be washed with lukewarm mild suds, but not scrubbed excessively.
- *Scrubbable*—Refers to a wallcovering more resistant to rubbing than washable types. Stains such as crayon marks can generally be removed from scrubbable wallpaper with cleaning agents recommended by the manufacturer or with soap and water.
- *Pretrimmed*—Refers to rolls of wallpaper from which the selvage has been trimmed.
- *Semitrimmed*—The selvage has been trimmed from only one edge of the wallpaper.
- *Prepasted*—Paper that has had paste applied during the manufacturing process. Detailed instructions for hanging are usually included. Generally, prepasted paper is soaked in water and applied to the wall while the paper is still wet.
- *Single roll*—Wallpaper is always priced by the single roll, but usually is sold by the double or triple roll. Regardless of width, a single roll usually contains 36 square feet. Eurorolls (wallcoverings produced in Europe and often used in the United States) typically contain 28 square feet per single roll.
- *Double and triple roll*—Regardless of width, a double roll (two single rolls) contains approximately 72 square feet, and a triple roll (three single rolls) contains 118 square feet. Generally, 18-inch and 20-inch-wide wallpapers come in triple rolls. Double or triple rolls are used to minimize waste when cutting wallpaper into strips.
- *Dye lot*—Refers to the production schedule of a color or colors. Each dye lot has a number. Because of color variations in different dye lots, all the wallcovering for a single space must come from the same dye lot. Designers should ensure that a sufficient quantity has been ordered to meet the client's needs. Attempting to reorder during installation may be impossible because the particular dye lot may be sold out.
- *Pattern repeat*—When a wallcovering has a pattern or motif, the pattern repeat is the distance from the beginning of the pattern to the point where it starts again. The patterns in the horizontal direction of the motif should match from the top to the bottom of the wall. The larger the pattern, the greater the wallcovering waste.
- *Sizing*—A liquid that is painted on the wall before the wallpaper is applied. Sizing prevents the wallpaper from absorbing too much paste or adhesive and helps the wallpaper adhere better to the wall.

Vinyl-Coated and Vinyl Wallcoverings

Numerous flexible wallcoverings are available that have been treated with varying thicknesses of vinyl. They are waterproof, highly durable, stain resistant, and may be washable or scrubbable. They can be used on nearly any type of wall and for any style. Vinyl-coated wallcoverings are applied using the same method appropriate for wallpaper.

Vinyl-Coated Wallcoverings

The following are the most common vinyl-coated wallcoverings:

- *Vinyl-protected wallcovering* is ordinary wallpaper with a coating of vinyl plastic to make it washable.
- *Vinyl-latex wallcovering* is a paper impregnated with vinyl, laminated to lightweight fabric or paper, then vinyl coated. The thickness of the vinyl may vary. This process produces a durable, scrubbable wallcovering.
- *Coated fabric* is a wallcovering with a woven cotton backing treated with an oil or plastic coating before the design is applied. This durable, tough, scrubbable material is ideal for kitchens and bathrooms.
- *Plastic foam* is a soft, flexible material available in rolls, squares, or rectangles. It absorbs sound, is soil and stain resistant, and insulates. It is easy to clean with soap and water. Although more expensive than some wallcoverings, plastic foam is ideal for television rooms or apartments with thin walls, and is particularly useful in commercial and institutional settings.

Vinyl Wallcoverings

True vinyl wallcoverings are composed of a backing, a vinyl layer, and a finish layer. Vinyl wallcoverings are commonly applied in commercial environments where building codes dictate their use (Figure 11.20).

Vinyl wallcoverings are rated based on their total weight per ounce. Type I wallcoverings weigh from 7 to 13 ounces per square yard and are best used in light traffic areas. Type II wallcoverings weigh from 13 to 22 ounces per square yard and can be used in high traffic areas such as hotel and commercial office corridors. Type III wallcoverings weigh more than 22 ounces per square yard and are used in extremely high traffic areas such as cafeteria lines and elevator lobbies (Figure 11.21). Type II and Type III wallcoverings are usually 54″ wide to expedite installation.

Figure 11.20 *A moiré print vinyl stripe wallcovering adds warmth, beauty, and durability to this hotel lounge renovation. (Designer: Gettys Group. Photograph by Bruce Van Inwegen.)*

Figure 11.21 *In this children's ophthalmologist's office a ribbed vinyl wallcovering in strong colors creates nonstop movement and provides durability. (Architect/Designer: Stuart Narofsky Architecture. Photograph by Ron Solomon.)*

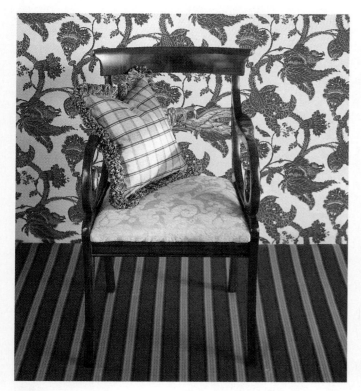

Figure 11.22 *Boldly patterned fabric can be applied to walls to create interest. Smaller scaled furnishings work best with a large wall pattern. (Courtesy of Schumacher. Photograph © F. Schumacher & Co. Permission has been granted by F. Schumacher & Co. to use copyrighted work. Background fabric: Pomegranate Resist, a Schumacher ® design from Colonial Williamsburg.)*

Fabric Wallcoverings

Many varieties of fabrics are used on walls (Figure 11.22). The best choice, except when using the shirred method of application (see below), is a mediumweight, closely woven fabric. For an informal look use fabrics such as sailcloth, ticking, Indian head, or glazed chintz; for a formal appearance use fabrics such as tapestry, brocade, or damask. Some fabrics come prepared for pasting on walls and are laminated to a paper backing. Nondirectional patterns are easier to use because they require no matching. Like patterned wallpaper, a repeat pattern requires allowance for matching. Fabrics can be applied to walls in a number of ways.

The *shirring method* is the simplest way to cover a wall with fabric. A lightweight fabric that drapes well is best. Cut-to-fit rods are fastened just above the baseboard and near the ceiling. The fabric is gathered, pleated, or folded and installed on the rods.

The *double-face masking tape method* is not permanent, because masking tape will dry out in time; however, this method may be appropriate for temporary or seasonal applications. Fabric is prepared by sewing panels together. Double-face tape is placed around the edges of the wall and

the fabric is applied to the tape first at the top and bottom, and then at the sides.

The *Velcro™ method* is similar to the masking tape method, except that one side of the Velcro™ tape is stitched along the edges of the fabric, then attached to the other side of the tape, which has been secured around the edges of the wall.

In the *staple method* the fabric is prepared as in the masking tape method. The top is stapled first, then the bottom, and the sides last. Exposed staples may be concealed with braid or molding.

The *paste method* is the most professional looking and most permanent method, but it requires special care and a set of wallpaper tools. The wall is prepared by applying a coat of liquid sealing or sizing to fill the pores in the wall surface. After the surface dries, a second coat of sealing is applied to the wall, and the strips of fabric are positioned like wallpaper. The fabric dries overnight and is then sprayed with a protective coating.

Fabric also can be applied to panels, which are then installed on the wall. Edges are often concealed with moldings.

Other Resilient Wallcoverings

Grass cloth or *hemp* wallcovering is flexible, long lasting, easy to care for, and provides suitable backgrounds for a variety of styles. Colored grass cloth, however, fades over time. Other woven reeds such as *sisal* can provide handsome and practical wallcoverings.

Wood veneer with fabric backing, another method of "papering" walls, produces a true wood surface and, once adhered to the wall, is difficult to distinguish from solid wood. One advantage over wood paneling is that this material can fit around corners or curves. It is available in sheets up to 24 inches wide and 12 feet long. The cost, however, is high (Figure 11.23).

Leather tile, made of top-grain cowhide, provides a soft, warm, rich surface. It comes in a variety of fade-resistant colors to blend with traditional or modern decor. The leather is permanently bonded to an aluminum tile base that has preapplied adhesive for easy installation. It is highly resistant to scuffing, and the only maintenance required is an occasional washing with mild soap and water. Leather tile in suede is also available on a custom-ordered basis. The depth of the brushed nap provides an interesting texture, but its high cost limits extensive use.

Cork is a moderately priced textured material producing a warm atmosphere in natural colors of brown. It is particularly adaptable for studies or rooms in which sound insulation is important. Unless plastic-impregnated, cork is not suitable for bathrooms, kitchens, and other moisture-prone areas.

A historical wallcovering embossed with intricate designs dating from the Victorian era is marketed under the trade name of *Anaglypta.* This wallcovering is commonly used on dadoes. It is neutral in color and is intended to be painted (Figure 11.24).

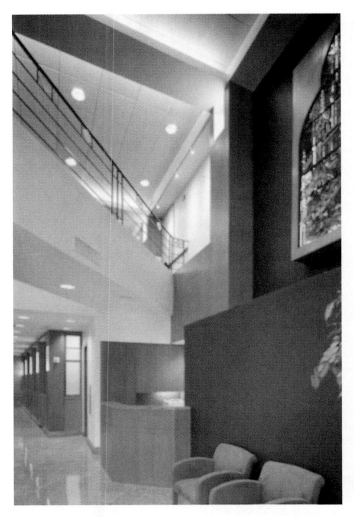

Figure 11.23 *The combination of painted Sheetrock walls and woven-backed wood veneer creates a welcoming reception area in the HealthCare Chaplaincy, New York, NY. (Designer: Descon Interiors Incorporated. Photograph by Durston Saylor.)*

Estimating Wallcovering Quantities

When working on a project, designers need to be able to estimate the quantity of wallcovering needed in order to calculate a budget. There are two generally accepted methods used to figure the quantity of wallcovering for a room.

The *general estimation method* is particularly helpful for quick "on the spot" estimates.

1. Total the wall area in the room. To do this multiply the height and width of each wall and then add the figures together.
2. Divide the total wall area by 30 square feet (slightly less than the average quantity per roll of wallcovering) to get the number of rolls of wallcovering necessary to cover the room.
3. Subtract 1 roll for every two openings such as doors and windows. Remember that wallcovering is usually packed in double rolls. Rolls cannot be split.

The *strip method* is more precise and should be used before making final purchases. It requires converting all dimensions into inches or centimeters. The designer will also need to know the *width, length,* and *pattern repeat length* of the selected paper. Once these dimensions are determined, proceed with the following steps:

1. Total the horizontal wall length for the entire room. To do this, measure the width of each wall in the room, add them together, and convert to inches.
2. Divide this amount by the width of the wallcovering. The answer indicates how many strips are needed to completely wrap the room in wallcovering. The next three steps will determine how long each strip should be to allow for a pattern repeat.
3. Determine the height of the room. Convert this to inches and divide by the pattern repeat. Round this number *up* to the nearest whole number.

Figure 11.24 *This historic building was renovated into a fine arts gallery. Anaglypta was used on the dado and painted a pale peach. (Designer: Lynn M. Jones. Photograph by J. J. Williams.)*

4. Multiply the number of repeats (answer to Step 3) by the repeat length. This answer determines the cut length for each strip of wallpaper.

5. Divide the total roll length (single, double, or triple roll length) by the length required for each cut (answer to Step 4). Round this number *down* to the nearest whole number. This determines how many strips will be available from each roll of wallcovering.

6. Divide the total number of strips (the answer from Step 2) by the number of strips per roll (answer to Step 5). Round this number *up* to the nearest whole number. This final answer determines how many rolls (either single, double, or triple) will be needed.

Selecting Wall Materials and Finishes

When selecting a finish for a wall, designers need an understanding of the functional, aesthetic, and economic requirements of the space. From a functional viewpoint, the amount of use or traffic in the area is a critical factor. For example, hospital, hotel, or other corridors frequented by large carts or wheelchairs require Type II or Type III wallcoverings. Chair rails made of molded plastics or metal also are appropriate in these areas.

Some rooms may require sound-absorbing wallcoverings. Libraries, studies, music rooms, and offices benefit from soft, absorbent wallcoverings. Large classrooms with hard surface flooring benefit from the use of cork walls or fabric panels, which also double as display areas.

In historic buildings, the designer may need to use materials that hide imperfections. Flat paint conceals flaws better than a semigloss. A vinyl wallcovering or product such as Anaglypta may also be appropriate.

Aesthetically, the architectural details of the room may direct the selection of the wall finish. An adobe fireplace would allow for a more casual finish, as would the use of a nubby material. A traditional fireplace may call for a more subdued wallcovering or paint. A traditional setting also may require an elaborate pattern or trompe l'oeil print. A strong contemporary structure may dictate the use of sleek metals and poured concrete walls (Figure 11.25). Large expanses of glass or glass block also may be appropriate.

Designers need to know whether the wall will serve as a focal point or as a backdrop for other objects. A strong, brilliant wallcovering may be appropriate for a kitchen; how-

Figure 11.25 *This unique contemporary interior has a shed ceiling. The sleek, structural materials include a concrete fireplace, custom wood entertainment center, and metal beams. (Architect/Designer: Lippert & Lippert Design, Palo Alto, CA. Photograph by Quadra Focus.)*

GREEN DESIGN

Wall Finishes

One of the worst problems with wallcoverings and paints is their toxicity level during production and application. When designing for environmentally conscious clients, interior designers should specify whenever possible paint, finishes, and wallcoverings that meet the following criteria:

- Use natural ingredients
- Are made in water-based manufacturing processes, especially with regard to printed wallcoverings
- Use renewable resources
- Contain no toxic solvents or VOCs (volatile organic chemicals)

Using paints with low levels of VOCs and without toxic solvents can limit color choices. First select a subtle background color and then add interest to the room through other accent items.

Natural products and materials for walls also must be chosen with care. As mentioned in Chapter 10, cork is a renewable resource and therefore works well in green design. Wood selected from sustainable forest management groups such as the Tropical Forest Foundation is also a wise choice. However, because wood usually requires a stain and/or finish, nonsolvent, low-toxicity finishes should be specified.

ever, in a gallery the wall material should be neutral so the focus is on the art.

When selecting patterned wallpaper, it is important to consider the scale of the room and select a pattern compatible with it. A small pin dot or petite floral may function well in a bathroom, but would be out of scale for a dining room or foyer. A wallcovering with a vertical stripe will increase the apparent height of a room, whereas a horizontal stripe will make the ceiling feel lower. Diagonal stripes on a wall can create confusion and disorientation and are not recommended unless vibrancy is the goal.

From an economic point of view, if the client is on a limited budget, or if time is a major consideration, a new coat of paint is probably the best solution. Paint is the least expensive and easiest interior wall finish to change. A new coat of paint will dramatically alter a room's presence. Accentuated moldings or doors also will create a new energizing effect.

Finally, designers concerned with environmental issues (or whose clients are) may wish to specify environmentally friendly products (see "Green Design: Wall Finishes").

Summary

In any interior environment, the ceilings and walls create a backdrop for the inhabitants. These surfaces provide security, enclose the mechanical systems, and create a comfortable living environment. Designers specify the materials and finishes that are applied to these surfaces. Care should be taken to ensure that the products used are durable and meet the functional needs of the space. Designers must also utilize the principles and elements of design when selecting surface finishes so that they coordinate with the architectural components and enhance the human experience.

12

Backgrounds:
Doors, Windows, and Fireplaces

Figure 12.1 *A soaring two-story angled bay window is framed with softly swagged white fabric. The inviting neoclassic wood fireplace is flanked by an armoire and cabinets, providing concealed storage for an entertainment center. (Photograph by Mark Boisclair.)*

Chapter 11 discussed walls and wall trim in relation to materials and appropriate finishes. Another important element in the design of walls is the fenestration. **Fenestration** refers to the arrangement, type, and design of openings in a wall or building. For example, many traditional homes built in the 1980s were called "five over four with a door," which referred to the pattern of windows (plus front door) on the **facade** (the front elevation of a building or object) of a two-story house.

In the interior environment, doors, windows, and even fireplaces create fenestration within a room (Figure 12.1). This chapter reviews the material and design selections for these components. Many times these architectural features are already in place and designers must work around the existing conditions. In other situations, the designer may select the style of the doors and windows. Usually, the designer is responsible for the selection of the window treatment, and occasionally is fortunate enough to be involved in designing the fireplace facade.

DOORS

Doors are powerful design elements in any interior. By their location, doors control traffic flow, which in turn controls the furniture arrangement. Doors provide privacy and sound barriers. They allow for ventilation and temperature control. They provide a sense of safety and security.

The main entrance door is generally the most important element and focal point in the facade. Traditional paneled period doors and leaded glass panels continue to be popular. Many contemporary exterior and interior doors are plain and flush, sheathed on both sides with a veneer. Metal exterior doors with insulating cores are effective in saving energy.

Door Construction

Doors are composed of three basic parts—the *door* itself, the *frame,* and the *hardware*. These components work together to form the design of the door and all should be considered when selecting the door style and type. Figure 12.2 indicates the various parts of the door.

Doors are available in a variety of styles, but are generally constructed of wood as hollow-core doors or solid-core doors. *Hollow-core doors* are composed of veneers laminated to a frame. *Solid-core doors,* also composed of veneers, have a particleboard, solid wood, or mineral core, all of which provide various degrees of fire resistance. Solid-core doors also provide better insulation and acoustical barriers.

Solid-core doors are the only acceptable solution for commercial interiors and for exterior doors on residences. Metal doors are also used in commercial (and occasionally residential) interiors, particularly in high traffic areas or in stairwells where fire codes dictate their use.

Door Frames

The doorframe supports the door and provides a *stop,* a *sill,* and a *jamb,* which allow the door to operate properly (Figure 12.3). Doorframes are made of wood or molded steel. Wood frames are generally used for residential interiors; steel frames are more often used in commercial construction. The *stop* is the vertical portion that prevents the door from swinging both ways. The *sill* is the horizontal member across the bottom of the opening. The *jamb* refers to the vertical members of the frame that support the door. Some frames also include trim around the jamb. In steel construction, the jamb may actually serve as the trim.

Figure 12.2 *Door parts and terminology.*

A. Panel door

B. Flush door

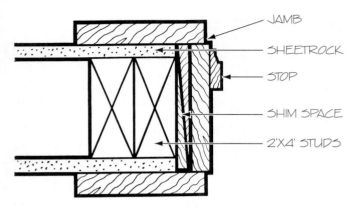

Figure 12.3 *Detail of standard wood doorframe.*

Door Hardware

The selection of the appropriate hardware is often left to the builder, who usually chooses the least expensive product available. This may not be the best design solution. Door hardware includes *latchsets* or *locksets* (handles), *push plates* or *pull bars, panic hardware, closers, hinges,* and *kickplates.*

Functional Hardware

Latchsets and *locksets* are usually shaped in the form of a knob or lever. They include a mechanism to operate the door and to hold it closed, and in the case of a lockset, to lock the door. Knobs are common in most residential environments, but lever handles are much easier to operate. A lever does not require a person to grip and rotate a knob to open a door, but simply to push the lever up or down. Because of their ease in manipulation, lever handles are required in commercial spaces. Many high-end residential interiors incorporate lever handles. They also are beneficial in homes for the elderly. These handles meet universal design standards.

Push plates or *pull bars* serve the same function as a knob or lever, allowing occupants to enter or exit a room. Push plates and pull bars, however, do not require the release of a latching mechanism.

Panic hardware and *closers* are usually used in commercial environments. *Panic hardware* includes a push bar that extends across the width of the door. When pushed, it releases the latches at the top and bottom of the door, allowing it to open. *Closers* automatically close a door, and are required by some building codes. Residential environments commonly use a similar hydraulic device to close storm doors.

Hinges attach the door to the frame and permit the swinging movement of the door. *Kick plates* protect the lower portion of the door and also can add a decorative touch.

Decorative Hardware

Hardware is obviously functional, but the selection of proper hardware also affects the character of the interior. Hardware can be finished in brass, antique brass, bright chrome, satin chrome, and a variety of other specialized finishes specific to each manufacturer. Flat-finished chrome hardware reflects a more contemporary interior, whereas a bright brass finish is

more traditional. Hardware also can be highly decorative, sleek, or finely crafted. Because the same hardware is normally used throughout the interior spaces, it adds a unifying element.

Hardware should also "feel good to the touch." This is referred to as the hand of the object (as discussed in Chapter 9 on textiles). Sharp edges and rough corners are inappropriate; a firm smooth finish would welcome a visitor.

Types of Doors by Operation

As seen in Figure 12.4, the three basic types of doors are swinging, folding, and sliding. These doors and their components may be constructed of wood, steel, aluminum, plastic, glass, or a combination of these materials, depending on design, location, and function.

Swinging Doors

Swinging doors are easy to install and operate, and are available in standard sizes. Most doors are single-hinged and swing only one way; a double-hinged door swings both ways. The latter is convenient between kitchens and dining rooms. A swinging door placed near a corner, with the arc swinging toward the adjacent wall, preserves wall space and directs traffic along the side of the room. Pairs of **French doors** are glass-paned single-hinged swinging doors that open the same way, leading to an outside area or an adjoining room. The **Dutch door** is a single-hinged door divided horizontally, making it possible to have ventilation and visual communication from the upper half while the lower half is closed.

Swinging doors are considered right-handed or left-handed. To determine the swing, walk through the door so that you are pushing the door open. If the hinges are on the right, it is a right-hand door, and vice-versa (Figure 12.5).

Folding Doors

Folding doors save space in a residential setting. They are available in sizes from a single door to a full wall divider, and they may be attached at both top and bottom or only at the top. Made in a wide variety of styles (such as louvered) and materials (including plastic and fiberglass), they are flexible and relatively inexpensive.

Sliding Doors

Sliding doors used on the exterior may be part of a glass wall or installed in pairs that slide one behind the other. They are popular in contemporary houses to make the patio or garden a visual part of the living area. Sliding-glass doors should be made of safety glass.

Interior sliding doors (known as *pocket doors*) slide into a pocket in the wall, or when paired may slide behind each other. Although not as flexible as folding doors, sliding doors (like folding doors) are great space savers for residential use. They can provide complete or partial privacy depending on their material, but they can be difficult to operate, especially for the physically challenged. The traditional Japanese shoji sliding panel is appropriate in both traditional and modern interiors, serving multiple uses (Figure 12.6).

Panel door   Wood molding   Flush   Dutch two piece   Batten (vertical and cross plank)   Louvered

Full glass center panel   French door   Glass insert at side   Glass insert at top   Double doors

Interior   Exterior   Double door

SWINGING DOORS

Folding accordion   Bifold folding door   Sliding glass door   Pocket door

Folding   Bifold   Sliding glass   Pocket

FOLDING DOORS   SLIDING DOORS

Figure 12.4 *Elevations and plan views of various types of doors.*

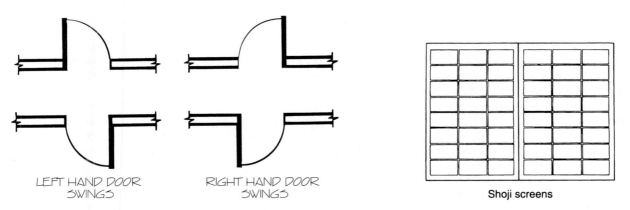

LEFT HAND DOOR SWINGS   RIGHT HAND DOOR SWINGS

Shoji screens

Figure 12.5 *Plan view of left-hand and right-hand door swings.*   **Figure 12.6** *Shoji panels can be used for screens or doors.*

Door Design and Placement

If doors are well placed to preserve wall space and direct traffic efficiently, they present no problem. But if a room has a surplus of doors, it may be necessary to camouflage them. One option (if other passageways exist) is to remove the hinges and fill the opening with shelves for books and small art objects. Relocating a door is also possible, and the result may be worth the effort and expense.

Door treatment depends on the design and style of the room. Doors are often painted to blend with the walls; wood doors may be stained or left natural. If a door has a particularly good design, painting it a contrasting color may augment the room's decoration. When walls are paneled, doors may conform to the walls or be painted in a contrasting color.

Doors come in standard widths. The most common are 2'-0", 2'-4", 2'-6", and 3'-0". All exterior doors should be a minimum of 3'-0" wide. Interior residential doors are commonly 2'-6". Standard door height is 6'-8", but doors are available that are 7'-0" and 8'-0". Additionally, doors may be custom designed to fit any space or shape.

As discussed in Chapter 6, barrier-free design requires doors to have a clear opening of 32". To obtain this dimension, doors used in handicap-accessible areas must be 36" wide. Additionally, the pull side of the door must have at least 18" clear of any obstruction; the push side needs 12" clear (see Figure 6.5).

WINDOWS

Although glass walls were known to the ancient Egyptians and Romans, historically, windows (or the "wind's eye") were merely small cutouts in the walls of a house. Over the years, many types of windows have been planned as an integral part of the structural design of a building. Although window treatments change with style trends, they are most attractive when attuned to the architectural spirit of the structure, both exterior and interior.

Windows perform three primary functions: they admit light, provide ventilation, and enhance visual communication. Even though light and airflow can now be mechanically controlled, and windows are not absolutely necessary, planning an interior without windows seems inconceivable. There are no substitutes for fresh air, natural light, and an outdoor view to create a psychological association with nature and provide a sense of well-being.

The window is a conspicuous element in both the exterior and interior design of a house. As a source of interior light, the window is the first point to which the eye is drawn during the daytime, while at night, a lighted window is the first thing seen from the outside.

The window is an important architectural and decorative element in a room. Traditionally, windows with small panes were often symmetrically placed in the facade of the house. With the development of modern architecture and technology, new types of window openings were planned as integral parts of the basic design.

Figure 12.7 *Window parts and treatment placement.*

Window Construction

Window terminologies are identified in Figure 12.7. Windows are composed of panes of glass. A casement window has only one pane, whereas a sash window is composed of at least two panes, one at the top and one at the bottom. Some sash windows have several panes and may be referred to based on their number of panes, such as six over six (written "6/6"). Originally, these panes were separated by wood **mullions and muntins** (Figure 12.7). *Mullions* form the vertical divisions of the panes; *muntins* form the horizontal divisions. It is a common practice today to divide the panes with pop-in plastic mullions and muntins. Although the plastic versions are not as rich looking as the wood, they do make cleaning the panes easier.

Glass

Architectural glass is available in single, double, or triple panes and is technically termed *annealed glass*. When the window consists of double or triple panes of glass that are separated by a layer of gas (air) that serves as an insulator, the glass is termed *insulated glass*. The air space also helps to prevent condensation on the glass. Insulated glass is sometimes called *thermopane glass*. For a further discussion of energy efficient glass, see "Green Design: Low-E Glass."

Glass can also be *tempered,* meaning that if it were to break, it would shatter into pebble-sized pieces instead of large sharp-edged pieces. *Laminated glass* is actually put together with a thin film laminated between the layers of glass. This is an excellent choice for overhead glazing.

In fire corridors or other hallways that are designed for fire egress, *wired glass* is used. Wired glass holds together when subjected to high temperatures or impacts.

Figure 12.8 *Various types of movable windows.*

Double-hung

Casements

French doors

Glazed wall with sliding door

Single pivoting pane

Awning or louvered

Jalousie

Frames

Glass panes are supported by wood, metal, or plastic frames. Each has particular advantages and disadvantages. *Wood* shrinks, swells, requires a protective finish, and is the most expensive. It discourages moisture condensation, however, and emits less heat than metal. Wood also has a richer appearance than metal or plastic. *Metal* is strong and does not shrink or swell perceptibly. Except for aluminum and stainless steel, however, it requires protective paint and causes moisture condensation in cold weather. Newer metal windows are designed to eliminate excessive heat loss and condensation. *Plastic* is stable and resists heat and cold, but may look inexpensive.

Types of Windows

Windows are available in standard sizes and can be movable, stationary, or a combination of both.

Movable Windows

Movable windows open to permit ventilation. Some of the most common movable window designs are illustrated in Figure 12.8.

Double-hung windows are made up of two **sashes** that may be raised or lowered to provide 50 percent ventilation. They are simple and inexpensive. *Casements* may swing inward or outward and permit up to 100 percent ventilation. (In-swinging casements must have special window treatments designed not to interfere with the window's operation.) *Horizontal sliding windows* may use two sliding panes or a large stationary central pane with a sliding pane on ei-

ther side or other combination. These windows work like a sliding glass door. *Awning* (or louvered) and *jalousie windows* consist of strips of glass, hinged at the top or bottom, that open outward or inward. Strips in jalousies are narrower than in the awning type. *Single-pivoting windows* are raised for ventilation by means of a hinged side. These windows are most often used as skylights or in light wells.

Stationary Windows

Stationary windows are built as an integral part of the wall construction. They may be made of plain or nonglare glass. Common stationary windows include fixed glazing, bow, and arch (Figure 12.9).

Fixed glazing (another name for a flat window) is a common feature of today's contemporary homes and may extend from floor to ceiling or begin a short distance above the floor. Hexagons, circles, and other geometrically shaped windows

Bow bay

Arched

Fixed

Figure 12.9 *Various types of stationary windows.*

Low-E Glass

Some windows can save energy without being bulky and heavy. Manufacturers are making glazed windows with a transparent, nonglare coating on the inside layers to help slow the transmission of heat energy through glass. Such windows are made with low-E (low emissivity) coatings. They help interior environments stay more comfortable.

Low-E glass treats sunlight's different wavelengths in different ways. The sun's energy spectrum is divided into three ranges of wavelengths: ultraviolet, visible light, and infrared, which can be felt as heat. (These heat-generating infrared rays are further divided into long wavelengths and short wavelengths.) The challenge is to let in visible light and control infrared transmittance.

Low-E glass, with its low-emissivity pyrolytic coating, lets in approximately 95 percent as much visible light as ordinary insulated glass, allowing the interior to look bright and the window to appear transparent. However, low-E glass reflects most of the long-wave infrared energy back toward its source, helping to keep summer heat out and winter heat in (Figure GD12.1).

Performance can be even better with the addition of argon gas (a superinsulator) between the layers of glass in the window unit. As a result of these new energy-efficient developments, windows can be practical as well as beautiful.

Figure GD12.1 *A: Low-E glass, coated on the inside layers, allows natural light and short-wave heat energy to enter freely. B: In summer, long-wave heat energy radiating from objects is reflected, lowering cooling costs. C: In winter, internal long-wave heat energy is reflected, lowering heating costs. (Courtesy of PPG Industries.)*

---

are occasionally used to provide a point of interest and additional light, and are also considered fixed glazing. The *bow window* is a smooth, sweeping curve of multiple panes. In *arched windows* the upper part of a rectangular opening is topped by an arch.

Combination and Custom Windows

Many window types combine movable and stationary sections (Figure 12.10).

The *picture window* is composed of fixed glazing, usually with movable end sections. *Palladian windows* feature a central arched window flanked by two smaller windows, often with movable sections. This window type is associated with the Federal style and today is used in a wide variety of settings. The *angled bay window* is made up of three or more windows that angle out of the room. The central pane may be stationary with movable side panes.

Clerestory windows may be straight or slanting windows set at the ceiling or high in a wall. Operable windows at this level provide for excellent air circulation when combined with windows opened at lower levels. The *corner window* consists of two windows of any style that meet or almost

meet in a corner. A single corner window can be thought of as a double window and treated accordingly. *Ranch* or *strip windows* can be any style and are wide and shallow. They are set far enough above the floor to allow furniture to be set against the wall, but they are not flush to the ceiling. *Dormer windows* are located in alcoves projecting out from the roof. Any style of window may be located in the dormer.

Skylights (windows placed in the ceiling) may be single or grouped panels of clear or translucent glass or plastic, either flat or domed, and fixed or movable for ventilation. Skylights in kitchens, laundries, and bathrooms have the special advantage of providing adequate daylight for inside rooms. In small areas light from above can expand visual space and make the sky and trees part of a room. The skylight window has a number of disadvantages, however, including problems with water seepage, insulation, and cleaning. Also, skylights present a security problem unless protected by safety-wired glass or other measures.

Architects and designers often create custom-designed windows for clients, as shown in Figure 12.11. They can be of various sizes and shapes and may be movable, stationary, or combinations of both types.

Fixed glazing with movable end sections

Palladian

Angled bay

Strip

Clerestory

Slanted clerestory

Corner

Dormer

Skylight

Figure 12.10 *Combination window types.*

Hard Window Treatments

All window treatments fall into two broad categories: *hard* and *soft*. Deciding on an appropriate window treatment from the almost unlimited options available can be challenging.

Blinds

Figure 12.12 shows several types of blinds. *Venetian blinds* were popular in ancient times, in colonial America, and during the Art Deco period. Today, modern adaptations of the blind have again become popular window treatments in both traditional- and contemporary-style homes and commercial settings. In most cases, blinds are constructed of aluminum, stainless steel, plastic, or wood. (The wooden slat blinds have been so popular that they are generally known just as *wooden blinds*.) These horizontally or sometimes vertically arranged strips can be adjusted precisely for light and privacy. Blinds can be mounted on the inside or outside of the window casing. They provide a clean, streamlined look and are available in a wide range of colors and sizes.

Miniblinds are narrow (about 1 inch wide) and create a sleek, trim look. Miniblinds are strong, lightweight, and come complete, requiring no supplementary hardware. Used alone they can add sophistication to a formal interior or be at home in a modest room. Miniblinds can be combined with a wide range of draw and side draperies for a more traditional look. These blinds are a little difficult to dust and clean; however, windows are made with miniblinds enclosed between two panes of glass to help eliminate

Figure 12.11 *Custom-designed fixed windows draw the outdoors into this eclectic French master bedroom. (Designer: Susan Lovelace, Lovelace Interiors. Photograph by Jack Gardner.)*

| Venetian blinds | Miniblinds | Vertical louvered blinds | Woven wood blinds Roman style | Bamboo blinds |

Figure 12.12 *Types of blinds.*

Figure 12.13 *These blinds are located between the pieces of glass within the window. This design is particularly beneficial for glass doors and anywhere dust is a problem. (Copyright: Permission has been granted by Hunter Douglas, Inc. to use copyrighted designs. Designs at Hunter Douglas Inc. Photograph by Joe Stawdart.)*

Figure 12.14 *Vertical blinds provide an efficient and simple window treatment that supports the modern style used in this bedroom. (Courtesy of Juan Montoya Design Corporation.)*

dust problems (Figure 12.13). This style, although expensive, provides better insulation. *Microminiblinds* have slats that measure about 1/2 inch. They are not as durable as miniblinds.

Vertical blinds are made of vertical strips that pivot at the top or at both the top and bottom (Figure 12.14). When drawn, the strips overlap to provide maximum privacy and light control. Usually made of plastic or metal, vertical blinds may have a different color on each side or may be covered with wallpaper or fabric. They are also available in wood. Vertical blinds provide a uniform, tailored appearance, and work particularly well on sliding glass doors.

Woven split-wood and *bamboo blinds* are slats of wood interwoven with colored or plain yarn. Woven split-wood and bamboo blinds allow some light through, and their warm natural texture is appropriate for many rooms and various styles (Figure 12.15). They may be used alone or combined with draperies and top treatments. This type of blind is raised by rolling or pleating.

Shutters

Figure 12.16 shows several types of shutters. *Louvered wood shutters* have been used since ancient times and continue to be a popular window treatment. They can substitute for drapery, be adjusted (by means of a vertical wooden support) for light and air (Figure 12.17), and are remarkably versatile. Shutters come in standard sizes and can be custom-made to

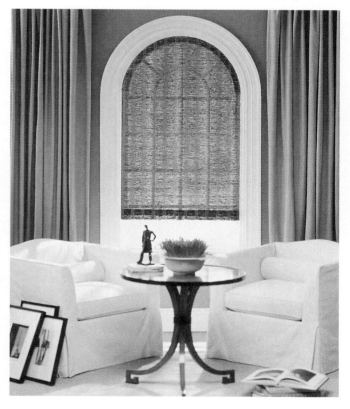

Figure 12.15 *These hand-woven shades conform to the arch-shaped window and provide contrast in texture to this formal interior. (Courtesy of Conrad Handwoven Window Coverings.)*

| Louvered shutters | Shutters with shirred fabric panels | Raised panel shutters | Vertical louvered shutters |

Figure 12.16 *Types of shutters.*

fit any window. Dark colors show dust more readily. Shutters can be used in tiers, have panels that are treated in the center with shirred fabric, have raised panel designs, or have vertical louvers. *Plantation shutters* have larger slats and are adaptable to many styles and window types. Although shutters can be expensive, they do provide good insulation.

Shoji Screens

The traditional Japanese shoji window or screen, with wood mullions and muntins supporting rice-paper panes, can slide or be stationary and may be used to establish an Asian or contemporary theme. The translucent rice-paper panes do not allow a view but do provide daytime privacy. Shoji screens are often fitted on a track to slide in front of a glass window.

Grills

Widely used in Spain and the Middle East for centuries, the pierced or grillwork screen can be an exotic window treatment. Privacy can be secured while light filters through, creating an appealing effect (Figure 12.18).

Specialty Glass

Glass block (also used for wall construction) is a translucent block of irregular glass, widely used during the periods of Art Deco and International Style in the 1920s and '30s. Glass block is also appropriate in contemporary commercial and residential environments (Figure 12.19). The blocks come in a variety of sizes and shapes and are

Figure 12.17 *This historical interior uses stained wood shutters to blend with the warm rich interior space. (Designer: Richard Warholic. Photograph by Gross & Daley.)*

Pierced screens

Figure 12.18 *Grill used as window or door treatment.*

made of two hollow half pieces joined together. The surface quality of the glass can be plain, frosted, mottled, or textured. A few companies produce glass block in triangular shapes to provide architects and designers with more design options.

Art glass, including *beveled* and *stained glass windows,* are common in both modern and traditional environments. *Beveled glass* refers to the angle ground into the edge of plate glass, reflecting the light in colorful ways. *Stained glass* is the art of arranging colorful pieces of glass into a pattern. Pieces of beveled or stained glass are joined by lead, zinc, or copper.

Beveled and stained glass panels are available for doors, windows, **sidelights** (windows beside doors), **transoms** (windows over doorways or above larger windows), and skylights. Used for the latter, they bring a brilliant glow into a room. Private craftworkers can provide custom designs.

Sandblasted and etched glass can create a variety of "frosted" designs. Such glass is often used as a design solution when a client specifies the need for privacy. Manufacturers also supply films that can be placed on existing glass for areas where sandblasting or chemical etching would be too messy. The films are meticulously cut in a variety of designs (Figure 12.20).

Liquid crystal is a glass technology that can change architectural glass from transparent to translucent and back again at the flick of a switch. A thin film coated with liquid crystal droplets is laminated between panels of heat-strengthened flat glass. When electricity is sent through the panel, the liquid crystals align to transmit light and the panel becomes clear like a normal window. When the power is switched off, the liquid crystals scatter and the panel becomes translucent. These glass panels are marketed for use in corporate conference rooms, offices, and presentation facilities where the ability to see through glass normally is desired, but at certain times privacy is required. As the price of liquid crystal panels decrease, their use in residential applications should increase.

Bare windows are sometimes beautiful in themselves and if privacy is not a problem, concealing them in layers of drapery can be a mistake. Triple glazing can help control energy costs.

Figure 12.19 *Translucent glass blocks in this large contemporary bath area allow additional light into the space without sacrificing privacy. (Courtesy of Pittsburgh Corning Corporation.)*

Figure 12.20 *The commons area in an educational facility was renovated from an existing bank. Large expanses of glass window were softened by the addition of rectangular-shaped film applied in a design similar to existing doors. (Designer: Lynn M. Jones. Photograph by J. J. Williams.)*

Soft Window Treatments

Draperies

Draperies are usually made of a heavier fabric than curtains, but the terms are used interchangeably. *Draw draperies* are made to draw over a window to control light, temperature, and privacy (Figure 12.21). Curtains and draperies terminate at one of three lengths: the windowsill, the bottom of the apron, or the floor; some draperies may be cut extra long to form a "puddle" effect on the floor (see Figures 12.22 and 13.11). They hang straight and may be used alone or combined with other curtains, blinds, or shades. For example, with a combination of draw sheers and draw drapery—the most common usage—the view can be exposed, and light, sound, temperature, and privacy can be controlled. Draperies that draw closed from both the right and left sides are called two-way traverse. Those that draw from one side only are called one-way traverse.

Side draperies or *stationary panels* remain at the sides of the window. Stationary panels may be hung straight or tied back. Their purpose is to bring beauty and style into the room. Because they are not designed to give privacy or provide insulation to a room, they may be combined with other window treatments (Figure 12.23).

Sheers or *semisheers* are used primarily to diffuse light and provide daytime privacy. They may be hung permanently against the glass or drawn back (Figure 12.24). Much of their beauty and efficiency depends on their fullness, most often three times the width of the window. When nighttime privacy is desired, sheers can be combined with draw draperies, blinds, or underdraws.

Casements are generally made of a loosely woven fabric and are heavier than a sheer. They may be used in residences, but are most often used singly in commercial environments and drawn to control light.

Underdraws, more commonly called *blackout draperies* or shades, are used in environments that require total darkness. Commercial office presentation and conference rooms may employ blackout window treatments. Some are controlled by mechanical devices. All underdraws should be concealed and are not considered decorative.

| Two-way traverse | One-way traverse | Draw draperies with sheers | Tieback side draperies | Bishop's sleeve or pouffed |

Figure 12.21 *Types of draperies.*

Figure 12.22 *Curtain and drapery lengths.*

To sill
(desirable)

To bottom
of apron
(desirable)

Between apron
and floor
(not desirable)

To floor
(desirable)

Figure 12.23 *Subtle custom hand-woven window coverings of natural flax are combined with draw draperies and side panels. The warmth of the materials is contrasted with the sleek glass table and silk pillows. (Courtesy of Conrad Imports, Inc., San Francisco. Design: Kneedler-Fauchère. Photograph by David Livingston.)*

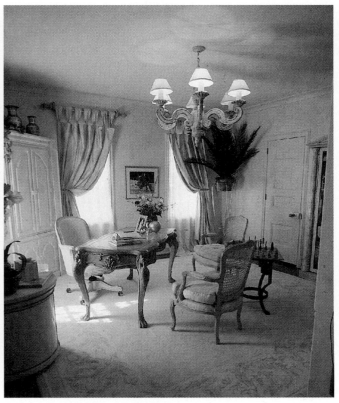

Figure 12.24 *This home office employs a custom-designed formal drapery with tab tops in front of a patterned sheer. (Designer: Pandy Agnew Interiors. Photograph by Lynn Barkley Photography.)*

| Center meet Priscilla curtains | Crisscross Priscilla curtains | Shirred curtains | Sash curtains |
| Cafe curtains, one tier | Cafe curtains, two tiers | Tiered curtains | Bishop's sleeve or pouffed |

Figure 12.25 *Types of curtains.*

Drapery lining serves several functions. Windows are viewed from two perspectives: outside and inside. Drapery lining provides a uniform and attractive view from the outside, covering patterns and colors seen more effectively from an interior perspective. When several windows face the street, it is best to coordinate their appearance through the use of drapery lining, especially for windows on the same level. Drapery lining also provides additional insulation from heat and cold, and protects the drapery from sunlight.

Ready-mades are draperies and curtains made to standard lengths and available in most drapery departments. Although often less full than custom-made draperies, ready-mades frequently give a satisfactory effect that belies their more modest cost.

Curtains

The most common types of curtains are illustrated in Figure 12.25. *Priscilla curtains* are ruffled tiebacks most often used in informal settings. They are usually made of light, sheer fabrics trimmed with a ruffle and shirred to a rod at the top of the window. One type of Priscilla curtain has panels over-

lapped in a crisscross fashion, and another has a symmetrical arrangement.

Shirred curtains are gathered on a rod and hung at the top of the window, letting the fabric drape softly. The amount of fabric used determines how full the effect of the curtains is.

Sash curtains are usually hung close to the glass. They are shirred at the top and often the bottom on sash rods.

Cafe curtains are hung over the lower part of the window. Usually used for privacy, they may draw or be stationary. Two or more tiers may be hung to cover the entire window, in which case the rods are concealed. Cafe curtains may be teamed with draw or side draperies, shades, blinds, or shutters. Cafe curtains are often embellished with a window top treatment.

Bishop's sleeves or "pouffed" curtains are similar to the stationary drapery type illustrated in Figure 12.21, but employ a sheerer fabric.

Shades

Some of the most common types of fabric shades are illustrated in Figures 12.26 and 12.27. *Roman shades* have a flat surface when extended down (Figure 12.28). When drawn

Shirred Roman

Shirred balloon

Flat Roman

Soft-pleated Roman

Balloon Roman

Accordion-pleated Roman

Figure 12.26 *Types of Roman shades.*

Austrian
shade

Honeycomb
shade

Fabric roller
shade

Fabric roller shade
with scallops

Figure 12.27 *Other types of shades.*

Figure 12.28 *Roman shades have been custom designed to fit the angles of this window, allowing a sweeping view of the city. The simple tailored effect complements the architecture and the room's Southwest decor. (Photograph by Mark Boisclair.)*

upward by a cord, the surface overlaps in horizontal folds made possible by a precreased rigid lining or by rings (or ring tape) and cords attached to the back of the shades. Roman shades come in a variety of styles, including shirred Roman, shirred balloon, flat Roman, soft-pleated Roman, balloon Roman, and accordion-pleated Roman.

Austrian shades consist of rows of lightweight fabric seamed to fall into deep scallops. The shade is operated by a draw cord and is similar in design to the shirred balloon Roman.

Pleated fabric shades are also called "accordion shades" and "soft shades." Pleated shades are factory manufactured, are available in a wide range of colors and finishes, and can be insulated. Fabrics vary from opaque to translucent and may be patterned or plain. *Honeycomb shades* have smaller pleats and are usually made of a heavy polyester fabric. They operate on the same principle as the single pleated shade except two pleated shades are bonded together, resulting in a "honeycomb" cross section (Figure 12.29). This construction provides an energy-efficient insulating air space. The exterior side of the shade is white to reflect the sun's rays and provide uniformity on the outside.

The *roller shade,* an old favorite, is an inexpensive window treatment. It may be installed between window casings or on the outside of the frame. The most common material is vinyl, which is available in a variety of weights. Traditionally, roller shades were white or off-white, but they are now available in

Figure 12.29 *These honeycomb shades provide privacy and insulation while allowing soft light to enter. A variety of pleat sizes, layers, and colors are available. (Copyright: Permission has been granted by Hunter Douglas, Inc. to use copyrighted designs. Designs at Hunter Douglas Inc.)*

the full spectrum of colors; however, colors do affect the exterior facade. Originally thought of as purely functional, the simple roller shade can be laminated with fabric and trimmed in a variety of ways. When mounted at the bottom of the window and drawn up, it is especially effective for privacy. Roller shades may be light filtering or room darkening, depending on the thickness of the material. Shades are easy to maintain, and insulate against heat and cold. Window quilts or thermal shades are made of additional layers of fabric, often have a decorative stitched pattern, and provide extra insulation.

Plants

Plants can be used successfully in lieu of other window treatments. Hung at varying heights and placed on pedestals or the floor, plants can form a border of greenery that softens hard-edged architecture, filters the light, and affords privacy.

A built-out window in a sunny location can become a greenhouse. Greenhouse windows are often used in kitchens and can provide a focal point.

Window Top Treatments

Many windows are embellished with treatments at the top or at the top and sides of the drapery or curtains. These treatments are of various designs and are made of soft or hard materials (Figure 12.30).

Soft Materials

The **valance** is generally a shirred, pleated, or draped soft treatment across the window top. A valance screens hardware and gives the drapery a finished look. It is used solely

Soft Materials

Pinch-pleated valance

Shirred valance

Asymmetrical valance with cascade

Flat panel valance with box pleats

Festoon, or swag, and jabot

Two swags with cascades

Flat fabric valance with scallops

Austrian valance

Hard Materials

Architectural cornice

Flat cornice with scallops

Lambrequin

Figure 12.30 *Types of top treatments for windows.*

for appearance; it does not change the function of the drapery. It can appear to extend the height and width of a window and unify windows of different sizes, thus altering the room's visual proportions. The valance may match the side or draw draperies and is often shaped by a stiff interlining. If the fabric is patterned, the shape of the valance looks best when it conforms to that pattern. The material in the valance should run the same direction as the drapery.

A *swag* is a type of valance treatment wherein fabric is draped over a rod at the top of the window. A *festoon* is a single draped member of a swag. A *cascade* drapes down from *under* the corners of the swag. The cascade has a vertical outside edge with an undulating edge closest to the swags. A *jabot* is similar to a cascade, but drapes over the edges of the swag. It is usually pleated and may be of varying lengths. Swags, jabots, and cascades may be hung over sheers, drapery, blinds, shutters, or shades, or at the top of bare windows (Figure 12.31).

Hard Materials

Cornices are generally made of wood, metal, or another hard material and are placed at the top of the window treatment. Often cornices are a continuation of an architectural molding or cornice around the top perimeter of the wall extending outward to accommodate the window top. Cornices may be simple or decorative, such as a scalloped or pierced design. They may be stained, painted, or covered with fab-

ric. A cornice with a fabric valance attached is an effective formal treatment.

Lambrequins are similar to cornices, but they also have a rigid treatment that extends vertically down both sides of the window. Lambrequins can be painted or covered with wallpaper or fabric, and used with or without draperies, curtains, blinds, or shades. They provide a tailored look and can alter the apparent size of the window.

Window Treatment Hardware

Functional Hardware

Figure 12.32 shows types of functional and decorative window hardware. Purely functional hardware should be inconspicuous. *Sash rods* are flat rods attached close to the sash (often both top and bottom) on which curtains are shirred. *Extension rods* are used for stationary curtains and drapery. They extend to various lengths and are available in single and double sets. *Traverse rods* operate on a pulley system. Available as either one- or two-way traverse types, they are used for drawing curtains and drapery. *Spring tension rods* fit inside the casing. *Swinging rods* are mounted on a mechanism that permits the rod to swing backward. These rods are suitable for in-swinging casements, dormers, and French doors. *Extender rods* extend outward to support stationary drapery beyond the sides of the window. *Ceiling tracks* with

Single curtain rod

Double curtain rod

Spring tension rod

Single traverse rod

Double traverse rod

Bay window curtain rod

Valance rod kit

Sash rod

Swinging rod

Corner curtain rod

Cafe rod

Decorative traverse rod

Curved curtain rod

Plain traverse rod set

Figure 12.32 *Curtain and drapery rods.*

concealed drawing mechanisms are especially popular in contemporary rooms. Small accessories such as hooks, rings, ring slides, brackets, and draw cords are all part of the unseen draw-drapery system. Rod placement on windows is illustrated in Figure 12.33. When drapery treatments are used in children's rooms, long dangling cords (such as those on blinds) present a danger to children and should be secured out of their reach.

Like doors, windows also require security hardware. Locking and opening mechanisms need to be of a durable finish that blends with the room's style.

Decorative Hardware

Decorative hardware is functional but also adds to the room's style. Rods may be wood (with natural, stained, or painted finishes) or metal (such as pewter, shiny or antique-finish brass, chrome, bronze, or wrought iron). Decorative hardware is equipped with a variety of **finials** (the decorative element attached to the end of a rod) to accommodate any style. Draperies suspended on rings may be cord operated or hand drawn. In the latter case, rings should be loose. Metal holdbacks that conform to the style of rods add a finishing touch.

Desirable

Desirable

Less desirable

Return

Figure 12.33 *Rod placement on window frame.*

Drapery and Curtain Headings

The *heading* is the pleating or gathering at the tops of curtains and draperies that forms the fold (providing the beauty of fullness for drawing). Headings are made in a number of ways. *French* or *pinch pleats* are made by stitching together three small pleats about 3 inches from the top. The pleats, which are spaced 3 to 4 inches apart, are held upright by an interlining. Ripplefold is a simple method of creating gentle, undulating folds by means of a compact track containing snap carriers. Folds are made from flat panels of fabric and are identical on both sides. *Accordion folds* are made by a combination of a compact track with snap carriers and a nylon heading tape. *Tailored pleats* form architectural-like folds. *Easy pleats* are made with a special tape attached to the inside top of the drapery. When pleater hooks are inserted in ready-made pockets, folds are automatically formed.

Shirred headings are made by stitching a pocket approximately 1 inch from the top, in which the rod is inserted. Tab top headings are similar to shirred headings, but the tabs are placed 2 to 4 inches apart so the decorative rod is exposed (see Figure 12.24).

Tiebacks hold back stationary draperies. They come in a wide variety of materials and styles and may be made of cords, tassels, metal, wood, or matching or contrasting fabric. Designers often tie back drapery somewhere between one-half and one-third from the bottom—employing the proportions of the golden mean (see Chapter 2). *Trimmings,* such as fringes, braids, edgings, cords, and tassels, can give a finished look to draperies, cornices, and valances.

Design and Placement of Windows and Window Treatments

The selection and placement of windows creates a powerful design statement. Poorly placed windows impede furniture arrangement and may allow for undesirable views. Whenever possible, designers should work with architects prior to construction. Furniture laid out in the schematic design and design development stages can help the architect determine where to locate windows. Window openings, however, are not always planned with indoor function in mind. A clever designer must work around these obstacles.

The following guidelines are important when selecting a window and treatment design:

- As with doors, consider the architectural background of the room. Architectural features may be enhanced or hidden.
- The exterior view also may need to be enhanced or hidden.
- Privacy may need to be created either at night, during the day, or both.
- Light may need to be blocked to prevent glare or to preserve precious furnishings.
- The window design should complement the furniture style and placement.
- The treatment may need to conserve energy (see "Green Design: Energy-Efficient Window Treatments").

In many cases, to serve a variety of functions a combination of treatments is required. These combinations should work together to become one design element.

GREEN DESIGN

Energy-Efficient Window Treatments

A window's treatment may cut down on heating and cooling costs. Curtain and drapery manufacturers are producing a variety of insulators for windows to save energy, such as double-woven multilayered fabrics that trap warm air in the room and insulated shades, draperies, and linings that protect against heat and cold, thus cutting down on utility bills.

Generally, natural materials do the finest job of insulating. The more yarn used in the fabric, the tighter the weave, the bulkier the material, and the fuller the drapery, the more air it will trap. Layered window treatments are effective insulators. One efficient combination is wooden blinds placed near the glass, with drawn sheers and lined draw draperies. To trap cold or hot air, the sides of the drapery may be anchored to the window frame or wall by double-faced fabric tape. Other effective energy-saving window treatments are quilted blinds, lambrequins, and cornices sealed at the top and sides, and window shades (which can be operated by a mechanical device) equipped with side channels to seal the cracks. Edge sealing is the most critical point for effective energy saving in window treatments.

FIREPLACES

The final form of fenestration discussed in this chapter is the fireplace. Fireplaces have served important functional roles through the centuries as a source of warmth and a place to cook meals. In simple homes the fireplace was the focus of the home and a place where the family congregated. In today's homes the fireplace may be a visual luxury serving primarily as a room's focal point or it may provide a source of heat.

Fireplaces can be expensive and hard to clean. They also require space for fuel storage. Gas fireplaces have become a common alternative, as have wood-burning heaters and stoves. A fireplace, however, is still considered a desirable asset; fireplaces in residential living spaces can add to a home's market value (Figure 12.34). Fireplaces in public settings like restaurants, hotels, and clubs can be particularly inviting, offering a friendly and intimate atmosphere.

Figure 12.34 *Before and after shots of this living room demonstrate the power of sensitive color usage and applied decoration. In both shots, however, the fireplace is the focal point. (Architect: Maresca & Assoc. Interiors: Louise Quinn. Photographs by Cheryl Dalton.)*

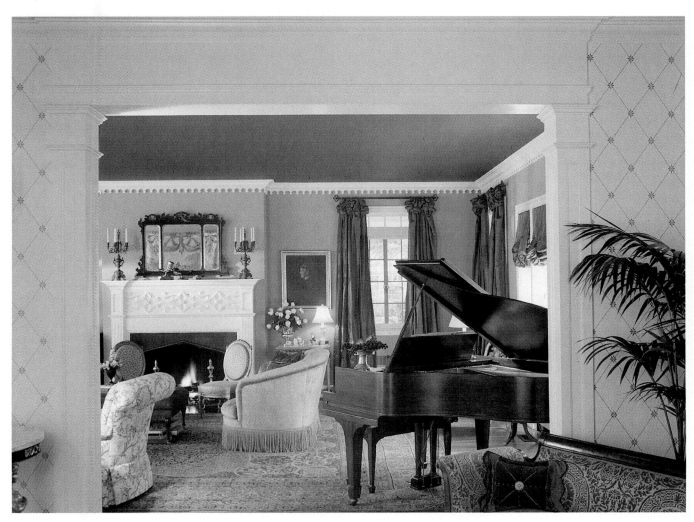

Fireplace Construction

Fireplaces may be constructed of masonry or be prefabricated from metal. Masonry fireplaces require space away from combustible materials. Some prefabricated units require no space between the fireplace and combustible materials, and can be installed within a regular stud wall. Models are available with openings on one, two, three, and even four sides.

The most common materials for fireplace surrounds include:

- *Brick,* available in many sizes, textures, and colors and laid in simple or intricate arrangements
- *Stone* of all types (marble, travertine, terrazzo, quartzite, fieldstone, granite, etc.)
- *Wood* of all varieties, either in strips (laid in numerous patterns and directions), panels, planks, or elaborately carved members, used on decorative surfaces
- *Facings* of plaster or stucco, painted or left plain
- *Concrete,* plain or with exposed aggregate accents
- *Tile* in a variety of colors, textures, and patterns.

Fireplace design often includes combinations of these materials. For example, a stone fireplace may have a handsome wood mantel, or a plaster fireplace may be outlined around the opening with colorfully patterned tile.

Types of Fireplaces

The wood-burning fireplace is the most prevalent fireplace design. However, faced with deteriorating air quality as well as wood-burning restrictions, many designers and homeowners are choosing alternatives to the wood-burning fireplace, such as *wood-burning heaters* and *stoves.* The Environmental Protection Agency (EPA) established strict codes in 1988 for wood-burning heaters and stoves: They may emit no more than eight grams of particulate per hour. (By comparison, an average wood-burning fireplace emits up to 1,000 grams of particulate per hour.) Today only certified wood heaters that meet the emission limits may be sold. Additionally, no person may install or operate a wood-burning heater or stove except in a manner consistent with the EPA's guidelines. Heating homes with these heaters and stoves instead of fireplaces can drastically cut down on air pollutants.

Wood-burning heaters and stoves are also much more energy efficient than wood-burning fireplaces. With the high cost of heating, wood-burning stoves and heaters have become popular and are available in a large range of styles (Figure 12.35).

Other alternatives to the traditional wood-burning fireplace are *natural gas fireplaces, fireplace inserts,* and *log sets.* These gas-burning devices provide the ambience of wood-burning fireplaces and stoves with none of the inconveniences. Compared to its wood-burning counterpart, natural gas fireplace equipment is cleaner burning, simpler to start, easier to keep clean, and has lower fuel costs. Although gas does not burn as hot as wood, a gas insert adds a substantial amount of heat to a room. Flueless gas logs are also available that require no venting to the outside.

Figure 12.35 *In this contemporary setting a wood stove enhances the interior architecture and provides a backup heating system. (Courtesy of Vermont Castings/Majestic Products Co.)*

Fireplace Design and Placement

The style of a fireplace is generally traditional or modern. Traditional styles for fireplace design provide charm and a feeling of authenticity. Modern fireplaces are often custom-designed for a particular space. Modern fireplaces may soar vertically, expand horizontally, or create a circular form. The fireplace may or may not have a mantel, the hearth may be on the floor or raised, and the fireplace may be set against the wall or project outward. The style of a fireplace is generally most successful when it complements the room's furnishings and background.

The size of the fireplace within a living space is flexible. Small fireplaces can have charm; an average- or medium-sized fireplace can be a focal point without overwhelming a room; and a very large fireplace can be a dramatic feature (Figure 12.36).

Designers may incorporate the fireplace as part of the total wall composition by using shelves or built-in furnishings, extending the fireplace material the full length and height of the wall. The fireplace may also be freestanding, independent of any wall. As with doors and windows, consideration of the scale and proportion of the room, the style, the materials to be employed, and the effect and function desired help to determine the most appropriate fireplace construction for a particular space.

Figure 12.36 *Michael Graves designed this Post-Modern residence in New Jersey in 1986. In the living room, the fireplace wall dominates the space. The placement of classic Villa Gallia chairs, designed by Josef Hoffman at the turn of the century, complements the fireplace wall. (Photograph by William Taylor.)*

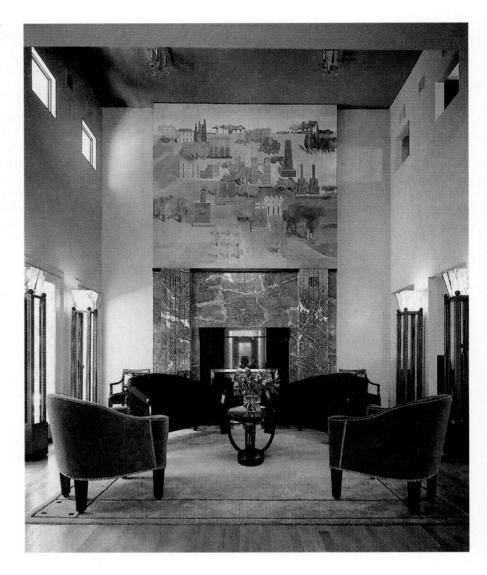

Summary

The fenestration of a room or building defines its style and creates natural divisions for interior zoning. Doors direct traffic and provide for privacy and security. Doors in combination with windows and fireplaces define furniture arrangements.

When given the opportunity, interior designers should work with architects and builders to determine the best furniture arrangements before the fenestration is established. However, in many cases this is not possible. Designers must cleverly apply the principles and elements of design, and where possible design window treatments or fireplace surrounds that enable the room to function properly.

Part V focused on the various components applied to an interior to create a space that functions within the client's aesthetic and economic preferences. The integration of these varying components is key to the creation of a successful interior environment. The accompanying Design Scenario illustrates how one design firm visually communicated their design solution for these various components to their client.

DESIGN SCENARIO RETIREMENT CONDOMINIUM

Project Description

Two sisters were moving into a retirement apartment. The sisters wished to reside in the same area of their community and had chosen a condominium that did not provide accessible apartment living. Rich Interiors was retained to adapt the physical environment and select furniture, furnishings, and equipment where needed.

Programming: The two-bedroom, one-bath apartment allowed for only minor wall changes in the bathroom and kitchen areas. Plumbing fixtures could only be moved within 5'-0" of their existing location in order to be near water lines.

The sisters were very fond of their existing bedroom furniture and wished to reuse it. Zoa realized her room would be tight for space because of the addition of the sewing table. Due to the size of the new apartment and their diverse existing furniture, the sisters wanted new living and dining room furniture. The Residential Programming Questionnaire and Furniture Inventory Sheet define other needs (Figures DS12.1 and DS12.2).

RESIDENTIAL PROGRAMMING QUESTIONNAIRE

I   **General Information**   **Date**

Client Name	*ZOA SMITH & ZONA LEE JONES*
Address	*100 ANY STREET*
Home Phone	*555-1212* Work Phone
Occupation(s)	*RETIRED*

II   **Family Members**

Name	Age	Universal Concerns
ZOA	*65+*	*WHEEL CHAIR ACCESSIBILITY*
ZONA LEE	*65+*	*GOOD LIGHTING*

III   **Family Members' Hobbies and Activities**

Activity	Family Member(s)	Where does activity take place
Computer		
Television	*BOTH*	*LIVING ROOM*
Stereo	*BOTH*	*NOTHING ELABORATE—LIVING ROOM*
Sewing	*ZOA*	*BEDROOM & LIVING*
Crafts		
Instruments		
Model Building		
Reading	*ZONA LEE*	*LIVING ROOM*
Other	*BOTH (GARDENING) FLOWERS*	

IV   **Room Requirements**

Living Room
Entertainment   Yes _____   No _X_   How Many? _____   How Often? _____

Dining Room
Formal/Casual/Both (circle one) *(Casual circled)*
Number of people maximum _*4*_
Comments

Breakfast Room
Number of people maximum _____
Comments _____

Living Room

Activities	*Shelves with doors to close off T.V. set/stereo. Straight firm chair for Zoa to sew in. Canister table to store sewing. Larger, softer, easy chair for Zona Lee. She requested this because this is what she is accustomed to.*

Figure DS12.1 *The residential programming questionnaire (see Appendix A) was used to define the needs and desires of the two sisters. (Courtesy of Tammie Roper, Rich Interiors.)*

Bedrooms

#	Who	Requirements
1	ZONA LEE	MUST BE ACCESSIBLE FOR WHEELCHAIR. BRINGING EXISTING FURNITURE
2	ZOA	BRINGING EXISTING FURNITURE (INCLUDING SEWING MACHINE) GOOD LIGHTING WITH CHAIR FOR SEWING.
3		
4		
5		

Baths

1	SHARED BATHROOM, REQUESTED MORE CONVENIENT TO ZONA LEE'S BEDROOM.
	ACCESSIBLE FOR WHEELCHAIR WITH ROLL IN SHOWER & BENCH
2	GRAB BARS, LOWERED SINK WITH KNEE SPACE.
3	
4	

Other Rooms

Rooms	Requirements
Laundry	
Kitchen	LOWERED WORK SPACE; ZONA LIKES TO COOK. KNEE SPACE UNDER SINK, STOVE. SIDE BY SIDE FRIG.
Office	AND SIDE OPEN RANGE.
Workshop	
Garage	
Play Room	
Study	
Music Room	

V   Design Preferences

Colors	THEY AGREE ON A SOFT, MELLOW GREEN THROUGHOUT
Mood	CHEERFUL NOT DRAB
Budget	MED.
Time Frame	3 MONTHS
Reuse items	BEDROOMS (if yes, see furniture inventory sheet)
Other	DON'T WANT HEAVY TRADITIONAL-LIKE A TRANSITIONAL LOOK MAYBE WITH SOME COUNTRY FRENCH—
	PREFER LIGHTER WOODS

VI   Other Information & Comments

ZONA LEE—RETIRED SCHOOL TEACHER. LOVES TO READ, COOK AND LOVES FLOWERS.

MUST HAVE OPEN SPACE FOR WHEELCHAIR TRAVEL. HARDWOOD FLOORS WITH NO RUGS.

BUILD IN BOOKSHELVES FOR BOOK COLLECTION.

LIKES PLUM FOR ACCENTS

ZOA—RETIRED HOUSEWIFE. LOVES TO SEW, COOK, & ALSO LOVES FLOWERS

MUST HAVE ROOM FOR SEWING MACHINE. FLORAL PATTERN FOR BEDROOM WITH SOME WALLPAPER. LIKES PURPLES AND GOLDS FOR ACCENTS

*BOTH REQUESTED NICE SEATING AND AREA FOR FLOWERS ON PATIO.

VII   Business Information
Travel Directions

NORTH ON MAIN

RIGHT ON ANY STREET

Fee Basis

FLAT FEE & PERCENTAGE OF PURCHASES

Figure DS12.1   *Continued*

FURNITURE INVENTORY SHEET

Item #	Description	Size W × D × H	Style	Comments
Zoa	Bedroom Furniture			
	Std Bed w/ head & footboard	54" × 86" × 48"	Empire/Sleigh Victorian	
	(2) Night stands	22" × 14" × 23"		
	Armoire	36" × 22" × 88"		Not for TV/ sewing-storage
	Dresser	48" × 22" × 40"		
	Sewing table/ chair	28" × 24" × 30"		
	Side chair	28" × 30" × 44"	Slipperchair uph to floor	Needs re-upholstery
Zona	Bedroom Furniture			
	Std Bed w/ headboard	54" × 82" × 46"	upholstery inset w/ wood trim	
	(2) Nightstands	22" × 20" × 22"	appears to have French Country influence	
	Dresser	48" × 20" × 40"		
	Chest	36" × 22" × 54"		
	Sidechair	30" × 32" × 48"	Armchair w/legs	Needs re-upholstery

Figure DS12.2 *The furniture inventory sheet (see Appendix B) was used to document existing furnishings that were to be reused. (Courtesy of Tammie Roper, Rich Interiors.)*

Conceptual/Schematic Design: Rich Interiors worked with the clients in developing a floor plan with minor wall changes. Additionally, Rich Interiors noted the following:

- Additional bathroom space would shrink Zona's room to the point where not all of the bedroom furniture would fit.
- A sage green color scheme with gold and plum accents was agreed to by the women.
- A built-in unit would be designed for the living room instead of open shelving.
- Custom cabinetry would be used in the kitchen, incorporating the design of the built-in bookshelves in the living room.

- All flooring would be in an oak finish, except for the tile in the bathroom.

Design Development: To visually communicate the proposed design, Rich Interiors developed three presentation boards. Figure DS12.3 shows the floor plan and furniture and finish selections for the dining and kitchen area. Figure DS12.4 illustrates the furniture and finishes for the living room and bath. Figure DS12.5 truly warmed the clients' hearts—their individual bedrooms were clearly defined in a three-dimensional rendering. Care was taken to include clients' personal items such as family portraits, lamps, and favorite accessories.

Designer: Tammie Roper, Rich Interiors.

Figure DS12.3 *Presentation floor plan and furnishings for the dining and kitchen areas. (Designer: Tammie Roper, Rich Interiors.)*

Figure DS12.4 *Presentation board for the living room and bath. (Designer: Tammie Roper, Rich Interiors.)*

Figure DS12.5 *Presentation board with axonometric renderings of the bedrooms. (Designer: Tammie Roper, Rich Interiors.)*

PART VI

The Profession of Interior Design

CHAPTER 13
Interior Design as a Career

Figure VI.1 *This Paris apartment focuses on the decorative nature of interior design, while incorporating architecturally significant interior details. Soaring ceilings and elaborate crown moldings set the stage for the embracing interior. See Figure VI.2 for other views of this apartment. (Designer: Manuel León Ponce, ASID. Photograph by Carlos Domenech. Courtesy of* Southern Accents.*)*

As discussed in Chapter 1, the interior design profession is a complex blend of technical design skills and creative artistic skills. Additionally, designers must possess strong business skills in order to be accurate and competitive in the design market. Interior designers must address the needs of their clients while balancing budget, environmental, aesthetic, and regulatory issues. Although many opportunities are open to the aspiring interior designer, a career should be based on a sound educational foundation that continues throughout the designer's career. Part VI addresses the path toward a career in interior design, professional involvement in design organizations, and specific issues relating to business practices, such as professional ethics.

Chapter 13 features outstanding interiors to inspire the beginning designer. These photographs were selected to represent a variety of specialty fields in residential and commercial design. Careful analysis of these interiors reveals professionals' accomplished use of the principles and elements of design. Figures VI.1, VI.2, and VI.3 begin this process by reviewing two residential design solutions.

In plan view, the two interiors are similar, containing a living area, study, and dining room. The design solutions, however, illustrate the distinct difference between decorative and structural design.

A.

B.

C.

D.

Figure VI.2 *The warm vibrant colors are cleverly blended with neoclassic motifs. A, the conversation grouping casually unites several chair designs. B, the study is encased by a custom-designed bookcase. C and D, the dining room opens into the conversation area and is highlighted by treasured accessories and art. Although lively, the interior also establishes a sense of serenity. The designer has created a "sense of place." (Designer: Manuel León Ponce, ASID. Photographs by Carlos Domenech. Courtesy of Southern Accents.)*

Figure VI.3 *This Virginia townhouse takes a more structural approach to its design solution. The calmer neutral color scheme is accented by bold black furnishings and sleek contemporary lines. A, tall French windows reflect similar qualities seen in the Paris apartment, as does the conversation area around the fireplace. B, the office/study area is defined by a polished, classic desk. C, the circular dining table opens onto the conversation area. The formal cool fabrics and subtle refined lighting are enhanced by the textural qualities of the carpet and drapery and by the primal coarse character of the accessories. (Designer: David Mitchell. Photographs by Scott Frances. Courtesy of Southern Accents.)*

A.

B.

C.

13

Interior Design as a Career

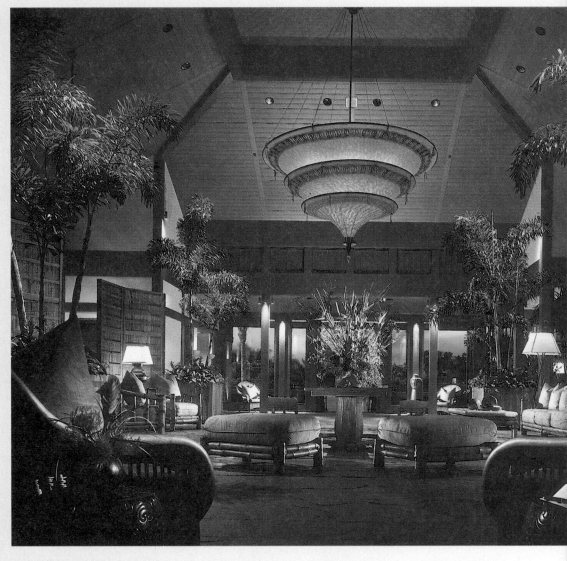

Figure 13.1 *Hospitality Design—Hotel: In this Hawaiian resort hotel, a custom silk and steel chandelier serves as the focal point. Furniture arrangements, floral designs, and architectural lighting add support to this locally inspired design. (Designer: James Northcutt/Wilson and Associates. Photograph by Robert Miller.)*

Career Progression

Deciding on a career is a search process that requires careful examination and evaluation of one's interests and capabilities as well as one's shortcomings. Creativity, sensitivity to the environment, and an interest in cultural heritage as well as contemporary design are all necessary traits for anyone who is seriously considering a career in interior design. Additionally, a designer is always concerned with improving the quality of the human environment.

As discussed in Part I, interior designers are qualified by education, experience, and examination. These three steps ensure the quality of the design professional and should be pursued *before* starting a business.

Education

One of the initial steps toward becoming a professional interior designer is to successfully complete an interior design program at a college, university, or design school. Programs are offered leading to an associate degree (usually two to three years) or a bachelor degree (four to five years). Advanced education is also possible. Master of science (M.S.) or master of art (M.A.) degrees require a minimum of one to two years of additional study. A master of fine art (M.F.A.) degree requires a minimum of two years of additional study, the acquisition of a fine arts skill, and a display of the resulting work. All master degrees in interior design may be considered terminal degrees. The M.F.A. is considered the equivalent of a doctor of philosophy degree (Ph.D.). Additionally, some universities are now offering a Ph.D. in interior design.

Curriculum

Associate- and bachelor-level programs teach a broad-based curriculum that prepares students for entry-level careers in the field of interior design. The Foundation for Interior Design Education Research (**FIDER),** founded in 1970, is a self-governing organization whose board of directors and teams of site visitors are composed of educators and practitioners who review educational programs in interior design. The standards developed by FIDER, with input from the practice community and educators, form a common body of knowledge required by all interior designers, regardless of their specific career direction. These standards include the following areas of knowledge:

- Art and design fundamentals
- Design theories
- Human behavior
- Design history
- Business principles and practices
- Laws, codes, regulations, and standards that protect the public health, safety, and welfare
- Building systems fundamentals
- Materials and products
- Communications skills, including oral, written, drawing, rendering, and drafting/CAD with regard to working drawings and construction documents

- Personal development, such as critical and creative thinking, listening, and ethical standards
- Professional responsibility, accountability, and effectiveness
- Application of the above areas of knowledge in an interior environment

Students are also required to be involved in team approaches to design solutions, and designs for multicultural and diverse populations, as well as adaptive use and historic preservation.

Of the approximately 200 bachelor-level interior design programs throughout the United States, approximately 60% are accredited by FIDER at the Professional Level. Some institutions may meet or exceed FIDER's list of standards and guidelines, but for financial or pedagogical reasons elect not to apply. Some states, as part of their registration process, require students to attend a FIDER-accredited school or its equivalent.

Internships

Most interior design programs require students to participate in an internship or work-study program as part of the requirements for graduation. Internship programs vary, but all have the same objective: to enable the student to experience the professional business world firsthand prior to graduation by combining classroom education with practice. Internship experience is invaluable to the student. By becoming actively involved in the professional world of interior design, students

- Experience operational procedures, policies, and various phases of design, such as client-designer relationships
- Learn about interactions of designers within a firm
- Observe and participate in design from concept to implementation
- Learn to be open to new and different attitudes and perspectives in all aspects of design
- Learn more about themselves in terms of their goals as a professional interior designer
- Acquire valuable experience that can be entered on a job résumé for use after graduation.

Experience

There is no better teacher than experience. All designers, whether just out of college or pursuing a career change, need to work with a licensed professional for a minimum of two years prior to establishing their own firm. Experience offers many advantages that simply cannot be achieved in an educational environment. Perhaps the most rewarding is the actual installation of one's design ideas.

In 1999, a structured work experience program called the Interior Design Experience Program (IDEP) started a pilot program. This program, developed and researched by Buie Harwood and outlined in the *Journal of Interior Design,* would link a graduate's internship experience to the FIDER and NCIDQ standards (discussed below). NCIDQ is coordinating this effort.

Figure 13.2 *Healthcare Design— Hospital: Sensitivity to the quality of life is put to the greatest test in the design of healthcare environments. Patients may heal faster in environments that are responsive to their physical and psychological needs. Right, in this children's hospital, color, animation, and movement create a fun, energizing atmosphere. Above, the atrium before. (Courtesy of Karlsberger Companies. "After" photograph by Robert Benson.)*

Examination

The National Council for Interior Design Qualifications **(NCIDQ)** was formed in 1972 to establish a professional level of competence for interior designers. Level of competence is determined through an examination that is accepted as the standard in all of North America. NCIDQ is also investigating the advantages and disadvantages of pursuing legal registration or certification of the profession.

To be eligible to sit for the exam, potential professional designers must meet one of the following educational and practice combinations:

- A four- or five-year degree in interior design or equivalent educational credit plus two years of practical professional experience

- A three-year certificate in interior design or equivalent educational credits plus three years of practical professional experience
- A two-year certificate in interior design or equivalent educational credits plus four years of practical professional experience.

Additionally, participants must submit three letters of recommendation and official college transcripts.

The six-part exam is given on a Friday and Saturday. On Friday, the *identification and application section* is a series of two multiple-choice tests. The *programming section* evaluates the candidate's ability to gather, assimilate, and interpret programmatic information into exercises. A *three-dimensional section* requires the candidate to apply the principles and elements of the theory of interior design within a three-dimensional volume of space.

1	ENTRY	4	LIVING
2	KITCHEN	5	OFFICE
3	DINING	6	BEDROOM

Figure 13.3 *Residential—City Apartment: This residence required many structural changes, including an expanded kitchen and visual division between the living and dining areas. Color and light are strong elements in this apartment, alternating the forms and adding an explosion of character. The floor plan illustrates the appropriate balance and clever use of relativity small space. (Designer: Hassan Abouseda. Photograph by John M. Hall.)*

On Saturday, the *problem solving section* requires the candidate to review a designer's drawings, to understand them, and to answer questions about a hypothetical situation. Next is a test covering *building and barrier-free codes*. The final test is a *project scenario*. Participants must interpret a programming statement and develop a space plan, furniture arrangement, and reflected ceiling plan for an office, residential, retail, institutional, or hospitality design.

The test is administered twice a year, and participants may elect to take from one to six sections at any given time. All six sections must be successfully completed within a five-year period.

Passage of the NCIDQ exam provides designers the opportunity for professional membership in other design organizations. (NCIDQ does not offer membership to individuals.) In fact, most of the professional design organizations *require* passage of the exam for professional membership. Additionally, passage of the NCIDQ exam is mandatory in those states and provinces that have licensing or registration statutes.

Licensing and Registration

Several states and provinces have passed some form of state registration, usually in the form of a title act or practice act.

A *title act* protects those who are competent to use particular "titles" such as "Certified" or "Registered" Interior Designer. Because of the title act, clients can be assured that persons using these titles are qualified professional interior designers.

A *practice act* requires those who qualify as professional interior designers and plan to practice this occupation to be licensed by a state board. The practice act is designed to legally recognize interior design as a profession, to ensure that designers work to protect the health, safety, and welfare of their clients, and to ensure that interior designers are qualified by education and experience to practice. In addition to passage of the NCIDQ exam, most of the acts require a combination of education and experience in order to qualify.

Continuing Education

To maintain their registration, professionals are required in most states and provinces to acquire Continuing Education Units, or CEUs. CEUs are awarded for coursework completed at the professional development level and must be recorded by the state or province. Designers also voluntarily attend sessions on new products, designs, and procedures in order to remain current in the field.

Figures 13.4 and 13.5 *Historic Preservation/Adaptive Use, Institutional—Community Center: These two photos illustrate the attention to detail required in a historic preservation/ adaptive use project. The courthouse was renovated to be used as a community center. Historical research uncovered the original paint colors and the judge's bench design. Figure 13.4 shows the renovated steps and custom handrail. The masculine design was typical in public buildings during the era. To allow multiple use of the renovated courtroom, the judge's bench in Figure 13.5 dismantles into three sections. A custom carpet, designed in the pattern of the era, improves acoustics in the large room. Figure 11.12 illustrates the courthouse corridor. (Architect: Office of Jack Pyburn, Architects, Inc. Designer: Lynn M. Jones. Photographs by J. J. Williams.)*

Professional Interior Design Organizations

Many professional organizations assist professionals in sharing information, continuing their education, promoting the profession, and serving the public. Most organizations require a combination of education and experience in order to join, with professional membership also requiring passage of the NCIDQ exam. Names and addresses of many of these organizations are found in Table 13.1.

ASID

The American Society of Interior Designers **(ASID)** is a professional international organization established to enact and maintain standards of excellence to enhance the growing recognition of interior design as a profession. ASID was formed in 1975 through the consolidation of the American Institute of Interior Designers and the National Society of Interior Designers, but its roots date back to the founding of the American Institute of Decorators in 1931. ASID is the largest organization of interior designers in the world, representing over 31,000 members in the United States and abroad. It represents interior design as a profession dedicated to serving people, and it provides a forum for its members to bring their differing points of view into harmony to promote unified action. ASID's mission statement is: "ASID means business by the promotion of design excellence through professional education, market expansion, information sharing, and the creation of a favorable business environment for the practice of interior design."

IIDA

The International Interior Design Association **(IIDA)** is an internationally established design organization founded in 1994 as a merger of the Institute of Business Designers, the

Table 13.1 *Professional Organizations*

American Institute of Architects, **AIA**
1735 New York Avenue NW
Washington, DC 20006
(202) 626-7300
www.aiaonline.com

American Society of Interior Designers,
 ASID
608 Massachusetts Avenue NE
Washington, DC 20002-6006
(202) 546-3480
www.asid.org

Business & Institutional Furniture
 Manufacturers' Assoc., **BIFMA**
2680 Horizon Drive SE, Suite A-1
Grand Rapids, MI 49546-7500
(616) 285-3963
www.bifma.com

Color Association of the United States
24 East 48th Street
New York, NY 10016
(212) 582-6889

Color Marketing Group
4001 North Ninth Street, Suite 102
Arlington, VA 22203

Design Communication Association, **DCA**
University of Arizona
College of Architecture
P.O. Box 210075
Tucson, AZ 85721-0075
(520) 621-9819

Environmental Design Research
 Association, Inc., **EDRA**
L'Enfant Plaza Station
P.O. Box 23129
Washington, DC 20024
(301) 657-2651

Foundation for Interior Design Education
 Research, **FIDER**
60 Monroe Center NW, Suite 300
Grand Rapids, MI 49503
(616) 458-0400
www.fider.org

Illuminating Engineering Society of North
 America, **IES**
120 Wall Street, 17th Floor
New York, NY 10005
(212) 248-5000
www.iesna.org

Institute of Store Planners, **ISP**
25 North Broadway
Tarrytown, NY 10591
(914) 332-1806
www.ispo.org

Interior Design Educators Council, **IDEC**
9202 North Meridian, Suite 200
Indianapolis, IN 46260
www.idec.org

The Interior Design Society, **IDS**
P.O. Box 2396
Highpoint, NC 27261
(336) 883-1650
www.interiordesignsociety.org

Interior Designers of Canada, **IDC**
260 King Street East, #414
Toronto, Ontario, Canada M5A 1K3
(416) 594-9310

International Association of Lighting
 Designers, **IALD**
Merchandise Mart
200 World Trade Center, Suite 487
Chicago, IL 60654
(312) 527-3677
www.iald.org

International Colour Authority
c/o Benjamin Dent & Company
33 Bedford Place
London WC1B 5JX, England

International Facilities Management
 Association, **IFMA**
One East Greenway Plaza, Suite 1100
Houston, TX 77046
(713) 623-4362
www.ifma.org

International Federation of Interior
 Designers, **IFI**
P.O. Box 19126
1000 CG Amsterdam, Nederland
(020) 276-820
www.interiorcity.com/IFI

International Furnishings and Design
 Association, **IFDA**
1200 19th Street, NW, Suite 300
Washington, DC 20036
(202) 857-1897
www.ifda.com

International Interior Design Association,
 IIDA
341 Merchandise Mart
Chicago, IL 60654
(312) 467-1950
www.iida.com

National Association of Home Builders,
 NAHB
1201 15th Street NW
Washington, DC 20005-2892
(202) 822-0200
www.nahb.com

National Association of Schools of Art
 and Design, **NASAD**
11250 Roger Bacon Drive, #21
Reston, VA 20190
(703) 437-0700
www.arts-accredit.org

National Council for Interior Design
 Qualification, **NCIDQ**
1200 18th Street NW, Suite 1001
Washington, DC 20036-2506
(202) 721-0220
www.ncidq.org

National Kitchen and Bath Association,
 NKBA
687 Willow Grove Street
Hackettstown, NJ 07840
(800) THE-NKBA (843-6522)
www.nkba.org

National Lighting Bureau, **NLB**
2101 L Street NW
Washington, DC 20037
(202) 457-8437

Council of Federal Interior Designers, and the International Society of Interior Designers. With over 9,000 members, the organization serves a broad base of professionals, industry members, and students. IIDA's mission "is to enhance the quality of life through excellence in interior design and to advance interior design through knowledge." In order to enact this mission, IIDA

- Supports members in the design services marketplace through continuing education and by upholding the industry's highest standards of professionalism
- Is the profession's advocate on issues of national and international importance
- Focuses on expanding the market for interior design services

Figure 13.6 *Environmental Design—Straw Bale House: Designed as a guest house, this 850-sq.-ft. straw bale home boasts 24"-thick walls with R values from R-40 to R-55. Custom niches, handmade tiles, and softly tinted plaster walls add to the cozy character. (Architect: Paul Weiner. Designer: Pam Tillman. Photographs by Bill Steen.)*

- Is the profession's local, national, and global information exchange
- Is the catalyst for expanding the body of interior design knowledge
- Supports excellence in design education and the continuous advancement of interior design professionals.

IDC

Interior Designers of Canada is the national professional association. It works with the provincial associations to advance the interior design profession and to promote quality in education and practice. Full professional membership requires passage of the NCIDQ exam.

IDEC

The Interior Design Educators Council (**IDEC**), incorporated in 1967, is dedicated to the development of interior design education. IDEC, according to Article 2 of its bylaws,

> is dedicated to the advancement of education and research in interior design. IDEC fosters exchange of information, improvement of educational standards, and development of the body of knowledge relative to the quality of life and human performance in the interior environment. IDEC concentrates on the establishment and strengthening of lines of communication among educators, practitioners, educational institutions, and other organizations concerned with interior design education.

The Business of Interior Design

Successful interior designers are not only creative artists but also perceptive business people. Designers must be aware of business practices, procedures, management, and marketing techniques in order to succeed in the profession. *Before starting a business, a designer should consult with an attorney, an accountant, an insurance agent, and a tax adviser.* The following section highlights the business issues involved in the practice of interior design.

The Business Plan

Most lending institutions require the submission of a business plan in order to qualify for a business loan. The plan describes the business, its market, competition, location, management, personnel, and projected revenue and expenses. The Small Business Administration can assist designers in developing this plan.

Business Structures

There are four basic ways to structure an interior design business. The *sole proprietorship* is the simplest. The individual and the company are basically one. The owner personally receives all the benefits of the business, but also bears all the risks. Personal belongings, such as an owner's home, car, and other valuables, may be garnished by a business loss. The *partnership* is similar to the sole proprietorship, except the benefits and risks are shared by two or more individuals.

In an *association* an individual "associates" with an existing or established firm. The associate may bring clients to the firm, and the firm may offer the associate a working environment and limited liability. Other forms of associations also exist.

The safest of all business types is the *corporation.* A corporation is a separate entity from its owners, who are the shareholders. Although more difficult to start, corporations offer limited liability to their owners.

Insurance

Before starting a business, the designer must research and decide upon necessary types of insurance. The two broad types of insurance include *property and liability insurance,* which protects the business, and *life and health insurance,* which protects the individuals. Another important type of business insurance, called *errors and omissions,* protects designers when errors are made in contract documents. Consulting with a trustworthy insurance agent and attorney is important.

Business Documents

Designers will find it necessary to acquire several business documents. Most municipalities require a *business license,* available from local city or county officials. A *resale certificate* or *tax number,* required in some states, allows designers to purchase products for clients; other states require alternative tax documentation.

Designers also will establish a separate business *checking account* to accurately track revenue and expenses. Other

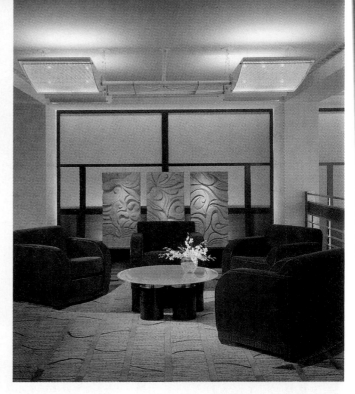

Figure 13.7 *Commercial Office Design—International Clients: At the Embassy of the Republic of Singapore in Washington, D.C., the designers were sensitive to the multicultural heritage of Singapore. The reception area is enhanced with naturalistic art and the adaptive grid pattern is accented by fine organic curved forms in the furniture and custom area rug. The floor plan, in the shape of a cross, reflects the typical residential floor plan in the "Garden City." (Architect/Designer: RTKL Associates. Photograph by Scott McDonald/Hedrich Blessing.)*

business documents may include items such as purchase orders, invoices, timesheets, and telephone logs. An accountant can be very helpful in identifying and tracking income and expenses.

Setting Up a Design Studio

There are generally three types of office arrangements when setting up a design studio: the home office, an office associated with retail sales, and the business office. The decision should be based on the goals and financial viability of the firm. For any office arrangement, budgets need to be considered for furnishings and equipment. One significant consideration is the cost of computers for business and computer-aided design work.

Technology in the Studio

Computers and related technologies have become essential pieces of equipment in all design firms. Aside from their obvious assistance with word processing and general office tasks, advanced computer systems can help in performing the following functions:

- *Estimating costs*—With cost information stored in the computer's memory, the task of projecting plan proposals into cost estimates is simplified.

Figure 13.8 *Furniture Design—Technology: The Personal Harbor is a 6' circular office space with a sliding door for total privacy. Designed for open office environments, the conservative space provides a quiet retreat. (Courtesy of Steelcase, Inc.)*

- *Preparing specifications*—The computer can store suppliers' catalog data, including prices and other valuable information, facilitating efficient preparation for project specifications. Manufacturers can supply electronic images of their products that can be introduced in plans and perspective drawings.
- *Ordering*—Orders for required furnishings can be placed directly through the computer to the manufacturer.
- *Drafting*—Computer-aided design (CAD) programs allow drafting on the computer. Although many firms develop initial programming and conceptual designs by hand, construction documents are commonly completed on the computer.
- *Drawing perspectives*—CAD systems are also extremely beneficial in creating three-dimensional design drawings (see Figures I.4 and 1.6 A and B). Some programs can render perspectives. Advanced computer systems perform immediate color changes, as well as changes in lighting design and location. Other advanced systems permit a client to visually walk through an interior by viewing the moving images on the computer screen.
- *Researching and communicating*—Because of the power of the Internet, manufacturers' data, new product information, current research data, and the ability to transfer mail and design files are all immediately available to the designer.

Design teams may consist of multiple firms located in different parts of the country or world. Designers and allied professionals frequently communicate via the computer. For instance, CAD files can be transferred via the Internet. Teleconferencing and digital cameras allow information to be quickly communicated on a global scale.

Obviously, technology is an essential tool in design firms. Before purchasing a particular software package, designers should thoroughly review the software marketplace. With prices ranging from $150 for basic software to over $15,000 for a complete system, a personalized hands-on class and demonstration are essential for understanding the possibilities and limitations of various programs.

The Source Library and Trade Relationships

A unique aspect of the design studio is the source room or resource library. The library contains catalogues of furnishings and furniture, along with actual samples of a variety of finishes and fabrics. The acquisition and organization of these materials require careful planning. A firm specializing in healthcare design will need to contact different sources than a firm specializing in residential design. A listing of manufacturers for specific sources is available through reputable design periodicals and their annual source guides. Various Web sites also display manufacturers' products.

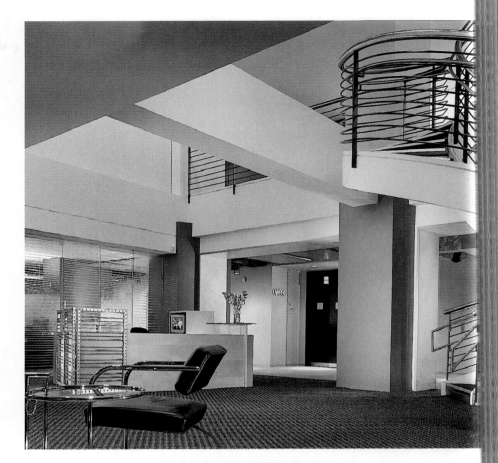

Figure 13.9 *Interior Design Studios: Designers frequently work in open office environments, as shown here and in Figure 13.10. Strong geometric forms and a keen sensitivity to natural light define the interiors of OWP & P in Chicago. (Architect/Designer: OWP & P. Photographs by Chris Barrett/Hedrich Blessing.)*

21st Floor

Legend

1. Main Street
2. Neighborhood
3. Town Square
4. Conference Room/Team Room
5. Central Resource Library
5. Central Resource Library
6. Office Services
7. Reception
8. Training Room
9. Information Technology

338

Figure 13.10 *Interior Design Studios: Intense colors and contrasting linear forms define the interiors of Quantrell Mullins & Associates in Atlanta. (Designers: Quantrell Mullins & Associates. Photographs by Brian Robbins Photography.)*

Industry representatives also supply designers with these source materials. For a wider array of samples or to view actual furniture pieces, designers work with design centers or merchandise marts. Many of these centers are open only to members of the design trade. Clients are brought to these establishments as guests of the designer to view specific furnishings. Establishing a working rapport with these trade sources provides for efficient business transactions. It is said that "designers are only as good as their sources."

Interiors of design firms are seen in Figures 13.9 and 13.10.

Marketing

Before starting any business, the owners must decide who their prospective clients are, how to reach them, and who the competition is. Useful marketing tools include the following, among others:

- A creative yet professional name
- A proper business location based on the firm's needs
- Letterhead, business cards, résumé, and related marketing brochures
- A Web site
- A professional portfolio of previous projects
- Signage
- Advertisements in the telephone book and other strategically placed locations.

Other places to advertise a firm include local chamber of commerce gatherings, community clubs and organizations, and professional interior design society referral networks.

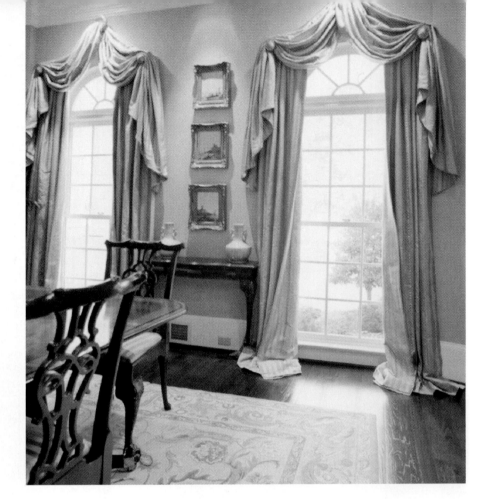

Figure 13.11 *Furnishings in Design, Attention to Detail—Window Treatment: Quality design requires attention to the finer points. In this formal dining room, the designer accents the window height through the use of a flowing window treatment. Custom lighting and carefully selected art and accessories add to the ambience. (Designer: Miner Details. Photograph by Deborah Whitlaw.)*

Business Contracts

Once the business has been established, designers must develop contracts with clients. Contracts consist of two basic types: the letter of agreement and the professional contract.

The *letter of agreement,* a simple contract written in the form of a letter, is legally binding. It is typically used for smaller residential projects. *Professional contracts* more thoroughly define the agreement between the owner and the client. Professional contracts are available to members through professional organizations, or can be developed in conjunction with an attorney.

Both forms of contracts should contain as a minimum the following information:

- Date
- Identification of parties involved
- Location of work, including an address and description
- Scope of services
- Cost of services and payment schedule
- Additional or reimbursed charges
- Arrangements for working with allied professionals
- Purchasing arrangements
- Expressed consent to photograph and publish project
- Time frame for completion
- Appropriate signatures with date
- Retainer due upon acceptance of contract

All contracts, regardless of their source, need to be reviewed by an attorney.

Fee Structures

One of the most complicated tasks in writing the contract is determining the cost of the services. Interior designers are compensated for their services in a number of ways. It is important that the designer and client agree on the terms of payment. Following are the most common fee systems:

- A designer who receives a *flat or fixed fee* determines the time and expense involved for the particular project and charges the client this specified amount.
- An *hourly fee* is a set rate for each hour of time spent on the project. This fee varies depending on many factors, including customary fees in a particular area, the competence and status of the designer, and the demand for his or her services. Sometimes this fee has a cap on the total cost of the design services.
- A designer who charges a *cost plus fee* buys merchandise at wholesale prices and sells the goods to clients for an additional percentage charge. The reverse of this is the *retail cost less a percentage fee:* The designer purchases merchandise at wholesale cost, but sells it to the client at a percentage off retail.
- A *fee based on the total square feet of the project* is generally used by experienced designers who are fairly knowledgeable in estimating costs involved in completing a space. The fee is charged for each square foot based on the square footage required for the entire project.

Figure 13.12 *Furnishings in Design, Attention to Detail— Bathroom Design: For this gentleman's bathroom, the original narrow room was gutted, and sleek, contemporary, moisture-resistant materials were used. (Designer: Jackie Naylor Interiors. Photograph ©Robert Thien.)*

- A designer may receive a *percentage of the total project expenditure*. This system provides a guaranteed fee regardless of what the project may cost. If the completed project has additional costs, the designer is financially protected.

Professional Ethics

Professional interior designers must maintain the highest level of integrity. Designers need a clear definition of right and wrong. Facts should not be muddied or glossed over to hide the truth. Designers have a responsibility to maintain the highest of standards with the public, the client, other interior design professionals, allied colleagues, and employers. ASID's Code of Ethics preamble states, "Members of the American Society of Interior Designers are required to conduct their professional practice in a manner that will inspire the respect of clients, suppliers of goods and services to the profession, and fellow professional designers, as well as the general public."

In regard to the public, designers must recognize that they are required to follow all building codes and regulations. Ignorance of codes is not an acceptable reason to skirt re-

quirements. Designers are responsible for researching codes for a project and then following those requirements.

When dealing with clients, the designer must clearly define the scope of work and compensation received for the project. Designers should not discuss one client's project with another client, and they should never accept a financial "kickback" from a vendor for specifying their product. Sources of revenue should be clearly defined to the client. Furthermore, designers should always let the client know the status of a job. If a specified product has been discontinued, designers must verify the appropriate substitution with the client.

Designers also have a responsibility to their design and allied professional colleagues. Designers should never criticize other designers' work. Designers should not solicit other designers' business. If freelancing for another designer, the freelancer must honor the employer's design decisions. Designers should work as a collaborative team with allied professionals. When problems arise, shifting blame does not solve the problem; teamwork does.

Additionally, designers have a responsibility to the profession of interior design. They should encourage the exchange of information and remain current in design practices. Designers should become involved in community projects and always present the interior design profession in the best possible light. Problems should be addressed in professional society meetings where true grassroots change can take place.

Finally, designers have a responsibility to their employers. Information completed at one firm should not be copied or taken to another firm or used in another freelance project without the consent of the employer. As designers leave a firm, every effort should be made to facilitate the exchange of information to the new employee.

Interior Design Forecast

The profession of interior design is relatively young, since the field of interior design has emerged only in the last 100 years. Possibilities for career specialization and advancement in the profession are numerous.

Emerging Career Specializations

Because of the recognition of the health benefits of a comfortable environment, the aging population, technological advancements, the need for energy conservation, and a move toward a simpler and more meaningful lifestyle, significant changes in the design industry have occurred. For example,

- Clients are better educated than in the past and are asking more questions.
- The aging population is aware of the need for accessible housing and buildings.
- The medical profession has recognized the need for aesthetics in the healthcare industry.
- Because of the Internet and networking capabilities, more people are working at home.
- The private office is shrinking and becoming portable. Open office environments are interspersed with conferencing areas and personal spaces.

Figure 13.13 *Specialty Design, Home Office: This open office has been designed with sophistication and practicality in mind. Task lighting and concealed technology equipment allow the office to blend with the dining and living areas. Figure 7.8 shows the breakfast nook. (Designer: Perla Lichi, Perla Lichi Design, ID 1727, Tamara, FL. Photograph by Barry Grossman. Courtesy of On Design. Residence: Condominium, private residence, Essex model at L'Hermitage, Ft. Lauderdale, FL.)*

- Clients place a high priority on prestigious locations and security.
- People are interested in saving the environment. In residential design in particular, owners want homes with high energy efficiency, low maintenance, labor-saving devices, and water-saving appliances, especially dishwashers, toilets, and shower heads.

These demands have created new career options that are leading to new and innovative design solutions in the healthcare/elderly care industry, in design technology, and in sustainable green design (see "Green Design: Solar Architecture and the Earthship"). The similarity among these specializations is the trend toward convenience in the work and home environment to improve the quality of life.

Healthcare Design and the Aging Population

Awareness has evolved in the medical profession for the need of quality aesthetics in the healing environment. Where possible, healthcare interiors are incorporating hospitality characteristics. Fabrics and furnishings have taken on a warmer and richer appearance. Hospital furnishings are now designed to conceal medical equipment and are losing their institutional appearance.

The aging population has recognized the importance of accessibility in housing as well as in the commercial environment. Because of the personal benefits of living at home and the high costs of institutional care, residences are adapted to allow the elderly to maintain independence (see the Design Scenario: Universal Design in Chapter 3). Retirement communities have also recognized the need for various levels of assistance to their occupants. Individual and community residences for the elderly are designed to accommodate wheelchairs; furnishings and cabinetry are readily available to meet universal needs.

Design Technology: The Virtual Office in Homes and Hotels

With the electronic developments of online networking, teleconferencing, and Internet access, going to work may no longer mean going to an office (Figure 13.13). The office furniture market has expanded to include ergonomically designed furniture available for home use. Designers should specify appropriate power and communication lines to all potential computer locations including bedrooms and kitchens.

The *virtual office* is a portable office. Furniture designed to be transported as luggage allows employees to take their office on the road. Consequently, the hospitality market is adapting to the electric and space needs of the virtual office in hotel rooms and restaurants. Conference centers are now equipped with teleconferencing and interactive video capabilities.

The airline industry has also recognized the needs of the commuting office and responded accordingly. Telephones are common amenities on airplanes, and airlines have begun to provide greater comfort via more first class and business seats and more gracious spacing in coach.

The portable office concept also affects the space requirements in commercial office designs. The private 12′ × 15′

Figure 13.14 *Specialty Design, Technology: This elaborate home theatre includes neon lights, a marquee, and a concession stand. The interior of the theatre includes an oversized movie screen, comfortable theatre seats, and speakers that surround the viewer. (Designer: Stevenson Design Group. Photograph by Robert Brantley.)*

office or personal open office cubicle may now be shared by various individuals (commonly called "hoteling"). Small conference rooms may be used when privacy is required.

Design Technology: The Smart House and the Home Theatre

A buzzword of the 1990s was the term "cocooning," and it has continued into the new millennium. Wishing to spend more time at home, people are investing substantial resources in home furnishings, accessories, entertainment, and other elements that contribute to a safer and more enjoyable environment. A continuing focus is the development of the "Smart House," a term that refers to an electronically controlled environment. For example, the amount of light for either nighttime or daytime illumination can be programmed to suit the occupants' particular needs. The custom-designed Smart House is planned to provide the latest developments in technology, including security systems, lighting, intercoms, central vacuums, entertainment systems, Internet access, and even equipment that can monitor children's activities within the home.

Because people desire to spend more time at home, the home theatre has become more prevalent in interior design. The theatre has evolved to include large-screen viewing, comfortable theatre seating, surround-sound, and accoutrements such as popcorn stands and soda dispensers (Figure 13.14).

Outlook for the Profession

The emerging career specializations just discussed result from the evolution of the profession of interior design. NCIDQ, FIDER, and the professional organizations often work together in analyzing the direction of this evolution.

A prominent view of the future of the interior design profession emerged through the efforts of FIDER. Having received funding from ASID, IIDA, and the Joel Polsky-Fixtures Furniture-FIDER Endowment, FIDER developed a research project called *The Future of Interior Design*. The first phase of the project required the selection of 15 to 18 visionaries from design practice, industry, education, and research to form a focus group. Individuals were carefully selected based on their varied backgrounds, interests, and cultural and regional diversity. This group defined which future trends, based on sociocultural, economic, political, environmental, and technological changes, will most likely affect interior design practice, education, and research.

Phase two of the project was the assimilation of the visionaries' findings into a survey and its distribution to a random sample of over 2,200 designers in the U.S. and Canada. Twelve trends were identified as the basis for the survey. Table 13.2 lists them in order of importance based on the survey results. Some of the more prominent trends from the project and other professional sources are discussed below.

Environmental Conservation

The need for environmental conservation has surfaced not only in interior design practice, but also as a relevant national

GREEN DESIGN

Solar Architecture and the Earthship

As discussed in Chapter 5, passive and active solar designs and earth-sheltered designs create living environments that require less energy to run and produce less waste. A cutting-edge design utilizing these principles, while incorporating waste materials as buildings blocks, is the Earthship.

The ecological consequences of the construction industry are well explored and documented. Old growth forests are vanishing forever. Generating electricity leaves nuclear waste and gasses that lead to acid rain. Sewage and chemicals contaminate the ground water necessary for all life to survive. The environment cannot indefinitely support the current methods of construction and their many hidden costs.

Michael Reynolds, the architect behind the Earthship philosophy and design, noted the direction of these wasteful construction methods over 30 years ago. He also noted the inordinate amount of time and effort that is required to obtain the "American dream" of home ownership. The average wage earner works 30 years to pay off the debt of the home, in addition to paying monthly bills to utility companies. Reynolds searched for a better solution to this seemingly endless cycle of bills and waste. His goals were far reaching:

- Develop construction methods that would reuse existing waste products as building blocks for construction.
- Design a building that would create its own energy and treat its own waste.
- Develop construction methods that can be executed with little training.
- Make the design affordable.

The major structural building component of the Earthship is recycled automobile tires filled with compacted earth to form a 3'-0" thick rammed earth brick enclosed in steel-belted rubber. The massive "brick" walls, and the method of incorporating them into the earth, create living spaces that retain a constant temperature. Thus, with natural ventilation systems built in, an Earthship will heat itself in the winter and cool itself in the summer without the use of fossil or nuclear fuels.

Earthships produce their own electricity through a photovoltaic power system; they also collect their own water from a unique metal roof, silt catch, and cistern system, and deal with their own sewage through food-producing greenhouse technology that allows contained-flush toilets.

Earthships have been designed and developed with an emphasis on global availability of all aspects of their construction. They exist now in Bolivia, Australia, Mexico, Japan, Canada, and all over the United States. Earthships are comparable in cost to typical frame construction; however, they are much more durable, better insulated, and have no utility bills.

The buildings look like Spanish adobe structures and can be designed in single or multifloor units (see Figures GD13.1–GD13.2). Interior walls, which can be painted or left in their natural color, are formed out of stacked aluminum cans. Walls can be pierced with clear or colored glass and formed in a variety of shapes. Figure I.3 illustrates a completed Earthship called the Suncatcher.

Figure GD13.1 *The exterior of an Earthship with glass sloping to the south. Facades can be customized utilizing various-sized tires, shaped retaining walls, and whimsical accoutrements. (Architect: Michael E. Reynolds.)*

GREEN DESIGN

Solar Architecture and the Earthship—cont'd

Figure GD13.2 *Rooms in Earthship are based on U-shaped modules grouped side by side or on two levels that can be added or deleted as needed. The sections through the designs illustrate construction and airflow. (Architect: Michael E. Reynolds.)*

Table 13.2 *Survey Results*

Environmental Conservation: Interior designers are likely to become increasingly responsible for ecological impacts of design decisions.

Accountability: Reliable performance standards and quantifiable measures of user satisfaction must demonstrate that interior design is a tangible benefit to clients.

Profession Gains Respect: The interior design profession is maturing as it deals with licensing, increasing codes and regulations, adjusting to an electronic age, and dealing with economic shifts. As a result, the profession will be more respected by the public.

Teams of Specialists: Teams of knowledgeable design specialists and experts with different backgrounds are likely to be required for future design projects.

Expand Studio Education: Studio teaching must change to emphasize broad-based general knowledge and critical thinking skills to solve complex problems of people and place.

Sharing Cost of High-Tech Education: Technology has increased costs and time required for undergraduate education. These costs need to be shared by industry, practice, and educational institutions.

Client Participation: Clients and design experts will work more closely and accommodation of clients' needs and desires will be the priority.

Preserve Cultural-Social Diversity: Interior designers are likely to become increasingly responsible for the cultural and social implications of design decisions.

Global Resource Competition: Design firms and companies are likely to face increasing competition from foreign companies for global markets and resources.

Graduate Education Gains Significance: In response to the rapid proliferation of new knowledge, graduate education gains importance.

Customization of Products: Industry will use large database systems so designers may work more directly with a manufacturer to specify a customized product.

Culturally Diverse Designers: Interior designers with cross-cultural language skills and international travel experiences will be in high demand.

For statistical analysis of these results, see FIDER, or *IDEC Conference Proceedings,* March 1996, pp. 15–20.

and global issue involving industry, manufacturing, and education. This trend, which began with the environmental movement of the 1960s, is still evolving. According to a 1994 Times Mirror-Roper study, approximately 42 percent of the American population donate their time or money to environmental causes.

As noted throughout this text, many manufacturers in the design industry also recognized this trend and are now producing green design products. Web sites and periodicals are dedicated to green products and green design. A true green design product mimics nature. All designs in nature are based on recycling; nothing is wasted. True green products are not only environmentally friendly, they also provide for the sustainability of the natural environment. Manufacturers and inventors are wise to follow in this direction; designers, as representatives of end-users, are wise to specify these green products.

Dennis Weaver, actor, humanitarian, and environmentalist, has developed an interesting approach in response to this trend by forming the Institute of Ecolonomics. "Ecolonomics" is a blend of the words *ecology* and *economics* in recognition of human dependence on both a healthy environment and a healthy economy. The institute advocates the use of responsible business practices—including design—to clean up the environment. In Weaver's words, "When we realize we can make a buck cleaning up the environment, it will be done."

Accountability

Another relevant trend in the future of the profession is the need to be accountable. Interior design professional organizations must work together to demonstrate the tangible benefits of interior design.

Kerwin Kettler, in *ASID Professional Designer,* surveyed 200 business owners and their opinions about productivity. Ninety percent believe productivity could be increased by improvements in office design. The top four factors influencing productivity included access, comfort, privacy, and flexibility. As designers work with commercial clients, a preliminary productivity analysis could be performed. The results of this analysis could be used as a baseline to measure productivity levels at the end of the design process. Designers must be able to document the benefit of their services to clients, particularly commercial clients. Research and programming analysis need to establish productivity baselines to document the quantifiable benefits of a quality interior environment.

Profession Gains Respect

As the profession engages in environmentally sustainable practices and develops quantifiable standards of accountability, respect for the profession will grow. According to White and Dickson in the *Journal of Interior Design,* sociologists have found that professions mature based on the development of their educational requirements and legal recognition. In the past 30 years the interior design profession has sought to define educational programs through FIDER and establish a basic competency level through NCIDQ. The continuing registration and licensing efforts, coupled with the ongoing development of an advanced research database, will enhance the profession's image and credibility.

Another key factor in establishing credibility (and thereby developing respect for the profession) is to ensure that the various voices of the professional design organizations blend as one to work with the public and represent the profession's goals, ideals, and visions. In the late 1980s and early '90s a move called the "Unified Voice" sought to establish a single organization. The move met with some success as three professional organizations merged to form IIDA. Perhaps future leadership and grassroots efforts will allow a truly unified voice to emerge.

Figure 13.15 *Retail Design: Form defines the character of this sweeping cosmetics showroom. The designer was charged with creating an interior environment that did not feel like a tunnel in this 24′W × 100′ L × 14′ H space. Undulating gypsumboard soffits draw clients into the retail establishment, adding interest and the appearance of width. (Designer: Yoshinari Matsuyama. Photographs by Paul Warchol.)*

Teams of Specialists

The breadth and depth of the design professions will continue to require the use of teams of specialists. Teams will consist of members with advanced degrees, or members who are involved in continuing education and research into uncharted areas; cooperation among allied professionals will be essential. Already ASID and IIDA have developed forums that focus on specialty areas of residential, hospitality, retail, healthcare, and commercial design, as well as facility planning, historic preservation, education, and research. According to Neal Frankel, IIDA, the connection between practitioners and researchers will continue to grow, creating an expanded body of knowledge.

Technology and the Human Factor

Global developments have surfaced in the areas of communication and computer technology, as well as in the understanding of human physical and cultural diversity. These two topics initially may appear to work against each other; however, in many cases it is the technology that is opening doors (both literally and figuratively) to human design issues.

Due to technological advances products are more readily customized, and design education has progressed to include teaching advanced computer skills. New knowledge made available by technology will expand the need for graduate education. Advances in telecommunications will enhance designers' understanding of cultural and social diversity and increase the demand for culturally diverse designers. According to Gary Wheeler, FASID, designers deal with the "human factor and the human spirit. We possess a profound responsibility to change the future."

Technology is a significant factor in achieving the sensitive adaptation of the human environment. The blending of technology to assist in the understanding of human needs will greatly affect the field of interior design.

Figure 13.16 *Restaurant Design: A playful intertwining of ribbons and grids defines the relaxed yet refined character of this main dining room. Playful light fixtures combine with architectural lighting to pinpoint tabletop displays. Live plants and cut flower arrangements bring human scale and natural warmth to the interior. (Designer: Kuleto Consulting & Design. Photographs by Cesar Rubio. Courtesy of Kimpton Group.)*

Summary

The progression of steps to becoming a professional interior designer include education, experience, and examination. Once established as a professional, the designer continues his or her education through advanced coursework and participation in professional organizations. The successful professional designer knows that the diverse nature of design, both as a science and as an art, also requires an advanced knowledge of business skills and ethical behavior.

The future of interior design will see the maturation of a young profession eager to provide for a multicultural community. Designers will work in specialized fields with allied design professionals in teams that encourage the sustainable use of products, materials, and space. Designers will actively search for universal design solutions that enhance the quality of life in all interior environments.

Chief Oren R. Lyons, traditional Faithkeeper of the Turtle Clan, speaking at the 20th Congress of the International Council of Societies of Industrial Design, said,

Each generation raises its intellectuals, heroes, and leaders. . . . We must raise leaders of vision who think and make decisions in the long term. Think positive, be courageous, be generous, share your wealth. Divest for the future.

Appendix A

Residential Programming Questionnaire

RESIDENTIAL PROGRAMMING QUESTIONNAIRE

I   General Information   **Date**

Client Name _____

Address _____

Home Phone _____ Work Phone _____

Occupation(s) _____

II   Family Members

Name	Age	Universal Concerns

III   Family Members' Hobbies and Activities

Activity	Family Member(s)	Where does activity take place?
Computer		
Television		
Stereo		
Sewing		
Crafts		
Instruments		
Model Building		
Reading		
Other		

IV   Room Requirements

Living Room

Entertainment   Yes _____   No _____   How Many? _____   How Often? _____

Dining Room

Formal/Casual/Both (circle one)

Number of people maximum ____

Comments _____

Breakfast Room

Number of people maximum _____

Comments _____

Family Room

Activities

_____
_____
_____
_____
_____
_____

Bedrooms

#	Who	Requirements
1		
2		
3		
4		
5		

Baths

1		
2		
3		
4		

Other Rooms

Rooms	Requirements
Laundry	
Kitchen	
Office	
Workshop	
Garage	
Playroom	
Study	
Music Room	

V   Design Preferences

Colors	
Mood	
Budget	
Time Frame	
Reuse Items	(if yes, see furniture inventory sheet)
Other	

VI   Other Information & Comments

_____
_____
_____
_____
_____
_____
_____
_____
_____
_____
_____
_____
_____
_____
_____
_____
_____
_____
_____
_____
_____
_____

VII   Business Information
Travel Directions

_____
_____
_____
_____

Fee Basis

_____
_____
_____

Appendix B

Furniture Inventory Sheet

FURNITURE INVENTORY SHEET

Item #	Description	Size W × D × H	Style	Comments

Appendix C

Typical Set of Residential Construction Drawings

Figure C.1 *Basement/foundation space use plan. (Courtesy of Santa & Associates)*

Figure C.2 *First floor space use plan. (Courtesy of Santa & Associates)*

Figure C.3 Foundation/basement floor plan. (Courtesy of Santa & Associates)

Figure C.4 *First floor construction plan. (Courtesy of Santa & Associates)*

357

Figure C.5 *Guest suite floor plan and exterior elevations. (Courtesy of Santa &*

Figure C.6 *Exterior elevations. (Courtesy of Santa & Associates)*

Figure C.7 *Interior elevations. (Courtesy of Santa & Associates)*

Figure C.8 *Interior elevations. (Courtesy of Santa & Associates)*

BUILDING SECTION "A" - "A"

DRAWING SCALE 3/8" = 1'-0"

SANTA & ASSOCIATES
SPACE PLANNING & DESIGN
706 754-5695
TURNERVILLE, GEORGIA 30580

PRELIMINARY BUILDING SECTION

XXXX RESIDENCE
THE ORCHARD
CLARKESVILLE, GA 30523

Figure C.9 *Building section. (Courtesy of Santa & Associates)*

Glossary

Also see pages 252 through 254 for textile terms.

Abacus Small slab found on top of the capital of a column.

Abstract A type of decorative design, modified so that the subject may not be recognizable.

Acanthus leaves A stylized design motif inspired by the acanthus plant and especially favored by the ancient Greeks and Romans.

Accent lighting Lighting used to focus and/or emphasize particular objects or features.

Accessible Unobstructive passage into and throughout a structure making it negotiable for wheelchair users and others with physical limitations.

Achromatic Hues "without color"; specifically, gray, black, and white.

Acoustics In design, the study of sound, including its properties and successful adaptation in a human environment.

Active solar energy system Mechanical systems particularly designed to collect and distribute solar heat.

Adaptation The modification of an item to make it fit more perfectly under conditions of its current environment. In furniture design, indicates that only some elements of the original have been adapted to the present design.

Adaptive reuse Historical structures redesigned for a current use.

Additive color Mixing or adding primary hues through the use of either dyes and pigments or lighting.

Adobe brick A brick of sun-dried earth and straw; most often used in the Southwest adobe–style dwelling.

A.F.F. Above finished floor.

Afterimage When the human eye focuses on a strong hue, the eye becomes saturated with that hue and an afterimage of that hue's complement can be seen when the eye focuses on a neutral surface.

Air-exchange unit A unit that allows fresh outside air to be drawn into a structure and discharges stale air. Contributes to a "healthy environment."

Aisle A hallway that runs parallel to the nave of a church and is separated from it by an arcade.

Ambient light A term interchangeable with general lighting; lighting that provides overall illumination.

Amp (or ampere) The measurement of electrical current in a particular circuit.

Analogous colors Hues adjacent on the color wheel.

Anodize The application of a protective oxide covering on metal.

Anthemion A radiating stylized honeysuckle flower motif used by the ancient Greeks and in Neoclassic design.

Anthropometrics The science of measuring the dimensions and proportions of the human body in various activities.

Antique A work of art, piece of furniture, or decorative object made at a much earlier period than the present, often at least 100 years old.

Apron The horizontal section beneath a table top, chair seat, chest of drawers, or window sill.

Apse A semicircular or polygonal recess at the end of a church plan.

Arabesque A leaf-and-scroll pattern with stems rising from a root or other motif branching in spiral form; usually in a vertical panel.

Arcade A series of adjoining arches with their supporting columns on piers.

Architectural lighting Permanently wired and architecturally fixed luminaires.

Architrave A horizontal member located above the column and capital in classical architecture.

Armoire The French term for a tall cupboard or wardrobe with doors.

Artesonado Ornately carved wood; usually used in Hispanic styles.

Ashlar Square or rectangular blocks of stone masonry used in the construction of a building.

ASID American Society of Interior Designers.

Asymmetrical balance Balance created by grouping objects or furnishings to give a sense of equilibrium.

Baffle A mechanism for deflecting light or directing it to reduce glare.

Balance Placing objects or furnishings in a symmetrical, asymmetrical, or radial approach to create a sense of equilibrium.

Balcony A projecting platform from the exterior or interior wall of a structure, enclosed by a railing.

Ballast An electrical transformer that converts current necessary for fluorescent lighting.

Balloon-frame construction A type of construction employing a simple, economical skeletal frame. Used most often for small wood houses with closely placed supportive elements with spaces in between for wiring, plumbing, and insulation.

Baluster A turned, upright support of a rail, as in the railing of a staircase.

Balustrade A row of balusters topped by a rail.

Banister A handrail.

Banquette Architecturally built-in seating units used in restaurants and sometimes in residential design.

Barrel vault An arched roof known since 4000 B.C. and perfected by the ancient Romans.

Barrier-free design Designs where no physical obstacles prevent access for wheelchair users to various facilities throughout a space.

Base molding   Moldings near or at the bottom of the wall along the floor's edge.

Bas-relief   A type of decoration in which the design is slightly raised from the surface or background.

Batik   A process of decorating fabric by wax coating the parts not to be dyed. After the fabric is dyed, the wax is removed.

Batten   A long strip of wood covering the joint between two larger wood strips.

Bay window   An angled window that projects outward from the wall surface.

Bead-and-reel   A convex classical Greek molding, with disks singly or in pairs, alternating with oblong beads.

Beam   A horizontal timber or metal bar supported on vertical posts, used to support a roof or ceiling.

Bell gambrel   A type of gambrel roof where the lower section splays outward to give the roof a "bell-shaped" appearance.

Beltcourse   See *stringcourse*.

Belvedere   See *cupola*.

Bentwood   A process of bending narrow strips of wood into various artistic forms; developed primarily by Austrian designer Michael Thonet during the latter half of the 19th century.

Bergère   A French armchair featuring a wood frame with upholstered arm panels, seat, and back.

Berm   A mound of soil. In solar design, placed against a building to add insulating qualities.

Bevel   The edge of any flat surface that has been cut at a slant to the main surface.

Bidet   A water-cleansing fixture.

Biodegradable   The ability of a material to decompose naturally.

Biotechnology   The use of new advancements in engineering and technology in product design and the environment.

Blocking   In construction, rough lumber is placed in a hidden location to support a joint or future object.

Blocking diagram   A visual drawing that groups individuals, departments, or spaces into block. Used in conceptual design.

Blueprint   A photographic print, formerly white lines on a bright blue ground, used for copying architectural plans. The standard today is blue lines on a white ground.

Board-and-batten construction   Construction employing wide upright boards placed side by side with joints covered by battens.

Boiserie   A French word generally used to designate elaborate carved wood paneling.

Bolection molding   A projecting molding with a rounded edge.

Bonnet roof   A type of French hipped roof with a bottom that covers a surrounding porch. The shape resembles a bonnet.

Bow window   A semicurved window that projects outward from the wall surface.

Breakfront   A large cabinet or bookcase with a center section projecting beyond the flanking end sections.

Brewster color theory   Another term for the Standard Color Wheel theory based on the three primary colors of blue, red, and yellow. May also be called the *Prang* or Palette system.

Broadloom   Carpet woven in 27-inch to 18-foot widths. Most commonly used in 12-foot widths.

Bubble diagram   A visual drawing indicating individuals, departments, or spaces with bubbles. Used in conceptual design.

Buffet   A cabinet for holding dining room accessories and from which food may be served.

Bullnose   A 180-degree rounded wooden edge on a table, step, or cabinet top.

Burl   A strong irregularity in the wood grain providing an interesting design and color; often used for veneering in furniture.

Burnish   To make shiny or lustrous by rubbing.

Butt joint   An expensive joint where two flush edges are joined by glue, screws, or other means.

Buttress   A supportive structure first used on the Gothic cathedral that splays from a wall to make it stable.

Cabriole leg   A furniture leg support designed in the form of a conventionalized animal leg with knee, ankle, and foot creating a double curve or *S* shape.

CAD (CADD)   Computer-aided design (and drafting).

Calendering   A finishing process for fabrics; the textile is pressed between rollers.

Candela   In lighting, the unit of measure for the intensity of light in a given direction directly from the lamp.

Caning   Flexible rattan or cane woven in open mesh for chair backs, seats, and other furniture members.

Canister   A small box or case for holding tea, coffee, flour, salt, or sugar.

Cantilever   A projecting beam or furniture member supported at one end only.

Capital   The top treatment of a column. In classical Greek architecture, the capitals were Doric, Ionic, or Corinthian in style.

Captain's walk   A balustraded observation platform built atop the roof of a coastal dwelling, providing an unobstructed view of the sea; also called a widow's walk.

Caryatid   The human form used as a structural support.

Casement window   A window hinged on one side only, allowing it to swing inward or outward.

Casepiece   A general term applied to furniture storage pieces that have no upholstered components.

Cathedral   In ceiling design, the vertical area formed by a pitched roof.

Cella   The interior space (or cell) of an ancient Greek or Roman temple, especially copied during the Greek Revival period.

Chair rail   The decorative trim horizontally positioned at about 3'-0" above the floor.

Chaise longue   A French term for a lounge chair (with or without arms) with an extended seat providing leg support for the occupant.

Chandelier   A lighting fixture suspended from the ceiling with branches to support candles or electric lamps.

Chase   A concealed channel in a wall that carries HVAC, electrical, or plumbing lines from floor to floor.

Chateau   A castle or large country house in France.

Chevron   A repeating *V* shape or zigzag motif consisting of diagonal bars meeting at a point.

Chimneypiece   The architectural design that sheathes the firebox and flue.

Chinoiserie (shinwá zor ee)   (French) Refers to Chinese lacquered designs, which were popularly employed during the 18th century on European furniture.

Chroma   The purity or saturation of a color. Also called *intensity*.

Circulation   The traffic patterns of occupants within an interior space, particularly important when planning rooms, stairways, hallways, etc.

Clapboard   A horizontal overlapping of thin wood boards used for the exterior sheathing of structures; popularly employed for 17th- and 18th-century colonial-style homes.

Classic A term generally applied to design of timeless quality that transcends changes in taste and fashion.

Classical A term relating to the arts of ancient Greece or Rome.

Clearance The planning of space required by building codes to clear combustible heating units such as fireplaces, stoves, or furnaces. Also, adequate clearance space between furnishings for the convenience of users.

Clerestory Windows placed at the top of a structure's wall allowing extra light.

Club foot A club-shaped or rounded foot on a cabriole leg, especially associated with Queen Anne furniture.

Cluster planning A method of arranging concentrated dwelling units, usually low-rise and either separate or attached, to take advantage of communal open spaces.

Code Federal, state, or local laws applied to the design of buildings in relation to safety and health standards.

Coffered ceiling Ornamental sunken panels between beams employed for a flat, vaulted, or domed ceiling providing a three-dimensional effect.

Colonnade Columns arranged in a straight or curved row, often supporting an entablature.

Colonnette A miniature colonnade used for decoration.

Color rendering index A measurement in graph form of a lamp's color spectrum.

Columned chimney (clustered chimney) A cluster or arrangement of a number of chimneys together.

C.O.M. Customer's own material. The customer purchases fabric for a job from another source.

Commode A French term referring to a low chest supported on legs with drawers.

Complementary colors Contrasting colors based on the opposite colors of the color wheel. Various combinations of cool and warm colors.

Computer network Computer terminals within an office that are connected by cables, permitting access to the same data.

Conceptual design The phase of the design process in which designers formulate preliminary broad-based concepts. May be called schematic design.

Condominium A multiunit structure, such as an apartment house, in which each unit is individually owned. Maintenance and services are paid for by the residents as a group.

Console table A table designed to be fixed on a wall; sometimes supported by two front legs.

Construction drawings Drawings that indicate how to build something.

Contemporary design Living or occurring at the same period of time. In furniture the term commonly refers to a modified type of modern or updated traditional design. Some styles are considered classic.

Contract administration A phase of design where the designer administers the contracts completed in construction documentation.

Contract documentation A design phase where the designer documents the design decisions approved by the client in previous design phases.

Corbel A bracket or projection from a wall used to support a molding or beam.

Corinthian The most ornate of the three Greek orders, characterized by its capital of small volutes (spiral, scroll-shaped ornaments) and acanthus leaves.

Cornice A horizontal and projecting member that crowns an architectural composition; a molding on a wall near the ceiling or under the eaves of the roof. Cornice board is a molding used with drapery instead of a valance.

Coromandel screen A large free-standing paneled lacquered screen with incised designs, made in China but originally imported from the Coromandel Coast of India.

Corridor Term used for a hallway, generally in a public building.

Coved ceiling A ceiling that meets the wall by means of a concave curve rather than a right angle.

Credenza A long, table-height cupboard with drawers and doors. Popular during the Italian Renaissance; today, a low storage unit with doors and often drawers, usually placed behind a desk.

Critical path A timetable or schedule used to determine the processes needed to complete a construction project.

Crown lintel An architectural detail used above windows, particularly in the late 18th and early 19th centuries. The lintel, often called a jack-arch lintel, features a crown-shaped keystone.

Crown molding The uppermost molding, usually joining the wall and ceiling.

Cruciform A cross-shaped form.

Crystal The finest quality of lead glass.

Cupola A small structure built on top of a roof for a lookout or to provide interior lighting; commonly used in Georgian, Federal, and Victorian structures.

Cyma curve A double curve formed by the union of a concave and convex line.

Dado The lower part of an interior wall when treated in a different manner from the wall above; usually defined by a molding called a dado cap or chair railing.

Daub A sticky or heavy mud or plaster infill between half-timber construction work with wattle.

Day-bed An extended type of couch or chair that can be used as a bed.

Decibel Unit by which sound is measured.

Design The planned arrangement of basic elements and principles that work together to create an image, object, or environment.

Design concept statement A statement outlining the goals and needs of the end users for a specific design project.

Design development A phase of design that involves specific selections of FF&E and illustrated 3-D designs.

Design process A progression of steps involving the analysis and synthesis of the design solution.

Direct lighting See *downlighting*.

Distressed Refers to a surface treatment for antique reproductions when the furniture is intentionally damaged to provide an aged appearance.

Doric Pertaining to the simplest of the three orders of ancient Greek architecture.

Dormer A window in a small gablelike projection built out from a sloping roof.

Double glazing A process of hermetically sealing two sheets of glass together with air trapped between. Provides efficient insulation against heat and cold.

Double-hung window A window divided into two sections, one lowering from the top and the other rising from the bottom. Each section is called a sash.

Dovetail joint A type of wood joint used in furniture construction consisting of two slotted fan-shaped pieces that interlock.

Dowel A round wood peg. Often used for furniture joinery, the peg is inserted into a cavity of the same size.

Dower chest   A chest to hold items for a prospective bride. In early Pennsylvania it took on distinctive characteristics.

Downlighting   Recessed or ceiling-mounted architectural lighting with lamps that direct the light downward. Sometimes called direct lighting. Downlights produce general lighting.

Dresden   Fine porcelain made in Meissen, near Dresden, Germany. Established 1710–1720, the factory produced some of the most famous china in Europe.

Drop-leaf table   A table with one or two hinged members that can drop to the sides or be supported to provide a larger tabletop surface.

Drywall   A type of wallboard applied to studs. May also be called Sheetrock, plasterboard, or gypsumboard.

Dutch door   A single-hinged door divided horizontally so each section can be opened independently.

Ears   Small squares or rectangles outlined with moldings. Found on the edges of some chimneypieces, doors, or other architectural details.

Eave   A protecting lower edge of a roof which overhangs the walls of a building.

Eclecticism   Mixing furnishings or borrowing styles from various sources and periods with an eye to compatibility.

Efficacy   In lighting, measures the efficiency of a lamp.

Egg-and-dart   A classical Greek molding consisting of ovoid (egg-shaped) forms alternating with dartlike designs.

Egress   The direct route to exit a building. Commonly used in life safety/fire codes.

Elements of design   The "tools" used by the designer to create an environment and achieve the goals or principles of design. The elements are space, line, shape and mass, texture, color, light, and pattern.

Elevation   Two-dimensional drawings of walls.

Ell   A wing or extension placed at a right angle to the structure.

Elliptical fanlight   A fan-shaped window that tops doorways or other windows.

End user   The client or the client's client; the person who ultimately uses the interior space.

Entablature   The upper part of a wall, usually supported by columns or pilasters and in classical orders consisting of the architrave, frieze, and cornice.

Ergonomics   The study of human beings in their responses to various working conditions and environments.

Escutcheon   In hardware, refers to a shaped plate for a keyhole or a metal fitting to which a handle or knob is attached.

Etagere   A series of shelves supported by vertical supports; used chiefly for display.

Eyeball   In lighting, a ceiling-mounted or recessed fixture with a pivoting spherical lamp that can be maneuvered to direct the light where desired.

Fabrics   Fibers and yarns made into cloth.

Facade   Refers to the exterior front of a building, either decorative or structural.

Fanlight   See *elliptical fanlight*.

Fascia   The vertical portion of the eave.

Fauteuil (fau tool)   The French term for an open armchair.

Faux finish   A "false" impression of a natural material. For example, to finish a surface so it looks like wood, marble, or granite.

Fenestration   The placement, type, and design of windows and other openings found on a building or wall.

Festoon   A carved, molded, or painted classical ornament representing a decorative chain, swag, or strip.

FF&E   Furniture, finishes, and equipment.

Fiber   A natural or synthetic substance processed into a thread or yarn of continuous length.

Fiberglass   Glass fibers used for fabric or molded for furniture, furniture parts, or skylights.

FIDER   Foundation for Interior Design Education Research.

Filament   A threadlike conductor (as of carbon or metal) that is rendered incandescent (brilliant) by the passage of an electric current.

Finial   An upright ornament that forms the upper extremity of an architectural detail, a piece of furniture, or an accessory.

Fish-scale shingles   Small pointed or rounded shingles that provide decorative interest on the exterior of the Queen Anne Victorian house.

Fixture   In lighting, the physical structure that supports the lamp and other necessary and decorative accoutrements.

Flemish gable   A gable composed of graceful curves or steps. An architectural detail especially used by the Dutch settlers.

Fluorescent lighting   Artificial light produced when a gaseous mixture of mercury and argon, sealed within a glass tube that is lined with a fluorescent coating, is activated by an electrical current.

Fluting   Parallel concave grooves commonly used on the shafts of columns.

Foil   Anything that serves, by contrast of color, pattern, texture, or other elements, to adorn or set off another thing to advantage; also, a wallpaper with the appearance of a thin sheet of metal; a background.

Footcandle   An international unit of light measurement. It is the illumination at a 1-ft distance from the light of one candle falling onto a 1-ft square surface. The intensity of light is calculated in footcandles.

Footings   Structural foundation of a building.

Footlambert   In lighting, the unit of measure for reflected light.

French doors   Single-hinged doors of paned glass, sometimes paired; a walk-through window that swings either inward or outward.

Fresco   The art of painting on moist lime plaster with water-based pigments.

Fretwork   Interlaced ornamental work either perforated or cut in low relief, usually in geometric patterns; also, tracery of glazed doors and windows.

Frieze   The horizontal decorative section found between the architrave and the cornice in classical architecture.

Fusuma screen   A sliding movable screen used in Japanese houses as a partition to define space.

Gable   The triangular-shaped end portion of a building formed by a pitched roof.

Galerie   A term for a covered porch found on the French home.

Gallery   A miniature railing placed along the edge of a tabletop or shelf.

Gambrel roof   A roof made from two lengths of lumber, the upper one being flatter and the lower one a steeper slope.

Generic   In textile use, a term pertaining to the characteristics of a particular type or class of fibers.

Geodesic dome   A dome of interlocking polygons held together by a self-supporting network of rods and covered with a variety of materials; usually a plastic membrane or glass.

Gingerbread   Lacy architectural detail.

Glass block   Hollow glass forms in a variety of sizes and textures used in building construction to emit light.

Glazing (paint treatment)   A type of painted surface treatment achieved by applying layers of colored transparent paint to produce a striated effect.

Glazing (windows)   Placement of window glass in an architectural opening.

Golden mean   The division of a line somewhere between $\frac{1}{2}$ and $\frac{1}{3}$ its length.

Golden rectangle   Rectangle with width to length proportion of 2:3.

Golden section   The division of a line or form in such a way that the ratio of the smaller portion to the larger is the same as that of the larger portion to the whole. Sometimes called the golden ratio.

Gradation   A type of rhythm produced by the succession of the size of an object from large to small or of a color from dark to light.

Grain   Refers to the vertical configurations or textural (coarse or fine) features of wood.

Gray goods or greige   Woven fabrics that have not been dyed, treated, or changed from their natural state.

Green design   Interiors and products designed to be environmentally friendly and sustainable.

Grotesques   Decorative architectural treatment incorporating fanciful human/animal forms.

Grout   A mortar (generally of cement) used to set tiles or fill in cavities.

Half-timber construction   Construction of timber frame, with the spaces filled with masonry or lath and plaster.

Hand or handle   The feel of an object or drape of a fabric.

Hardware   Metal fittings used for furniture such as keyholes, drawer, and cupboard pulls.

Header   In construction, the structural member over a door, window, or other opening that transfers the weight to the side supports.

HID   High-intensity discharge lighting.

Hieroglyphics   Inscriptions on walls, some telling pictorial stories.

Highboy   A tall chest of drawers supported on tall legs and divided horizontally into two sections; particularly popular during the Georgian period.

Hip roof   A roof with sloping ends and sloping sides.

Hue   The distinct name of a color such as blue, orange, or yellow. One of the three dimensions of color in the Munsell color system.

Hutch   An informal chest or cabinet common to many countries, which came to America from England. The type most commonly used has bottom doors and open upper shelves.

HVAC   Heating, ventilating, and air conditioning systems.

IAQ   Indoor Air Quality.

IDC   Interior Designers of Canada.

IDEC   Interior Design Educators Council.

IIDA   International Interior Design Association.

Ikebana   The Japanese term for the art of arranging flowers according to precise rules.

Incandescent lighting   Light produced by heating a filament sealed in a light bulb.

Indigenous   Inherent; native to or living naturally in an environment.

Indirect lighting   See *uplighting*.

Ingress   A term referring to the entrance into a building.

Inlay   Pieces of stone, wood, shell, metal, or ivory arranged in a design composition and set into another piece of wood or other material for a decorative effect.

Intensity   A dimension of color that denotes the dullness or brightness of a hue. Also referred to as *chroma*.

Ionic   The Greek order designated by the spiral volutes of its capital.

Jack-arch lintel   See *crown lintel*.

Jacquard   A special loom designed by Joseph-Marie Jacquard to produce intricate weaves. Weaves produced on the loom, such as damasks and tapestries, are called jacquard weaves.

Jalousie window   A window made of narrow horizontal and adjustable glass louvers that control ventilation and light.

Jamb   The vertical side sections of a window or door.

Jetty   The overhang produced when a second floor of a building extends over the first.

Kelvin   A measurement of a light's temperature.

Ladderback   A term describing a chair with a back composed of horizontal slats resembling a ladder.

Lambrequin   An ornamental window treatment, usually in the form of a wooden frame across the top and down the sides of the window, either painted or covered with fabric.

Laminate   The binding of layers of materials together. In paneling, several layers are laid alternately across the grain for strength and durability. For decorative purposes, a thin layer of fine wood (veneer) is glued to the surface of the base wood; a process also used for plastics.

Lamp   The light source (bulb or tube) of artificial lighting.

Lath   Thin strips of wood or a metal mesh attached to the structural frame of a building to support plaster, tile, reinforced concrete, or other material.

Lathe   A machine used to turn wood or metal into various shapes.

Latillas   Crude sticks laid between the vigas (pole beams) in the Southwest adobe–style home.

Law of chromatic distribution   The large areas should be covered in the most neutralized colors of the scheme. As the areas reduce in size, the chromatic intensity may be proportionally increased.

Life-cycle costing   Analysis of a product's total costs from conception through disposal.

Linenfold   A Gothic decorative detail depicting a stylized folded linen fabric.

Lintel   The horizontal beam or component that spans the area between openings such as columns, windows, and doors.

Louver   A slatted panel (usually wood) for controlling the flow of air and the radiation of light; most often used as a window treatment.

Lowboy   A low chest of drawers supported on legs; particularly associated with the Georgian style.

Lumen   A measure of the flow of light produced by one lamp.

Luminaire   A complete light fixture including the lamp and all supportive elements.

Mansard roof   A roof having two slopes on all sides, the lower one steeper than the upper one. The roof usually conceals a second or third floor.

Mantel   The shelf that projects from a chimneypiece.

Marbleizing   A painted surface treatment that imitates the texture of polished marble.

Marlborough leg   A square straight leg with a square foot most often associated with Chippendale furniture.

Marquetry   A decorative inlay design glued into furniture and floors employing a variety of woods or other materials.

Masonry   Construction materials of stone, bricks, tiles, blocks, or other material joined with mortar.

Matrix   A diagram indicating adjacencies between individuals, departments, or spaces.

Matte   A dull finish.

Metamerism   The effect of various types of light in changing the appearance of a color.

Metope   In classic architecture, the square panels between the triglyphs found on the entablature of the Doric order.

Miter   Joining two members of material at a 45-degree angle to form a corner.

Modern style   A new art form that breaks all ties with previous design forms and styles.

Modillion   An ornamental bracket (usually console shaped) that often supports a cornice or soffit.

Modular   Constructed with standardized units or modules.

Module   One in a series of standardized units to be integrated together, such as building construction units or a set of furniture.

Molding   An architectural wood strip, usually decorative, that projects from the ceiling or wall surface; may also be of metal, plaster, or plastic.

Monochromatic   A color scheme that uses one color with varying value and chroma.

Monotone   A color scheme that uses one color of very low chroma, neutralized.

Mordant   Any substance that serves to produce a fixed color in a textile fiber, leather, or other similar material.

Mortise and tenon   A type of joint used in furniture construction with a projecting tenon that fits into the mortise or cavity.

Mosaic   A floor or wall decoration made up of small pieces of stone or glass arranged in a design.

Mottle   A dripped or irregular color.

Mullion   A vertical member dividing glazed doors, windows, or bookcases.

Munsell color theory   A color theory based on three dimensions of color: hue, value, and chroma. Each color has a number notation.

Muntin   A horizontal bar dividing the panes of a window, door, or bookcase. The term is often used interchangeably with mullion.

Nap   A fuzzy surface found on fabrics composed of short fibers or hairs.

Nave   The principal section of a church, usually flanked by the aisles and extending from the entrance to the altar or chancel.

NCIDQ   National Council for Interior Design Qualification.

Newel post   The main post at the foot of a stairway.

Niche   A shallow recess in an exterior or interior wall; usually with a rounded head.

Nogging   The brickwork (or infill) found between half-timber construction.

Nonarchitectural lighting   Any type of luminaire that is portable.

Nosing   The projecting edge at the top of a stair's riser.

Open office planning   A large office space where divisions are made by modular furnishings to create workstations.

Orders of architecture   In classical Grecian architecture: the Doric, Ionic, and Corinthian styles of columns.

Organic design or architecture   Modern architectural approach put forth by Frank Lloyd Wright. The house should "grow out of the land."

Orientation   Placement or arrangement of various elements such as buildings, windows, rooms, or furnishings in relation to points on the compass or other elements.

Ormolu mount   A decorative treatment usually applied to furniture; made from copper and zinc alloy to look like gold. Common in French design.

Ostwald color theory   A color theory based on the yellow, red, blue, and green and the amount of black and white added to a hue.

Ottoman   A general term for a large upholstered footstool.

Palladian window   A window consisting of three vertical parts with the central section higher than the flanking ones and surmounted by a fanlight.

Panic hardware   In commercial design, hardware on a door that opens when pushed against.

Parapet   A low wall or protective railing at the edge of a roof or platform.

PAR lamp   Reflective parabolic aluminized reflector lamp.

Parquetry   A mosaic of wood laid in geometric patterns.

Passive solar energy system   A system of collecting, storing, and distributing solar heat by employing elements of the structure.

Paterae   Oval or round decorative details, particularly used during the Neoclassic era.

Patina   A mellow surface often developed with age.

Patio   A courtyard.

Pavilion   A part of a building projecting from the main structure.

Pedestal   A support at the base of a column; any base or foundation on which to display an art object.

Pediment   A triangular architectural structure above a portico, window, or door.

Pembroke table   A small table with one drawer and drop leaves.

Pendant   An object suspended from above.

Pendant chandelier   A light suspended from the ceiling with a single fixture.

Pent roof   A small projected eave found above the first story.

Period style   A term used to designate a single item or a complete interior including the architectural background, furniture, and decorative arts prevalent in a specific country or at a particular time in history.

Peristyle   A series of columns surrounding a structure. Also a garden surrounded by columns at the back of an ancient Roman house.

Piece dyeing   Color is added to a fabric after it is woven.

Pier   A rectangular pillar devoid of detail.

Pilaster   An upright rectangular or circular projection or partial column fixed to a wall, architecturally treated as a column.

Pitched roof   A sloping roof, either a low or high pitch.

Plan   A drawn arrangement of elements in a structure indicating walls, rooms, spaces, and so forth shown looking down at the floor.

Plenum   Area between the ceiling of one level and the floor of the next. Usually conceals mechanical, electrical, and plumbing systems.

Plywood   A process of laminating layers of wood with alternating grain direction. Usually the top layer or veneer is of a finer quality; used for furniture and paneling.

POE   Postoccupancy evaluation.

Portfolio   A flexible case used by designers containing renderings, pictures, and other design-related projects.

Portico   A projection from the main structure of a building over the front entrance, supported by columns and often capped by a pediment.

Prang color wheel   Another term for the standard color wheel.

Prefabricated (prefab)   Mass-produced in standardized modules or parts for later assembly at the factory or building site.

Principles of design   The goals of a design composition consisting of scale, proportion, balance, rhythm, emphasis, and harmony.

Programming The information-gathering phase of the design process.

Proxemics A study of spatial needs of humans relating to personal and cultural aspects.

Pueblo One of the Indian tribes of New Mexico; an Indian village built in the form of apartment houses.

Punch list A final list indicating all items still to be completed on a construction or design project.

Quoin A solid material at the corner of a building distinguished from the adjoining surface by material, color, size, or projection.

Rabbeted A type of joint where one edge has a groove cut the entire width to accommodate a straight edge piece.

Radial balance Balance created from a central point.

Ragging and rag rolling A wall surface treatment where paint is partially wiped or rolled off with a rag.

Rail The horizontal member of a door frame or panel.

Ranch style Also known as a California ranch or rambler home; a ground-hugging single-level plan with a low-pitched overhanging roof supported by posts.

Random plank Wood planks laid in a manner disregarding the width of individual boards.

Reeding A small convex molding, the reverse of fluting; used on columns, pilasters, and furniture.

Reflected ceiling plan Commercial design lighting plan in a set of construction drawings. May include HVAC and sprinkler information.

Replica An accurate reproduction.

Repoussé Relief work done on metal, created by hammering the material on the reverse side.

Reproduction A precise duplication of a historic style; a replica.

Resilience The ability of a particular material to give or spring back when pressed.

Rhythm Elements in a room that assist the eye in moving easily from one area to another.

Riser The upright member between two stair treads.

Sash The framework (in a window or door) in which the glass is set. It may constitute a movable part.

Schematic design See *conceptual design*.

Sconce A lighting fixture secured to the wall.

Section A cut-through view of a building, interior wall, cabinet, or other interior component.

Shade A color that has been darkened by adding black; a low value.

Shed In ceiling design, the area formed by one wall extended higher than the opposite wall, also called a lean-to.

Shibui (shih BOO ee) Japanese approach to beauty; appreciation of serenity, not ostentation.

Shoji A basic element of a Japanese house, made of panes of rice paper and wooden mullions and used as an exterior window. Shoji panels are also employed as wall partitions and freestanding screens.

Sick building syndrome An unhealthy environment with stale or polluted air.

Sidelight A vertical window placed beside a door.

Sillplate Construction member that secures the floor to the foundation.

Simultaneous contrast When a hue, value, or chroma is perceived as different as a result of being viewed beside or on a different colored background.

Soffit A lower section of a ceiling; area underneath this section.

Solution dyeing Color is added to the fiber in its liquid state.

Space planning The process of determining square footage requirements and then manipulating the spaces into an appropriate arrangement to meet the client's needs. May involve the use of a matrix, bubble, blocking, and stacking diagrams, and furniture plans.

Specifications or spec book Written directions indicating appropriate means to produce or purchase furniture, furnishings, and equipment.

Spinneret A device (similar to a showerhead in appearance) through which liquid viscose is forced to form manufactured fibers.

Stacking diagram A chart or graph indicating on which floors individuals, departments, or spaces will be placed. Used in conceptual design.

Standard milled items Items of various kinds (e.g., doors, door frames, windows, window frames, and mantels) made in standard sizes in large quantities in the factory, thus making the cost much less than for custom-made items.

Stepped gable A gable in which the sides ascend to the peak in steps.

Stile The vertical or upright supportive frame for a door.

Stock dyeing Color is added to fibers before they are processed into yarns.

Stretcher The horizontal supportive crosspiece spanning the area between the legs of a chair or table.

Stringcourse A narrow horizontal band placed on the exterior of the Georgian house between the first and the second floors.

Stucco A type of plaster surface treatment used on exterior or interior walls.

Subtractive color Color that is visible to the eye via the reflection of wavelength not absorbed by an object.

Swag A festoon of flowers or fruit. May also refer to a gathering of fabric at the top of a window, gently draped over each end.

Symmetrical balance Balance is created by objects arranged equally on either side of an imaginary line.

Synthetic Something artificial simulating the genuine piece.

Systems furniture Flexible type of component furniture that can be arranged and rearranged to accommodate various needs for workstations.

Tambour The front of a piece of furniture made with strips of wood attached to fabric and adjusted on a track, allowing it to open and close.

Task light Lighting designed for specific types of work or tasks.

Tatami mat A soft straw mat, approximately 3 ft by 6 ft by 1 in., which is the basic element of the Japanese house and serves as a unit of measurement, determining the size and proportion of all spaces. The dark lines of its binding form an overall grid pattern, according to which rooms are sized.

Templates Small patterns of furniture (either to cut or trace) used as guides in planning rooms.

Terrace Usually refers to a relatively level paved area adjoining a building.

Tint A color that is lightened by adding white; a high value.

Tokonoma A sacred recessed niche or alcove in the Japanese house.

Tone A neutralized hue produced by adding gray or the color's complement.

Tongue-and-groove joint The rib on one edge of a board is made to fit into a corresponding groove in the edge of another board to make a flush joint.

Torchère A tall floor lamp with a design that casts light in an upward direction. Particularly popular for Art Deco and Post-Modern styles.

Trabeated construction Post and lintel design for structural support; developed by the Egyptians.

Tracery Decorative carved stone or wood openwork; associated with Gothic design.

Traffic lanes In design, refers to the walkways or passages.

Transept The lateral arms (across the nave) of cruciform churches.

Transom Small window above a door or window.

Tray In ceiling design, the area that extends vertically above the lower ceiling. Usually a 6″–18″ rise.

Tread The horizontal section of a stair.

Trompe l'oeil French expression meaning "to fool the eye"; a term applied to two-dimensional decoration showing a three-dimensional drawing or effect.

Truss system A triangular construction system for structural support; developed by the Greeks.

Tryglyph Greek for "thrice grooved." On a Doric frieze, the blocks that alternate with the metopes.

Tudor arch A low or flattened elliptical arch.

Turning See *lathe*.

Universal design Spaces and furnishings created to meet the needs of individuals regardless of age and ability.

Uplighting Suspended or wall-mounted lighting with lamps that direct the light up. Sometimes called indirect lighting.

Valance A short decorative fabric treatment at the top of a window that conceals drapery, curtains, and often lighting.

Value The lightness or darkness of a color, on a scale from white to black.

Vaulted In ceiling design, the area formed beneath the arch.

Veneer Thin sheets of wood or other material (usually of fine quality) used as a top surface over other more ordinary materials such as particleboard.

Veranda An open galley or portico (usually roofed) attached to the exterior of a building.

Vernacular Reference to the distinguishing attributes or qualities of a certain culture.

Vigas The large exposed pole beams that support the roof in the Southwest adobe structure.

Villa (Italian) A large residential structure.

Visual communications The drawings, plans, and presentation materials designers create to visually explain the design to the client prior to implementation.

Volume The area that occupies any space including the width, depth, and height.

Volute The spiral-shaped decoration that tops the capital of the Ionic column.

Wainscoting Wood paneling that extends partway to the ceiling, associated with the medieval-style interior.

Wall washer In lighting, a ceiling mounted or recessed fixture with a lens that focuses the light on the wall or object.

Warp Vertical or lengthwise threads in a woven fabric.

Wattle Interlacing twigs that function as infilling for timber-framed structures. Wattle and daub often work together.

Weft Horizontal threads in a woven fabric, also called filling threads.

Working drawings See *construction drawings*.

Wrought iron Ornamental iron that has been worked into a decorative shape or design.

Yarn Twisted or assembled fibers that produce cloth.

Yarn dyeing Color is added to yarns before they are woven into fabrics.

Zapata A carved decorative supportive bracket found on the Southwest adobe house.

References

Texts and Internet Resources

Building Codes, Accessibility, and Universal Design (Also see code book references in Chapter 4)

American National Standard for Buildings and Facilities—Providing Accessibility and Usability for Physically Handicapped People. A11.1–1986. Washington, DC: U.S. Department of Housing and Urban Development, 1986.

American National Standard Specifications for Making Buildings and Facilities Accessible to and Usable by Physically Handicapped People, ANSI A117.1–1980. New York: American National Standards Institute, 1980.

Harmon, Sharon Koomen. *The Codes Guidebook for Interiors.* New York: Wiley, 1994.

Harness, S., and J. Groom. *Building without Barriers for the Disabled.* New York: Whitney Library of Design, 1976.

Leibrock, Cynthia. *Beautiful Barrier Free.* New York: Van Nostrand Reinhold, 1993.

Minimum Guidelines and Requirements for Accessible Design. Washington, DC: U.S. Architectural & Transportation Barriers Compliance Board, 1982.

NFPA 101® Life Safety Code® 1991. Quincy, MA: National Fire Protection Association, 1991.

Perry, Lawrence G., Michael A. Jawer, John T. Murdoch, and James C. Dinegar. *ADA Compliance Guidebook: A Checklist for Your Building.* Washington, DC: BOMA, 1992.

Wilkoff, W.M.L., James S. Brady, and Laura W. Abed. *Practicing Universal Design: An Interpretation of the ADA.* New York: Wiley, 1997.

Business Profession

Farren, Carol E. *Planning and Managing Interior Projects.* Kingston, MA: R.S. Means, 1988.

Knackstedt, Mary V. *The Interior Design Business Handbook: A Complete Guide to Profitability.* 2d ed. New York: Van Nostrand Reinhold, 1992.

Loebelson, Andrew. *How to Profit in Contract Design.* New York: Van Nostrand Reinhold, 1983.

Morgan, Jim. *Marketing for the Small Design Firm.* New York: Whitney Library of Design/Watson-Guptill Publications, 1984.

Murphy, Dennis Grant. *The Business Management of Interior Design.* North Hollywood, CA: Stratford House Publishing Company, 1988.

Piotrowski, Christine. *Interior Design Management: A Handbook for Owners and Managers.* New York: Van Nostrand Reinhold, 1992.

_____ . *Professional Practice for Interior Designers.* 2d ed. New York: Van Nostrand Reinhold, 1994.

Rose, Stuart W. *Achieving Excellence in Your Design Practice.* New York: Whitney Library of Design/Watson-Guptill Publications, 1987.

Siegel, Harry. *Business Guide for Interior Designers.* New York: Whitney Library of Design, 1976.

Siegel, Harry, and Alan Siegel. *A Guide to Business Principles and Practices for Interior Designers.* Rev. ed. New York: Whitney Library of Design, 1982.

Stasiowski, Frank, and David Burstein. *Project Management for the Design Professional.* New York: Whitney Library of Design/Watson-Guptill Publications, 1982.

Thompson, Jo Ann Asher, ed. *ASID Professional Practice Manual.* New York: Whitney Library of Design, 1992.

Veitch, Ronald, et al. *Professional Practice.* Winnipeg, Canada: Peguis, 1990.

Color

Birren, Faber. *Color and Human Response.* New York: Van Nostrand Reinhold, 1984.

Hope, Augustine, and Margaret Walch. *The Color Compendium.* New York: Van Nostrand Reinhold, 1990.

Kaufman, Donald. *Color: Color Palettes for Painted Rooms.* New York: Clarkson Potter, 1992.

Ladau, Robert F., Brent K. Smith, and Jennifer Place. *Color in Interior Design and Architecture.* New York: Van Nostrand Reinhold, 1989.

Mahnke, Frank H., and Rudolf H. Mahnke. *Color and Light in Manmade Environments.* New York: Van Nostrand Reinhold, 1987.

Ostwald, Wilhelm. *The Color Primer.* New York: Van Nostrand Reinhold, 1969.

Sharpe, Deborah T. *The Psychology of Color and Design.* Chicago: Nelson-Hall, 1975.

Verity, Enid. *Color Observed.* New York: Van Nostrand Reinhold, 1982.

Fundamentals and Theory

Abercrombie, Stanley. *A Philosophy of Interior Design.* New York: Harper & Row, 1990.

Bevlin, Marjorie Elliott. *Design Through Discovery.* New York: Holt, Rinehart & Winston, 1985.

Carpenter, James M. *Visual Art: A Critical Introduction.* New York: Harcourt Brace Jovanovich, 1982.

Cheatham, Frank R., Jane Hart Cheatham, and Sheryl A. Haler. *Design Concepts and Applications.* Englewood Cliffs, NJ: Prentice Hall, 1983.

Ching, Francis D.K. *Architecture: Space, Form, and Order.* New York: Van Nostrand Reinhold, 1980.

De Sausmarez, Maurice. *Basic Design: The Dynamics of Visual Form.* New York: Van Nostrand Reinhold, 1983.

Kleeman, Walter B. *The Challenge of Interior Design.* New York: Van Nostrand Reinhold, 1981.

Lauer, David A., and Stephen Pentak. *Design Basics.* 4th ed. Fort Worth, TX: Harcourt Brace College Publishers, 1995.

Malnar, Joy Monice, and Frank Vodvarka. *The Interior Dimension: A Theoretical Approach to Enclosed Space.* New York: Van Nostrand Reinhold, 1992.

Ocvirk, Otto G., Robert E. Stinson, Philip R. Wigg, Robert O. Bone, and David L. Cayton. *Art Fundamentals: Theory & Practice.* 8th ed. New York: McGraw-Hill, 1998.

Pena, William. *Problem Seeking.* Washington, DC: AIA Press, 1989.

Rybczynski, Witold. *Home: A Short History of an Idea.* New York: Penguin Books, 1987.

Zelanski, Paul, and Mary Pat Fisher. *Shaping Space.* Fort Worth, TX: Harcourt Brace College Publishers, 1995.

Furniture and Accessories

Aronson, Joseph. *The Encyclopedia of Furniture.* 3d ed. New York: Crown, 1965.

Battersby, Martin, et al. *History of Furniture.* New York: Morrow, 1976.

Boger, Louise Ade. *The Complete Guide to Furniture Styles.* Prospect Heights, IL: Waveland Press, 1997.

Boyce, Charles. *Dictionary of Furniture.* New York: Roundtable Press, 1985.

Butler, Joseph T. *Field Guide to American Antique Furniture.* New York: Henry Holt and Company, 1985.

Deasy, C. M., and Thomas E. Lasswell. *Designing Places for People.* New York: Whitney Library of Design, 1985.

Emery, Marc. *Furniture by Architects.* New York: Harry N. Abrams, 1983.

Fitzgerald, Oscar P. *Three Centuries of American Furniture.* Englewood Cliffs, NJ: Prentice Hall, 1982.

Furuta, Tok. *Interior Landscaping.* Reston, VA: Reston Pub. Co., 1983.

Gandy, Charles D., and Susan Zimmermann-Stidham. *Contemporary Classics: Furniture of the Masters.* New York: McGraw-Hill, 1981.

Garner, Philippe. *Twentieth-Century Furniture.* New York: Van Nostrand Reinhold, 1980.

Hanks, David A. *Innovative Furniture in America from 1800 to the Present.* New York: Horizon, 1981.

Lucie-Smith, Edward. *Furniture: A Concise History.* London: Thames & Hudson, 1985.

Mackay, James. *Turn-of-the-Century Antiques: An Encyclopedia.* New York: Dutton, 1974.

Mang, Karl. *History of Modern Furniture.* New York: Harry N. Abrams, 1979.

Meadmore, Clement. *The Modern Chair.* New York: Van Nostrand Reinhold, 1975.

Russell, Frank, Philippe Garner, and John Read. *A Century of Chair Design.* New York: Rizzoli International, 1980.

Stimpson, Miriam. *Modern Furniture Classics.* New York: Whitney Library of Design, 1987.

Watson, Sir Francis. *The History of Furniture.* London: Orbio, 1982.

www.finefurnitureintl.com Based on periodical of same name.
www.homearts.com Furniture information.

General

Allen, Edward, and Joseph Iano. *The Architect's Studio Companion.* New York: Wiley, 1989.

Ball, Victoria Kloss. *The Art of Interior Design.* 2d ed. New York: Wiley, 1982.

Ballast, David K. *Interior Design Reference Manual.* Belmont, CA: Professional Publications, 1992.

Ching, Francis D. K. *Interior Design Illustrated.* New York: Van Nostrand Reinhold, 1987.

DeChiara, Joseph, Julius Panero, and Martin Zelnik. *Time-Saver Standards for Interior Design and Space Planning.* New York: McGraw-Hill, 1991.

Dizik, A. Allen. *Concise Encyclopedia of Interior Design.* 2d ed. New York: Van Nostrand Reinhold, 1988.

Faulkner, Ray, Sarah Faulkner, and LuAnn Nissen. *Inside Today's Home.* 5th ed. New York: Holt, Rinehart & Winston, 1986.

Friedmann, Arnold, John F. Pile, and Forrest Wilson. *Interior Design: An Introduction to Architectural Interiors.* 3d ed. New York: Elsevier, 1982.

Kilmer, Rosemary, and W. Otie Kilmer. *Designing Interiors.* Fort Worth, TX: Harcourt Brace Jovanovich College Publishers, 1992.

National Council for Interior Design Qualification. *NCIDQ Examination Guide.* New York: National Council for Interior Design Qualification, 1989.

Nielson, Karla J., and David A. Taylor. *Interiors: An Introduction.* 2d ed. Madison, WI: Brown & Benchmark, 1994.

Nissen, LuAnn, Ray Faulkner, and Sarah Faulkner. *Inside Today's Home.* 6th ed. Fort Worth, TX: Harcourt Brace College Publishers, 1994.

Pile, John. *Dictionary of 20th-Century Design.* New York: Facts on File, 1990.

———. *Interior Design.* 2d ed. Englewood Cliffs, NJ: Prentice Hall; New York: Harry N. Abrams, 1995.

Ramsey, Charles George, and Harold Reeve Sleeper. *Architectural Graphic Standards.* 8th ed. New York: Wiley, 1988.

Reznikoff, S. C. *Interior Graphic and Design Standards.* New York: Whitney Library of Design, 1986.

Russell, Beverly. *Architecture and Design.* New York: Harry N. Abrams, 1989.

Tate, Allen. *The Making of Interiors: An Introduction.* New York: Harper & Row, 1987.

www.designare.com General interior design information.
www.dezign.com General interior design information.

Green Design

Hawkseed Group. *The Passive Solar House Book.* New York: Rand McNally, 1980.

Pilatowicz, Grazyna. *Eco-Interiors.* New York: Wiley, 1995.

Reynolds, Michael. *EARTHSHIP Vol. I—How to Build Your Own.* Taos, NM: Solar Survival Press, 1990.

———. *EARTHSHIP Vol. II—Systems and Components.* Taos, NM: Solar Survival Press, 1990.

———. *EARTHSHIP Vol. III—Evolution Beyond Economics.* Taos, NM: Solar Survival Press, 1993.

Wright, David. *Natural Solar Architecture: The Passive Solar Primer.* 3d ed. New York: Van Nostrand Reinhold, 1984.

Zeiher, Laura C. *The Ecology of Architecture.* New York: Whitney Library of Design, 1996.

Historic Preservation

Debaigts, Jacques. *Interiors for Old Houses.* New York: Van Nostrand Reinhold, 1973.

Duerksen, Christopher J. (ed.). *A Handbook on Historic Preservation Law*. Washington, DC: The Conservation Foundation and The National Center for Preservation Law, 1983.

Gottfried, Herbert, and Jan Jennings. *American Vernacular Design: 1870–1940*. Ames, IA: Iowa State University Press, 1988.

Guidelines for Local Surveys: A Basis for Preservation Planning. Washington, DC: National Register of Historic Places, 1985.

Hiss, Tony. *The Experience of Place*. New York: Vintage Books, 1990.

Maddex, Diane (ed.). *All About Old Buildings*. Washington, DC: The Preservation Press, 1985.

Murtagh, William J. *Keeping Time: The History & Theory of Preservation in America*. Rev. ed. New York: Wiley, 1997.

Respectful Rehabilitation: Answers to Your Questions about Old Buildings. Washington, DC: The Preservation Press, 1982.

Shopsin, William C. *Restoring Old Buildings for Contemporary Uses*. New York: Whitney Library of Design, 1986.

Stipe, Robert E., and Antoinette J. Lee (eds.). *The American Mosaic: Preserving a Nation's Heritage*. Washington, DC: United States Committee of the International Council on Monuments and Sites, 1987.

Vale, Thomas R., and Geraldine R. Vale. *U.S. 40 Today: Thirty Years of Landscape Change in America*. Madison, WI: University of Wisconsin Press, 1983.

History

Anscombe, Isabelle. *Arts and Crafts Style*. New York: Rizzoli, 1991.

Ball, Victoria Kloss. *Architecture and Interior Design: A Basic History Through the Seventeenth Century*. New York: Wiley, 1980.

_____ . *Architecture and Interior Design: Europe and America from the Colonial Era to Today*. New York: Wiley, 1980.

Blakemore, Robbie G. *History of Interior Design Furniture*. New York: Van Nostrand Reinhold, 1997.

Blumenson, John J.-G. *Identifying American Architecture*. New York: W. W. Norton, 1981.

Brown, Erica. *Sixty Years of Interior Design*. New York: Viking Press, 1982.

Bush, Donald J. *The Streamlined Decade*. New York: George Braziller, 1975.

Clark, Robert Judson (ed.). *Arts and Crafts Movement in America, 1876–1916*. Princeton, NJ: Princeton University Press, 1972.

Curtis, William J. R. *Modern Architecture Since 1900*. 3d ed. Upper Saddle River, NJ: Prentice Hall, 1996.

de la Croix, Horst, Richard G. Tansey, and Diane Kirkpatrick. *Art Through the Ages*. 9th ed. Fort Worth, TX: Harcourt Brace Jovanovich College Publishers, 1991.

Fehrman, Cherie, and Kenneth Fehrman. *Post-War Interior Design, 1945–1960*. New York: Van Nostrand Reinhold, 1986.

Ferebee, Ann. *A History of Design from the Victorian Era to the Present*. New York: Van Nostrand Reinhold, 1970.

Foley, Mary Mix. *The American House*. New York: Harper & Row, 1980.

Garner, Philippe. *Contemporary Decorative Arts*. New York: Facts on File, 1980.

Gaynor, Elizabeth. *Scandinavia Living Design*. New York: Stewart, Tabori & Chang, 1987.

Gowans, Alan. *Styles and Types of North American Architecture*. New York: Harper Collins, 1992.

Hicks, David. *Style and Design*. Boston: Little, Brown, 1987.

Hitchcock, Henry-Russell, and Philip Johnson. *The International Style*. (1932, reprint). New York: Norton, 1966.

Horn, Richard. *Memphis: Objects, Furniture, and Patterns*. Philadelphia: Rushing Press, 1985.

Itten, Johannes. *Design and Form: The Basic Course at the Bauhaus*. New York: Van Nostrand Reinhold, 1964.

Jaffe, Hans L. C. *De Stijl*. New York: Harry N. Abrams, 1967.

Janson, H. W. *History of Art*. 2 vols. 5th ed. Englewood Cliffs, NJ: Prentice Hall; New York: Harry N. Abrams, 1995.

Jordan, R. Furneaux. *A Concise History of Western Architecture*. London: Thames & Hudson, 1969.

Klein, Dan. *Art Deco*. New York: Crown, 1974.

Kostof, Spiro. *History of Architecture*. New York: Oxford University Press, 1985.

Kron, Joan, and Suzanne Slesin. *High Tech: The Industrial Style and Source Book for the Home*. New York: Clarkson N. Potter, 1978.

Maass, John. *The Victorian Home in America*. New York: Hawthorn, 1972.

Massey, Anne. *Interior Design of the 20th Century*. New York: Thames and Hudson, 1990.

Mather, Christine, and Sharon Woods. *Santa Fe Style*. New York: Rizzoli International, 1986.

McAlester, Virginia, and Lee McAlester. *A Field Guide to American Houses*. New York: Alfred A. Knopf, 1984.

McFadden, David. *Scandinavian Modern Design*. New York: Harry N. Abrams, 1982.

Naylor, Gillian. *The Bauhaus*. New York: Dutton, 1968.

Pevsner, Nikolaus. *Pioneers of Modern Design from William Morris to Walter Gropius*. 2d ed. New York: Museum of Modern Art, 1975.

Pierson, William H., Jr. *American Buildings and Their Architects: The Colonial and Neoclassical Styles*. New York: Doubleday, 1970.

Radice, Barbara. *Memphis*. New York: Rizzoli International, 1984.

Sharp, Denis. *Showcase of Interior Design—Pacific Edition*. Grand Rapids, MI: Vitae, 1992.

_____ . *Twentieth Century Architecture*. New York: Facts on File, 1991.

Smith, C. Ray. *A History of Interior Design in 20th Century America*. New York: Harper & Row, 1987.

Smith, S. Jane. *Elsie de Wolfe: A Life in the High Style*. New York: Atheneum, 1982.

Tate, Allen, and C. Ray Smith. *Interior Design in the 20th Century*. New York: Harper & Row, 1986.

Trachtenberg, Marvin, and Isabelle Hyman. *Architecture from Prehistory to Post-Modernism*. New York: Harry N. Abrams, 1986.

Warren, Geoffrey. *Art Nouveau Style*. London: Octopus, 1972.

Whiffen, Marcus, and Frederick Koeper. *American Architecture, 1607–1976*. 2 vols. Cambridge, MA: The MIT Press, 1983.

Whiton, Sherrill. *Interior Design and Decoration*. 4th ed. New York: J. B. Lippincott, 1974.

Wright, Frank Lloyd. *The Natural House*. New York: Bramhall House, 1954.

Lighting

Design Criteria for Lighting Interior Living Spaces. New York: Illuminating Engineering Society of North America, 1980.

Gardner, Carl, and Barry Hannaford. *Lighting Design: An Introductory Guide for Professionals*. New York: Wiley, 1993.

General Electric. *The Light Book.* Cleveland, OH: Nela Park, 1981.

Grosslight, Jane. *Light: Effective Use of Daylight and Electric Lighting in Residential and Commercial Projects.* Englewood Cliffs, NJ: Prentice Hall, 1984.

Jankowski, Wanda. *Designing with Light.* Glen Cove, NY: P. B. C. International, 1992.

Jones, Frederic H. *Architectural Lighting Design.* Los Altos, CA: Crisp Publications, 1989.

Kaufmann, John E. *IES Lighting Handbook Reference Volume.* New York: Illuminating Engineering Society of North America (IESNA), 1981.

Lightolier. *The Light Book.* Jersey City, NJ: Lightolier, 1981.

Michel, Lou. *Light: The Shape of Space.* New York: Van Nostrand Reinhold, 1996.

Moore, Fuller. *Concepts and Practice of Architectural Daylighting.* New York: Van Nostrand Reinhold, 1985.

Nuckolls, James L. *Interior Lighting for Environmental Designers.* 2d ed. New York: Wiley, 1983.

Robbins, C. C. *Daylighting Design and Analysis.* New York: Van Nostrand Reinhold, 1986.

Rooney, William F. *Practical Guide to Home Lighting.* New York: Van Nostrand Reinhold, 1980.

Smith, Fran Kellogg, and Fred J. Bertolone. *Bringing Interiors to Light.* New York: Whitney Library of Design, 1986.

Sorcar, Prafulla C. *Architectural Lighting for Commercial Interiors.* New York: Wiley-Interscience, 1987.

Steffy, Gary R. *Architectural Lighting Design.* New York: Van Nostrand Reinhold, 1990.

www.qualitylight.com Lighting information.

Materials (Floors, Walls, Window Treatments, Etc.)

Commercial & Residential Wallcoverings Reference Manual, Created for Design Schools. Chicago: Wallcoverings Association, 1997.

Conran, Terence. *New House Book.* New York: Random House, Villard Books, 1985.

_____ . *The Bed and Bath Book.* New York: Crown, 1978.

_____ . *The House Book.* New York: Crown, 1976.

Eiland, Murray L. *Oriental Rugs: A Comprehensive Study.* Greenwich, CT: New York Graphic Society, 1973.

Hall, William R. *Contract Interior Finishes: A Handbook of Materials, Products, and Applications.* New York: Whitney Library of Design, 1993.

Jacobson, Charles W. *Check Points on How to Buy Oriental Rugs.* Rutland, VT: Charles E. Tuttle, 1969.

Kahlenberg, Mary Hunt, and Anthony Berlant. *Navajo Blanket.* New York: Praeger, 1972.

Kopp, Joel, and Kate Kopp. *American Hooked and Sewn Rugs.* New York: Dutton, 1975.

Neal, Mary. *Custom Draperies in Interior Design.* New York: Elsevier, 1982.

Nielson, Karla J. *Window Treatments.* New York: Van Nostrand Reinhold, 1990.

Radford, Penny. *Designer's Guide to Surfaces and Finishes.* New York: Watson-Guptill, 1984.

Reznikoff, S. C. *Specifications for Commercial Interiors.* Rev. ed. New York: Whitney Library of Design, 1989.

Riggs, J. Rosemary. *Materials and Components of Interior Architecture.* 5th ed. Upper Saddle River, NJ: Prentice Hall, 1999.

Rupp, William, and Arnold Friedmann. *Construction Materials for Interior Design.* New York: Whitney Library of Design/Watson-Guptill Publications, 1989.

Wrey, Lady Caroline. *Complete Book of Curtains and Draperies.* London: Ebury/Random Century, 1991.

www.internetdesigncenter.com Source information.

Space Planning/Human Scale

Hall, Edward T. *The Hidden Dimension.* Garden City, NJ: Doubleday, 1969.

Harrigan, J. E. *Human Factors Research: Methods & Applications for Architects & Interior Designers.* New York: Elsevier Dutton, 1987.

Karlen, Mark. *Space Planning Basics.* New York: Van Nostrand Reinhold, 1993.

Laseau, Paul. *Graphic Problem Solving for Architects & Designers.* 2d ed. New York: Van Nostrand Reinhold, 1986.

Niels, Diffrient. *Humanscale Four-Five-Six.* Cambridge, MA: MIT Press, 1981.

_____ . *Humanscale One-Two-Three.* Cambridge, MA: MIT Press, 1974.

_____ . *Humanscale Seven-Eight-Nine.* Cambridge, MA: MIT Press, 1981.

Panero, Julius, and Martin Zelnick. *Human Dimensions and Interior Space.* New York: Whitney Library of Design, 1979.

Papanek, Victor. *Design for Human Scale.* New York: Van Nostrand Reinhold, 1983.

Preiser, Wolfgang. *Post-Occupancy Evaluation.* New York: Van Nostrand Reinhold, 1988.

_____ . *Programming the Built Environment.* New York: Van Nostrand Reinhold, 1985.

Scott-Webber, Lennie. *Programming: A Problem-Solving Approach for Users of Interior Spaces.* Houston: Dame Publications, 1998.

Temple, Nancy. *Interior Design Workbook.* New York: Van Nostrand Reinhold, 1993.

Specialty Design

Baraban, Regina S., and Joseph F. Durocher. *Successful Restaurant Design.* New York: Van Nostrand Reinhold, 1989.

Barr, Wilma, and Charles Broudy. *Designing to Sell: A Complete Guide to Retail Store Planning and Design.* New York: McGraw-Hill, 1985.

Boykin, Paula Jo. *Hotel Guestroom Design.* Dubuque, IA: Kendall/Hunt Publishing, 1991.

Bush-Brown, Albert. *Hospitable Design for Healthcare and Senior Communities.* New York: Van Nostrand Reinhold, 1992.

Gosling, David, and Barry Maitland. *Design and Planning of Retail Systems.* New York: Whitney Library of Design, 1976.

Howell, Sandra C. *Designing for Aging: Patterns of Use.* Cambridge, MA: MIT Press, 1987.

Jones, Lynn M. *The Design of National Park Visitor Centers: The Relationships Between Buildings and Their Sites.* Athens, GA: University of Georgia, 1990.

Logrippo, Ro. *In My World: Designing Living & Learning Environments for the Young.* New York: Wiley, 1995.

Malkin, Jain. *Hospital Interior Architecture: Creating Healing Environments.* New York: Van Nostrand Reinhold, 1992.

Mazzurco, Philip. *Bath Design.* New York: Whitney Library of Design, 1986.

Mount, Charles Morris. *Residential Interiors.* Glen Cove, NY: P. B. C. International, 1992.

Novak, Adolph. *Store Planning and Design.* New York: Lebhar Friedman, 1977.

Pile, John. *Open Office Planning: A Handbook for Interior Designers and Architects.* New York: Whitney Library of Design/Watson-Guptill Publications, 1986.

Piotrowski, Christine. *Open Office Planning: A Handbook for Interior Designers and Architects.* New York: Whitney Library of Design, 1986.

Raschko, Bettyann. *Housing Interiors for the Disabled and Elderly.* New York: Van Nostrand Reinhold, 1982.

Russell, Beverly. *The Interiors Book of Shops and Restaurants.* New York: Watson-Guptill, 1981.

Weinhold, Virginia. *Interior Finish Materials for Health Care Facilities.* Springfield, IL: Charles C. Thomas, 1988.

Weishar, Joseph. *Design for Effective Selling Space.* New York: McGraw-Hill, 1992.

Technical Data (Construction)

Anderson, L. O. *How to Build a Wood-Frame House.* New York: Dover Publications, 1973.

Ballast, David Kent. *Interior Construction & Detailing for Designers and Architects.* Belmont, CA: Professional Publications, 1994.

_____ . *Practical Guide to Computer Applications for Architecture and Design.* Englewood Cliffs, NJ: Prentice Hall, 1986.

Browning, Hugh C. *The Principles of Architectural Drafting.* New York: Whitney Library of Design, 1996.

Ching, Francis D. K. *Building Construction Illustrated.* New York: Van Nostrand Reinhold, 1975.

The Encyclopedia of Wood. New York: Sterling, 1989.

Flynn, John E., A. Segil, and G. Steffy. *Architectural Interior Systems.* 2d ed. New York: Van Nostrand Reinhold, 1988.

Graf, Don. *Basic Building Data.* 3d ed. New York: Van Nostrand Reinhold, 1985.

Huth, Mark W. *Understanding Construction Drawings.* Albany, NY: Delmar Publishers, 1983.

Indoor Air Quality Programs: A Two-Part Program Package for the Design Professions. Washington, DC: American Society of Interior Designers, 1994.

Jones, Frederic H. *Interior Architecture Drafting and Perspective.* Menlo Park, CA: Crisp Publications, 1986.

Kicklighter, Clois E., Ronald J. Baird, and Joan C. Kicklighter. *Architecture: Residential Drawing and Design.* South Holland, IL: The Goodheart-Wilcox Company, 1990.

Kicklighter, Clois E., and Joan C. Kicklighter. *Residential Interiors.* South Holland, IL: Goodheart-Wilcox, 1986.

Lamit, Louis Gary. *Technical Drawing and Design.* Minneapolis/St. Paul: West Publishing Company, 1994.

Muller, Edward J., and James G. Fausett. *Architectural Drawing and Light Construction.* Englewood Cliffs, NJ: Prentice Hall, 1993.

Smith, R. C. *Materials of Construction.* 3d ed. New York: McGraw-Hill, 1979.

Staebler, Wendy. *Architectural Detailing in Contract Interiors.* New York: Whitney Library of Design/Watson-Guptill Publications, 1988.

Stein, Ben M., Frederick H. Reynolds, and William McGuiness. *Mechanical and Electrical Equipment for Building.* New York: Wiley, 1986.

Veitch, Ronald M. *Detailing Fundamentals for Interior Design.* Winnipeg, Canada: Peguis, 1994.

Wakita, Dr. Osamu A., and Richard M. Linde. *The Professional Practice of Architectural Working Drawings.* 2d ed. New York: Wiley, 1994.

Wakita, Osamu A., and Richard M. Linde. *The Professional Practice of Architectural Detailing.* 2d ed. New York: Wiley, 1987.

Wallach, Paul I., and Donald E. Helper. *Reading Construction Drawings.* New York: McGraw-Hill, 1979.

www.codecheck.com Field guide to building codes.

www.InteriorsTechnology.com Industry link.

Textiles

Corbman, Bernard P. *Fiber to Fabric.* New York: McGraw-Hill, 1983.

Jackman, Dianne R., and Mary K. Dixon. *The Guide to Textiles for Interior Designers.* 2d ed. Winnipeg, Canada: Peguis, 1988.

Joseph, Marjory L. *Essentials of Textiles.* 3d ed. New York: Holt, Rinehart & Winston, 1984.

Kadolph, Sara J., and Anna L. Langford. *Textiles.* 8th ed. Upper Saddle River, NJ: Merrill/Prentice Hall, 1998.

Larsen, Jack Lenor, and Jeanne Weeks. *Fabrics for Interiors.* New York: Van Nostrand Reinhold, 1975.

Lyle, Dorothy Siegert. *Modern Textiles.* New York: John Wiley, 1983.

Tortora, Phyllis G., and Billie J. Collier. *Understanding Textiles.* 5th ed. Upper Saddle River, NJ: Merrill/Prentice Hall, 1997.

Yeager, Jan. *Textiles for Residential and Commercial Interiors.* New York: Harper & Row, 1988.

Visual Communications

Burde, Ernest. *Design Presentation Techniques.* New York: McGraw-Hill, 1992.

Dong, Wei. *Color Rendering: A Guide for Interior Designers and Architects.* New York: McGraw-Hill, 1997.

Doyle, Michael E. *Color Drawing.* New York: Van Nostrand Reinhold, 1981.

Evans, Larry. *Illustration Guide, Vol. Two.* New York: Van Nostrand Reinhold, 1988.

Gerds, Donald A. *Markers: Interiors, Exteriors, Product Design.* Santa Monica, CA: DAG Design, 1983.

Laseau, Paul. *Graphic Thinking for Architects & Designers.* 2d ed. New York: Van Nostrand Reinhold, 1988.

McGarry, Richard, and Greg Madsen. *Marker Magic: The Rendering Problem Solver for Designers.* New York: Van Nostrand Reinhold, 1993.

Porter, Tom, and Sue Goodman. *Manual of Graphic Techniques 2.* New York: Charles Scribner's Sons, 1982.

Walker, Theodore D. *Perspective Sketches II.* West Lafayette, IN: P. D. A. Publishers, 1975.

_____ . *Plan Graphics.* West Lafayette, IN: P. D. A. Publishers, 1975.

Wang, Thomas C. *Plan and Section Drawing.* New York: Van Nostrand Reinhold, 1979.

Selected Periodicals, Trade Journals, Product Publications, and Professional Journals

Abitare

American Craft

American Homestyle & Gardening

Architectural Digest

Architectural Lighting

Architectural Record

Art and Antiques

Atlanta Homes & Lifestyles

Audio/Video Interiors

Conference Proceedings—Interior Design Educators Council

Contract Design

Design Solutions

The Designer Magazine

Domus

Elle Decor

Facilities Design and Management

Fine Furniture International

Florida Design

Home

Home Building

Hospitality Design

Interior Design

Interiors

Interiors & Sources

Journal of Interior Design

Kitchen and Bath Business

Luxury Kitchen and Bath

Metropolis

Metropolitan Home

National Trust for Historic Preservation

Old House Journal

On Design

Professional Builder

Progressive Architecture

Sighting Dimensions

Southern Accents

Traditional Home

Veranda

Current catalogs and brochures are published by and available from major manufacturers of fabrics, wallpaper, wall paneling, hard floor coverings, carpets, and furniture.

Index